BURNING CITY

POEMS OF METROPOLITAN MODERNITY

EDITED BY

JED RASULA

&

TIM CONLEY

ACTION BOOKS, NOTRE DAME, INDIANA, 2012

Burning City: Poems of Metropolitan Modernity
Edited by Jed Rasula and Tim Conley
ISBN 978-0-9831480-2-9
Library of Congress Control Number: 2011939610

Action Books
Joyelle McSweeney and Johannes Göransson, Founding Editors
Derek White, Book Design
Kimberly Koga, Ji-Yoon Lee and Megan Komorowski, Editorial Assistants

Action Books titles are distributed by Small Press Distribution (spdbooks.org).
Our mailing address is 356 O'Shaughnessy Hall, Notre Dame, IN, 46556.
Visit us online at actionbooks.org, actionyes.org, and montevidayo.com.

Action Books is grateful to the Department of English, the College of Arts and Letters, and the University of Notre Dame for instrumental support of this publication.

◈ CONTENTS ◈

Overtures

Poetic Circulation

Paris

Interlude

Multiple City

Interlude

Cineland: Matinee

Postcards

Whipcracks & Megaphone Chants

Music Hall

Parade of the Eccentric

Postcards

Cineland: Evening Show

Electric Man

Ports of Call

Interlude

New York

Cineland: Chaplinade

A New Mythology

Postcards

Lunar Baedeker

◈ INTRODUCTION ◈

We are creatures of great cities; it is in the city,
and there only, that the Muses exult and grieve.[1]
— Gottfried Benn

Shortly before his first book appeared, Langston Hughes published a prose sketch called "The Fascination of Cities"[2] in *The Crisis.* "The fascination of cities seizes me, burning like a fever in the blood," he declares in response to a childhood trip to Kansas City. Chicago, Mexico City, New York and Paris follow, exposing him to "the ecstasy of crowds; the joy of lights,"[3] "the thundering subways, the arch of the bridges,"[4] until Hughes finds himself "ecstasy-wearied" but always ready for more. His is one of many pledges to the urban muses animated by modernity. The international reach of Modernism—that often radical and mutative recalibration of aesthetic and sensory sensibilities—is bound up with the growth of the great cities that Benn salutes. Mere mention of metropolitan modernity conjures up a constellation of ghosts led by Edgar Allan Poe's "man of the crowd" negotiating an urban "forest of symbols" as Charles Baudelaire memorably put it. In Baudelaire's vision, the Parisian promenade transforms the simple American prototype into the dandy and the flâneur "botanizing on the asphalt,"[5] as Walter Benjamin characterized a practice of urban peregrination that fascinated him and fellow cultural theorists Georg Simmel and Siegfried Kracauer—not to mention the Surrealists in 1920s Paris. As Baudelaire christened the concept of modernity as a combination of the eternal and the transient, the durable and the ephemeral, so Baudelaire himself strikes Marshall Berman as "remarkably fresh and contemporary" and at the same time "almost exotically archaic."[6] Such contradictions have consistently informed the profile of "metropolitan modernity" with its voluptuous austerities, its familiar shocks, its regressive progress culminating after World War One in the "urban jungle" energized by skyscraper primitivism. The period in question (1910-1939, commonly designated as the

---

[1] Gottfried Benn, from *Double Life* tr. E. B. Ashton, in *Primal Vision: Selected Writings of Gottfried Benn* (New York: New Directions, 1971), 177.
[2] Langston Hughes, "The Fascination of Cities," *The Crisis* (Jan. 1926), 138.
[3] Hughes, 139.
[4] Hughes, 140.
[5] Walter Benjamin, Charles Baudelaire: A Lyric Poet in the Era of High Capitalism tr. Harry Zohn (London: Verso, 1973), 36.
[6] Marshall Berman, All That Is Solid Melts Into Air: The Experience of Modernity (New York: Simon and Schuster, 1988), 164.

heyday of the avant-gardes) is now nearly a century old, yet we still inhabit metropolitan configurations pioneered under the auspices of Modernism: subways and automobiles and other forms of mass transit, airplanes, radio and telephone, the experience of the crowd as both alienating and exhilarating, the flux of spoken languages, billboards and advertising culture, cinema and the dominance of popular music. We are still very much the creatures of great cities.

"The city is replacing nature and the elements,"[7] Vladimir Mayakovsky observed in 1914. "The city itself is becoming elemental, and in its womb a new urban individual is born.... The flowing, peaceful, unhurried rhythms of old-fashioned poetry do not correspond to the psychology of the contemporary city dweller.... In the city there are no flowing, measured, rounded-off lines: angles, breaks, and zigzags are what characterize the city picture. Poetry should thus correspond to the new psychological elements of the contemporary city." These "new psychological elements"—dance halls and cafés, jazz bands and circuses, subways and arcades, skyscrapers and streetcars– necessitated both new forms in poetry and new interactions between poets. The adherents of the early twentieth-century avant-garde experienced the city as "a domain of aesthetic contention,"[8] not just a habitat. Furthermore, the big cities were *"laboratories of the modern."*[9] These were shared experiences integral to a Modernism comprised of an array of differing vanguard "isms" and their attendant, sectarian rivalries: the city is the prism which reveals the full range of the spectrum within the same slant of light.

In "the distinctive modern attitude developed in post-war Europe,"[10] observed *Broom* editor Matthew Josephson in 1922, "The writer arms himself with new material. There is no logical direction or growth. It is rather that many unexpected zones of experience have been discovered to him within the monstrous expansion of human activity, and he is concerned for the moment with reaching for and gathering these impressions." *Burning City* is a gathering of such impressions, a directory of poetic discriminations. Unlike anthologies that rank poets based on posthumous representations, and which thereby mute (if not entirely erase) any sense of poetry as cooperative and historically contingent, the present volume acts as a multi-sensory Baedeker to the complex traffic of aesthetic impulses—commonly known by such avant-garde labels as Paroxysm, Expressionism, Cubism, Futurism, Orphism, Simultaneism, Dada, Surrealism, and Constructivism—unfolding in the streets of Berlin, Moscow, London, Barcelona, Antwerp, Lisbon, Madrid, New

[7] Vladimir Mayakovsky, quoted in Tim Harte, *Fast Forward: The Aesthetics and Ideology of Speed in Russian Avant-Garde Culture, 1910-1930* (Madison: University of Wisconsin Press, 2009), 56.
[8] Peter Jukes, *A Shout in the Street: An Excursion into the Modern City* (Berkeley: University of California Press, 1991), xvii.
[9] Joachim Schlör, *Nights in the Big City: Paris, Berlin, London 1840-1930* tr. Pierre Gottfried Imhof and Dafydd Rees Roberts (London: Reaktion Books, 1998), 18.
[10] Matthew Josephson, "After and Beyond Dada," *Broom* 2: 4 (July 1922), 346-347.

York, and Paris. Moreover the scope of this gathering includes regions often overlooked in Anglo-American pictures of Modernism, and so the milieu extends from Prague, Cracow and Belgrade to Sao Paolo and Buenos Aires. The most cursory survey of this book's "Passports" section (wherein appear basic biographical data for each author) will reveal what an international assembly this is: we share Federico García Lorca's experience of exhilaration and dread in Harlem, we negotiate the traffic of Vienna and Shanghai with Robert Musil and Mao Tun, respectively, and gaze upon the Eiffel Tower, that modernist beacon called a "living machine" by Nicolas Beauduin, with any number of poets. The reader is hereby advised to pack for many different climates and cultures.

An accelerating world glimpsed through train windows or oceanliner portholes also expanded with crowds and was launched upward into the sky. In 1913 Ezra Pound observed how, as one looks down from the heights of a New York skyscraper, such buildings "take on their magical powers. They are immaterial; that is one sees but their lighted windows. Squares after squares of flame, set and cut into the ether. Here is our poetry, for we have pulled down the stars to our will."[11] By the time the American mania of building ever higher culminated in the erection of the Empire State Building in 1931 (all 1,250 feet of it), *The New York Times* reported that within a month of its opening an average of 3,000 visitors paid the one dollar fee to "view the broad panorama of the metropolitan area."[12] The view from below was just as staggering, and prompted Gertrude Stein to judge the enormity "right because why end anything."[13] As American as this expression may seem, similar ambitions propelled Vladimir Tatlin's planned *Monument to the Third International* (1920) in the USSR and Yvan Goll's conception of poets atop the Eiffel Tower beholding (or perhaps themselves forming) a "symphony orchestra of clouds."

Engaged by what one called "the exasperated rhythm of modern life," poets no longer wrote "verse" as such, but allowed the exultations and grievances felt in the cities to expand their palette of compositional practices. In this new dynamic, the poem imperceptibly becomes manifesto, prose manifests the inner poetry of the sentence, and the visible arrangement of typographic materials yields texts in the process of becoming ideograms of modernity. The "poetic," purged of its decorative connotations, affirms a broader conception of "making" that remakes and documents the world in concert with railways and movie cameras. Narrative likewise splinters into accelerated data: Cocteau, for example, excitedly indexes

[11] Ezra Pound, *Patria Mia* (Chicago: Ralph Fletcher Seymour, 1950), 32-33.
[12] "$1,000,000 a Year to See City from Tower Being Paid by Visitors to the Empire State Building," *The New York Times* (6 June 1931): 19.
[13] Gertrude Stein, *Everybody's Autobiography* (Cambridge: Exact Change, 1993), 209.

"steamship apparatus–*The New York Herald*–dynamos–airplanes" next to "the telegraph operator from Los Angeles who marries the detective in the end" and "my room on the seventeenth floor"[14] without copula or further explanation, a gesture as extravagant as it is symptomatic. Contiguous works like James Joyce's *Ulysses* (1922), Rainer Maria Rilke's *Notebooks of Malte Laurids Brigge* (1910), Virginia Woolf's *Mrs Dalloway* (1925), John Dos Passos' *U.S.A.* (1936), Martín Adán's *The Cardboard House* (1928), and Louis Aragon's *Paris Peasant* (1926), conventionally understood as novels, appear here in excerpts as revelatory glimpses of a trans-generic poetics. In a similar strategy, *Burning City* pointedly includes poetry by figures known better for other accomplishments, like filmmakers Dziga Vertov and Jean Epstein, visual artists Hans Arp, Fortunato Depero, Francis Picabia, Kurt Schwitters, and Theo van Doesburg.

That so many poets of the era were tuned in to what might be called the Apollinaire frequency on the metropolitan wavelength provides initial clues into an understanding of the history of the international cross-fertilization of urban modernism. As the embodiment of what he called "the new spirit" (from which Le Corbusier's influential architectural journal *L'Esprit Nouveau* took its name in 1920) Apollinaire was a powerful vortex of innovation, including "poem-promenades," "conversation-poems," and the pictorial dynamism of calligrams. Roger Shattuck calls Apollinaire "a ringmaster of the arts": the tag is apt, evoking as it does the circus, the music-hall, and other venues of modernity before and after the Great War. Locating the far-flung associates of Apollinaire reveals an astonishing network, including, among many others, Blaise Cendrars, Pierre Albert-Birot, Jean Cocteau, Philippe Soupault, Max Jacob, and Tristan Tzara in France; Clément Pansaers in Belgium; Paul van Ostaijen in Flanders, and Theo van Doesburg in Holland; Yvan Goll, Alfred Richard Meyer, and Franz Richard Behrens in Germany; Vitěslev Nežval and Jaroslav Seifert in Czechoslovakia; Lajos Kassák in Hungary; Anatol Stern in Poland; Mykhail Semenko in the Ukraine; Joan Salvat-Papasseit and Joaquim Folguera in Catalonia; Guillermo de Torre in Spain; Mario de Sá-Carneiro in Portugal; Mário de Andrade in Brazil, and Vicente Huidobro, the Chilean poet who spent long periods in Paris and Barcelona. Yet "the Apollinaire movement" and its modernizing instigations proved to be only a starting point, and the variety of modernisms percolating in so many locations at once, broadly united by a collective fixation on city life, became apparent as we trawled through the dozens of vanguard journals of the early twentieth century, discovering forgotten works and neglected authors as well as rethinking the established bulwarks of literary Modernism.

Although scholarship and museum exhibits of the past decade have dramatically expanded the profile of the historical avant-garde and enhanced

[14] Jean Cocteau, quoted in Frederick Brown, *An Impersonation of Angels: A Biography of Jean Cocteau* (New York: Viking, 1968), 128-129.

understanding of the "social text" and texture informing artistic activity, the lack of ready (and readily comparative) access to many texts has left a conspicuous gap in awareness of early twentieth-century avant-garde poetry as a shared encounter with the phenomena of metropolitan modernity. A return to primary documents reveals how quickly and richly this gap may be filled, and *Burning City* is a feast of discoveries. Many of the texts retrieved here come from such journals as *transition*, *SIC*, *Grecia*, *The Little Review*, *The Crisis*, *Der Sturm*, *Orpheu*, *De Stijl*, *Contact*, *Integral*, *Montparnasse*, and *Zenit*. *Burning City* offers a return to the typographic versatility of the original publications environment (sometimes abandoned without explanation in reprints), both by retaining the look of the original texts in translation, and by judiciously selecting from the numerous, sometimes explosive typographic displays—even devoid of semantic content– characteristic of these and other vanguard publications. This re-presentation restores the emphasis on visual composition and permits the reader to see these experiments not as aesthetic idiosyncrasies but as constituent efforts in an international lingua franca. Moreover, the examination of such a wide cross-section of publications yields a recognition of discrete genres of urban modernist poetry recurring in different geographical, political, and linguistic contexts: conversation poems, street poems, café poems, flight poems, jazz and blues poems, and so on. Thus, while this volume as a whole offers the opportunity to transition quickly and freely from one section to another, and thus obtain a panoramic view or even a flying tour of urban modernism, consecutive reading within designated sections (galleries in which poems are arranged by inter-animating principles) will reveal constellations of details, interplay between selected texts and authors.

For example, the new technologies and media that transformed worldwide communication and facilitated the networks of influence and dissemination discussed above are reflected in this book's structural topoi. "Electric Man" tunes into the ubiquity of wireless radio, emblazoned in so many poems with the acronym TSF (*télégraphie sans fil*), the ringing telephones, the live current of the newly electrified metropolis. F. T. Marinetti's advocacy for "words in freedom" and André Breton's celebration of the "wireless imagination," Futurist and Surrealist propositions respectively, attest to the inspirational power of electric transmission. "Aviograms" display how communication fused with the vertical axis, as messages from distant ships at sea and written in the sky by smoke-trailing airplanes awed and transfixed crowds and individuals alike. The "Postcards" that punctuate *Burning City* bring greetings from various travelers in a medium staggeringly popular in this period: some 140 billion postcards[15] crossed the globe between 1894 and 1919,

[15] Lisa Z. Sigel, "Filth in the Wrong People's Hands: Postcards and the Expansion of Pornography in Britain and the Atlantic World," *Journal of History* 33.4 (2000): 561.

seven billion of them in 1905 alone[16]. These were mobile reminders of cities, for the most popular images were "photomechanical reproductions based on hand-tinted black and white photographs showing cities and tourist attractions in the United States and Europe."[17]

The wild variety of entertainments—cheering on the heroes of boxing, knocking back stylish cocktails, frenetically dancing to jazz—appear in *Burning City* like a culinary menu, a parade of enticements. Among the most popular sources for urban thrills were the circuses, both those that roamed the continents by railways and, later, those of fixed locations. Replete with acrobats, orchestras, and exotic animals, circuses offered fantasies and marvels to adults well before they gradually became "family entertainment," and depended upon industrial urbanization, the booming railways, rising wages, and the growth of women's employment. In its first five years (1904-09), Luna Park at Coney Island had 31 million visitors, each of whom paid a dime to get in (only to discover individual attractions inside had their own admission prices). Even literature might be found performing in its own ring alongside the tigers and clowns: the Spaniard Ramón Gómez de la Serna delivered lectures[18] in this environment, and Vasiliy Kamensky, dressed as folk hero Stepan Razin, recited his poetry on horseback[19] in Moscow's Nikitin Circus.

Film's stimulating effect on poetry, represented here chiefly in three "Cineland" sections (populated by such internationally recognized stars as Douglas Fairbanks, Asta Nielsen, Harold Lloyd, Barbara La Marr, and of course Charlie Chaplin, known in Europe simply as "Charlot"), ought to be understood as a close relationship of exchanges of influence. By the time Sergei Eisenstein was theorizing the cinematic practice of montage, montage had become an international idiom of modern poetry. In 1920 Yvan Goll declared, "The basis for all new developments in the arts is film" (Goll's own poem "Paris Burns" was compared to a film) and the following year Guillermo de Torre observed how "cinema aspires to become . . . the Art that is synthetic, muscular, integral, dynamic, and clearly expressive of our accelerated and vorticist era."[20] If poetry was becoming filmic, it was no less true that (and perhaps because) film was the newest evolution in poetry, an extension of cinema's history as an urban phenomenon.

---

[16] Bjarne Rogan, "An Entangled Object: The Picture Postcard as Souvenir and Collectible, Exchangeable, and Ritual Communication," *Cultural Analysis* (2005): 4.

[17] Rosamond B. Vaule, *As We Were: American Photographic Postcards 1905-1930* (Boston: David R. Godine, 2004), 51.

[18] Miguel Gonzalez-Gerth, Introduction, *Aphorisms* (Pittsburgh: Latin American Literary Review Press, 1989), 11.

[19] Harte, *Fast Forward*, 64.

[20] Guillermo de Torre, "El Cinema y la novísima literatura: Sus conexiones," Cosmopolis 33 (1921); reprinted in Documents of the Spanish Vanguard, ed. Paul Ilie (Chapel Hill: U of North Carolina P, 1969), 401-9 (trans. Tim Conley).

Readers will perceive topical and geographically localized arrangements within these and the other titled sections, where we have sought to animate a particular line of conversation between poets. “Multiple City” might be seen as a promenade through the “unreal city” commemorated in *The Waste Land* (1922), although a particular city may come into momentary focus the way London does in Eliot’s poem (Berlin, for instance, in the overlapping visions of Alfred Döblin, Walter Mehring, Basil Bunting, and Bertolt Brecht). “Whipcracks and Megaphone Chants,” along with “Parade of the Eccentric,” sets a carnivalesque spirit in motion. Later, a festival of Chaplin films—in which the icon trips from his earliest slapstick to his simultaneous zenith and nadir of celebrity—leads to a compendium of “A New Mythology,” disclosing Brooklyn Bridge and Eiffel Tower as icons of modernity along with the boxing ring and honking taxi cabs, twentieth-century sirens in which the myths of antiquity have come to nestle. Late-night meandering leads from one display or encounter to another in “Lunar Baedeker,” as the “Twentieth Century Blues” follow as sober reckoning after a night of prowling and carousing.

Burning City offers the reader a journey commensurate with the challenge and exhilaration of early Modernism, a crisscrossing of continents and oceans. The excited pulse of the cities, beating in these pages, will provide a traveling rhythm.

◈ OVERTURES ◈

NICOLAS BEAUDUIN: The City in Me [from *Cosmological Man*]

1

Centre of rotation: abyss to which everything is drawn
The buses wing their way
City in madness tramways and cars
City in frenzy seem to soar.

Crude and colored posted sheets
on the walls of the immense City
All along the streets café-bars peddle
poison and insanity.

Ha whirling
flames and clamour
synchronous images New unity of time.
engines mad with rage
dazzling panic

Brothels bazaars theatres
breaths of mint and pepper
shops in the eyes of millions
electricity
gas Palette of odors.
acetylene
Hypertension of batteries
jettisons bodies to fiery kisses
waves of machines
darkness that spooks
rotation of beacons
in the night assassinated by their two-edged electrical sword.

Turmoil of affairs
golden magnetism = in a design of sounds – lights

which electrifies me
and gives my flesh
Life with its power and its lightning.

2

Translation, algebra of forces — *within me*
without me

smashing their gangue and their crust
and vaulting into flights of faith.

Without end — Product
movements — Masses
assail me — Speed

$$\sum m\frac{dx}{dt} - \sum {}_{o}m\frac{dx}{dt} = \sum \int_{to}^{t} F\,dt$$

The immense City torments me,
(*fire-violence*)
bursts my heart.

Suddenly everything becomes internal
and my heart
at the rhythm of the motors
beats, *victory tocsin,*
at the Center of the Capital.

bars cinemas
deluge of crowds

3

My aroused being leaps up
in the fever of automobiles
whose wheels chew the pavement
My flesh is elated fran-tic-al-ly

A new soul — *passion movement*
penetrates me.
I sense another being
with another understanding
with not 5, but 6, 7, 8, 9
new senses (*subtler ones*)

aerials projecting for the Wireless.

I perceive an identical soul
(*range of electromagnetic vibrations*)
in the gleam of luminous-chemical waves
among parking lots, boxing rings
cinemas, meeting rooms,
theatres, music halls
where the City scrambles and flies
and dilates
A BOMB THAT EXPLODES in golden coils.

Forces *migrations mutations*
are *powers rays*
within me *myriads of lives*

Ho that this night should go on without end
the City growing more desperate ! . . .
Artillery of vertigo combining
(*rapid fire*) violence
VERTICALLY desire
madness.

4

To lie Swollen with an incomparable world,
in within me Machines rumble
child-bed and suns whirl.

Torture-joy
force that creates force that destroys

Numbers rays
Lights images } pound my soul with blows of rage.

All of your desires haunt my blood

Furnace City
where iron burns
where air wheezes } *paroxysm of matter*

where it all explodes

green
blue
red Infinite apotheosis.
gold

Ha my body reigns un-lim-it-ed
World, I am enlarged by your forms
and my spirit *shadow and light*
draws back, fearful at the sight
(*law of equivalents*)
(*synchronisms upon several plains*)
in myself appears

$$\frac{\mathbf{1}}{\mathbf{1}} = \mathbf{I}$$

(*mathematics of identity*)

OF BEING
the Cosmogonic Unity
OF BEING

CLAIRE GOLL: Twentieth Century

Oh my century!

Propellers churn in your heavens,
the bird-man of Romantic adventure
fighting with God.

From the gramophones
comes the metallic phoenix
singing an automatic song;
but what about the actual bird?

The woods are already subsiding
into cities.

What are ponds verdant with willows to us?
(There's too much sorrow in the world to dream of that!)
What of those yellow points, the stars?
What of the sunset
sifting each day?
Against magic X-rays
and solar-art violets?

We need the new urban landscape,
the dance of turbines,
the oily atoms of machines.
Petrol engines and radium alone protect
against the threats of existence.
Electric billboards are more efficient
than the moon,
a pianola in a suburban roadhouse
is better balm for my malaise
than all the nightingales.
The elevated rail is more intoxicating
than the heavenly cathedral.
We pray in cinemas
for the sprocketed gods of destiny,
in every express train
our longing finds a seat.
The heart functions electrically,
its red signal . . .

Oh cosmic sensation of speed!

You my century!
electrical gears,
speedway racer to the sun,
headlights on the stars,
I'm yours!

FRANCISCO AND GUILLERMO RELLO: The Voices of Life

Daybreak.
The sun throws down its lazy rays
practically rubbing them in your eyes
like a pair of hands.
And the voices of life start up,
those shapeless voices
that separately are strident shrieks
or harsh words
or breaths that escape the lips
like souls
or disgusting belches.
And all together, they make up a buzzing
of invisible bees
that make the eardrum wince
with their circular stingers.
A similar shriek in the dust of the roads
that from afar resembles a compact mass
but, looking closely,
dissolves in the retina.
And it blends with the honking horns
with the cries of the vendors,
with the songs of the blind,
with the barking dogs,
with the braying donkeys
and the church prayers.
And all form a single voice,
one sonorous zone
surrounding the city,
mingling with factory smoke,
and the higher you go the deeper it sounds
and the lower you go the higher it sounds.
And in this way, second by second,
and minute by minute
and hour by hour
with a tired and idiotic buzzing,
heavy and stupid as time,
always the same, always the same.

And so it goes until night descends
and the moon appears, wrapped
in the halo of light
that surrounds it
just as the voices and factory smoke
envelops the cities.
And the noise of the city abates
in the silence of the night,
just as Life is undone in Death
and the voices switch off little by little
like the stars dim out
with the dawn.
And now no more noise will be heard
until the sun rises again
and throws down its lazy rays
practically rubbing them in your eyes
and plucking out the sleep.

Gunnar Björling

I want to live in a city just like it is
with a W. C., electric light, a gas stove
and well-swept streets
a rich man's park at every other corner
and palaces and cafés, with wealth on display in the windows,
and at five marks or two marks rectilinear
glory.
A sea of light and gaudy colors
and faces, destinies
and the light of heaven—irritating my thoughts and a struggle and fresh-kindled love
for one at a time
and for all, all!
to be like a herb in the spring meadow
to stand like a tree among trees
filling one's place like a brick among the bricks
of the building,
to know that thousands love and are happy and have worries

and that the same beautiful eyes smile tears and burn and suffocate, dream, stumble, and are destroyed
but are going to a land for all and to a heroic deed with bright perspectives.
—I am happy with the streets and factories of the cities
and there is beauty without and within.
The heavens and the waters remain the same
and the night is not so dark under the lamps round streets and waters.
The emptiness comes alive with the sound of the collected dancing, cries, despair, and solidarity with all the well-known things,
and loneliness is a destiny to be borne alone among a thousand eyes, and struggling in the teeming crowd
is like walking under the heavy vault of the forest
with the vault of the stars hidden in your heart.
The thundering roar of the cities—all of them!
the like and brother of all
and the struggle for thousands to thousands
and the struggle against all
and finally the eyes, many eyes
known,
not known,
which we carry as in a bowl
which must not be spilled.

HAGIWARA SAKUTARO: Longing I Walk in a Crowd

Always I long for a city
long to be in a city's bustling crowd
a crowd is like a wave with a large emotion
a *group* of active wills and lusts that flow where they will
ah in the wistful spring twilight
how delightful to walk jostled about in a large crowd
longing for the shadows between labyrinthine city buildings
look at the way this crowd flows
one wave piles on another
waves make countless shadows   the shadows wavering spread and advance
the melancholy and sorrow I have for every one of the people   have vanished in the shadows there, without a trace
ah   with what a peaceful heart   I'm walking this street as well

ah merry shadow of my all-encompassing love and innocence
the way I feel, carried away by you, a merry wave, moves me almost to tears.
In the twilight of a pensive spring day
this throng of people swimming under the eaves of buildings
where, and how, is it going to flow
one large shadow on the ground that wraps my sad melancholy
flow of the drifting, innocent wave
ah however far it may be I'd like to walk jostled in this crowd this wave
where the wave goes on the horizon hazy
let us flow only in one just in one Direction

EMIL BØNNELYCKE: Century

I love you, mysterious age, rich in unguessed vicissitudes, rich in chaos, confusion beauty velocity splendor, rich in hard headed pluck and progress, rich in horror at its murderous overture War's guns trombones drums proclaiming World Revolution.

I love your technical sprawl, I love the machines mapping the land, a propeller age in which humanity for the first time rises above the earth, and who knows, other planets may be next . . . become human . . .

I love everything that happens and must happen.

I love the electro-technical alchemists, inventors gushing ideas in ceaseless marathon, those possessed with the critical love for production, fertility, roots, blood, sun, health.

I love the organizers, administrators, for their straight reckoning with necessity. I love the statisticians for their exclusive calculating logic.

I love mathematical equations, polytechnics. I think charts and graphs are poetry. The carefully applied strokes are pure poetry!

I love the expansive future, new spheres to conquer. I love train tracks for their bright blue rails. Railway track, chattering precision, English production.

I love the signal system, bridges, viaducts, drains and tunnels. The electric coordination is on a par with "Romeo and Juliet" . . . There are already enough treatises on "The Merchant of Venice" . . . these exceptional plays are crossed out . . .

I love the streetcar sidings, the poster pillar, a cigarette and a match better than any of Christian Winther's poems. (He really is an awful poet.) Isn't a sheer factory chimney in reinforced concrete a pretty profile? Simple, solid, precise. Isn't asphalt more fetching than greenery? Are trolleys, cars, bikes, kiosks, shops, ads, newspapers not a lush new dimension of the human psyche?

Is not the click of the telegraph, telephones, arc lights, elevators, cranes, trains, airplanes not a blossoming after millennia of terrestrial monotony? Oh, you young earth, you're like an infant taking first steps, just starting to talk. Think of your future. Imagine yourself as a cool, mature, dazzling orator . . .

I love ships, steamers. Oceanliners with four stacks, the broad decks and interior luxury shine. Radio operator, navigator. I love shipping lanes and their wonderful names: "Imperator," "Britannic." Cunard Line, Ø. K. United. Hamburg America Line. East Indian Lloyd.

I love trains. The locomotive is a better sculpture than any masterpiece by Michelangelo . . . I love the dining car sliding flexible along the rails singing songs with steel wheels. There's something homey in the sleeping compartment . . .

I love these migrant chambers, in which I'm at home . . .

I gaze into the majestic express, plundering distance by the kilometer, a runaway unicorn.

I love airplanes plowing the ether, given over to the clouds and risen to unbelievable heights. I love the irrepressible power and explosive noise of a Gnomotor, 1918 model, for its sound is the sound of the future. Propeller Song, deafening velocity hymn humming into the distance.

I love the sleek Propel design, its finely shaped limbs, the sweeping fuselage.

I love airplane wings, glittering oil tanks, struts and cables and guy ropes, carburetor, gears and spark plugs. These white and gold butterflies, gnats and sailing blimps that must populate the blue sky with unprecedented traffic, a giant vision. Oh, you nearby moment when transatlantic airmen launch from the aerodromes. American boats zoom into the Town Hall Square. Oh you age when streetcars make elegant spirals curving around City Hall. Line 42 the feeling of movement in curves, the ground flying by underfoot, the sense of being lifted and borne along, the feeling of moving in curves, rhythms, and the expanding evolving circle of man!

So, you century, radical clutch of space and beauty and terror, of fear and joy, of horrible reckoning. Humans are frightened by the power they gain from these forces... your depths have led to murderous swamp of war, that abyss from which greatness germinates. Impotent in the face of aberration they raise themselves up into rebirth in our Renaissance time.

Why are you, century, a Bigtime, Specialtime, Horrortime, Joytime. Such drama humans have never seen, to such a fierce World Atmosphere never submitted. Therefore, you century, youth time, spiritual contest, wild new dreams, sacred gamble emitting life, sport, speed, business, penetrating turmoil, competition. Woe to who fails to *choose.* He dies a second death. Falling away from the new age spirit relay runners...

I love you, happy Accidenttime . . .
I love you, you obvious Specialtime . . .
I love you, you riotous Crazytime . . .
I love you, chaotic Systemtime . . .
I love you, Darktime, Resurrectiontime,
Vast era Contradictiontime . . .

Valery Larbaud: from *Europe* [III]

Europe! You satisfy the infinite appetites
Of the mind, and those of the flesh
And of the stomach, and the unspeakable
And more than imperial appetites of Poets,
And all the pride of Hell.
(Sometimes I've wondered if you weren't one of those borderlands, a country
adjacent to Hell.)
O my Muse, daughter of the great capitals! You recognize your rhythms
In the constant rumbling of these endless streets.
Come on, let's get out of our evening clothes,

Here's an old jacket for me and this wool dress for you:
Let's mix with the common people we don't know anything about.
Let's go down where the students dance, and to the dime-a-dance halls,
Slumming in night-spots!
Tell yourself
That we're just passing through
Leaving shallow footprints
Disappearing in this shining mud.
For whenever we want we'll go back to the virgin forests,
The desert, the prairie, the colossal Andes,
The White Nile, Teheran, Timor, the South Seas,
The entire planetary surface ours for the asking!
Because if I were one of these people who stay in one place,
Working morning, noon and night in a factory,
Or an office, going out evenings,
Or playing a part in a theater for the hundredth time,
Or in clubs, or at the races,
I couldn't stand it! And like a farmer
Who comes back after selling his crops in town,
I'd leave,
Walking-stick in hand, and I'd go, I'd go,
I'd walk straight toward the Equator without stopping!
For me
Europe is like one big town
Filled with goods and all the urban pleasures,
And the rest of the world
Is an open country where, hatless,
I rush into the wind with a wild wahoo!

Jaroslav Seifert: All the Beauties of the World

At night, the black skies of streets were ablaze with lights,
how beautiful were the ballet dancers on bills between black type,
low, very low gray aeroplanes like doves had swooped down
and the poet remained alone among flowers, stupefied.
Poet, perish with the stars, wither with the flower,
today no one will mourn your loss even for an hour,
your art, your fame will wane forever and decline,

because they resemble flowers in a graveyard;
for aeroplanes, which are fiercely roaring up to the stars,
in your stead now sing the song of steely sounds
and beautiful they are, just as lovelier are the jolly electric blossoms
on the houses in the street than the flower-bed variety.

For our poetry we found utterly new kinds of beauty,
you moon, island of vain dreams, burning out, cease to shine.
Be silent violins and ring you horns of automobiles,
may people crossing the street suddenly begin to dream;
aeroplanes, sing the song of evening like a nightingale,
ballet dancers, dance on bills between black typeface,
the sun may not shine,—from towers floodlights beam
into the street they will cast a new flaming day.

Falling stars were trapped in the iron constructions of lookout towers,
before the cinema screen today we dream our fairest dream,
the engineer builds bridges in the wide Russian plains
and high above the waters will travel our trains
and on rooftops of skyscrapers when the lights burn brightly,
we take walks, without feeling the need to recite poetry
and like a rosary during prayer between bony fingers will bead,
the elevator rises between floors a hundred times a day,
and gazing from above you will behold all the beauties of the world.
And that which was sacred art only yesterday
suddenly was transformed into things real and plain,
and the loveliest pictures of today were painted by no one,
the street is a flute and it plays its song from dawn till night
and high above the town to the stars aeroplanes glide.

Well then, adieu, allow us to leave you invented beauty,
the frigate heads for the distance across the open sea,
muses, let down your long hair in grief,
art is dead, the world exists without it.

For greater truth is even in this little butterfly,
which, from its cocoon, having gnawed the book of verse, will rise to the sun,
than in the poet's verses, which are written on each its page.

And that is a fact that no one can deny.

LAJOS KASSÁK: Craftsmen

We are neither scientists nor abstract priestly Chrysostoms
nor are we heroes driven with crazy clamor to battle
and left sprawling senseless on sea-floor and sunny hilltop
and all over the thunder-beaten fields, all over the world.
Now the hours bathe in bad blood under the blue firmament . . .
But we are far from everything. We sit deep in the dark peace-barracks:
wordless and undivided as indissoluble matter itself.
Yesterday we still cried and tomorrow, tomorrow maybe the century will admire
our work.
Yes! Because quick force jets from our ugly stubby fingers,
and tomorrow we shall toast our triumphs on the new walls.
Tomorrow we shall throw life onto the ruins from asbestos and iron and titanic
granite
and away with the gilded dream-swags! the moonlight! the music-halls!
We'll soon set up great skyscrapers, an Eiffel Tower will be our toy.
Basalt-based bridges. New myths from singing steel in the squares
and shrieking blazing trains thrust onto the dead tracks
to shine and run their course like meteors dazzling the sky.
New colors we mix, new cables we lay undersea,
and we seduce ripe unmarried women to make each nurse new types
and the new poets can rejoice as they sing the face of the new times coming:
in Rome, Paris, Moscow, Berlin, London, and Budapest.

ILARIE VORONCA

AVIOGRAM

(instead of a Manifesto)

HERMETIC SLEEP OF THE TRAIN ENGINE OVER BALCONIES EQUATOR
PULSE MUST BE BIG **ANNOUNCEMENT** DYNAMIC MARITIME SERVICE
THE ARTIST DOESN'T IMITATE THE ARTIST CREATES
LINE OF THE WORD COLOR YOU WON'T FIND IN A DICTIONARY
VIBRATES CENTURY TUNING FORK
HORSE RACES ELEVATOR DACTYLOGICAL-CINEMA
I N V E N T I N V E N T

ART SURPRISE
GRAMMAR LOGIC SENTIMENTALISM AS LAUNDRY PINS
ON ROPES THE KINGDOM OF LUMINOUS POSTER CALLS
CHERRY-BRANDY WINE TRANSURBAN RAILWAYS THE MOST
BEAUTIFUL POEM: THE FLUCTUATING DOLLAR
THE TELEGRAPH HAS WOVEN WIRE RAINBOWS
IRRADIATOR STARTS OFF STIGMA AND **a b c** DENTAL ALPHABET
ASTRAL STENOGRAPHER
BLEEDING WORD TO COME
METALLIC THE DENIAL OF PURGING
FORMULAS AND WHEN
WHAT WE'RE DOING
BECOMES FORMULA
WE'LL DENY OURSELVES TOO.
IN THE ANAESTHETIZED AIR
CABLEGRAMS SINGING DIASTOLE OF STARS THOUGHT UNPACKED
THE MECHANICAL PIANO IS SERVING COFFEE WITH ELEGANT MILK
OH! RECITALS OH! CHARITY BALLS A LICENCE FOR SUICIDE
3 DINARS THE SIDEWALK HAS FILLED ITS TEETH IN A SPIRAL
MILK DIET THE CRANK IN THE DRUM
BOULEVARD READ ORIENT EXPRESS ANTHRACITE EMBRYO BUS

75H.P.

READER, DEBUG YOUR BRAIN!

HYDROCHLORIC MIRAGE IMPOSSIBLY ACHIEVED WHAT LITTLE EYES
LIKE POUNDED SUGAR INCEST PROCESSION
ABSTRACT TRANSATLANTIC NEWS AGENCIES
COLLIDE LIKE BILLIARD AIRPLANES

THEY GO DOWN LIKE BAROMETERS THE EUROPE LIGHTHOUSE NECKLACE IS BURNING
HAS CRAMPS SWALLOWS PILLARS USELESS COMFORTABLE AS BEST YOU CAN
THE INFINITE IN SLIPPERS MAKES AN ANNOUNCEMENT
BISEXUALITY ATHLETE FOLLOW THE RECIPROCAL DISCOURSE NEWSPAPERS OPEN
LIKE WINDOWS THE CONCERT OF THE CENTURY BEGINS
ELEVATOR RINGS INTER-BANK JAZZ JUGGLER

HORN
F FLAT
D
F FLAT
IN
PAJAMAS
FOOTBALL

Manuel Maples Arce: Metropolis

Here is my poem
gruff
multiple
of the new city.

O city all tense
with cables and strains
all humming with motors and wings.

Simultaneous explosion
of new theories
a little beyond
in the diagram of space
Whitman and Turner
a little this side
of Maples Arce.

The great lungs of Russia
breathe towards us
the wind of social revolution.
What does it matter if literary inkspitters
fail to understand
the untouchable beauty
of a sweaty century,

or the moons
deadripe
falling?
They are the bilge
that squirts
out of the spigots of solid intellect.
Here is my poem:
O strong city
multiple city
built all of iron and steel.
The wharves, the drydocks.
The cranes.

And the sexual fever
of factories.

Metropolis:
Escorts of trolleycars
running up and down the insurrectionary streets.
The show windows carry the sidewalks by storm
and the sun is sacking the long avenues.

On the margin of the days
marked off with telegraph poles
instantaneous landscapes flit
through systems of pneumatic tubes.

Suddenly,
O the green
powderflash of their eyes.
Under the noonhour's coy blinds
pass the red batallions.
The cannibal romance of Yankee music
has made its nest in all the ariels,
O international city,
towards what remote meridian
did that steamer set its course?
Everything is slipping far away.
Corrugated twilights film
the masonry of hills and woods.
Spectral trains wind away
into the far distance
puffing out civilizations.

The multitude broken out of doors
ripples musically through the streets.

And now the thievish bourgeoisie begin to tremble
for the leaders
who robbed the people;
but someone hid under his dreams
the spiritual pentagram of dynamite.

Here is my poem:

Garlands of hurrahs streaming in the wind,
flaring hair,
captive mornings in all eyes.

O city
full of music
built all out of mechanical rhythm.

Tomorrow perhaps
only the live embers of my verse
will glow to the trodden horizons.

2.

This new depth of landscape
is a projection into inner mirrorings.

Roaring crowds
today overflow the city squares
and the triumphal hurrahs
of the Obregonistas
rattle in the sun of the façades.

O romantic girl
all a flareup of gold,
perhaps between my hands
only these live moments will remain.

The hills dressed in yellow
were asleep behind the windowglass
and the trammeled city
has been left trembling in the wires.
That wall is all handclapping.

"Good God".
"Don't be afraid, it's the tidal wave of the crowd,
later on the fringe of silence
we'll see the Aztec night grow to immensity.

Put out the light in the chandelier.
Among the mechanisms of sleeplessness
desire with a million eyes
strokes the poor flesh."

A steel bird
has set its course for a star.
The harbor:
burning distances,
factory smoke,
above the orchestra tent
her memory suns itself.

An overseas farewell leapt out from the shore.

The motors sing
across the slaughtered landscape.

3.

The afternoon shot full of windows
floats above the telephone wires
and among the inverted
girders of this hour
hang bunches of mechanical goodbyes.

Her marvelous youth
went off one morning
between my fingers
and in the empty ponds
of looking glasses
shipwreck forgotten faces.

The poor sindicalist city
scaffolded all over
with cries and hurrahing.

Workmen
are red

and yellow.

Pistols have burst again into bloom
after the trample of speeches,

and while the lungs
of the sick wind
suppurate,
lost in the obscure corridors of music
some white sweetheart
shatters into withered petals.

4.

Among the thickets of silence
dust licks up the blood of twilight.
The fallen stars
are dead birds
in the dreamless water
of the mirror.

And the sonorous
artillery of the Atlantic
faded away at last
into the distance.

Over the autumn trees
breathes the night wind
the wind off Russia,
wind of immense tragedies.

And the garden
yellowing
founders in shadow.
Suddenly the recollection of her
sparks in the dull room.

Her gold words
sift over my memory.

The rivers of blue overalls
overflow the dams of the factories
and the agitator trees
gesticulate speeches.
Strikers pelt each other
with stones and insults
and life is one tumultuous
conversion to the left.

At the edge of the pillow
the night is a sheer cliff
and sleeplessness
stays whirring in my brain.

Whose are these voices
skimming over the dark?

And those trains howling
towards gutted horizons.
The soldiers
will sleep in hell tonight.

God,
of all this disaster
only a few scraps
so white
of her memory
are left in my hands.

5.

The savage hordes of the black night
threw themselves on the shuddering town.

The bay
all flowering
with masts and moons
pours out
over the gentle piano-score
her hands play,

and the far away cry
of a steamboat
towards the northern sea:

Goodbye
to a shipwrecked continent.

Between the wires of her name
fluttered feathers of birds.

Poor Cecilia Maria Dolores;
The landscape inside us.
Under the axestrokes of silence
the cast-iron buildings crumble.

The waves are of blood and the great hating clouds.

Desolation.

The speeches doped with marihuana
of the deputies
splatter crap on her memory,
but
over the surging crowds of my soul
she has sifted her gentleness.

Ocotlan
there in the distance.

Voices.

Detonations
go pecking among the trenches.

Desire threw stones all night
at the darkened windows of some virginity.

Machinegun fire
hacks off hunks of silence.

The streets
reverberating, empty
are rivers of darkness
pouring into the sea
and the sky
threadbare
is the new
flag
that flares
over the city.

◈ POETIC CIRCULATION ◈

RAOUL HAUSMANN

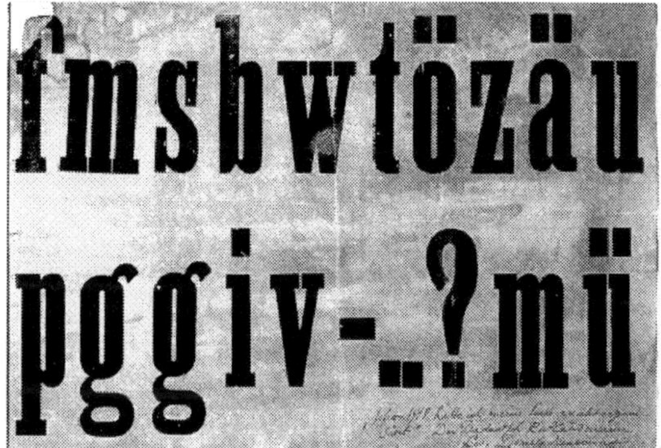

OFFEAHBDC

BDQ☞,,qjyE!

Josep-Maria Junoy

ARS POETICA

Z

SAȘA PANĂ

MANIFESTO

s a ș a p a n ă

"readers, disinfect your brains!"
kettledrum cry
airplane
wireless telegraphy—radio
television
76 h.p.
marinetti
breton
vinea
tzara
ribemont-dessaignes
arghezi
brancusi
theo van doesburg
huraaaah hurraaaaaa hurrraaaaaaaa

the library garbage is burning
a. et p. Chr. n.
12345678900000000000000 kg.
or rats get fat
scribes
dodges
sterility
amanita muscaria
eftimihalachisms
brontosaurs
Boooooooooooooooooooo

Combine verb
abcdefghijklmnopqrstuvwxyz
= art rhythm speed unexpected granite

gutenberg you're reviving

Álvaro de Campos [Fernando Pessoa]

The true modern poem is life without poems,
It's the train itself and not verses that sing of it,
It's the iron of the rails, the hot rails, the iron of the wheels, their actual spin,
And not my poems that talk about rails and wheels they don't have.

Srečko Kosovel: Rhymes

Rhymes have lost their value.
Rhymes do not convince.
Have you heard the friction of wheels?
Let a poem be the friction of grief.

Where to with clichés, dear speaker!
Put clichés in museums.
Your words must have friction
to seize the human heart.

Everything has lost its value.
The white sea of a spring night
spilling through fields, gardens.
An inkling of the future is passing us by.

Marianne Moore: The Past is the Present

If external action is effete
    and rhyme is outmoded,
        I shall revert to you,
    Habakkuk, as on a recent occasion I was goaded
            into doing, by XY, who was speaking of unrhymed
                    verse.
This man said—I think that I repeat
    his identical words:
        "Hebrew poetry is

prose with a sort of heightened consciousness. 'Ecstasy
affords
the occasion and expediency determines the form'."

GUILLERMO DE TORRE: Pentagram

Leaping in the pentagram
I multiply oceanic cables

The millipede magician
hides the streets in his hat

The surging skyscrapers
breathe through luminous electric eyes

Grand residue of faded nights

Laugh = healthy fan
Sonority   Impulse   Grimaces
Lovely picturesque anamorphosis
Clouds   alert for airplane songs

Periscopes   rip through
the horizontal mirrors of the sea
The horizon launches its daily show
The hours dance a rag-time
to the tune of my typewriter keyboard

Listen to the unprecedented 25th hour

Daily release of life's high tide

Round trip
Coming soon
On the polyhedral platform
of our new art
everything's going to be decontorted

MIHAIL COSMA: Preface for a Baedeker

Geographical atlas the loveliest poem
corrosive chuckle under the train tracks and oceans
Life or a series of railway sidings and docks
my thoughts cast out beyond where a suitcase can go

GEORGES RIBEMONT-DESSAIGNES: Poetic Circulation

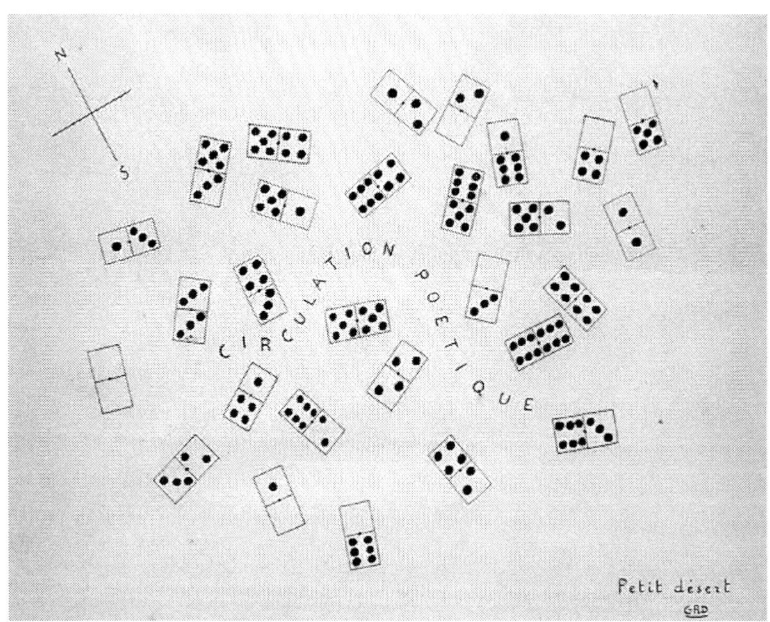

VADIM SHERSHENEVICH: The Rhythm of the Future

Every epoch differs from every other not in terms of individual episodes, anecdotes or facts, but in terms of its special rhythm.

We have lived through the age of foot transport, the age of horse transport and the age of the motor car (the twentieth century); soon we will have the age of the aeroplane.

If the rhythm of motion in the eighteenth century might be represented as a, then that of the nineteenth century might be represented as $a + x$, and that of the twentieth century as $a + x + y$.

Accordingly, the rhythm of the art of those centuries will be equal to a, $a + x$ and $a + x + y$ respectively.

The task of the contemporary poet is to express the dynamics of the contemporary city. That dynamics cannot be conveyed with the aid of content. That is: we cannot convey the city merely by talking about it. The rhythm of reality is a question of form and for that reason the appropriate formal method must be found.

Let us consider how earlier poets wrote. They usually selected some image as the basis of the piece, an image as leitmotif, so to speak, and the whole poem developed and illuminated that image quite logically. All the other images were subordinated to it, and dependent upon, that one leading image.

This strategy, which was a legitimate and essentially correct one when the old, slow and strictly orderly tempo of life was being communicated, is utterly useless today.

The chaos of streets, the movements of towns, the roars of stations and harbors, the whole fill, the quick of contemporary life, cannot be communicated other than by the internal motion of the verse.

This motion is brought into being by the multi-thematic or polythematic character of a poem. It is achieved because the images are no longer subordinated to a leading image. Every line is pregnant with a new image, sometimes one that directly contradicts the one in the line before. Images are heaped upon each other as messily as possible; they compete with each other for attention, and this increases the sense of tension and the notice taken of each individual image. If one image happens to be weaker and more anemic than the others, then the others will gang up and rub it out, trample it to death, leaving an empty space that defaces the whole line and indeed the whole poem. The images should not lie down next to each other tidily, like convent schoolgirls retiring to bed in the dormitory of the reader's mind. What is tidy and sequential is incapable of capturing a synthesis of the city; its motion is that of a horse being made to canter in circles on a lunging-rein. It does not matter if one image crowds out the one before because it contradicts this; that will mean that the reader is forced to be on his guard, forced to hunt down the crude and dominating lyricism of the images as a borzoi hunts down a wolf.

On the city street, hundreds of motor cars, electric trams and bicycles flash before my eyes every moment, yet I retain all of these in my mind at once; why, then, is the view commonly held that such disorder and speed in poetry makes it meaningless for the reader?

VASILY KAMENSKY: From Hieroglyphics to A

On the ceiling of the soul there rocks
with a tail of a smile
an electric chandelier
a sister of morning-evening
rusty coachman Zarathustra
betroths brides
hundreds of poems
ferroconcrete ones
in dresses made of fabrics
XRAYS
of bubbling energy
WORLD MORNINGS = it will raise
a florid advertisement
on blue velvet of
lines of letters
trolley sparks
crystal thawing
RECORDS OF HEIGHTS
    + 3.15
        of oxygen
to carry up like yokes the fate
        of news
OF THE RADIOTELEGRAPH
        from the island of ravath
where for the sake of the count or lord
they destroyed the warring tribe
        OF PEOPLE-PLANTS
        with wings
of mountain-peak birds
    Hamatsu-havu
OF THE FIRST AVIATORS
        who have flown to
Solomon
for the building of a temple
of the first to have read
from above THE PATH OF THE EARTH——————

Alexei Kruchenykh

And the chartered plane will hum
Carrying my fresh pomestrophics away
Over the Eiffel Tower over the fugitive ocean
There the backs of busses are waiting for them,
And newly-cooked I'll be a competitor for frozen pork!

Greasy vehicles with delicate hands will grab
My songsqueals conveying them throughout the world of quarters
Over the Citease, over the High Stars
Astonished people will stop cars and cablecars
And the sun will hang down like a butterfly from the frame!

Everyone will start reading Zaum
Studying my poetic gellescence,
So be happy till I'm with you
And don't wear that hangdog look.

Ion Vinea: Tip

And the constant clamor of the telephone sputtering utterly in vain.
My warm handclasp to whoever plants the flag.
Poetic art: to give the next guy a thrill.

Bruno Jasiénski: Song of Hunger [Prologue (Fragment)]

In hundredstreet multithousand cities
every day thousands of newspapers come out,
long, black columns of words,
are announced loudly in all the boulevards
they are written by little middle-aged men in spectacles
wrong
they are written by the City

in the shorthand of thousands of accidents
in its rhythm, pulse, blood
long forty-column poems
ticked out by multithousand machines
which feel the pulse of the world millions of miles away .
agencies: reuter, havas, pat,
kilometer-long rolls of papertape
messages
the city hears it all
it knows whom the spanish princess is marrying
and knows about the latest conspiracy of the germans in danzig
what new viaduct is being built in the himalayan mountains
radiotelegrams from California
and weather reports from Timbuktu
all this the city writes in its forty-column poems
this is true gigantic poetry
the only one ever new, every twenty-four hours
one that affects me as a strong electric current
how ridiculous is all other poetry in front of it
poets you are superfluous!

WALTER MEHRING: Prologue to "Berlin—Paree"

Poetry?
I spit on thee
And your moony idylleries
The ideal?
Unreal—
We sing in distilleries!
And if it ain't pretty, if it has the effect
Of shocking the burrjwa and such,
And if it doesn't taste holy,
It's still smelly—after all, it's holy-smoke hooch!
Maybe you love us, maybe you hate us—hey!
We're still singing with glee
From Berlin to Paree
In the cabaret—the cabaret—the cabaret!

In the dance halls
On the Spree canals
Surrounded by smoldering smokestacks
In Tierra del Fuego
On beaches where the gulls go
And high up in the Adirondacks,
Where a drunken sailor babbles
In the midst of stolen goods
On a barge full of apples,
In Potsdam behind the woods,
In the big-city ocean, on the high seas, hey!
We're still singing with glee
From Berlin to Paree
In the cabaret—the cabaret—the cabaret!

In the coal pits
And the suburban bits
On stages short and long
The old cardboard-box brothers
and the discovery of dead mothers
They all have their songs—
And what ripens behind the gate
With yellow bones lying about
And what the fancy man whistles late
When somebody gets rubbed out!
In the coziest booths in the slammer, hey!
We're still here singing with glee
From Berlin to Paree
In the cabaret—the cabaret—the cabaret!

Poetry?
I spit on thee
It's always the same old song—
A political song
An invidious song
The bank vultures sing it all night long!
And if it ain't pretty, we understand it, when
It's only our ears that ring!
We can write it ourselves, we can
Sing a song about anything!

As long as the green Spree still runs, hey!
We're still singing with glee
From Berlin to Paree
In the cabaret—the cabaret—the cabaret!

GUNNAR BJÖRLING: from *4711: Universalistic Dada-Individualism*

My songdoodle.
Capsized in the chair.
Finger the cigarette.
Exhale smoke.
Arms legs vents saxophones
what do I
know!
Dance
with cheek!
—Final march applaud
and I writhe jump
with everyone, things are rocking beneath the tables.
What is smile,
when a nerve can smile in the eye?

*

Jazzcleverness world press telephone café ensemble—
we need foreign faces around us the temptation of the unknown:
We found the salt in our coffee cup
and turned homeward in the distant travels.

*   *for Henry Parland*

"Gape roll" that's the philosophy, Dada's square well-groomed
lip fundamentals—
walk on the streets
be a facial nerve
talk with uncontrollable
thumbs

ANDOR SUGÁR

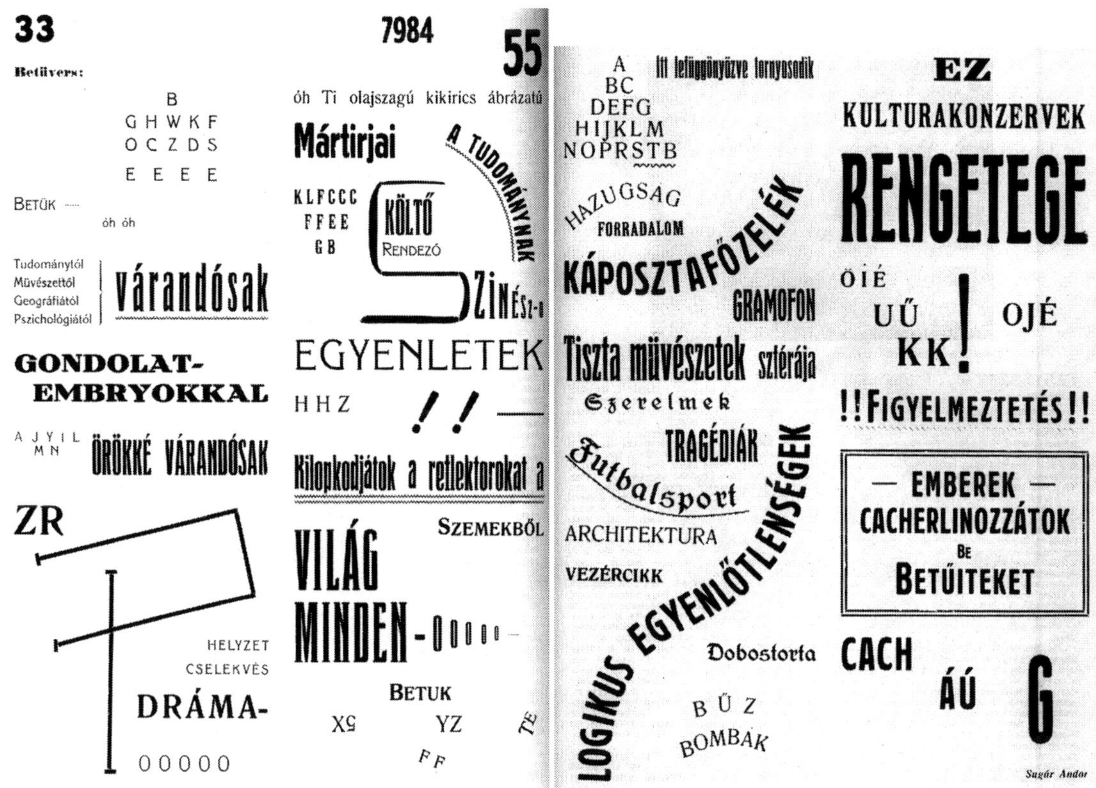

WALTER BENJAMIN: This Space for Rent [from *One Way Street*]

Fools lament the decay of criticism. For its day is long past. Criticism is a matter of correct distancing. It was at home in a world where perspectives and prospects counted and where it was still possible to adopt a standpoint. Now things press too urgently on human society. The "unclouded," "innocent" eye has become a lie, perhaps the whole naïve mode of expression sheer incompetence. Today the most real, mercantile gaze into the heart of things is the advertisement. It tears down the stage upon which contemplation moved, and all but hits us between the eyes with things as a car, growing to gigantic proportions, careens at us out of a film screen. And just as the film does not present furniture and façades in completed forms for critical inspection, their insistent, jerky nearness alone being sensational, the genuine advertisement hurls things at us with the tempo of a good film. Thereby "matter-of-factness" is finally dispatched, and in the face of the huge images spread across the walls of houses, where toothpaste and cosmetics lie handy for giants, sentimentality is restored to health and liberated in American style, just as people whom nothing moves or touches any longer are taught to cry again by films. For the man in the street, however, it is money that affects him in this way, brings him into perceived contact with things. And the paid reviewer, manipulating paintings in the dealer's exhibition room, knows more important if not better things about them than the art lover viewing them in the gallery window. The warmth of the subject is communicated to him, stirs sentient springs. What, in the end, makes advertisements superior to criticism? Not what the moving red neon sign says—but the fiery pool reflecting it in the asphalt.

LOUIS ARAGON: Imagination's Speech [from *Paris Peasant*]

One must take the rough with the smooth; each of you has in his own way put a brave face on things without relying on me. Moving from one illusion to the next, you have repeatedly fallen prey to the illusion, Reality. Yet I have given you everything: sky blue, the Pyramids, motor cars. With my magic lantern at your disposal, why do you despair? I've reserved an infinity of infinite surprises. As I said to the students of Germany in 1819, one can anticipate everything from the power of mind. Already its pure, fantastic inventions have, to giddy effect, given you mastery over yourselves; I have invented memory, writing, infinitesimal calculus. As the word distinguishes man from mute creatures, so other discoveries, not yet imagined, will make him unrecognizably different from his present image. What are you mumbling there? It's not a question of progress: I am just a cocaine pusher; my snow, your manna—whether memory or the experimental method—has the intoxicating properties of a mirage. Everything stems from the imagination, and all that is imaginary sheds light. The telephone is purportedly *useful*: don't believe a word of it; just observe man convulsing over the receiver as he shouts "Hello?" What is he if not an addict of sound, dead drunk on conquered space and the transmitted voice? My poisons are yours: here is love, strength, speed. Do you want pains, death or songs?

NICOLAS BEAUDUIN: The New Beauty

vibration
Art bursting forth from perceptible forces
powerful cries
new chromatism
transmutation
potential values

O the modern beauty
speed — daring — truth
you saw it TRANSPORTING RHYTHM

(New equation of forces)
vanquishing doubts – torpors
pulling you, spheroid, with horsepower,
covering the entire world with iron networks,
throwing up towers, tunnels and depots
in the assault upon two hemispheres.

Ardent *Insatiate*
Always reaching for the vastest life,
nothing resists you

DYNAMIC BEAUTY
of speed *of hope*

"Air Express"

pushing (*golden propellers on red and black background*)
the new humanity is paroxyst.

Beauty of brass *Beauty of fire*
GEOMETRIC BEAUTY
decorated with
purple and gold

THE ELECTRIC CITIES

thrown into spirals of pride:
heat of dynamos and winches,
bubbling of toiling vats,
multiple effort of the machines,
roaring airplanes in the sky
and flying over you, frontiers of hatred,
the lightning flight of hertzian waves.

BOŠKO TOKIN: Cinema Poems

1

Life: buildup of power.
Thwarted power is worked off daily.
American, our—life—certainly three films:
Charlie Chaplin, Douglas, Rio Jim.
Our America, three triumphs:
life (being alive), struggle (struggling), creation.
Accumulated powers, emotions, creating, raging,
the jazzband rages.
Owing to the play of Romanticism—mourning:
    Thirsting after freedom in my dreams
    Seeking new men, crazed, through the world.
When will my work see the light of the world?
The jazzband rages.
Our film (*title: The Standard Intensity of Life*)
is projected.
Our America: *wins.*

2

There, as here, a happy industry thrives:
Staša, Kraša, Tosa, Dada, Tin,
Mima, Rastko, Pera, Hipnos, Stop.
With "Paris" Douglas, happy dynamic.
Paris
city of isms and my friends.
Our heart's biplane.
Our soul's monoplane.

The new generation takes flight.
Striking women,
gallant thoughts,
have taken us far.
There.
Mainly we keep our noses clean.
We defeat
ourselves, yourself, every minute. Mainly.
Line. Victory. Style.

3

Life for most:
Question Answer, Answer Question.
Always: Question Answer.
Our life, a diminishing life?
Airplane, department store,
cinema, sports,
speed and art.
Art.

4

In a drawing a thousand lines
In an airplane a hundred possibilities
In a film a million flickers.
Embrace. Be an artist.
Always.

BOB BROWN: from *The Readies*

A dot and an angosturian dash with an hermaphroditic hypodermic hyphen is all that's needed nowadays, with maybe a word here and a blind spot there to help the heavy-heads out of their frowsy mental beds. Here's a poem, believe it or not:

—
. — 00
(Explain yourself)
— (Title)

. (Bullet)   — (Hyphen) O (Head)
00 (Heads)
Bullet-Heads
—
. — 00

...

In our aeroplane age radio is rushing in television, tomorrow it will be a commonplace. All the arts are having their faces lifted, painting [Picasso], sculpture [Brancusi], music [Antheil], architecture [zoning law], drama [Strange Interlude], dancing [just look around you tonight], writing [Joyce, Stein, Cummings, Hemingway]. Only the reading half of Literature lags behind, stays old-fashioned, frumpish, beskirted. Present day reading methods are as cumbersome as they were in the time of Caxton and Jimmy the Ink. Though we have advanced from Gutenberg's moveable type through the linotype and monotype to photo-composing we still consult the book in its original archaic form as the only oracular means we know for carrying the word mystically to the eye. Writing has been bottled up in books since the start. It is time to pull out the stopper.

...

Let's see words machinewise, let useless ones drop out and fresh Spring pansy winking ones pop up.

Without any whirr or splutter writing is readable at the speed of the day—1930—not 1450, without being broken by conventional columns confined to pages and pickled in books, a READIE runs on before the eye continuously—on forever in-a-single-line-I-see-1450-invention-moveable-type-Gutenberg-Wynkyn-de-Worde-Jimmy-the-Ink-Caxton-though-Chinese-centuries-before-printed-thousand-page-books-on-silk-leaves-furnished-by-local-silk-worms-no-two-leaves-tinted-alike-printing-from-dainty-porcelain-type-same-stuff-makes-teacups- - -dreams-Shakespeare-bending-over-workbench-making-language-laboriously- - -bellowing-blacksmith-turning-out-grotesqueries-at-forge-all-onhisown-to-keep-UP-interest-in-job- - -Spenstream-of-lusty-steamy-bigfisted-word- - - -moulders-flit-by- - - - - - Rabelais-BenJohnson-DanDefoe-Sterne-WaltWhitman-GertStein-JimJoyce-Stephen-Crane's-Black-Riders-Crash-by-hell-bent-for-leather-uppercase-LOWERCASE-both-together-chanting-valorously-Print-in-action-at-longlast-moveable-type-at-breakneck-gallop-Cummings-Boyle-Sandburg-flash-through-daredevil-commaless-Cossacks-astride-mustang-bronco-vocabularies-leaning-farout-into-inky-night-picking-up-carefully-placed-phrases-with-flashing-Afric-teeth—Myself-I-see-motherfather-newscope-Optical-Writers-running-round-newhorizon-rims-rhythmically-Eye-Writers-writing-endless-lines-for-reading-machines-more-optical-mental-more-colorful-readable-than-books- - - -simple-foolproof-Readie-Machine-conveying-breathless-type-do-eager-eyereaders-tickling-Inner-ears-dumping-Inner-ear-Eyefuls-of-wriggling-writer-right-before-receptive-ocular-brain-portals-bringing-closer-hugging-readerwriter-now-there-is-more-mental-necking-radioactivity-television-readievision-going-on-more-moving-reading-more-moving -

LUIS ARANHA: Cocktail

HOTEL RESTAURANT BAR
A chair squeaks
Waiter
In the mirror «try our COCKTAIL»
Champagne cocktail
Whisky cocktail
Alcohol
Absinthe
Sugar
Aromatics
Shaken in a metal tube
Cold and strong
Cocktail
Cocteau
Cendrars
Rimbaud
Cabaret'd
Spontaneity
Simultaneity
The intellectual plane is just confusing
Association
Rapidity
Happiness
Poem
Modern art
FOR A COCKTAIL!
NO: FOR ALL
COME FILL THE CUP OF MY HEART WITH A SENTIMENTAL COCKTAIL
Sentimental?!

IGOR TERENTEV: from *17 Nonsensical Tools*

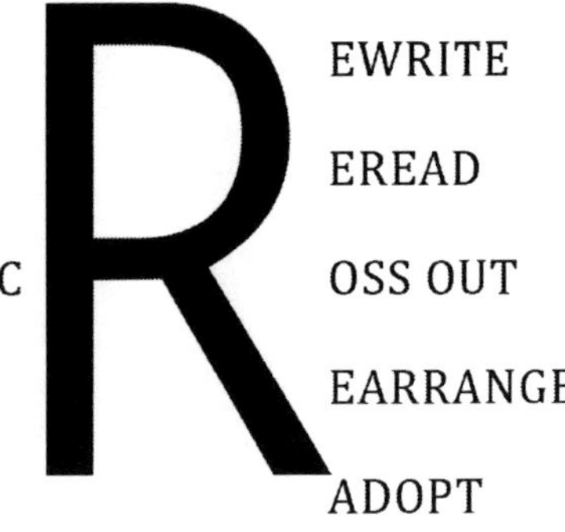

EWRITE

EREAD

C OSS OUT

EARRANGE

ADOPT

JUMP OVER AND SKEEDADDLE

двѣНадцатое

ЕрепиСаТь

ереЧиТать

ЕречеРкнУть

ереСтаВитЬ

ЕреНЯТь

еРэпрЫгнутЬ и УДРАть

◈ FUTURIST HOPE ◈

ARDENGO SOFFICI: Typography

BRUNO CORRA: Futurist Hope

Paris London New York monstrously engaged anxious scooptures machines insane speed refinement let's tentacularize ourselves romance yourself nickel-izingly absorb yourself torrid laughters perflumes catastrophes autocontrol will-power fashion elegance smile of a copper hand snipped from a wrist and abandoned in a basket of swallows futurism surgery Bonnot detach-ism and all the immobility of all the intensity of all the steel of all the madness assuming the appearance of deformed spheres will spring forth through the spiral track of all the chasms total review polygynists supermusculism speed speed towards the future extremely violent germusic

F. T. Marinetti: from *Destruction of Syntax— Wireless Imagination— Words in Freedom*

Futurism is based on the complete renovation of human sensibility brought about by the great scientific discoveries. Those people who now use the telegraph, the telephone, the gramophone, the train, the bicycle, the motorcycle, the automobile, the ocean liner, the dirigible, the airplane, the cinema, the great newspaper (synthesis of a day in the world's life), never imagine the decisive influence these things have on the psyche.

The train affords any provincial the chance to get away from his moribund little village, whose desert places are the playground of sun and dust and silence, to a great metropolis bristling with action, lights, and hubbub. The inhabitant of a mountain village, by means of a paper costing a pittance, can get all hot and bothered following a Chinese revolt, suffragettes in London or New York, Doctor Carrel, or the heroic dogsleds of the polar explorers. The sedentary dweller of any provincial town can get a kick out of danger by going to the movies and watching a game hunt in the Congo. He can admire Japanese athletes, black boxers, American jugglers with their bottomless bag of tricks, and elegant Parisian women, all for the cost of a franc at the music hall. Tucked up later in his bourgeois bed, he can enjoy the farflung voice of Caruso.

...

The wireless imagination and words-in-freedom will take us to the heart of matter. Discovering new analogies between distant and seemingly contrary things, we will approach them far more intimately. Instead of *humanizing* animals, vegetables, and minerals (as it used to be said) we will be able to *animalize, vegetalize, mineralize, electrify*, or *liquefy* style, making it live the life of matter itself. For instance, a blade of grass can be rendered: "I'll be greener tomorrow." So we have: *Condensed metaphors. —Telegraphic images. —Sum of vibrations. — Nodes of thought. —Closed or open fans of movement. —Shortcut analogies. —Color balances. —Dimensions, weights, measures, and speed of sensations. —The plunge of the essential word into the water of sensibility without the concentric circles made by the word. —Relaxed intuition. —Movements in two, three, four, five different rhythms. —Analytical explanatory poles that hold up the cables of intuition.*

AURO D'ALBA: Brush Strokes

Melee of streets   factories   gardens   hazy brilliance of windows
the mist of curtains
        the monotone dance of silence dressed like a drunk found out by a
searchlight
        crackling of stars drum-beats of resonant matter   (ground-bass for
the symphony of night)   lamp-posts
        like weeping willows in the fog   globes in drug-store windows
flayed red skulls   arcades of enormous reach their tension of arches
streets running terror-stricken to the city limits
        At every corner sound of footsteps echoes in a cathedral   the town's
square an impassable theaterpit of the night.
        Terraces glittering with stars for garlands   the campaniles are
rosaries of prayer
        the cities a bead-work of hearts strung like bridges from station to
station over gleaming railroad tracks.
        Gardens an ambush of spears   (a child's remembrance of soldiers of brawls in the
sunlight)   their lassitude perked up by the whips of fountains   some
windows alight
        policemen their shakos stabbed by prisms mirrored in visors   drunks
somnambulist strutters lolling by cab-stands   in the sky's dark loges the
ripple of constellations   the heart fluttering like a fugue
        From the city's highest tower the peal of a bell shatters the stillness
the bursting of a giant electric bulb.

VELIMIR KHLEBNIKOV

Cresting spines
of towering stronghold-books,
pages of glass habitats
on which to print inhabitants.

Here are cities: living books
ruffling their own pages,
towering stronghold-surfaces,
books set upright, bound in black,
where thundercloud plough-horses
shake sheets of blue lightning from their manes.
O write of rights, uprighting rites!
People gathered into human haystacks,
stowed as cozily as drying hay.
In the glass canyons of this city's streets
the balladeer calls us to play.
A city undefiled by scabby walls!
Habitable, populated pages,
glass woven into habitats,
shiny flatirons, pleating their inhabitants
into crisp, unwrinkled folds of symmetry.
Shelves of books, whose author's name is Sound,
whose common carcass—those who read the book.

FILLIA: Typography

fantastic rotary presses print electric snapshots of feelings on original white paper.

machine-subject in the lyric din set the technical composition to music, spasmodically, like songs that explode in your throat seeking a greater resonance.

modern linotypes dominating in movement. Lunatic sensibility of colors.

RED YELLOW BLUE BLACK

dancing figures-rainbows in a bright elegant merry-go-round between violences of forms.

brilliant totality of colors
ocular lust

— — — — —

Typography opens shouting at the crowd hungry for the future.

newspaper-poetry, a mass of feelings and colors, dedicated to the miraculous new LIGHT.

GINO SEVERINI

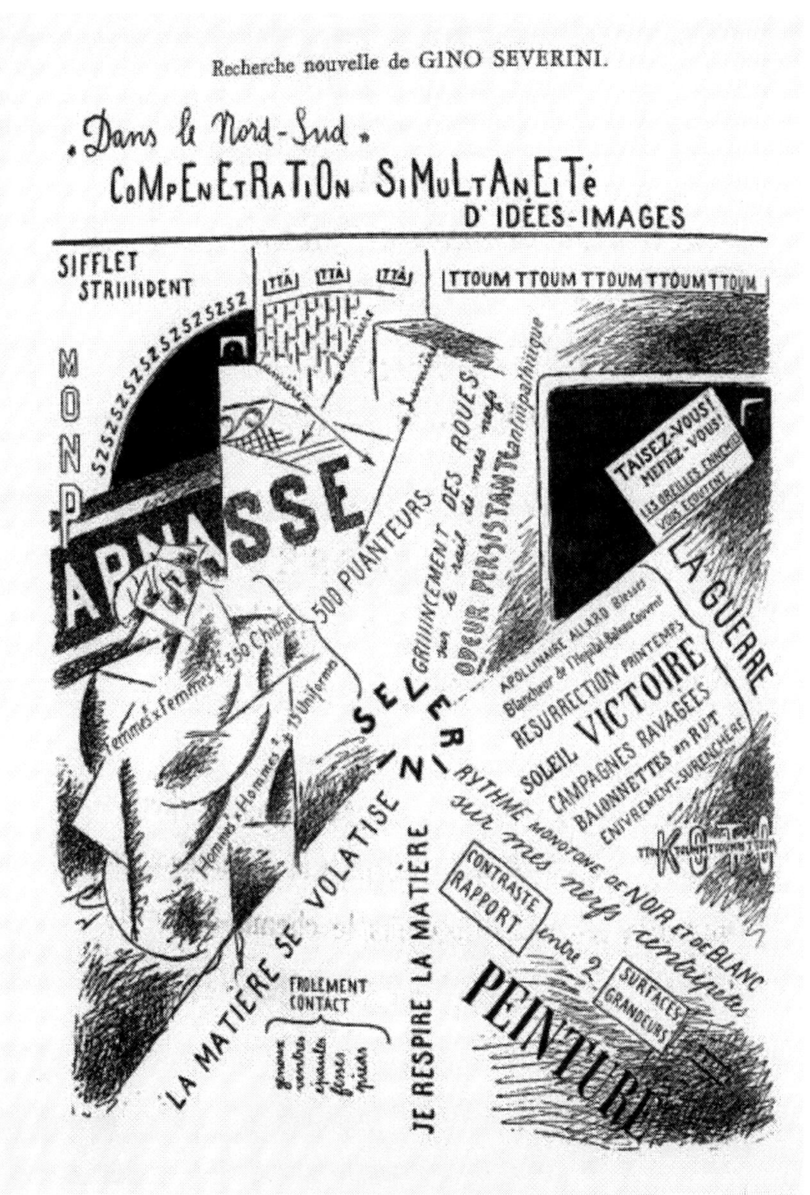

SHRIIIILL WHISTLE

women^5 x women^5 + chichis
stink
men^2 x men^2 + 15 uniforms

MATTER IS VOLATILE

knee GRIIIIIINDING WHEELS
belly TOUCH
shoulder CONTACT *on the rail of my nerves*
buttocks
feet *unpleasant* PERSISTENT ODOR

I BREATHE MATTER

HUSH!
BEWARE!
THE EARS OF THE ENEMY
CAN HEAR YOU

APOLLINAIRE ALLARD WOUNDED
Whiteness of the Hospital-Ship
SPRING RESURRECTION
SUN VICTORY THE WAR
COMPANIONS RAVAGED
BAYONETS IN RUT
INTOXICATION-UPMANSHIP

MONOTONOUS RHYTHM OF BLACK & WHITE
on my centripetal nerves

CONTRAST *between* 2 SURFACE
RAPPORT MAGNITUDE

P A I N T I N G

dirigible + sky

METROPOLIS

TUFTS OF CLOUDS CRYSTAL CURTAINS

VIRGIN OFFERING

DIRIGIBLE = LACE PILLOW
DRILL
HYPODERMIC NEEDLE
TORPEDO

CUTTING FLUID TUNNEL IN THE SKY

CRACKLING CASTANETS MACHINE GUN-ENGINE

FLUTTERING LOTTO ARABESQUE

Noise fades
fades faaaades

VASILY KAMENSKY: Summons

CACoPHoNy of SOUL

symphony of MoTOrS

———frrrrrrrrr

it is **I** it is **I**

futurISt-SONGWARRIOR and

PILOT-AVIATOr*)

VASILIKAMENSKY

with eLaAsTic pRopelLer

SCREWED into THe CLouds

for the visit

TO the FaT COURTESAN death

sewn from Pity

A TAngO MaNtLe and

STOCKINGS

with

PAnTIES

FORTUNATO DEPERO: Abstract Transcription of a Woman

SYNOPSIS: The portrait begins with hair, curls, "filamentous sensations." "She is neurasthenic"; there's a "brilliance of neurotic glances and fits." More hair and "lyric sympathy." "She's built—I like her a lot—inside of me a dialogue forms—vague—intimate—confused": as corroborated by bits of floundering exclamations. "Her clothes are adorned with lace, embroidery, jewels and trinkets. She's near me, speaking with a friend while I absent-mindedly think about her. She goes away and I hear her still absent mindedly." More linguistic debris ensues, following in the lady's wake. "What's more, I hear the rustle of her skirt."

VERBALIZZAZIONE astratta di SIGNORA

capelli

sensazioni filamentose:	*riccioli:*	*masse:*	*essa è nevrastenica — luminosità degli sguardi e scatti nevrotici:*			
simpilli	liri biri	CHIOMOLLE	ROSLUCI	pic	sss	PIZZZZ
carilli	ciri lilliri	MOCOLLE	ACUCI	pic	sss	PIZZZZ
billi	rirriri	OLLOME	VIDICIP	SGUIC	sss	PIZZZZ
occhilli	birrriri	OLLO	CILOPIC		sss	PIZZZZ
mirilli	ciriri ri	ELLE	SPRIZZZZZ		sss	PIZZZZ
ollichi	pirilliri	MELLECO	LUCIZZZZZ	FISS	sss	PIZZZZ
	ri ri ri ri	NELLOLLE	SBRIZICIZZZ		sss	PIZZZZ

Essa è ben fatta — mi piace assai — dentro di me nasce e si sviluppa un dialogo—vago—intimo—confuso:

CHE BE! AMA CHI BA! NOBI..... PERSICOSI'... NO MAI TE!..
COSTI.... MANO.... SI CHE VOI SI.... NO CHE SE.... PER.... IO.... MI
CHE SI PER PER PER SI-SI-SI....... PERSI'................. COSI'.......

Essa ha gli abiti adorni di pizzi — ricami — gioielli e gingilli:

TRI BLI CRI
RODRI NORIDLI **ORINDI**
RIVLI clodoli **CLODLO**
CORINDILINDOLI
BLO BLI
CODOL BIBLO

Mi è vicina, parla con l'amica mentre io distrattamente la contemplo:

IO MI SA SI SA
SASI SASI GIÀ MA
POI SE FORSE
MA LA SETA il COTO
che so se poi essa
MI SA SI
SASI SASI la seta
che se forse cheso cheso
Se io MI SA SI

Si allontana e l'ascolto sempre distrattamente:

ESEORIALACAMI
ONOEFICICABALA
NOTIBACILOFRONICHI
MISIBERONICO
LA MANISECHERO'
chirullimaconi

inoltre odo il frusciare della gonna:

aefffff-ififfff-uvofff-
BLO—CLONOBLO ***novolovo - sovonosovvvvv***
COBLOVV—VLO—BLO—MNOLOVLO zzZLOWOMMMO

ROMA 1916

STEPHAN ROLL: F. T. Marinetti

interrupted your silhouette skyscrapers gripped between the teeth like a dagger
I want to stroke your neck like I climb the Eiffel Tower the way I guzzle vitriol
the submarine passes across your eyes (what a handsome metal cowboy)
from great distances words add alcohol to glands

sometimes shoulders crackle like iron bridges
old century assassinated in a unique gesture of apoplexy
the globe sweats under the trains like the grimiest of miners
and fifteen acres of heart stuffed in our poetic upholstery

and if trains serenely pierce actual mountains
steamships had best replace the mythic sirens
futurists we bite the sun like an apple
in the air everywhere disheveled antennas and planets

I swim 50 meters in you—and before and behind
what body cyclone sweeping the raspberry villages off the map
at every step the sky melts howling into us
and we crack open books in windows like fissures in the clouds of art

the prospect rapidly opens in the middle of the racetrack
body traversed like gold mines of the American West
from time to time I torch your petroleum regions
and Thursday I'm your globe-trotter in the bloodstream

after that, Marinetti,

integralists we sky up the air in a plane
amuse ourselves igniting constellations with coal
ultra-poets we make our descent into stadiums
to write poems and do ten rounds of boxing

ION VINEA: Empty Words

Metro, metronome, mechanical, constructive: nickel,
express, radium, telephone, radio, cable,
elevator, thermometer, petroleum, integral
calculus, vermouth, speed, passport,
radiator, voltaic arc, pneumatic, motor,
alcohol, turbine, etc.
—in current opinion it's ok
to use all these industrial terms
dressed up as words in
freedom, to be a modern
poet...
It's a lexical revolution.
It's a hairdresser understudy's notion.
To what revolution of sensibility, really?

◈ AVIOGRAMS ◈

VIRGINIA WOOLF: from *Mrs Dalloway*

The sound of an aeroplane bored ominously into the ears of the crowd. There it was coming over the trees, letting out white smoke from behind, which curled and twisted, actually writing something! making letters in the sky! Everyone looked up.

Dropping dead down, the aeroplane soared straight up, curved in a loop, raced, sank, rose, and whatever it did, wherever it went, out fluttered behind it a thick ruffled bar of white smoke which curled and wreathed upon the sky in letters. But what letters? A C was it? an E, then an L? Only for a moment did they lie still; then they moved and melted and were rubbed up in the sky, and the aeroplane shot further away and again, in a fresh space of sky, began writing a K, and E, a Y perhaps?

VASSILY KAMENSKY: Flight

i
io
io
epzy
a little more
fog [fragment]
or [fragment]
greatness trembles
higher than the city, into deep blue
turn steeply toward the sun
horizons grow light
strips of fields run higher
suddenly lightly the earth departed
the wings reeled in the wind
the contact propeller is set
aerodrome crowd mechanic hustles

Flight of Vasya Kamensky on an airplane in Warsaw
(read from bottom to top)

PAOLO BUZZI: Highway to the Stars

We were flying at a hundred miles an hour.
The night advanced a thousand miles a minute.
Whorls of lead, clouds shifted in the sky;
the mountains reared their peaks of anthracite.
The lake below us looked like a basin filled
with the ink of cuttle-fish.
Lights began to flicker along the shore.
On and on we sped, as through a mighty sea,
cross-hatched with lines and shadows,
our nostrils flaring in the windy mist.
The landscape rumbled to our engine's roar,
and my heart sang an ode impossible to repeat.
Behind us the women chattered gaily, like fountains,
their veils caught in the blow, and trailing perfume.
Suddenly, lights flaring—
we streamed away, a comet with a tail,
on a highway of bright abysses of stone and water and air
fixed in the devil-prism of our beam.
The rain poured, spilling diamonds.
Blackness all about,
the women's eyes shot sparks,
and in that wide and glowing orbit
we lived through a grand vertigo of whirlpools
like strange creatures of fire
from another part of the far-flung galaxy.

Later,
bone-drunk on starry metaphysics,
how like gods—in the stillness of the spirit's cloister—
did we warm our flanks and our dreams
by the glowing meteors in the fireplace!

PIERRE ALBERT-BIROT: Poem for Voice and Dance

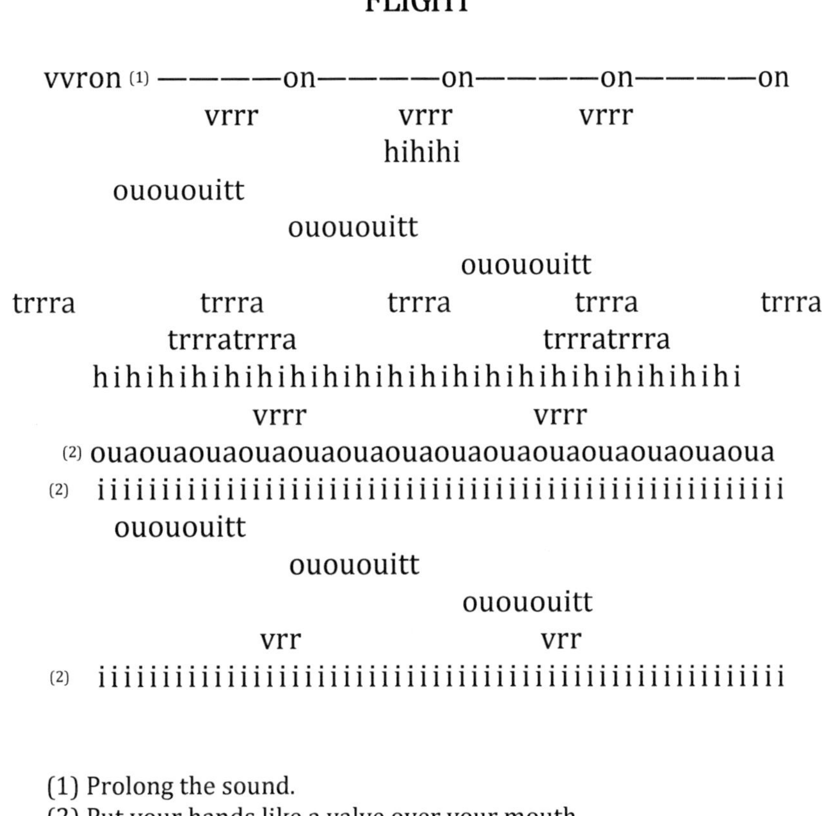

FLIGHT

vvron (1) ————on————on————on————on
vrrr vrrr vrrr
hihihi
ouououitt
ouououitt
ouououitt
trrra trrra trrra trrra trrra
trrratrrra trrratrrra
hihihihihihihihihihihihihihihihihihihihihi
vrrr vrrr
(2) ouaouaouaouaouaouaouaouaouaouaouaouaouaouaoua
(2) iiiiiiiiiiiiiiiiiiiiiiiiiiiiiiiiiiiiiiiiiiiiiiiiii
ouououitt
ouououitt
ouououitt
vrr vrr
(2) iiiiiiiiiiiiiiiiiiiiiiiiiiiiiiiiiiiiiiiiiiiiiiiiii

(1) Prolong the sound.
(2) Put your hands like a valve over your mouth

GUILLERMO DE TORRE: Upon Landing

And I have avidly beheld, in euphoric visual spasm, a beautiful view of the future,
reflected in the laminated awareness of your helix,
oh, augural sailing boat!
Returning from your extratelluric raid you landed vibrating with a flutter of wings,
in my erect cranial hangar...
The multi-souled city opens its central viscera and extends its peripheral members
like tentacles.

The infinity of crystal buildings—vertical villages—capped by domes of agricultural stations, traverses convulsive dynamism of clear rectilinear avenues.
In its vortex-shaped estuary traditional glances sink.
And the flow of polyrhythmic human tide jostles with noisy machines and telegraphic gestures.
Sensory perceptions flow out osmotically.
Surgical locomotives advance on huge bridges over clouds of smoke, drilling the mountain torsos.
Over celestial hills, covered with living stars, squadrons of grand airbuses pilot the azure.
The passengers, leaning on orographical perches, behold the lyrical posters stars skillfully beam down on crystal prairies.
The arms, like wings, of adolescents row in the sapphire blue ocean.
Their tarsi, adorned with stars as if they were jewels, punctuate a horizon with dactylic stress.
And libertarian lovers swing in the pentagram of telegraphic wires!
In the blue boulevards, golden-pink boys wrap their fingers in the wires of tamed planes!
Androgynous girls manipulate electrical switches of morning stars!
A trolley, its soul hanging on the horns of the moon, blooms in the insurgent cranial vaults of rebellious transients!
In the hemihedric night, electric necklaces of women light up!
And behind their breasts, in the endocardium, the compass of erotic whims sets a course into the future!
Dynamic Propeller Impulses
Striations of light liquefy creationist hypervitality.
Sunlit yearnings of Ultraist Lucifers crystallize electric charges!
Auras have a mental taste—exiting the propellers where the engines crash the dialectic—.
On the pedestals of mythological icons, flex your muscles, living gymnastic statues.
Hypertropic branchiated nerves, clipped in spring gardens, emanate arousing fragrances.
And in the gauges the needles press beyond the limit, revealing supreme emotional pressure!
Fiber bundles of jubilant flesh burn like sheaves on the great night of pyrotechnical scorching desires.
Bellowing senses flap like a banner over the insurgent instincts.

All that is sensed in the limpid landscape is smooth, dynamic, *happyized.*

Art returns to its pure cosmic infancy. Released from the school of Fine Arts,
painters move like a magic paddle to the undigressed chromatic polyphony.
And others, lyrical newborns, handle on a dictionary tablet, as on a typewriter,
roaring plastic verbosity . . .

Oceanic aortas flow from a newborn tide.
And the dionysiac rhythm of life vibrates to the pulse of the Zodiac.

Gino Soggetti

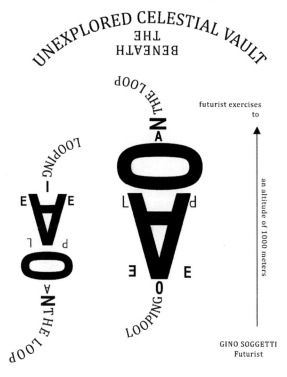

ATHLETES OF THE AIR

WORDS IN FREEDOM

UNEXPLORED CELESTIAL VAULT
THE
BENEATH

THE LOOP
N
A
O
L A P
E E
O
LOOPING

LOOPING
I
E A E
L P
O
A
N THE LOOP

futurist exercises
to
an altitude of 1000 meters

GINO SOGGETTI
Futurist

F. T. MARINETTI

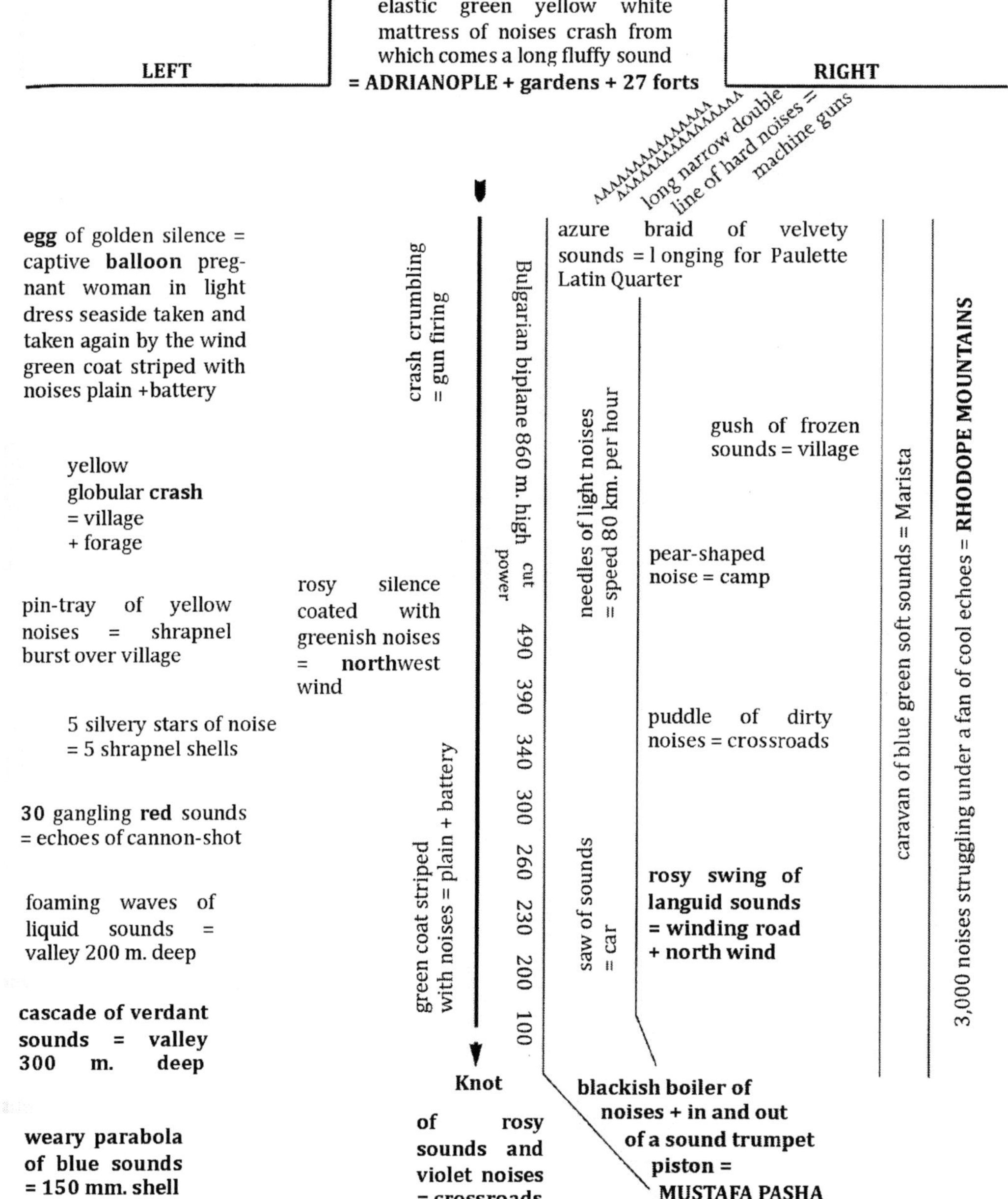

SYNCHRONIC CHART
of sounds noises colors images smells
hopes desires energies longings
drawn up by the aviator Y.M.
elastic green yellow white mattress of noises crash from which comes a long fluffy sound = ADRIANOPLE + gardens + 27 forts
LEFT
RIGHT
long narrow double line of hard noises = machine guns
egg of golden silence = captive balloon pregnant woman in light dress seaside taken and taken again by the wind green coat striped with noises plain +battery
yellow globular crash = village + forage
pin-tray of yellow noises = shrapnel burst over village
5 silvery stars of noise = 5 shrapnel shells
30 gangling red sounds = echoes of cannon-shot
foaming waves of liquid sounds = valley 200 m. deep
cascade of verdant sounds = valley 300 m. deep
weary parabola of blue sounds = 150 mm. shell
crash crumbling = gun firing
rosy silence coated with greenish noises = northwest wind
green coat striped with noises = plain + battery
Bulgarian biplane 860 m. high
cut power
490 390 340 300 260 230 200 100
Knot
of rosy sounds and violet noises = crossroads
azure braid of velvety sounds = longing for Paulette Latin Quarter
needles of light noises = speed 80 km. per hour
saw of sounds = car
gush of frozen sounds = village
pear-shaped noise = camp
puddle of dirty noises = crossroads
rosy swing of languid sounds = winding road + north wind
blackish boiler of noises + in and out of a sound trumpet piston = MUSTAFA PASHA
caravan of blue green soft sounds = Marista
3,000 noises struggling under a fan of cool echoes = RHODOPE MOUNTAINS

W. H. AUDEN: The Airman's Alphabet

ACE—	Pride of parent and photographed person and laughter in leather.
BOMB—	Curse from cloud and coming to crook and saddest to steeple.
COCKPIT—	Soft seat and support of soldier and hold for hero.
DEATH—	Award for wildness and worst in the west and painful to pilots.
ENGINE—	Darling of designers and dirty dragon and revolving roarer.
FLYING—	Habit of hawks and unholy hunting and ghostly journey.
GAUGE—	Informer about oil and important to eye and graduated glass.
HANGAR—	Mansion of machine and motherly to metal and house of handshaking.
INSTRUMENT—	Dial on dashboard and destroyer of doubt and father of fact.
JOYSTICK—	Pivot of power

	and responder to pressure and grip for the glove.
Kiss—	Touch taking off and tenderness in time and firmness on flesh.
Looping—	Flying folly and feat at fairs and brave to boys.
Mechanic—	Owner of overalls and interested in iron and trusted with tools.
Nose-Dive—	Nightmare to nerves and needed by no one and dash toward death.
Observer—	Peeper through periscope and peerer at pasture and eye in the air.
Propeller—	Wooden wind-oar and twister whirler and lifter of load.
Quiet—	Absent from airmen and easy to horses and got in the grave.
Rudder—	Deflector of flight and flexible pin and pointer of path.
Storm—	Night from the north and numbness nearing and hail ahead.
Time—	Expression of alarm

and used by the ill
and personal space.

UNDERCARRIAGE— Softener of shock
and seat on the soil
and easy to injure.

VICTIM— Corpse after crash
and carried through country
and atonement for aircraft.

WIRELESS— Sender of signal
and speaker of sorrow
and news from nowhere.

X— Mark upon map
and meaning mischief
and lovers' lingo.

YOUTH— Daydream of devils
and dear to the damned
and always to us.

ZERO— Love before leaving
and touch of terror
and time of attack.

JEAN COCTEAU: Parable of the Prodigal Sun

where the poet tells of Garros' famous flight and his return to earth

Sport

dawn

a dim awakening of Aphitrite

a hanging morning

chilly waves
one after the other
bathe on the sea side
playing bones

ebb and flow
systole   diastole

the stitch of cold foam
the froth between the pebbles

those eggs those hearts those little loaves those skeletons
petrified alive by water

the wind tests its pulleys
a bird shrieks and escapes

pine trees

that sailboat without a Mizzen without a Topsail
without a Spanker
without a Jib without a Flying Jib
without a Crossjack
the little stiffwinged boat
on the down
like a seal

The naval officers
and the young woman with the fur cloak
                              anguish sinks
                              into the bosoms

seaweed

the new yawl by the rail
in her christening robes
her hull ready for other waves

furs   tow   Eskimo

the pilot
pulls down leather over his ears
puts on his gloves
                calm
                steady
the newly fitted Morane machine
he examines
the red propeller
that can split
astern the palmed tail of the wheels
the bolts   the tank
without a word
foresee the least accident

cigarette

the morning fleet
            manoeuvres   westward

Fréjus

I shall have to go

a belt around the loins
the opossum hump
the map and the route in ink on
the yellow islands
compass

The two young sailors quite moved
although they have been through many squalls
where they could not weigh anchor
      a smile
      to these captives of soil
and farewell to the lady
before the mask   a dumbness
            aquarium
cinematograph   hypnosis
chloroform
sixth sense

the prodigal son
felt his span
down to the tips of his wings
like a blind man
down to the tips of his wide-stretched arms

the beech
the pier

the creek

goodbye
turn the propeller

already far away jolts detonates
and bellows in a semi-circle
tearing off sods
motor explosions
battle with the earth
to destroy a rail of planetary
obedience

at last
witnessed only by officials
and by a pack of cows one of which
throws itself into the water
as if it had a hornet in its ear
the young man
pulls off the artificial bird
from the dune

and the sun after it

South
he flies away
immense heat

of the day

a convict free from prison

peninsula of the Esterel

the gradually indistinct bellowing restores
already
a marble silence of statue
attesting the incipient exploit

how would this astonish you
old Mediterranean
fundamental mirror of myth
giddiness and its censers
reverberation
lark

the sea
glitters
bob-sleigh lift
swing scenic railway
pink Esterel
on the right
cheers of all things to light
dazzled polish of a wing
one plane more and more distinct
rejoicings after deluge
hashish of emptiness
enchanted canoe
seat so narrow
strap

The adventures of the Grand Vizier
and of a Manchurian magician
the Prince
looks at his compass
and at various implements of magic
under his turban
of leather
of fur

of glass
of cork
of aluminum
and of rubber

starry roof of the palace of octopi
of sponges

a click

the propeller one blade then
another then
the blades

he sees the
blades

where blazes
a lottery of sky

the motor is silent

the airplane
dives steep down

into emptiness

helpless a mythic dive
at four thousand from earth

the fishfed gull
falls
beak-heavy
on its deep
prey

this world's end tar
and pastorals of foam

Ganymede victorious
over the eagle Jupiter
returns to his bleeting flock

the shadow of the wings   covers the sea

but the propeller
in its fall
starts turning
and revives the motor
watchful of the sublime fate

just a little short of it

floating airplane wreckage
water sepulcher

the pilot feels at his neck a silver
medal
gift of the bravest
beloved

free
                    a
          keen Iliad air

leather cuirassed Pallas
over fleets
over riots

the pilot escapes anew

the prison of weight
on the fleeing captive's track
lets loose its soldiers and its pack

                                        higher

higher
a secret wheelwork broken   is the motor
going to stop

slopes of the void
its warm rivers
its gulfs   where   he   turns
its pumps of icy moraine
its Guadalquivirs   its Gulf Streams
its Lake Tchads

its Zuydersees

the right road he loses
where are those islands
one ought to see in front

nothing here gives bearings
nothing shows
the landward road
neither map
nor compass   febrile blue
insect
at the heart of the Rose

rearing he aims at
the falls of the sun
which
following the same road faster
gives the time

a sirocco cyclone

brass blazes

leather boils
sea sunstroke
blind he soars   hothouse
his nostrils bleed
his legs are numb
in the furs and wools

cramped hand

the varnish on the wings shrivels

exhausted is it going at once
to take fire in full flight
like a boat soaked in petrol
a moth at a gas lamp
and Sieur Roland
                the other one
blowing his horn bursts an artery
at Ronceveaux Pass

and the new one

son of the
ever loving pregnant earth
forges
with the fire of the sky
without an anvil
like Durandal and Joyeuse

feathers   wax

a marvelous revenge
on Dedalus and on the child
daubed with the honey from the hives of Minos

JOSEP-MARIA JUNOY: Guynemar

SKY
OF
FRANCE
in the mortally wounded aircraft the engine still roars brightly while the soul of the intrepid young hero is already flying aloft to the constellations

JUAN MARÍN: Looping

to "LOOPING" puppy
mascot of naval aviators

going up 5000 meters
this morning I wanted to do a looping
accompanied by "Saxophone"
a black Pekinese, my mascot
and my main concern
the track was so lovely
limpid as decoration
without wind without fog

without a single tremor
working it up a bit
old Motor
let's have fun like before
with Marion
while passing her window
shooting a kiss in "medium roll"
doing the clown and we see
the gigolettes of Orion
and as though it understood
the old plane frolicked and bounced
it's all a question of speeding up
and "pecking" with love
while a strong firm hand
opens the throttle to "full"
how do the struts whistle in the wind
how do the wings sing their song
good rain needling the face
and in the ears the lyric trumpet
of Nebuchadnezzar
control is getting hard
the land rises toward the "capeaux"
whoa! a chessboard spins
into a fantasy of the Charleston
the propeller's bent on reaping
the sheaves of the sun
the moment is here!!
the heart throbbing seesaw
righting the feet
to a straight line
hand tight on the control
it's a knock!
a sharp knock
and so the eyes won't close
switch heels
the engine draws an agile crescent
without the slightest hesitation
now
rising up into space
like a bubble or an electron

is mounting to be steadied
with nerve
                    the eyes see the sky clearly
                    like a sea of Japan
the fixed vacancy in the seat
in a great pressure
already the machine is crossing
the vertical
its voice
has the anguish of a tense rope
string of a giant guitar
the old Rolls-Royce gasps
in the windshield glass
I see the face and astonished ophthalmology
of "Saxophone"
                    the hand
now closing on contact
pressing a button
                    that will dampen
                    like a line
stopping the engine
is a breath of entangled music
from the wings at the helm
feet firmly in command
going to spin "Saxophone"
                    no sensation that something turns
                    above or below
                    the two of us
that mountain so high
that snow
sliding
matrix that glides in delirium
into a new dimension
the city a ruin on a
mah-jong board
                    we're suspended in the air
                    in our belts
                    silence licking the auricles
                    in a sweet frisson
                    leaving us in this dream

of Nafta and Mobiloil
oh how suavely the acrobatics come to a close!
the silver bumblebee
is horizontal
open contact
rev up the engine
hey! old Pekinese!!
you're looking pale
like a Pierrot
we're at 3,000 oh! how much longer
to enter the kingdom of God
the propeller cheerfully claps
a tireless ovation
I will break the mirror
of the day
and pop the cork
of this morning's blonde champagne
like the curls of Marion
the girl that makes us both
a little wicked, "Saxophone"
but it's time to descend
"chop"
and time to say adios
down
all is always the same
the home
the trams
Marion

PEDRO GARFIAS: Storm

A monstrous airplane snorts above the night
And the wind hits me with its fists
The souls of forgotten dead
dance on the telegraph wires.
And the aviator fires
his automatic pistol.
Still night.

But the day already forces its windows.
The powder-keg of the camps exploded,
a crazy crow
will rip out chunks of the sky with its beak.
There are birds absorbed
above rapid clouds.
Passing over me
the night has thrashed me with its wings.

JOHANNES R. BECHER: The New Syntax

The Bengal adjective butterflies
Circle attuned around the lofty substantive noun Squarebuild.
A participle must bridge the gap. Bridge!
Meanwhile the bold verb screws into the buzzing plane up high.

The dancing article pulls snug the pendulum legs.
Chickpea rhythms rock the floor.
But a pure strophe springs in metallic
tones from the trapeze. The warp

of the streetlamps splinter into each other.
Despite every colorful lady a holy vocative.
A young poet cements subjects.
Drills of the object tunnel. Imperative

Stands upright. Fantastic sentence-vistas reined in.
Seven tubes of the Hydra blow. The cloud falls.
And blue flows. Penetrating ironclad mountains.
So we bloom in the May lit glimpse of the overworld.

◈ POSTCARDS ◈

PIERRE ALBERT-BIROT: Poem-Poster

PLACARD-POEM.

THE SUN
IS IN THE STAIRCASE

FOR INFORMATION
CONTACT THE WINE MERCHANT
DOWN THE ROAD

EZRA POUND: In a Station of the Metro

The apparition   of these faces   in the crowd   :
Petals   on a wet, black   bough   .

ALEXEI KRUCHENYKH

I'm blissing off into infashomnia
—YANK!—
like the Eiffel Tower on a string!
I'll bathe and scrub POWDERHIP eyes,
INFINITE OBSCENITIES
for the ripening soul!
(May-June 1919)

ATTILA JÓZSEF: Postcard from Paris

The *patron* is never up in the morning,
in Paris the Berthas are called Jeanettes,
and even at the barber's you can buy
candles, spinach and suzettes.

Along the Boulevard Saint Michel
sixty nudes sing to the sky.
Notre Dame is cold inside:
it's five francs to see from on high.

The Eiffel Tower reclines at night,
wrapped in its foggy sheets,
and the *gendarmes* kiss the girls
and the toilets have no seats.

◈ PARIS ◈

MARY BUTTS: from *Mappa Mundi*

Paris is not a safe city. It is never supposed to be, but so often for the wrong reasons. Perhaps the only place in the world that is really and truly both a sink of iniquity and a fountain of life at one and the same time; in the same quarter, in the same place, at the same hour, with the same properties—to even the same person.

It is no use, or not much use, to know it only as a spree, or as an aesthetic jolt, returning very sophisticated about it. Like all the great feminine places, behind its first dazzling free display, you come quickly upon profound reserves. After the spree a veil is drawn, a sober, *noli me tangere* veil. Isis, whose face on a first swift initiation you think you have seen, even to the color of her eyes, Isis you believe you have kissed, withdraws, well wrapped-up, grown instantly to her own height—as is the property of a Goddess.

GUILLAUME APOLLINAIRE: Windows

From red to green all the yellow dies
When parakeets sing in their native forests
Giblets of pihis
There's a poem to be done on the bird with only one wing
We'll send it by telephone
Giant traumatism
It makes your eyes run
Do you see that pretty girl among the young women of Turin
The poor young man blew his nose with his white tie
You'll raise the curtain
And now see the window opening
Spiders when hands wove the light
Beauty paleness fathomless violets
Vainly we'll try to take some rest
We'll begin at midnight
When you have time you have liberty
Winkles Codfish multiple Suns and the Sea Urchin of sunset

An old pair of yellow boots in front of the window
Towers
Towers are the streets
Well
Wells are the squares
Wells
Hollow trees sheltering vagabond mulattoes
The Chabins sing melancholy songs
To brown Chabines
And the wa-wa wild goose honks to the north
Where raccoon hunters
Scrape the fur skins
Glittering diamond
Vancouver
Where the train white with snow and lights flashing through the dark runs away from winter
Oh Paris
From red to green all the yellow dies
Paris Vancouver Hyères Maintenon New York and the Antilles
The window opens like an orange
The lovely fruit of light

Ardengo Soffici: Studio

A phone-box assembled from deep red planks of the sun
receives all messages;
each quarter a window on madness.
I myself am an opener of windows and senses:
colors sing like birds:
an instrument, a passion,
blue, yellow, green, cobalt,
vermillion, black and soft pink.
My eyes attract light and memory
from all points;
unraveling the rainbow.

Abandon objects, people, countries,
approach me as simple virgins,

drape yourselves about—everything has its place in the frame:
bottles of exotic liqueur, their labels,
Sher Tvui Cèsa;
a ripe fig;
watermelon that marbles the mouth;
red nipples, resting from love in the shade of summer brushwood;
flasks of wine, toys, newspapers,
naked bodies, florid posters:
Mèdrano Circus,
La Gaïté-Rochechouart;
the most sublime creations of international chaos
scattered over tables, pinned to the walls.

Unanswered letters,
telegrams,
business appointments, invitations:
here is the Russian footman with the gold top-hat
brought back from Kiev in Marinetti's pocket;
a guitar,
the white pipe
labeled Gambier of Paris reg. trade mark,
and the young tulip stem
of a woman gone forever.
The words "Je t'aime" have been repeated too often
in too many languages;
these shelves of books are repulsive as the cadavers of old friends
Stendhal alone is still readable,
but the charcoal and chalk inscriptions
on the door and walls
echo sharply today's weird music:
"I'm at the café opposite";
"A. called at 5. Will come again";
"You lack appointments (like the rabbits)! Germaine";
"Anita Caputo, model, 57 rue de Vaugirard";
(Rue de Vaugirard! It's half my sorrow
to have wasted time down there, on a perfumed divan of Jichy and ether)
"R.R.L., phone 375";
"Remember to write to Irene, Fondukleskaja, D.27"
"N.V., 104, Prussian blue 3"

Cheap mysteries
paid for with 24 hours of youth per day.
Studios of pink twenty-year-olds;
a profound blend of joy, beauty, misery and zits,
in these cubicles of the palace of art.

Enough to open the panes to break this spell;
take down the tent of the undulating street;
the white bowl of decaying
smokestacks, towers, chimneys, stars,
cities of Europe at the end of the night, and trains,
lined up, wired like theaters; trainfuls of nostalgia.
The whole earth nods off
in surfeit of desire; our hearts
spread out like flags.

MINA LOY: Café du Néant

Little tapers leaning   lighted diagonally
Stuck in coffin tables of the Café du Néant
Leaning to the breath of baited bodies
Like young poplars fringing the Loire

Eyes that are full of love
And eyes that are full of kohl
Projecting light across the fulsome ambiente
Trailing the rest of the animal behind them
Telling of tales without words
And lies of no consequence
One way or another

The young lovers hermetically buttoned up in black
To black cravat
To the blue powder edge dusting the yellow throat
What color could have been your bodies
When last you put them away

Nostalgic youth
Holding your mistress's pricked finger

In the indifferent flame of the taper
Synthetic symbol of LIFE
In this factitious chamber of DEATH
The woman
As usual
Is smiling as bravely
As it is given her to be brave
While the brandy cherries
In winking glasses
Are decomposing
Harmoniously
With the flesh of spectators
And at a given spot
There is one
Who
Having the concentric lighting focussed precisely upon her
Prophetically blossoms in perfect putrefaction
Yes there are cabs outside the door.

Francis Picabia: Magic City

A dangerous and enticing wind of sublime nihilism
pursued us with incredible exhilaration.
Unexpected ideal.
Break in equilibrium.
Growing irritation.
Emancipations.
Everywhere men and women with music I enjoy
publicly or in secret
unleash their sterile passions.
Opium.
Whisky.
Tango.
Increasingly discerning
spectators and actors
overcome crude satisfactions.
Women less strong
more beautiful and more unconscious.

The men with silent ulterior motives
gaze at their pleasure.
Years of genius and eastern sun,
1913-1914.

PIERRE ALBERT-BIROT: Jazz Chronicle

The 10th at 9:16
I came in at no. 13
Where there was light and people and a piano
And next to the piano
Framing Bass Drum and Drum
A little informal everyday portico
Little glasses and children's toys
Were hanging there at the ends of strings
A little like the poor Christmas tree
It was the Jazz-Bandesque opening
of Francis Picabia's exhibition
History Painter
Upon arriving a smile and hand signals
Told me from afar Good evening dear Friend
And I unknotted my muffler
And that night all the hands and all the faces
Were always ready to say Good evening dear Friend
And maybe a little the hearts too
When it was impossible to turn your head
Or even to put your hand in your pocket
Twenty fingers on the piano gaily panicked
While the poet Jean
Dear to the cock
Recommended brand
With that my dear
You won't be chicken
Tapped on the bass drum and on the drum
In time
Sometimes he even tapped on the glasses
And blew in the Christmas trumpets
Which were hanging in front of him

On the ends of their strings
And to kill the off-beat
A botany professor
Leaning against the music
Gave us a lesson on philosophy and one on art
Or maybe on the philosophy of art
Delivered very patiently
Listened to a bit impatiently
Doubtless due to its form
Too academic
And its quality
Truthfully
Too substantial
Not to forget a certain recipe
to make apple soufflés
Which could soon well
even make Letters inflate
It was there noble instruction
Dancing on an air of dancing
And I left with a ballroom in my heart
And then it happened that some time later
One day it was Sunday
That day of the dead that always inserts itself
Between Saturday and Monday
I followed the boulevards
Which didn't seem real
And I was, I think, myself
An imitation of myself
And yet at the door of a grocery
I saw a dog smoking a pipe
But I think there wasn't even any tobacco
In his smokeless pipe
At the end there was the Emperor's tomb
And we went in with those who were going in
We went around
this sun in a hole
And we went out with those who were going out
And soon we saw that the Rodin Museum
Was on our left
In a garden

In the middle of this Sunday
I had never visited
This new prison of winter and summer
Since it didn't matter where we were going
We were going to the museum
No sorry
To the Hôtel Biron
As soon as we faced
This sonnet
This poem in space
It was no longer Sunday
And the house and its big brother the garden
Recognized us immediately
And the whole time that we stayed with them
They stayed with us
They complained
We are sad they told us
We, beloved sons of men
And created to live with them
We are given to statues that we don't know
Never a word between them and us
Because these statues don't talk
For the people who visit us
We always receive our guests kindly
Because we were born and we know how to behave
But it's no longer anything but a façade
In truth we are dying of boredom
With these old stones night and day
Ah Poet who has almost the same name as us
You who live in a compartment
Entangled in the disorder of the faubourgs
We would so have liked
To be your house
To be your garden
And I felt sorry for the Hôtel Biron
And I think he's right eighteen times over
For without the Palace of my age
That Brancusi the initiate was supposed to build for me
Brancusi who makes spirit and matter speak
The intimate friend of Marble and of Bronze

The beauty of the hotel
Could suit me well, while I wait
And since it would mean that at the same time
We would please each other
I would claim triply—
as living being, as poet, and as Birot
These curves these living rooms these gardens
For at bottom Birot and Biron
Are the same name
Have pity, have pity on the Hôtel Biron
May the larvae that drive it to despair be removed
May it be given to my creative joy
Which might get dirty in my lair
It is made for high ceilings
At least for ducal architecture
But happily, happily
Sunday doesn't stick around forever
Like praise for Malherbe
Not more by the way
Than the true days of the week
Than Mondays and Tuesdays
Than other days and other Sundays
Pass by
Like telegraph poles
To people on trains
For those who wanted it
And those who didn't want it
Arrived on the 22nd day of January
Gallery opening of the Independents
But will I speak in my chronicle
Of the Independents
Of this year
Don't you find, my dear sirs, Visitors,
That it's enough to visit
And that this habit of hanging
Paintings upon paintings
That touch each other
In rooms upon rooms
That follow upon one another
Is really barbaric

And bound to outrage the nature
Of painting
I think it's about time
That we become civilized
Here is my plan
Next year the 4 salons
Will be up high
And each one will carpet, from the base to the tip,
One of the four sides
Of our Eiffel Tower
So that its four sides
From bottom to top
Will be nothing but paintings
This will be more than beautiful and new
And all the people will be massed
From the Champs-de-Mars gardens
To the terraces of St-Cloud
And on all the hills all around
To see
And we'll do the tour by airplane
Of the Tower Salon
But I think that the wires
Of the wireless telegraph
Might cast shadows on the paintings
And who knows if they would survive
Discussions
On the subject of the chair-rail
So I will let this first project
Go
For projects always have a natural tendency
To go
Then I will inflate another one
That I will hold onto very tightly
Because it's a pretty color
Painting having no fear of air currents
On the Invalides-Versailles line
On each side of the tracks
When it is Spring
We'll hang all the paintings
In this Salon-hallway

It will be the longest Salon
Anyone has ever seen
Each painting will make itself at home
On the chair rail
Of this new Sacred Way
The people will buy one
Or more round-trip tickets
And will pass through in electric cars
This super-gallery of paintings
And this salon will be so long
That the people and the painters
Upon coming to the end will say
It's the last Salon
And immediately we'll enter
The great, promised epoch
Of invisible painting
And masterpieces will be born
Without anyone paying attention
And the people will thank me
But as I insist
That they say thank you to me
Starting today
I will regale them with
This Franc-Comtois soup—thinly slice 2/3 potatoes 1/3 new turnips braise with butter add a handful of finely chopped sorrel and lettuce and melted butter pour milk over everything finish by poaching at the last moment vermicelli double cream and chervil fluff
This young fatted chicken à la Derby—stuff a young fatted chicken with 200 grams of rice cooked for 12 minutes to which is added 100 grams of foie gras and 100 grams of truffles cut into large cubes tie up the chicken fry it in herbs and spices then deglaze with fine Madeira champagne truffle juice and veal juice place the chicken upright surround it with escalopes of foie gras sautéed in butter and large whole truffles cooked in champagne put aside the juice of the young fatted chicken
Alas these two poems are not by me
Farewell Franc-Comtois soup
Farewell young fatted chicken

ÉMILE MALESPINE: Montparnasse

Cardboard target left bank
Railway-arrows
are refracted
in the magnifying glasses unknown horizons
toward the chromatic foyer
irridescent with dreams.
Montparnasse.
Airplane dreams nosedive
towards the electro-magnet.
Polyglot Eiffel Tower
stuttering
the T.S.F. literatures of tomorrow.
Drang nach Osten!
Nach Paris!
It's much quicker by express
There's a dining car.
The Cossack chef doubles
his dreams, of furs
NITCHEVO!
What's the use; I'd give the world
for a kiss.
Spanish amarilla flowers of pesetas
Gold Louis apoplectic transatlantic
Kisses to order
from pasteboard women
red-lead Spanish fly
sliding from kohl.
Al restaurante
si lo quiere usted
vamos!
Orangeade rainbow stocked room
Eye oilcloth Indian parchment
hair ballet Oriental dyes
Sapphire satellite in spirals
of smoke
Commercial offers of a night of love.
Are you ready?

Play!
Shuttlecock garlands of conversation thrown
from one mouth to the other.
Center of the world's gravity.
International sex.

Claire Goll: To Bus No. 12

Bus No. 12
Take my nostalgia
From Montmartre to Grenelle
Or from Calvaire to L'Étoile
You who never reach the terminal!
Your motor-heart beats in accord with mine
While you are winging
The hydrants
Cry: Fire!
Feeling the burning essence
Of your soul
The Posters of Cook and Sons smile:
"From Paris to Cairo in 7 days—
Steamers de luxe: France
Leaves the 27th
Casino to Tahiti . . ."
The Pathéphone sings
Two bars of Il Trovatore.
And farther along
The scent of the Market-Place:
Coral, sea-fish,
The dunes of youth,
Sea-shells of youth
O pineapple forests
And adventure!

— — — — — — — — — — — — — — — — —

Wait, Bus No. 12, stop!
But it rolls steadily on
Like destiny.

Pithecanthropus
Antediluvian, mystic bird
Take my nostalgia
From Calvaire to L'Étoile
Without terminal,
Bus No. 12,
My lover!

YVAN GOLL: Paris is Burning

for Georg Kaiser

Scarlet ship "PARIS"
Go to God, upon the plasterwork of all the town halls
upon the flanks of all the trams!
The sign LIBERTÉ ÉGALITÉ FRATERNITÉ
swings in the draughts from the prisons
Angels fly from the towers of Saint-Sulpice
in invisible elevators
The pianolas sing in the veils
Angelus
5 in the morning
The apocalypse of freight trains
slowly enters the station in the rain
and carry oranges golden dawn
One catches the first bus
going to Châtelet

The white crows the daily news
squabble about the lures of the night
The world judges in three lines
Subway gospel
« A hairdresser hangs himself with his wife's hair
12 negroes on board the Suffren shot for denominational reasons
General strike at the Vatican: The Pope suffers intestinal pains
In New York a comet revives 3,000,000 dead
They enjoy ten years of hard labor »

Republican boulevards

the morning cafés blink
the houses raise blinds heavy with sleep
Urinals pleasant springs
as though thyme grew there!
And the last widows of the night
button up the mist upon their breasts

Night in your honor
On Arago Boulevard we raise
the Guillotine statue
where a blue blackbird comes to perch
The curly-haired assassin smiles
on the front page of *Matin*
in all the dairies
grief of all the trains of Europe's suburbs
Already the head rolls
in the gold dust
rolls and rises
at humanity's back
round
red
SUN!
You will not kill at all!
But the sun is not a death's head
It's the humble dandelion
It's the blonde chignon of my typist
It's the pin of my necktie
And in Paris
in all the bakeries
which smell of the blueberry patch
it is this three-kilo
round loaf

The good housekeepers hide
a bottle of vitriol
behind the bedpost
for when the postman comes
with grave news

The skin disease specialist

writes out a death certificate
on the ground floor of furnished hotels
and gives the manicurists a discount

But at all the tram stops
A stranger awaits me
The buses drive off
completely in tears
At first she smiles: then
I set her heart in raspberry ice cream
Three hundred times she was called Isabelle
But yesterday it was Zouzou
fallen in a hotel room
Her heart is a doll
that closes its eyes when you tilt it
But when she cries
the old dame shows through
Her eyelids are autumn leaves
afraid to fall into the grass

Together we discover nature
little vapors from St. Cloud
Veritable primroses around the gas factory
Under the armpits the marble goddesses are wearing moss
The mornings age quickly
The tree flies
Turn around, it's no longer time
to be Greek

Turn, spinning-top of the world
Circus
Phony pantheon
Fouetté of pink garters!
Upon the Great Wheel we raffle off the stars

A carousel of electric heads turns
around your metal geyser
Eiffel Tower

From month to month

the drive belts tighten
Sun on a unicycle
at the astronomical cycling track
pursues your handicap
Noon
Zenith

He perspires in his yellow sweater
This race is eternal
The milky way is a new tire
And at Longchamp
lemon gold jockeys
take off
HURRAH!
The man defies the divine champion
All the hairdressers of Europe put
their soul into Paris Mutuel

NOON

High tension
700,000 volts
Batteries of nerve impulses
The platinum spire of the Eiffel Tower
punctures the abscesses of the clouds
Fever
Isolated typhus
Blast furnaces
snowtrains incandescence 44º C
more or less 0
The forests burn like cigarette papers
The icebergs glide along the equator
The comets thrash their tails
Aluminum eagles
fall
A hundred years turn like a loose wheel
on the dial
Chronometer guaranteed gold
Sun
And I'm afraid

that my heart
which has no safety catch
like a revolver
may fire by itself

The brickmade sphinxes
command: *Work Work*
The prostituted sirens factories whine push cut weld turn plow drive sweep knit
lift die
O socialist Sebastian with flaming beard
Perched atop your streetlamp
hoarse prophet
pointing out the new Tuileries
The cloud is lifting in Belleville
Red flags burning down the prisons

LIBERTÉ ÉGALITÉ FRATERNITÉ

The Sower has put her Phrygian cap on askew
Pensioners, your girlfriend
is dancing the tango
on each forty-sou piece
Smiling virgins of the Folies-Bergères
in your oregano scent
The dreadnoughts come ashore in France
Your blue-white-red hair
lights up the beacons of Europe

Yet I know your humility
virgin of inconsolable mornings
who haggles over second-hand blouses
and on an oil lamp
quickly prepare two eggs à la coq

But there are the fortune tellers
on a piano stool
these Pythias inhale the vapors
of a cheap tea
and sell to poor girls
the lucky star

the ace of diamonds for hope
three nines for marriage
the queen of spades wants it for you
and behind the Japanese partition
the king of hearts is smoking
Maryland
Oh Place de la Concorde
where a pyramid is missing
At the Admiralty
in a mildewed office
there's Madagascar
in a painting
the blue Prussian admirals
with handsome beards
magnetized by their pencils
the battleships around Gibraltar
Official departure
Alphonso XIII clutches his top hat
The Presidents of the Republic appear in all the windows
Alone the prince and heir Hirohito
with a cynical smile
executes all of the diplomatic corps

VIVE LA FRANCE!

There: an accident
Rumors
One-second film
One head
One hat
One head among fifty thousand heads
parted on the left
which falls
which rolls
under the pitiless wheel
Head with paternal beard
Perhaps Jochanaan
gone from the abyss of the metro
Or some other head
Maybe my head . . .

All the reporters' blue ink fades
The photograph bows to the story
The rotaries
spew out grey reptiles
all the newspaper offices
are Pandora's boxes
above the stock markets of London and Brussels
a hand that is strong
white
fleshy
greasy
cuffs and mother-of-pearl links
anathema which gets up and convulses
All the gramophones know the price of Royal Dutch
La Marseillaise

ALLONS ENFANTS DE LA PATRIE

On the Boulevards
one recites the litany of the saints numbers of the era
Oracle
606
69
75
Civilization's poker
In Chicago the famous tile falls from the roofs
In Greenland a seal dies
In Shantung the Minister of Finance sings:

I have atop my tooth
A golden crown

I have 100 shares
In Olympia Mines

I have a family vault
For 20 centuries

I have

I have

And he tenders his resignation

Moscow telegraphs Gomorrah

REVOLUTION!

workers in a blue tramway-tank attack the Louvre
On all of the café terraces
the first of May cockades are blooming
“Machine guns sewn by Singer”
The railwaymen are on strike
The express trains rest in the pine forests
for four days
The radio-telegrams buzz
in their hive the Eiffel Tower
The Mont-Blanc station gleams in the distance
Diamond signals
“Special edition!”

Ideal of ideals
Boxing match in Jersey City
The new era of the law of the fist
The Haberdashers’ Union sends a delegation over the Ocean
Hear hear! Round one!
Europe and the negro Zeus shake hands
Tricolour shorts
The human chest bends a steel rose
The Morse telegraphs are fevered
Four fists form the honor of the world
U.S.A. all of the watches have stopped
The munitions factories have shut down
The oceanliners halt in the middle of the Atlantic
Round four
Mountains have vertigo
Ransacked banks
77 suicides
300 assassination attempts
Knock-out

The STATUE OF LIBERTY smiles
so a war breaks out
skeletons beat the drum
the price of sugar rises
free burials
heroes laurelled in bandages
heaped in cattle carts
carry their dried-up heart
between two stamped sheets of paper
The Rome-Stockholm express line
is made up exclusively of coffin cars

At that instant
at a café table
a GENIUS discovers
the love of mankind
Café ESPRIT
Centre of the world
Brothers and sisters exchange cigarettes
CAFÉ DES WESTENS
CAFÉ TERRASSE
CAFÉ STEFANIE
CAFÉ DE LA ROTONDE
CAFÉ PRAGUE
CAFÉ DES TROIS MONDES
Within the pistachio ices
swim the unexplored planets
The brains' fans are raging
in the two-way mirrors
the poets drown, fishermen of dreams
the painters add ultramarine balconies to the sky
Fernand Léger's scarlet dynamos
crack the concrete walls
Lipchitz makes to sing of new sphinxes
while at the Louvre cemetery
the grass grows in the ears of the gothic statues

Meanwhile
the café waiter
sells contraband
brotherhood
for 50 centimes

Paris
Diamond upon the neck of Europe
made iridescent by a hundred thousand arc- & oil lamps
Jazz plays on the Arc de Triomphe
Pantheon cymbals
Trocadéro organ
Paris foxtrot
Soft flute in the wind
hear the Eiffel Tower
The magician in a sports cap, Monsieur Eiffel
on the hundredth storey of his tower
personally receives to dinner
the poets of Europe
Symphonic orchestra of clouds
Interplanetary acoustics
After the third course
lightning-grilled stars
toasts

This poetry gathering went on all night
To each Monsieur Eiffel made a gift of three shares in his Anonymous Society
Paris was always burning
The clasps of the Grand Boulevards were platinum
And the war widow Seine was dragging her shimmering
black pearls
All the jewellers got the Nobel Prize
The Opera House
undermined with Maggi cubes
was guarded by dancers from the Ballet Corps

Berlitz-School Academy of the Fifth International

At the Musée Grévin Marat demanded three francs for an interview
Café de Madrid: conference of travelling piano salesmen
And all of the adulterers marry their detective
Oh Queen of Romania sell me your love
because I am named Ivan
Like a good European
I shall kill you tomorrow!
I shall seek my final despair

at the cinema guarded by the Swiss of Notre-Dame
Charlotte Corday laughs on the posters
And the flaming airships
project the photo of Lenin
onto Saturn

Here violet Zouzou
silently blossoms
on the shelf
of the Printemps stationery shop
In exchange for this poem
will you sell me a notepad?
And since the skylarks died
I pitch into the air
pink checks

In our Jacob's ladders the elevators
we ascend into our meagre Eden (Hotel)
Insipid telephone
Menus
to weep upon
and fringed in black
The janitor is only a worried family's father
Where is Australia found?
When do the boats leave for Saint-Cloud?
The police arrive in a sky-blue car
The freight trains
lurch and rear
with their cargo of rotten oranges
The sunrise is cancelled for today
Last
red light
of the transcontinental Express
my heart
gives out

What time is it?

Blaise Cendrars: Contrasts

The windows of my poetry are wide open to the boulevards and its showcases
Shine
Jewels of light
Listen to the limousines' violins and the linotypists' xylophones
The inept painter washes with the sky's wash cloth
Everything is splashes of color
And the hats of the women passersby are comets in the evening bonfire

Unity
There is no more unity
All the clocks are now showing midnight after having been set back ten minutes
There is no more time.
There's no more money.
In the legislature
They're spoiling the marvelous elements of elemental matter

In the corner bar
The workmen in blue shirts are drinking red wine
Every Saturday chicken in the pot
They play
They bet
From time to time a bandit passes in a car
Or a child plays with the Arch of Triumph . . .
I advise Mr. Big to quarter his protegés at the Eiffel Tower

Today
Change of owner

The Holy Ghost is on sale in the smallest shops
With increasing delight I read the strips of calico
Of marigold
Only the Sorbonne pumice stones are never in bloom
The "Samaritan's" signboard ploughs the Seine
And over by Saint Severin
I can hear
The trolley's excited clanging

It's raining electric light bulbs

MARCEL SAUVAGE: from *Bus Trip*

PLACE
Ste-OPPORTUNE
or
PLAN FOR A FESTIVAL
BELOW
THE FLYING CIRCUS

Colorful planes
in thousand of colors

Paris from 100 to 10,000 meters below
as far as millions of spectacles can see

The silent motors
Flying squads in reserve behind the clouds

All of the sky is sequined cloth
—of fluttering emblems—
Rivers are born, burst forth
sheds leaves—on the wing
ocellated on the wing

CIRCLE OF PEACOCKS

From slow and heavy cages
they write the legend d.o.t.t.e.d.

Torn into confetti
the sun in seven figures of light
—DUSTMOTES—

Behold the gladiators
jinglingly looping the loop

and when the machine gun has no teeth left
the hippocampus escapes into the smoke

TOURNAMENTS OF DEATH	staltic fires the harnessed cadavers the Morgue with the cold faucets ..... endless intestines

But the joy multiplies the gravel stones of the sun
blows bubbles . . .

Behind the scenes in high places
The street is mad, the square mad
the quay and the river
the risen river

At the sky's false bottom
the cloths fade
The bistros strive
The sky like a pebble
house

Night quadrilles of the stars
to the discordant jazz band of the motors
Conga-line avalanches

Below the Pantheon
the projectors cross swords
«TOUCHÉ!»
arches of light
Paris is a basket of applause
(all that is required in good order)

. . . Is it the wind in the wires? . . .

Planes hooked on midnight's summit
. . . stars
and the star that sings

spin

JULIAN PRZYBOŚ: Four Quarters

1

My shadow flashed by passing me on a double avenue.
I go,
with the top of my head I feel the flickering touch
of leaves, pure lightness,
not here, where I am, but there, to where I see.
The bottom of the distance is filled after sunset by a windstorm,
red rose of the winds outspread on a stem;
the factory chimney wanders far away with me.

From there the cars endlessly spin out the perspective, perspective,
which
breaks suddenly at the knees.

From the anthill of wingless cars pure speed will fly away:
an airplane.

2

Traffic swarmed with cars, iron and the wall ground glass on the curves,
the sparking material spattered me from close by.
It is here.
The last man disappeared devoured by the crowd,
only a policeman remained like a marmot whistling on a molehill.

Touched by his wand the square spurted out with a fountain.

M'sieur! Plant the pit jumping in your whistle!
Only a nail sprouted in the roadway . . .
Smoke, the sprout of gasoline, withered before it unfolded,
battered down in a hail of buildings.

It is here the golden current spends the triumphant night.

I watch for when the poem will change into a skyrocket.

3

From the packed hall, with the symphony falling toward the door like a bullet,
winged by the music I struggle along the boulevards.
I hear the houses like ruins after a bombardment.

Below a plank fence a street musician, blind angel
sheds
one wing of his hat
feather after feather
slowly . . .

he stretches and shrinks floors with the steps on the bellows of his accordion.

Nike
in a victorious flight beats against the pavement with an invisible head,
with a pink vacuum,
the light.
On the Seine dawn moves the flood held by chords.

Vincent van Gogh with a branch of blossoming almond
restored my sight of the world.

4

A shadow staggered at the muzzles of the streets.
A volley of cars pierced it through,
aiming
at the jumping dot.

The policeman froze in the whirling sphere.
And again he waved with his arms, rewrapped,
bandaged the wounded place—

The traffic overgrew
the pavement with rubber wheels.
The heart of the tree beat in the raised wand.

The audible aspen, entirely made of the trembling of motors
began to tremble,
and, transparent with the air, with distance and spreading,

sank into the depth of the forest out of sight,
no one's—

Ney from the monument raised his sword, ordering his own death.

VLADIMIR MAYAKOVSKY: Paris (Chatting with the Eiffel Tower)

Pounded by a million feet.
Swished by thousands of tires.
The streets of Paris I roam—
appalled here not to meet
a familiar face or soul,
abysmally alone.
Round me
motor-cars are dancing,
round me
from the fountain-jaws
of Royal fish
jets are prancing.
I emerge
on the Place de la Concorde.
I await the appointed hour
when,
dodging the cops,
through thick
fog
comes the Eiffel Tower
to meet me,
a Bolshevik.
"They'll spot you,
psst,
don't shuffle so!"
The guillotine-noon breeds fear.
"Now listen
to me!"
(On tiptoe
I whisper
in her

radio ear)
"I've been busy
propagandizing.
Every building is with us,
but we
need you!
Will you head the uprising?
We'll vote you leader
if you agree.
Such a fine piece of engineering
rotting here
in Apollinaire moods!
Not for you
is the Paris
of bleary
bards,
stockbrokers,
Moulin Rouge nudes.
The Metro's agreed
to go with us.
It will spit the gentlefolk
from its tiled halls,
the perfume and face-powder posters
with blood
it will wash
from its walls.
It thinks:
'Why should my carriages
serve plutocrats?'
It won't be oppressed!
It finds now
our posters
and placards
of class struggle
suit it best.
Do not fear the streets!
Should the roads
block
the Metro rising,
cause delays,

the tracks will give them a thrashing.
I'll call a revolt of the rails.
You're afraid?
Of the tavern brawlers?
To our aid
the Left Bank will come.
Fear not!
I've agreed with the bridges—
and the river's
not easily
swum!
The bridges
on the Seine embankment
in fury
together shall rear,
at the first call to rebellion
shed pedestrians on every pier.
Not a thing but shall rise—
life's unbearable—
In fifteen
or twenty
years' time
steel
shall age,
and to Montmartre repairing
sell its favors
at night
for a dime!
To my land,
tower,
come!
There
we
need
you.
To steel's glitter,
smoke billowing above,
with more tender care
we'll greet you
than first lovers greet their loves.

To Moscow let's go!
There
there's space.
You'll have
your own streets—
every one!
We'll coddle you—
a hundred times
a day
polish you
till you glow like the sun.
Let
the Paris
of fops and hussies,
of boulevard loafers lie alone
in the morgue of the Louvre, mid the lumber
of museums and the Bois de Boulogne.
Come!
Stride with the powerful paws
Eiffel drew you for you to stand on,
so your brow in our sky rap out Morse
and the stars their proud airs abandon!
Make your mind up!
Rise, all as you are,
let revolt shake the city and seize her!
Come
to us
in the USSR!
I'll see to it
you all get a visa!

LOUIS ARAGON: from *Paris Peasant*

"CERTA"

TARIF

DES CONSOMMATIONS

Martini Cocktail	3 F.	Porto Flipp	3 F. 50
Perfect »		Brandy	
Rose »		Sherry	
Brandy »		Egg Nogs	4 F.
Champagne »		Fizzes	
Gin »		Sours	
Grillon »		Sangarees	3 F. 50
St-James »		Pick me Hup	
Derby »		Kiss me Quick	
Omnium »		Pousse Café	5 F.
Max »		Pêle-Mêle Mixture	2 F. 50
Waller's »		Grillon Cup	3 F. 50
Manhattan »	4 F.	John Collins Gin	3 F. 50
Oscar »		Brom	
Dada »		Clover Club	
Sherry Cobler		Mousse Moka	2 F. 50
Champagne »		Florio	
Porto »			
Café Glacé	1 F. 50		

Whisky
Soda
— 5 F —

This list is displayed in the little room, and above it, advertising a drink whose name escapes me, there used to hang a poster designed by one of the former waiters in the style of Francis Picabia's mechanistic drawings; it vanished some time ago. One of the café's charms resides in the little signs posted everywhere, vaunting Martini, Bovril, Carola mineral water, or W. M. Youngers Scotch Ale. Sometimes they form a cascading sequence:

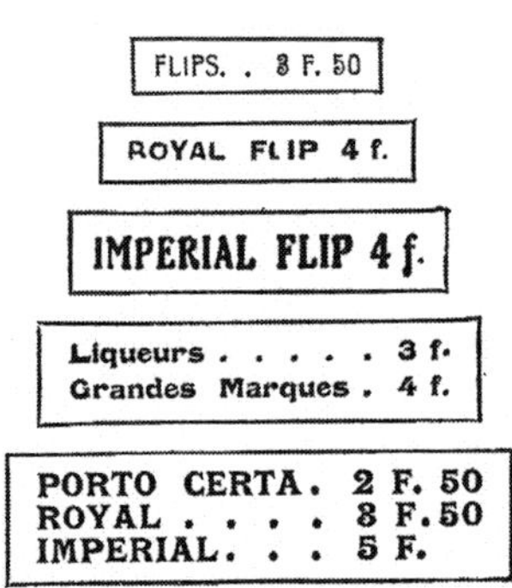

They are all excellent, impeccable. And if you have a craving for some beef broth, order Bovril; it will come with salt and delectable stalks of celery, which you must eat unstintingly.

ELSA VON FREYTAG-LORINGHOVEN: Café du Dôme

For the love of Mike!
Look at that—
Marcelled—
Be-whiskered—
Be-spatted—
Pathetic—
Lymphatic—
Aesthetic—
Pigpink—
Quaint—
Natty—
Saintkyk!

Garçon

Un pneumatic cross avec suctiondiscs topped avec thistle-tire...s'il vous plait.

PIERRE REVERDY: Paris in Play

In the city there are at times those who no longer move
    between walls blackened like full pages
        The illumined frame passing on the sidewalks
In that Parisian landscape russet at the hour before you
    switch the light on in the shop windows
        There are those who pass by leaves and people
        Against the background of the well-ordered garden under the sky
                To the right the beautiful streets
                To the left the great river
Those who do not move and who talk on the flag-

stoned terrace near the black balustrade's green reflection
The city turns around the obelisk and the province
looks at pictures
Pictures in relief and in color
There is deep in the air this major algae
This bare head under the lightning flashes
This figure precise more refined and more real that demarcates itself clearly
Against the fog

CÉSAR VALLEJO: Hat, Overcoat, Gloves

Across from the Comédie Française is the Regency
Café, in which there's a separate
room, with armchair and table.
When I come in, the lifeless dust is already up on its feet.

Between my lips of rubber, the spark
of a cigarette smolders, and in the smoke
are two intensive fumes, the Café's thorax,
and in this thorax a bottomless oxide of sorrow.

It's important that autumn graft itself to autumns,
important that autumn complete itself with buds,
the cloud, with semesters; the cheek, with wrinkle.

It's important to reek like a lunatic declaring
how warm the snow, how quick the turtle,
how simple the how, how explosive the when!

FRANZ KAFKA: from *Travel Diaries*

The subway seemed very empty to me then, especially in comparison with the time when, sick and alone, I had ridden out to the races. Even apart from the number of passengers, the fact that it was Sunday influenced the way the subway looked. The dark color of the steel sides of the cars predominated. The conductors did their work —opening and closing the car doors and swinging themselves in and out between times— in a Sunday afternoon manner. Everyone walked the long distances between branch connections in leisurely fashion. The unnatural indifference with which passengers submit to a ride in the subway was more noticeable. People seemed to face the door, or get off at unfamiliar stations far from the Opéra, as the impulse moved them. In spite of the electric lights you can definitely see the changing light of day in the stations; you notice it immediately after you've walked down, the afternoon light particularly, just before it gets dark. Arrival at the empty terminal of Porte Dauphine, a lot of tubes become visible, view into the loop where the trains make the curve they are permitted after their long trip in a straight line. Going through railroad tunnels is much worse; in the subway there isn't that feeling of oppression which a railroad passenger has under the weight—though held in check—of mountains. Then too, you aren't far off somewhere, away from people; it is rather an urban contrivance, like water pipes, for example. Tiny offices, most of them deserted, with telephones and bell systems, control the traffic. Max liked to look into them. The first time in my life I rode the subway, from Montmartre to the main boulevards, the noise was horrible. Otherwise it hasn't been bad, even intensifies the calm, pleasant sense of speed. Subway system does away with speech; you don't have to speak either when you pay or when you get in and out. Because it is so easy to understand, the subway is a frail and hopeful stranger's best chance to think that he has quickly and correctly, at the first attempt, penetrated the essence of Paris.

Vladimir Mayakovsky: Last Farewell

Off in a cab,
having changed the last of my francs.
"Is this the train to Marseilles?"
I ask the official.
Seeing me off
Paris
runs alongside,
in all her
unbearable beauty.
But heartsob
wells up in my eyes
when I know
I must go!
In Paris

I'd love to live
and die
if it weren't
for such a place
as Moscow.

Henry Miller: from *Tropic of Cancer*

Walking down the Rue Lhomond one night in a fit of unusual anguish and desolation, certain things were revealed to me with poignant clarity. Whether it was that I had so often walked this street in bitterness and despair or whether it was the remembrance of a phrase which she had dropped one night as we stood at the Place Lucien-Herr I do not know. "Why don't you show me that Paris," she said, "that you have written about?" One thing I know, that at the recollection of these words I suddenly realized the impossibility of revealing to her that Paris I had gotten to know, the Paris whose arrondissements are undefined, a Paris that has never existed except by virtue of my loneliness, my hunger for her. Such a huge Paris! It would take a lifetime to explore it again. This Paris, to which I alone had the key, hardly lends itself to a tour, even with the best of intentions; it is a Paris that has to be lived, that has to be experienced each day in a thousand different forms of torture, a Paris that grows inside you like a cancer, and grows and grows until you are eaten away by it.

INTERLUDE

PHILIPPE SOUPAULT: Westwego

All the cities of the world
oases of our starving plights
offer refreshing drinks
to the memories of loners and maniacs
and sedentary types
Cities of the continents
you're flags
stars fallen to earth
without really knowing why
and the mistresses of the poets of our day

I was walking around London one summer
feet burning and my heart in my eyes
near black walls near red walls
near the massive docks
where the giant policemen
were pricked like question marks
One could play with the sun
that would pose like a bird
on all the monuments
passenger pigeon
everyday pigeon
I went into this district called Whitechapel
my childhood pilgrimage
where I ran into
only people all dressed up
and wearing top hats
just merchants of matchsticks
wearing boaters
who hollered like the farmers of France
to get some clients to come
penny penny penny

I went into a bar
third-class cabin where
Daisy Mary Poppy
had sat at the table
next to the fishmongers
who chewed tobacco while closing an eye
to forget about the night
the night that approached with a wolfish step
an owl's stealth
the night and the smell of the river and of the tide
the night tearing sleep apart

it was a sad day
of copper and sand
that slowly leaked between the souvenirs
deserted islands storms of dust
for the animals snarling with wrath
who lower their heads
like you and like me
because we are alone in this city
red and black
where all the boutiques are delicatessens
where the best folks have very blue eyes

It's hot outside and it's Sunday today
it's sad out
the river is really unhappy
and the residents stayed home
I walk along the Thames
a single boat glides to garner the sky
the sky unmoving
because it's Sunday
and the wind wasn't up
it's noon it's five o'clock
we don't know where to go any more
a man sings without knowing why
like I walk
when one is young it's for life
my childhood encaged
in this sonic museum

Madame Tussauds
it's Nick Carter and his bowler hat
in his pocket he's got a full set of pistols
and shiny handcuffs like four-letter words
Next to him the knight Bayard
who resembles him like a brother
it's sacred history and the history of England
near to the big time criminals who no longer have any names
When I left where did I go
there are no cafés
no lights that make the words whisk off
there are no tables you can lean on
to see nothing to look at nothing
there are no glasses
there are no vapors
only the sidewalks as long as the years
where blood stains bloom at dusk
I saw in this city
so many flowers so many birds
because I was alone with my memory
near to all its gates
that hide the gardens and the eyes
along the banks of the River Thames
in February, on a beautiful morn
three English blokes in shirt sleeves
were crooning 'til the cows came home
tra la la tra la la tra la lay
Bus tea-rooms Leicester Square
I recognize you I've never seen you
except on postcards
my maid used to get
dead leaves
Mary Daisy Poppy
little flames
in this rinky-dink bar
you're the friends a poet fifteen years old
gently admires
thinking of Paris
at a window ledge
a cloud goes by

it's twelve o'clock noon
next to the sun
Let's walk to be silly
let's run to be glad
let's laugh to be powerful

Strange traveler traveling luggageless
I never left Paris behind
my memory would saunter wherever I walked
my memory trailed me like a little dog
I was stupider than the sheep
that blaze in the sky at midnight
it's very hot
I whisper to myself real seriously
I'm terribly thirsty I'm really quite thirsty
I've got nothing but my hat
key to the fields key to the dreams
father of memories
have I never quit Paris
but tonight I'm in this city
behind each tree of the avenues
a memory watches out for my wandering by
It's you my old Paris
but tonight at last I'm in this city
your monuments are the kilometer markers of my fatigue
I recognize your clouds
which cling to the chimneys
to tell me goodbye or hello
at night you are phosphorescent
I love you like one loves an elephant
all your cries are to me as cries of tenderness
I'm like Aladdin in his garden
where the magic lamp was alight
I'm in search of nothing
I'm right here
I'm sitting at a café terrace
and I flash a toothy smile
thinking of all my famous trips
I'd like to go to New York or Buenos Aires
to know the Moscow snow

to set out one night aboard an ocean liner
for Madagascar or Shanghai
trek back up the Mississippi
I went to Barbizon
and reread the voyages of Captain Cook
I lay down to sleep on the cushiony moss
I wrote poems near a wood anemone
gathering the words that hung from the branches
the little railroad put me in mind of the Trans-Canada
and tonight I smile because I'm here
in front of this trembling glass
where I see the universe
while laughing
on the boulevards in the streets
all the hoodlums walk past singing
the dry trees touch the sky
provided it rains
one can walk without getting tired
to the ocean or farther on
over there the sea beats like a heart
nearer the humdrum tenderness
of lights and barking
the sky has discovered the earth
and the world is blue
provided it rains
and the world will be content
there are also women who laugh when they see me
women whose names I don't even know
the children shout in their aviary of Luxemburg
the sun has changed a lot in six months
there are so many things that dance before me
my friends asleep all over the world
I will see them tomorrow
André of the planet colored eyes
Jacques Louis Théodore
the great Paul my dear tree
and Tristan whose laugh is a big peacock
you're all living
I forgot your gestures and your true voice
but this evening I'm alone I'm Philippe Soupault

I walk slowly down the Boulevard Saint-Michel
I think about nothing
I count the streetlamps I know so well
coming close to the Seine
alongside the Bridges of Paris
and I speak out loud
all the streets are tributaries
when one loves this river where all the blood of Paris flows
and that's dirty like a dirty whore
but also simply the Seine
to whom one speaks as if to his mom
I was right next to her
who took off with no regret and no flourish
her extinguished memory was a malady
I was leaning against the parapet
like one kneels down to pray
the words were falling like tears
sweet like bonbons
Hello Rimbaud how're you
Hello Lautréamont how are you faring
I was twenty not a nickel more
my father was born in Saint-Malo
and my mother lives during the daytime in Normandy
me I was baptized in Canada
Hello me
The rug vendors and beautiful ladies
who hang around at night on the streets
those who guard the grace of the lamps in their eyes
those to whom pipe smoke and the glass of wine
seem all the same a bit drab
know me without knowing my name
and in passing say Hello you
and nevertheless there is in my chest
small suns that turn with a sound of lead
tall giant of the boulevard
caring man from the courthouse
the lightning is it prettier in spring
Its eyes my lightning are scissors
chauffeurs I have seven cartridges left
not one more not one less

not one of them is for you
you're ugly like interrogations
and I read on all the walls
carpet carpet carpet and carpet
the great convoys of experiences
near to us near to me
Swedish matches

The Paris nights have these pungent odors   identification through flags
that regrets and headaches leave behind
and I knew it was late
and that the night
the Paris night was going to end
like holidays
everything was well in order
and no one said a word
I awaited the three strokes
the sun comes up like a flower
we call I believe a dandelion
the great mechanical vegetation
that expected only encouragements
climbs and develops
faithfully
we no longer know whether to compare it
to ivy
or grasshoppers
has the fatigue up and gone   - moving towards a poetic moment, pushing forward in his new identity
I see bargemen who exit
to clean up the charcoal
the tugboat mechanics
who roll a first cigarette
before lighting the boiler
over there in a port
a captain pulls out his handkerchief
to daub his head
by force of habit
and me the first this morning
I say anyhow
Hello → not in french, doesn't fit in

◈ MULTIPLE CITY ◈

Dragan Aleksić

Humberto Rivas: The Multiple City

The city stretched like an octopus
plunges the thousand arms
of its streets in the ground

The apartments propping up the city's shoulders
leap out of the balconies
and rush about in trolleys and buses

All the streetcars

do new math
with luminous digits

All the streetcars
have a circus on the roof
and on its spinning ring
take inverted steps
under the wires

Every doorway's a mouth
that chews and belches urban high tide

On the skin of walls
posters like ivy
deafen pedestrians with proclamations

Posters are small lizards
that lick the wall with flickering tongues,
wet with blood of the press

There's a parade of exotic locales
sunken in display windows
like a submarine realm

Sidewalks
move vertiginously
in the stained glass windows

The asphalt rises up
beating multicolored time

A regiment passes by
quivering
under the banner of the sky

And the beehive, fluttering its wings
and lighting up in space,
oozes golden honey

A prayer from a church

sinks in the rising sea
and freezes over in the skyscrapered ice floes

A church is a devotee
that threads and mends with her needles
the blue garment of her prayers

A clump of myopic trees
is groping amidst the strolling foliage

And the evening is closing,
snuffing out with its eyelashes
the sunset wick

The keel of the cars
cleaves the surface of the breakers
sailing in the sea froth
its pupils aglow

Horns,
with the happy noise of street organs,
flood the air with fireworks

On the blackboard of night
an oscillating hand
sketches fireflies

The city dozes off,
its huge arms extended

The city twisting its exhausted arteries
becomes still as a corpse
wrapped in the convex, moth-eaten
shroud of the sky

The dynamic city
the multiple city
the dromedary-city
dragging the caravan on its back

Marcel Sauvage: "...and Marcadet!" [from *Bus Trip*]

The car creaks and groans
like Moses robed in clouds
That line won't go to the promised land
Hello? Canaan? crash

We are thrust forward like lights
trembling

I am the clown
king of wires that adorn
the plains and the mountains
and the world
with a dress of electric stars . . .

To the four points of the compass
the orthographies rolling around the oceans
        . . . wandering sparks
        stories of love mining affairs
        the fangs of famine
        and the novels of the film . . .

Barefooted
the dawn
was going
dancing
along
the telegraph wires

Jean Cocteau

The café quivers, dazed in light
The immigrants huddle in the hold
The cashier rows between waterlilies
Saucers' pale hatching

I can see it's nine but Christ how I hate
Being in a café
I ponder a great auto-da-fé
Drop the anchor! Toss the ballast!

Wake up, crew, it's morning:
The siren besotted who sleep off their opium
Come up from the humid
Metro aquarium

Today we need more frantic muses
Like that telegrapher in Los Angeles
Who boxing, galloping, riding the rails
Grabs the eye of the young detective

Álvaro de Campos [Fernando Pessoa]

Bright bugle of morning on the outer edge
Of the horizon's cold half circle,
Tenuous distant bugle like hazy flags
Unfurled beyond where colors are visible . . .

Tremulous bugle, dust that hovers where the night ends,
Golden dust hovering on the edge of visibility . . .

Car that cleanly screeches, steamer that whistles,
Crane that begins to swivel in my ear,
Hacking cough announcing that the man's going out,
Light morning shiver of the joy of living,
Burst of laughter veiled in some strange way by the mist,
Seamstress destined for worse than the morning she feels,
Consumptive laborer dying of happiness in this
Inevitably vital hour
In which the contours of things are soft, friendly, and sure,
In which the walls are cool to the hand's touch, and the houses
Here and there open their white-curtained eyes . . .

Every morning is a gently waving curtain

Reviving illusions and memories in my passerby soul,
In my exiled, epidermically spirited heart,
In my tired and veiled . . . . .

. . . . . and everything proceeds
Toward the light-filled hour when shops lower their eyelids
And noise traffic pushcart train I-feel sun resounds

Vertigo of midday framed in vertigos—
Sun in the heights . . . . . of my striated vision,
Of the frozen whirl of my parched memory,
Of the faint steady glimmer of my consciousness of living.

Noise traffic train pushcart cars I-feel sun street,
Hoops crates streetcar shop street shopwindows skirt eyes
Quick tracks pushcarts crates street crossing street
Sidewalks shopkeepers "excuse me" street
Street strolling over me strolling down the street over me
All is mirrors shops on this side in the shops on that side
The speed of the cars upside down in the tilted shopwindow mirrors,
The ground in the air the sun underfoot street watering flowers in the basket street
My past street shaking truck street I don't remember street
Me headfirst in the center of my consciousness of myself
Street unable to pinpoint just one sensation street
Street behind and ahead under my feet
Street in *x* in *y* in *z* in my arms
Street through my monocle in circles of a small movie projector,
Kaleidoscope in distinct iridescent curves street.

Drunk from the street and from feeling seeing hearing everything at once,
My temples throbbing from coming here and going there at the same time . . . . .

MAXWELL BODENHEIM: Sunlight on the Avenue

The sunlight marches like a crystal-thighed,
Cubistic, balanced, and relentless mind,
With slow, long steps that travel on beside
The short and rapid steps of coward-sounds.

The sunlight is a never-satisfied
Analysis of men and women thick
Upon this street—its fingers slimly creep
Below the scurrilous renown of clothes.
The sunlight thrusts an old, judicial glare
Against the purposeless and spongy bloom
Of faces, reaching in and pulling out
Perversions, servitudes, and appetites
That wait for sneaking auctions held by night.
One shred of explanation on each face
Eludes the sunlight and, less confident
Than small psychologists, the light resumes
Its sheer, composed, and brutal inquiries,
And makes the morning known to hordes of men
Whose inward strolls of light do not preserve
An independent visit and retreat.
Immensely unconvinced, the sunlight tries
To find a reason for the delicate,
Sequestered sprays of nerves that grew in beasts
And turned them to the comical dismay
Of men with half-impeded claws and teeth.
The reason dodges underneath a long
And insubstantial shadow partly caused
By the response of objects to the light
That seeks to rob them of their dark defence.
When men turn midnight into afternoon,
With minds that hold a fresh, capricious glare,
And when they seize the morning and coerce
Its light to blackness serving as a road
For mornings less confined and regular,
The outer sunlight on this avenue
Will drop upon its knees and be content.

JULES ROMAINS: The City

"There is a joyful streaming of bodies."

My smoke arches their blue chests,
Shakes their heads, twists their torsos,

Stamps on the chimneys, rears up
In a brutal desire to gallop.
It rained just now. The trees,
The roofs, the sidewalks hold a little water
Where the sun melts like honey.
The uneven lightning rods
Suddenly discharge against the dawn
My most youthful urban will.
It seems to me that down in my streets
The passersby run in the same direction,
And, unraveling the neutral crossroads,
Straighten out the twisted boulevards
So that, diverging less and less,
In spite of the walls, in spite of the buildings' frames,
The countless forces flow together
And, abruptly, the total momentum
Sets all the houses in motion.
The city is going to move, this morning
It is going to wrest itself from the earth,
Uproot its foundations,
Extricate them from the thick clay
Carry away the stones in the flesh;
Swarm like beasts; cover
The space with its heavy creeping;
Brandishing towers, swelling crowds
Under the multicolor clouds;
And then leave for the Ocean or for the Dawn.

ADRIANO DEL VALLE: Gyrating City

Land of blue silk paper with yellow days and white nights
The citizens play polo with golden mallets
The clouds of perfect blankness play hoops with the moon
The innocent verses go back to their nests with folded wings
The regimental colonel orders up some Ultraist poems
The archbishop distributes benedictions and Swiss chocolates
Jewelers come up with necklaces of pale maggots for the freshly deceased!
At dawn the coffee shoots out like trains from the roundhouse

Flabbylip Lucifer's pennants bear the standards of the luminous city
Rosy trollops hatching numbers on their fingers croon like clerics
Wild alms make gymnastics with their coils of laughter
All the nights herd their stars to the celestial prairie!
The blessed mothers comb their daughters' hair like solar teeth
Laughter—Carnival—Pantomime—breaking crystal
In the great plaza the glacial juggler conjures images
The modern poets munch angel hair and celestial apples
And in bed, at the peak of the carousel, braided into my brain is the Ballets Russes

---

Ardengo Soffici: Crossroad

Dissolving in the powder of goldenight
With the sudden clamor of electricity gas acetylene and other lights
Blossoming in the shop windows
In other windows and in the firmament's airplane
Shoes trailing diamond and gold droplets along vernal sidewalks
Like the mouths and eyes
Of all those women victims of solitary hysteria
Automobiles arriving from everywhere
Royal carriages and streetcars chirping like machine-gunned birds

Nous n'avons plus d'amour que pour nous-mêmes enfin

'Speaking to the driver is prohibited'

Oh to swim like a fish in love drinking emeralds
In this net of perfume and fireworks!

Andrei Bely: from *Petersburg*

There were no people on Nevsky Prospect; but a creeping, wailing myriapod was there; into a single damp space multivarious voices were poured—a multivariety of words; articulate phrases broke there one against the other, and horribly there did the words fly apart like the shards of bottles that were empty and had all been broken in one single place: all of them, jumbled up together, again wove into a sentence that flew into infinity without end or beginning; this sentence seemed meaningless and woven from fantasies: the ceaseless flow of the sentence that was formed from meaninglessness hung above the Nevsky like black soot; above the expanse stood the black smoke of fantasies.

And with these fantasies, swelling out from time to time, the Neva roared and struggled between its massive walls of granite. . . . And beyond them, beyond: ones, twos, threes and couple after couple—they blow their noses, cough, shuffle, laughing and maliciously gossiping, and they pour into the damp expanse with multifarious voices a multivariety of words that have been torn loose from the sense that gave them birth: bowler hats, feathers, service caps; service caps, cockades, feathers; tricorne, top hat, service cap; umbrella, shawl, feather.

OLIVERIO GIRONDO: Street-Sketch

On the terrace of a café there is a gray family. Some cross-eyed breasts pass looking for a smile over the tables. The noise of the automobiles dyes the leaves of the trees. On the fifth floor, somebody crucifies themselves by opening the window wide.

I think of where I'll keep the stands, the street lights, the passers-by, which come into me by my pupils. I feel so full that I am afraid of exploding . . . I'd need to leave some cement on the sidewalk . . .

Arriving at a corner, my shadow separates itself from me, and suddenly, it hurls itself beneath the wheels of a streetcar.

ROBERT MUSIL: from *The Man Without Qualities*

Automobiles shot out of deep, narrow streets into the shallows of bright squares. Dark clusters of pedestrians formed cloudlike strings. Where more powerful lines of speed cut across their casual haste they clotted up, then trickled on faster and, after a few oscillations, resumed their steady rhythm. Hundreds of noises wove themselves into a wiry texture of sound with barbs protruding here and there, smart edges running along it and subsiding again, with clear notes splintering off and dissipating. . . . All in all, it was like a boiling bubble inside a pot made of the durable stuff of buildings, laws, regulations, and historical traditions.

JULIAN PRZYBOŚ: Buildings

POET,
EXCLAIM THE STREET!

half suspended masses, from which the builder
hijacked motion: frozen floors.
roofs'
suspended pitch.
walls
just inferred.
human packed intensity:

buildings.

think:
each brick pressed on a bare hand.

– represents buildings itself

XAVIER BÓVEDA: An Automobile Passes

Oú, oú, oú:
    slowly an automobile passes . . .
Oú, oú, oú:
    the automobile's continuous song.
And the motor
accompanies
frisky.

Trrrrrrr
Trrrrrrr
There's an ultraviolet light
inside the car
where an older lady reposes
between the "oú" and the "trrr", evoking
suave memories of the past . . .

As a girl, she remembers
a blond boy, the sweetheart
dancing partner, with whom
that "fox-trot" was the tops.
Oú, oú, oú.
The auto heaves,
frenetic...
Trrrrrrrr
And all of a sudden
it's off, purring in the background...
Po-po-po-pöe.

XAVIER ABRIL: Chronic

There goes a friend if needed, to hasten the collapse of morale.

This other guy is useless. Already with a second mortgage: forty-five years without a decent home, no car, and the sad tale leaked out about his wife with the protestant pastor.

That one there is the rogue of the city. Decked out in a gallant mustache picked up in a movie from 1913. But he must be a hero if he can manage to survive amidst the great con artists of the postwar era.

But of all this: men, women, money, happiness, fame or oblivion, the purest of all is the odor of petrol for automobiles.

The odor of petrol is the bride of the city.

Alfredo Mario Ferreiro: Poem Without Traffic Obstacles

TRAFFIC LIGHT

Cart,
        Limousine,
                Double-Carriage,
                                A Truck,
20 Taxis,
        8 Motors,
                2 Trams,
                        Bus.

Traffic cop

All a lone.

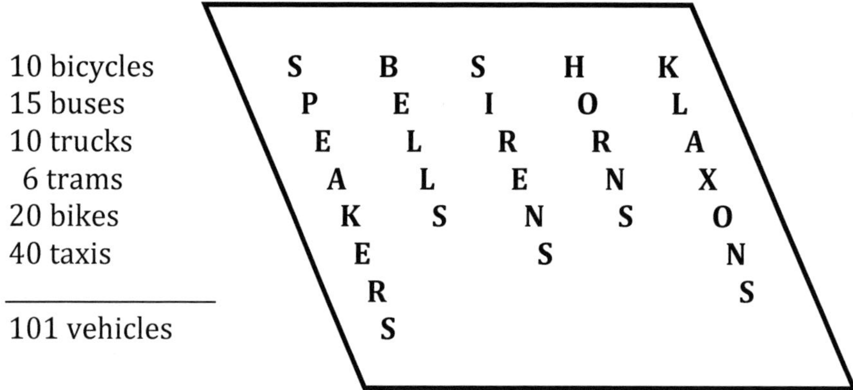

The traffic cop,
    with an elegant turn of the hand,
    opens up the transit spigot.
Lackluster storm — Reflections — Noise
        Engines — engines —
    Honking, horns, bells,
    Shouts, dust, thumps.
    The windows of the buildings
    look up terrified,
    begging for peace.

FORTUNATO DEPERO: Streetcar

SYNOPSIS: "I had such an appetite that my senses were electrified, and I had a voracious desire to eat." For 7.75 lire, boiled beef and soup are devoured, breaking up the language in the process. After that, "I had such a thirst that I wanted to drink myself unconscious." After indulging, "All of a sudden I remembered an appointment at 1:20 and paid the bill of 10.50. I went to meet the tram and gave it a metallic greeting," to which the tram responds ("PLOMMO-PLAMMO") The "ferocious machine-like tram" merges with "trame" (story plot). Apparently the tram has run down a pedestrian, and "the distant mewling echo of the funeral" with Latinate mumbo-jumbo is "dispersed in vocal arabesques."

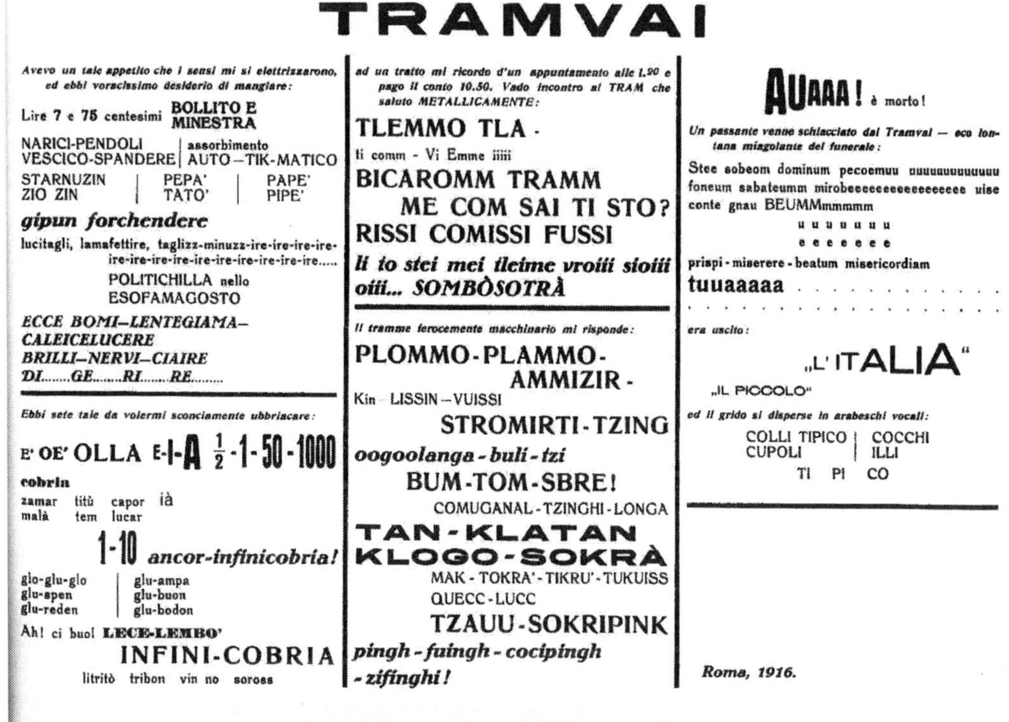

TRAMVAI

Avevo un tale appetito che i sensi mi si elettrizzarono, ed ebbi voracissimo desiderio di mangiare:

Lire 7 e 75 centesimi BOLLITO E MINESTRA

NARICI-PENDOLI | assorbimento
VESCICO-SPANDERE | AUTO—TIK-MATICO

STARNUZIN | PEPA' | PAPE'
ZIO ZIN | TATO' | PIPE'

gipun forchendere

lucitagli, lamafettire, taglizz-minuzz-ire-ire-ire-ire-ire-ire-ire-ire-ire-ire-ire-ire-ire-ire.....
POLITICHILLA nello
ESOFAMAGOSTO

ECCE BOMI—LENTEGIAMA—
CALEICELUCERE
BRILLI—NERVI—CIAIRE
DI.......GE.......RI.......RE........

Ebbi sete tale da volermi sconciamente ubbriacare:

E' OE' OLLA E-I-A ½-1-50-1000

cobrin

zamar titù capor ià
malà tem lucar

1-10 *ancor-infinicobria!*

glo-glu-glo | glu-ampa
glu-spen | glu-buon
glu-reden | glu-bodon

Ah! ci buol **LECE-LEMBO'**
INFINI-COBRIA
litritò tribon vin no soross

ad un tratto mi ricordo d'un appuntamento alle 1.20 e pago il conto 10.50. Vado incontro al TRAM che saluto METALLICAMENTE:

TLEMMO TLA -
li comm - Vi Emme iiiii
BICAROMM TRAMM
ME COM SAI TI STO?
RISSI COMISSI FUSSI
li to stei mei tleime vroiii sioiii oiii... SOMBÒSOTRÀ

Il tramme ferocemente macchinario mi risponde:

PLOMMO-PLAMMO-
AMMIZIR -
Kin LISSIN—VUISSI
STROMIRTI-TZING
oogoolanga - buli - tzi
BUM-TOM-SBRE!
COMUGANAL-TZINGHI-LONGA
TAN-KLATAN
KLOGO-SOKRÀ
MAK-TOKRA'-TIKRU'-TUKUISS
QUECC-LUCC
TZAUU-SOKRIPINK
pingh - fuingh - cocipingh - zifinghi!

AUAAA! è morto!

Un passante venne schiacciato dal Tramvai — eco lontana miagolante del funerale:

Stee sobeom dominum pecoemuu uuuuuuuuuuuu foneum sabateumm mirobeeeeeeeeeeeeeeeee uise conte gnau BEUMMmmmmm
u u u u u u u
e e e e e e e
prispi - miserere - beatum misericordiam
tuuaaaaa . . . .

era uscito:

„L' ITALIA"
„IL PICCOLO"

ed il grido si disperse in arabeschi vocali:

COLLI TIPICO | COCCHI
CUPOLI | ILLI
TI PI CO

Roma, 1916.

MAO TUN: from *Midnight*

The car was racing along like mad. He peered through the wind-screen. Good Heavens! the towering skyscrapers, their countless lighted windows gleaming like the eyes of devils, seemed to be rushing down on him like an avalanche at one moment and vanishing at the next. The smooth road stretched before him, and street-lamps flashed past on either side, springing up and vanishing in endless succession, A snake-like stream of black monsters, each with a pair of blinding lights for eyes, their horns blaring, bore down on him, nearer and nearer! He closed his eyes tight in terror, trembling all over. He felt as if his head were spinning and his eyes swam before a kaleidoscope of red, yellow, green, black, shiny, square, cylindrical, leaping, dancing shapes, while his ears rang in a pandemonium of honking, hooting and jarring, till his heart was in his mouth.

JOHN GOULD FLETCHER: 'Bus-Top

Black shapes bending,
Taxicabs crush in the crowd.
The tops are each a shining square
Shuttles that steadily press through woolly fabric.

Drooping blossom,
Gas-standards over
Spray out jingling tumult
Of white-hot rays.

Monotonous domes of bowler-hats
Vibrate in the heat.

Silently, easily we sway through braying traffic,
Down the crowded street.
The tumult crouches over us,
Or suddenly drifts to one side.

PIERRE ALBERT-BIROT

METRO
POEM FOR TWO VOICES

Mercerou Dupleix Ferris Wheel thermogenic there is a place
he's so ugly green light this coat doesn't go with the hat

a lantern
police station
Zenith
Du onnet
Dubonnet
women
with children
dirty
fellow
in front of me

to fall is to love the center beings and
things love the center the whole earth
loves the center this love made the
earth the earth Mobility the wheel
what a stroke of genius! My right glove
backwards could very well be on my
left glove to get off is also to get on
when it is day it is night furs
mousseline parasol umbrella the
blue of the sky the clouds the storms
the hurricanes might be the mass of
human thoughts.
mustn't forget my hat

a red
pompon on
a blue cap
this whistle
blast!
hand
sale
where do we
get off?

exit armond Ah he's gone transfer
socialist delegate type a collection of old heads
Bon Marché

GUILLAUME APOLLINAIRE: Monday in Christine Street

The concierge's mother and the concierge will let everyone through
If you're a man you'll come with me tonight
All we need is one guy to watch the main entrance
While the other goes upstairs

Three gas burners lit
The proprietress is consumptive
When you've finished we'll play a game of backgammon
An orchestra leader who has a sore throat
When you come through Tunis we'll smoke some hashish

That almost rhymes

Piles of saucers flowers a calendar
Bing bang bong
I owe damn almost 300 francs to my landlady
I'd rather cut off you know what than give them to her

I'm leaving at 8:27 P.M.
Six mirrors keep staring at one another
I think we're going to get into an even worse mess
Dear sir
You are a crummy fellow
That dame has a nose like a tapeworm
Louise forgot her fur piece
Well I don't have a fur piece and I'm not cold
The Dane is smoking his cigarette while he consults the schedule
The black cat crosses the restaurant

Those pancakes were divine
The water's running
Dress black as her nails
It's absolutely impossible
Here sir
The malachite ring
The ground is covered with sawdust
Then it's true

The redheaded waitress eloped with a bookseller

A journalist whom I really hardly know

Look Jacques it's extremely serious what I'm going to tell you

Shipping company combine

He says to me sir would you care to see what I can do in etchings and pictures
All I have is a little maid

After lunch at the Café du Luxembourg
When we get there he introduces me to a big fellow
Who says to me
Look that's charming
In Smyrna in Naples in Tunisia
But in God's name where is it
The last time I was in China
That was eight or nine years ago
Honor often depends on the time of day
The winning hand

PAUL MORAND

CARLOS OQUENDO DE AMAT: Advertisement

Today the moon is out shopping

From a trolley
the sun like a passenger
reads the city

corners
thin the walkers

and wind pushes
the cabs

Programs dropped from the moon
(the earth will be given)

sports footage plays twice
p s
e m
r u
f b
u l
m a
e
s n
e
o p
of international gazes

A cop tames the breeze
r and the sound of the horns has turned the dresses blue.
o
t News Flash
a All the poets have come out of the Underwood's U. key
v
e
l
e

n
a bought the moon five meters of poems

Conrad Aiken: Inscriptions in Sundry Places

On a billboard
smoke Sweet Caporals

In a street-car
do not speak to the motorman

On a vending machine
insert one cent then press the rod
push push push push

On a weighing machine
give yourself a weigh

On the schoolhouse
Morton Grammar School Founded 1886

In gilt letters on a swinging black sign
Dr. William F. Jones M.D.

On a tombstone
memento mori

On a coin
e pluribus unum

On the fence of a vacant lot
commit no nuisance

In a library
silence

At the entrance to a graveyard
dogs admitted only on leash

At a zoo
do not feed the animals

On a cotton wharf
no smoking

On a crocheted bookmarker in a Bible
time is short

On a sailor cap
U. S. S. Oregon

At a railway-crossing
stop look and listen

At the end of a road
private way dangerous passing

Beside a pond
no fishing

In a park
keep off the grass

In a train
spitting prohibited $100 fine

On a celluloid button
remember the Maine

On a brick wall
trespassers will be prosecuted to the full extent of the law

Outside a theatre
standing room only

At the foot of a companionway leading to the bridge of a ship
officers only

In a subway
the cough and sneeze
both spread disease
and so does spit
take care of it

Over the gateway to a college yard
What is the man that thou art mindful of him?

Ditto
enter to grow in wisdom

On a sign hung with two lanterns beside a frozen river
no skating

Beside a wood
no shooting

Behind a building in a dark alley
No sir, carry your water up the street

In a public lavatory
fools' names and fools' faces
always show in public places
and this I'll add if you don't know it
that Shakspeare was no backhouse poet

Ditto
Mabel Waters 26 John Street

Ditto
do not deface

Ditto
say when you'll meet me

Ditto
it was down in the Lehigh Valley—me and my saucy Sue

In a museum
visitors are requested not to touch the objects

In a concert hall
no admission after doors are closed

On an office door
Peter Jones

In a saloon
no treating allowed

Laundry-mark on linen
B69

In a window
board and room

On a ship
first class passengers not allowed aft of this sign

In a train
ne pas se pencher au dehors

On an apartment-house door
all deliveries must be made at side entrance

Over a door in a hospital
staff only

Joaquín Torres-García: from *The City With No Name*

Us, because the world would have to be cured first, since all our ills stem from its being out of kilter. Correcting this deficiency, then, through heat or cold, seems to be his method of healing, which he apparently applies with admirable results. He gave me a boost after the catastrophe you know of, and continues to sustain me. I advertise for his clinic. It occurred to him that what might attract the most attention in this city of shorn men was a bearded one. Now, take a look at my back and see what is written there.

The sign read: "Dr. Sharpaine. Mental illnesses. Specialist in Bypass B (the businessman's disease) and Superbypass C (the politician's), etc. Repair shop for repetitive-stress injuries . . ."

— Ah! So I've been strolling along in the company of a walking advertisement?
— Is that bad? Doesn't everyone who passes through these streets?
— I'm sure you're right. I'd be interested in meeting the man.
— Are you feeling poorly?
— No, my head is clear . . . but you've piqued my curiosity. He must be an interesting person.
— He is, and you'll meet him soon. Let's move on, though. I'm going to leave the tools of my trade here, but I'll be back. Wait for me in the café out front. After a while he returned and ordered a coffee on the patio.
— Great observation deck, I said.
— Yes, all the city's fauna passes by here.

M. G. Shelley: Poème Mécanique

Go to hell yes no yes no
Goodmorning hello hello

How do you do yes no yes no
Goodbye go to hell.

Nice day yes no yes no
Operator sorry of course goodnight
See you tomorrow yes no yes no
Twelve o'clock ten o'clock two o'clock
Turn out the light a new moon
Quarter moon half moon it is raining
The sun is out yes no yes no nice day.

I had a lovely time so did I come again
Yes no yes no thank you no yes
Yes no yes no a quart of milk
A dozen eggs a pound of coffee
And a loaf of bread it is percolating
Dinner is ready supper's ready yes no yes no
Breakfast is ready it is late time to get up
You have the wrong number I am sorry
Are you ready yes yes no yes no.

II

Autos honk down and up the streets
Bridges rattle lovers sigh contacts of bodies
Springs giving kissings relaxations
And sleep sleep sleep sleep.

Whistles blow bells ring
Somebody hollers help
Somebody else hollers murder
Somebody says oh
Women dress bands play trains run
Lights go on and off and stay on stay off
Clocks tickTOCK tickTOCK tickTOCK
Rain falls stars shine minds think
Eyes close people dream

III

Singsong singsong singsong singsong
Count the bars count the bars

Yes no yes no you'll never get out
You'll never get out yes no yes no
Count the bars count the bars you'll never
Get out you'll never get out singsong
Singsong singsong singsong.

And BUT and PERHAPS and YES and NO
Yes no yes no and THIS and THAT and AND and THE
Andandand Smithsmithsmith Mr.
Mrs. Miss. Yes sir no sir yes no yes no
No yes bang-bang
O God help me won't he never come yes
No yes no the doctor the doctor
It aint right shut your goddamned mouth will you
Let's have a drink yes no yes no a hamsandwich coffee and
Pay the cashier will you marry me no yes yes no
Yes no I'm sleepy kiss me again
What have you been doing nothing much
And you the same
Weatherclear weathercloudy weatherrain what are you doing
Tonight I have an engagement busy line goodbye
Yes no yes no see you again sometime
Thank you guilty not guilty thirty days
Dismissed yes no yes no yes no oh
Hell.

KURT SCHWITTERS: High Fashion Furs

Leonine Pharmacy, Edward Goldacre (custom-made intestine boilers)
Clocks clock art, three miles to go
Gold acres
Boil intestines, A-1 intestines
Custom-made gold boilers (run by steam)
The Red Cross Bakers run by steam (The Boil Intestines Pharmacy)
Umbrellas, canes, men's underwear
Boil intestines (beer in cans)
Telephones broadcast baskets
(City Employment License)

Intestines at old prices, artwork in cans
Leonine Pharmacy (custom-made basket boilers)
Bicycles boil artworks in intestines (installation is our job)

František Halas: The World in the Telephone

1634
Stock Exchange Copper's up? Then buy!

999
Barracks František! Come and get baptized

1756
Bedroom Bon jour mon ami

13
Office Hihi—it's from the party

12775
Telephone Cell Hellooo — Hellooo — Hellooo

335
Café Forget it! A hundred with the pharaoh

691
Circus Trainer—You've broken my heart

554
Editorial Strike? Explosion in the mine?

3399
Hotel Please! How many beds? Two

17
Hospital Dead! And the mattress?
Come along then

MALCOLM COWLEY: Buy 300 Steel

Buy 300 steel at the
market, buy 300 steel
at the market, buy 300
steel.

His face melted into the telephone,
his lips curled with hello, and dreamed
his vulcanized-rubber eyes,

with a hello . . . there was a lake beneath
the Bowling Green 6000 trees
and hello, Bowling Green, the noise of waters

under a curdled sky, hello,
I dove into the lake, hello,
into the lake as green, hello,
as Mr. Kahn, hello, hello,
as green as Bowling Green.

I'll make a note of it, good-by, and rain
suddenly falling, down fell railways, coppers,
motors, industrials, Rebecca Steel,
Calumet, Monkey-Ward, and Chrysler falling,
rain steadily falling, public utilities
. . . always a good buy,

a good, I'll make a note of it,
buy, good-by, good-by.

PAUL MORAND: Business

5,000 dollars
To whoever can demonstrate
That a word can be heard in the factory
Where tubular furnaces are made.

The steel frames soar, suspended;
The head explodes under the pile driver.
I like that.
I run my days at the speed of an aerial express,
I call up my friends by megaphone,
I lunch standing up,
The stock market tickertape unwinds on the floor;
The subway shakes inside the legs.
I like that.
All the while,
On a black divan,
My wife extends her breasts to a friend.

Alfred Döblin

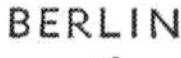

Walter Mehring: Advertising is the Parasite of Life

Coming out, evenings . . . *All along the Linden!* Flagged with placards
"The flying Brothers"
"Sous les Ponts de Paris"
and "Fisher-girl, little one . . ."
[5 % savings on electricity]
"Ace of Spades at the *Zauberkönig*"
"The Man Without Nose Cartilage"
leers at "The Lady Without a Lower Body"
And the young miss smiles
In "Steiner's Paradise Bed"
House-high
"*Hanewaker*, the pure and natural herbal liqueur
in huntsman's hat with Tyrolean feather"
Holdrioh! There's no such thing as sin in the mountains—
only "Condensed Milk from the Alps"
"The Secret to a Voluptuous Bosom"
Oriental vices
[Previously forbidden—to youth under 80]
"Babel-Berlin"
"Even in Hell they use Kaiser Briquettes"
Look out!
—Rubber goods! Golden Swan Drugstore
"The Leda from the Wannsee-Lido"
Certified masseuse
for spinal-cord syphilis—feudal with seven jags—
"The count's sweetheart"
—La Bibliothèque Rose—
Volume 25: "The Language of Flowers"
. . . in the penal code: The seduction of minors . . .
"Suffer the little children to come unto me!" Oh, Tannenbaum—
Mayflower
The *Old Trapper* looks up
over the guardrail
to the thousand candles of the starry
sky in the "Wintergarten"
Variété—
Nick Carter's already on the trail.

This man knows your fate!
"The art of captivation"
"The Yellow Peril"
and "How the Jews Are to Blame for the Great War"
Thus: *"Recruit for the Freikorps!"*
The "Trumpeter from Säckingen" sounds the alarm!
on roundel windows for the silver wedding anniversary—
his blonde love on his arm
A poignant fate
out of "Belgium's sporting houses"
—Who's driving so late?—
Jack the Ripper's chauffeuring
"Only with death's-head—accept no imitations"
on *"Dralle's Birch Water"*
wave
the Erl-daughters of the inventor
through the great city's deeps.

BASIL BUNTING: Aus dem Zweiten Reich

I

Women swarm in Tauentsienstrasse.
Clients of Nollendorferplatz cafés,
shadows on sweaty glass,
hum, drum on the table
        to the negerband's faint jazz.
Humdrum on the table.

Hour and hour
meeting against me,
efficiently whipped cream,
efficiently metropolitan chatter and snap,
transparent glistening wrapper
        for a candy pack.

Automatic, somewhat too clean,
body and soul similarly scented,

on time,
rapid, dogmatic, automatic and efficient,
ganz modern.

'Sturm über Asien' is off, some other flicker . . .
Kiss me in the taxi, twist fingers in the dark.
A box of chocolates is necessary.
I am preoccupied with Sie and Du.
        The person on the screen,
divorced and twenty-five, must pass for fourteen
for the story's sake, an insipidity
contrived to dress her in shorts
and a widenecked shirt with nothing underneath
so that you see her small breasts when she
often bends towards the camera.
Audience mainly male stirs,
        I am teased too,
I like this public blonde better than my brunette,
        but that will never do.
—Let's go,
arm in arm on foot over gleaming snow
past the Gedächtnis Kirche
to the loud crowded cafés near the Bahnhof Zoo.

Better hugged together ('to keep warm')
under street trees whimpering to the keen wind
over snow whispering to many feet,
find out a consolingly mediocre
neighborhood without music, varnished faces
bright and sagacious against varnished walls,
youngsters red from skating,
businessmen reading the papers:
no need to talk—much:
what indolence supplies.
'If, smoothing this silk shirt, you pinch my thighs,
that will be fabelhalf'.

II

Herr Lignitz knows Old Berlin. It is near the Post Office
with several rather disorderly public houses.

'You have no naked pictures in your English magazines.
It is shocking. Berlin is very shocking to the English. Are you shocked?
Would you like to see the naked cabarets
in Jaegerstrasse? I think there is
nothing like that in Paris.
Or a department store? They are said to be
almost equal to Macy's in America'.

III

The renowned author of
more plays than Shakespeare
stopped and did his hair
with a pocket glass
before entering the village,
afraid they wouldnt recognize
caricature and picturepostcard,
that windswept chevelure.

Who talked about poetry,
and he said nothing at all;
plays,
and he said nothing at all;
politics,
and he stirred as if a flea
bit him
but wouldnt let on in company;
and the frost in Berlin,
muttered: **Schrecklich**

Viennese bow from the hips,
notorieties
contorted laudatory lips,
wreaths and bouquets surround
the mindless menopause.
Stillborn fecundities,
frostbound applause.

KURT SCHWITTERS: Subway Poem

Houses eyeball millions cudgel lamps
Windows crunch on eyes
Bellow light the subway-shuttle teeth
German Daily News sleds past and music (super shoeshines)
Adding machines spew numbers, Garden City
Songs tender cannons' gold (physician tested)
Windows live sans light grow numb
Sans coal glass woodens
Flames glass up
Bellow crunch on light the window
Flames glass flames
Houses eyeball millions sparkle lamps
And fire woodens coal light bellows forth
(In case of crowds step to the center aisle)

TADEUSZ PEIPER: The Street

The street.
Two rectangles of brick over the rectangle of cement.
Hymn of the vertical.
Light slips through the tollgates of the roofs
to the thieves of day—punishment.
A tramway, peacock of tin, . . . gl-gl . . . gaggles its vanity.
Sun = only gasoline or vapor.
Man = bird of coal.

JORGE LUIS BORGES: Butcher Shop

More vile than a brothel
the meat market flaunts itself like an insult to the street.
Over the door
a blind steer's head

rules the coven
of primping meat and marble counters
with the haughty majesty of an idol.

Oliverio Girondo: Pedestrian

At the end of the street, a public building breathes in the bad odor of the city.

The shadows bend their spines in doorways, lie down to fornicate on the sidewalk.

With an arm stuck against the wall, a lightless streetlamp has a convex vision of people passing by automobile.

The looks of passers-by dirty the things exhibiting themselves in shop windows, make thin the legs hanging beneath victory capes.

Next to the curb a kiosk has just swallowed a woman.

Passing: an Englishwoman identical to a streetlamp. A streetcar that is a school on wheels. A failed dog, with eyes of a prostitute shaming us to look at it and let it go.*

Suddenly: the corner watchman stops with a swing of a baton all of the shiverings of the city, so that a single whisper is heard, the whisper of all the breasts brushing against each other.

* The failed dogs have lost their owners for raising their legs like mandolins, their skin has become much too big for them, they have aphonic voices, of alcoholics, and are capable only of stretching in doorways, so that they sweep them together with the trash.

JOAQUIM FOLGUERA: Blind Street Musicians

to Guillaume Apollinaire

TEARS OF MUSIC GLIDING ON RESIN
VIBRATION OF STRINGS AND NERVES AND AIR
TURBID, TURBULENT WATERS THAT HAVE A FOUL SMELL
GREEN CLOTH YELLOW HANDS WHITE STRINGS
EYES OF SERENE AND POLISHED AGATE
MAXIMUM PRESSURE OF THE MUSICAL MOAN
GUTTER OF OILY MELODY
TANGENT MULTITUDE
LITERARY VALVE
BEGGARY
PUCCINI

GUILLAUME APOLLINAIRE: Phantom of Clouds

Since it was the day before July fourteenth
Around four in the afternoon
I went down to the street to see the jugglers

Those people who give open-air performances
Are beginning to be rare in Paris
In my youth you saw many more of them
They've nearly all gone to the provinces

I took the Boulevard Saint-Germain
And in a little square between Saint-Germain-des-Prés and Danton's statue
I found the jugglers

The crowd surrounding them was silent and resigned to waiting
I found a place in the circle where I could see everything
Tremendous weights
Belgian cities raised at arm's length by a Russian worker from Longwy
Hollow black dumbbells whose stem is a frozen stream
Fingers rolling a ciagarette as bittersweet as life

A number of dirty rugs covered the ground

Rugs with wrinkles that won't come out
Rugs that are almost entirely dust-colored
And with some yellow or green stains persistent
Like a tune that pursues you

Do you see the man who's savage and lean
His father's ashes sprouted in his graying beard
And he bore his whole heredity in his face
He seemed to be dreaming about the future
Turning his barrel organ all the while
Its lingering voice lamented in marvelous
Glug-glugs squawks and muffled groans

The jugglers didn't move
The oldest wore a sweater the rose-violet color you see in the fresh cheeks of young
girls who are dying

That rose nestles above all in the creases surrounding their mouths
Or near their nostrils
It's a rose full of treachery

Thus he bore on his back
The lowly hue of his lungs

Arms arms everywhere mounted guard

The second juggler
Wore only his shadow
I watched him for a long time
His features escape me entirely
He's a headless man

Then there was another who resembled a tough thug
With a kind heart and a dirty mind
With his baggy trousers and garters to hold up his socks
Didn't he look dressed up like a pimp

The music stopped and there were negotiations with the public
Who sou by sou threw down on the rug the sum of two and a half francs
Instead of the three francs the old man had set as the price of the show

But when it was clear no one was going to give any more
They decided to begin the performance
From beneath the organ appeared a tiny juggler dressed in pulmonary pink

With fur at his wrists and ankles
He gave little cries
And saluted by gracefully lifting his forearms
And spreading wide his fingers

One leg back ready to kneel
He saluted the four points of the compass
And when he balanced on a sphere
His thin body became such delicate music that none of the onlookers could resist it
A small inhuman sprite
Each of them thought
And that music of shapes
Destroyed the music of the mechanical organ
That the man with the ancestor-covered face was grinding out

The tiny juggler turned cartwheels
With such harmony
That the organ stopped playing
And the organist held his face in his hands
His fingers resembled descendents of his destiny
Miniscule fetuses appearing in his beard
New cries like Redskins
Angelic music of the trees
Vanishing of the child

The jugglers raised the huge dumbbells at arms' length
They juggled with weights
But every spectator searched in himself for the miraculous child
Century oh century of clouds

Pierre Reverdy: Acrobats

In the middle of the crowd there is, with a dancing child, a man lifting weights. His arms tattooed in blue call on the sky to bear witness to their useless strength.

Lightly, the child dances, in tights which are too big for him; lighter than the balls he balances on. And when he holds out his purse, no one gives anything. No one gives for fear of making it too heavy. He is so thin.

TRISTAN TZARA: The Showmen

the brains swell up flatten out
heavy balloons tire shrivel up
(ventriloquist's words)
swell up flatten out swell up flatten out
flatten out
dissolved organs
clouds have these shapes sometimes too
widows grow nervous looking at them
sometimes
listen to dizziness
acrobatics of numbers
in the mathematician's head
NTOUCA leaping
cap and bells
which is dada which is DADA
the static poem is a new invention
MBOCO the asthmatic HwS2
10054 moumbimba
there is a machine
machine
the vowels are white globules
the vowels stretch out
stretch out
gnaw at us clock
stick
AND LOOK A LIGHT IS RUNNING ALONG THE ROPES
smoke curls out from the rope-walker's head
my aunt squats on the trapeze in the gymroom
her nipples are herring heads
she has flippers
and draws draws draws the accordion from her breast
she draws draws draws the accordion from her breast glwa wawa prohahab
in the little towns the sun hatches under the carts before the inn
nf nf nf tataï
the little children break wind looking at the circus props
and there are lice
and grandmothers covered with soft tumors that is to say polyps

LÉON-PAUL FARGUE: The Boulevard

The boulevard unfurls and yawns . . . A train wails behind the hedge . . .

Girls in bright colors sew and wait in the doorways of brothels. At the noise of black footsteps approaching, their eyes turn like stars . . . Germaine and her friend idle against a billboard at the end of an empty street under stormy skies . . .

Remember the hotels barred by a red-painted half-gate where an iron cornet tinkles, in some lane where houses lift a patch of dusky sky as though it were a jade cup in the tips of dirty hands . . .

The walls gaze upon each other with the weariness of old partners, or of endless confrontations in a miserable dance . . . Tattered clothes cackle on ropes in the windows.—Corners conceal strange faces. I hear the tail ends of quarrels and staring eyes defy me.

Children shriek in the shadow and fall down: A scolding voice lifts them up again.—The lane is so badly paved that everyone seems to limp along it. The back of an old woman rounds the end of a passageway . . . A cat breaks cover—two lozenges of moonlight . . .

The sky darkens between the walls like a large flower, up above, in an iron vase . . . A crooked Argand lamp, the color of burnt onion. Its thin arm. Its tinkling kindles it . . . Short blue flames sprout in kitchens . . . Street stalls light up, lower and tremble . . .

A girl opens her window. And I see her lamp, coiffed in pink like a tall flamingo standing on one leg . . .

Remember our muffled descents down yellow stairways awash with the breath of uncovered drains open to the sulfur of the courtyards, the slanting rays of the sky in a gutter, the blue corner of a roof where a pipe dripped, and that woman with her dark crown of hair, her legs gloved in red stockings, and your heart pounding when you took the girl—and the soldiers who walked along the railway—and that gaze of a woman at her window—wise and heavy as purple grapes . . .

HAGIWARA SAKUTARO: Yoshiwara

Enclosed in tall board fences
it's a shadowy gloomy district.
Nevertheless in a vacant lot a ditch flows
trees grow
and everywhere the smell of white carbolic acid.

Yoshiwara!
Like a frog lying dead on an embankment
it's a pleasure zone, its belly exposed white.

In the sad enclosure of board fences
I heard the woman I fancy weeping
all night long.
Then she ate indigestible noodles
and was lying under a sooty electric lamp.
"Come again, please!"

Even on a day of cloudy weather of despair
a photograph is posted on the brothel billboard.

Vadim Shershenevich

Garrulous motors babbled briskly and onto
The hanging jaw of a tram, which had crashed into the sheen of the wooden
    pavement,
Came an awkward, one-sided, clumsily structured sound,
And the evening gave a look more cunning than the eye of corpse.

The electric frames and doors opened up, like wounds, and
From them oozed the purulent masses of pale straw-colored ladies;
Some warmed up their soul with newspaper headlines,
And others conjugated love in all the cases and genders.
And when the city began to list to the side and
Ran off along the roofs of crumbling homes,
When the lamps served up gas apples
Over a compote of sour yawns and words,

When I got carried away with this mad game of macau,
Myself shuffling the facts of the marked deck of cards,—
Over the champing, moment-enduring chaos,
You arose, spilling iodine from your heart.

HAGIWARA KYOJIRO

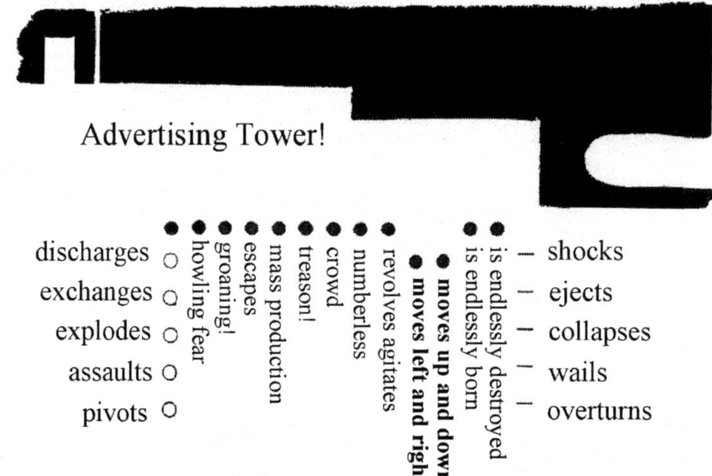

Advertising Tower!
discharges
exchanges
explodes
assaults
pivots
howling fear
groaning!
escapes
mass production
treason!
crowd
numberless
revolves agitates
moves left and right
moves up and down
is endlessly born
is endlessly destroyed
shocks
ejects
collapses
wails
overturns

The languid brains sing a song
I'm listening to the noise of the water
Everything is the ocean's sunless black abyss!
With no beginning and no end!
Each thing comes and passes!
Life? Who has a clue?! The face of a hobby-horse!
Ah, Pierrot!
I can believe in neither freedom, nor God, nor mankind!
Only, I find the utmost fissure in the Dadaists!
You want to find a meaning?! Go ahead!
All is but a series of affectations!
I'm tired of this continual boredom!
The melancholy gospel washes over bones on the ocean floor!
Why? ! Must I keep on living?!
Now, I don't believe we'll return to the earth or the sky!
Even my passion is listless!
I desire neither growth nor individuality!
Even cinema and pigments are dark!
Sadness, joy, and sentiment fossilize!
I'm a wood-block, an ornament!
I only rattle along!

A noise-making comforter!
Why must I keep on living? !
I'm a dead man!
I'm a moving thing!
The only thing that touches me is death!

He laughs! He drives the carriage! She gives thanks to God!
He cries! He is cold and gray! She turns to bones!
He walks! He saw her! She walks the path of thorns!
He rejoices! He is a cosmopolitan! She withers with fatigue!
He sleeps! He also spies! She keeps it a secret!
He eats! He holds the ticket! She is a fine wine!
He rages! He smokes a cigar! She is the shade of death!
He runs! He is a gambler! She is delicate!
He sinks! He set up a seat! She has no husband!
He births! He chatters happily! She drips with blood!
He fattens! He swells and walks! She commits a sin!
He steals! He tied up the woman! She embraces him!
He comes! He refuses the interview! She believes steadfastly!
He goes! He makes it into a game! She is naked!
He rips! He is just as we asked! She has a premonition!
He collapses! He shoots at everything! She plucks his beard!
He rides! He is an assassin! She trembles her breast!
He bends! He was birthed by explosion! She drops her shoulders!
He leaks! He was piled up! She goes to the rear!
He falls! He laughs at folly! She is a great miracle!
He dies! He is a realist! She slides along!
He echoes! He is a wish! She wipes her face!
He embraces! He is a demand! She has painful eyes!
He receives! He is assertion! She has black legs!
He pains! He is negation! She is dust!
He chirps! He is affirmation! She is a distant rose!

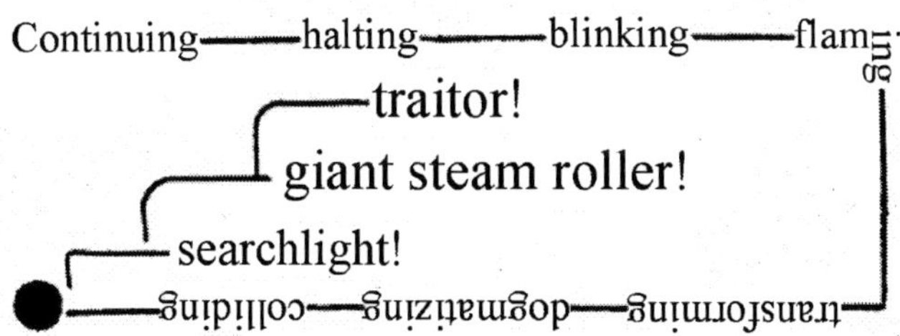

In the road, on the streets, on the rooftops, in the rooms,
the warehouses, the cafes, I----------------------●
--------I live like a pig!
--------I live like a spy!
--------I live like an informer!
--------I live like a butcher!
--------I live like an emperor!
--------I'm listening to the pale gloomy cartridge tear apart!
--------I'm watching the changes and ornaments of the life outside myself!

Advertising tower
A huge gamble
A forest of chimneys, pouring out black smoke

----------------------Several bodily cavities and a bumpy face and several round sticks and
yellow and hair and *springs* and a *compass* and tendons
and a *tapeworm* and socks and a calling card!
A dirty *shirt* with several *buttons* coming off and *pants* that look like I just changed—
--that instrument called me!

Ah ha ha ha ha-----ha ha ha

Mário Sá-Carneiro: Manicure

In the sensation of polishing my nails,
Sudden sensation, inexplicably tender,
All of me I include in Me—piously.
And so alone, I go to the Café:
In the morning, like always, with yellowed yawns.
In leaving, the tables just—ungrateful
And hard, cornered in their awkwardness:
The Negroid, in the New Land, square and, free-thinker . . .

Outside: May day in light
And sun—brutal day, provincial and democratic,
Which my delicate eyes, refined and urban,
Can't stand—and when forced to, are
Supported by nausea. This offends my whole
Sensibility, this day, that may as well have singers
Among the friends I sometimes hang out with—
Their bushy moustaches, their naturally tan skin—
They write, but have their political party,
And aid republican assemblies;
And buy women, and like red wine,
Apples, and fried sardines . . .

And all the while I, in that sensation of polishing my nails
And painting them a Parisian gloss,
Move closer and closer, to being moved,
Until I cry for Me . . .
A thousand colors in the Air, a thousand vibrations beating,
Foggy plans unrealized,
Abating and bent; voluble listings, flexible discs,
Come tenuously, lining up before me
All the tenderness I could have lived,
All the greatness I could have felt,
All those scenarios that nonetheless, Went . . .
Bit by bit, as if they brought into focus
For me the dim obsession of one smile,
Which hollow mirrors might have reflected . . .
And carry in the sinews of their inflections . . .

Thin crystallizing chills . . .
Dislocatedly unattainable . . .
Quick, atmospheric flash . . .

And everything, everything just like that, is driving me into space
Through innumerable intersections of multiple
Plans, free: and slipped away.

And there, in that great Mirror of ghosts
Undulating and engulfing my entire past,
And crumbling down my present,
Is my future, already in dust . . .
....

So I lay out my files,
My clippers, my polish,
The polish of my feelings—
 and dispose of them
And free my eyes, growing wild in the Air!
Oh! to have the power to waste it all,
 the air, encrusting himself in everything—
To thrash, and thwack your Beauty—unsupported, in short! —
To sing of what He spins, and whets, impregnates,
And spills out, expanding, in vibrations:
Splaying out its subtleties, successively—perpetually, towards Infinity! . . .

What tricks, suspended in the ruined ribs of arches,
What triangular solid, atop the broken ships!
What helixes trail behind that skyward flight!
What funny spheres become that tennis ball! —
What blonde waves laugh, from out the player's mouth . . .
What red wreath, what fan, moves the half-naked Russian
Dancer, her hands painted up like Salomé,
On a big, Gold stage!
—What lace, the other dancers!

Ah! but what ruined inflections, strident, and blinding,
What savage peaks diverge, and creak,

Apache blades, criss-cross

The cold high dawn . . .

And through the stations and docking ports,
Accumulating large crates,
And suitcases, and bales—pell-mell . . .
All of it, inserted in Air,
His friend and, his divorcer,
Split from him by every nook of time and space,
Towards the place I feel my Soul, a'rambling off to! . . .

—The wonderful wares of futurism!

—Bale canvas,
How I wish to shawl myself in You!
—Crate wood,
How I long to drive my teeth into You!
And the nails, and the ropes, and the flanges...—
But, above everything, is that dance, sparkling
For my eyes, bold, from the Beauty
Of the labels on all those crates and bales—
Black or red or blue or green—
The very screams of Commerce & Industry
In transit, cosmopolitan:

FRAGIL ! FRAGIL !

843 — AG LISBON

492 — WR MADRID

Eager, towards that new, atmospheric Beauty,
My sight winding, watching, absorbs the frenzies
All around me. And o what magic, no lie; everything
Crossing over, thrashing about that
Treacherous, insidious fluid;
From grotesque, returns—rapid,
Imponderable, svelte, flippant . . .
—Look at the tables... Go on! Go on!

Up they go, into the Air, somersaulting
Frames-by-square-frames-per-second,
There—and now, and further away, in stray geometrical diamonds . . .
And engulf even the unengulfable strings they do engulf,
And at the tables, blend them, in clamoring insinuations,
Invocations round huddled seats of red velvet
That run along the whole Café . . .
And even loftier, with plans oblique,
With airborne symbols from tenuous heraldries,
Illumination set-to-stun, they illuminate
The cross-hatched straw bottoms of the chairs that,
Startled from their horizontal sleep, go on,
Go-on, up into the saraband . . .

My eyes anointed, anew,
Yes!—my futurist eyes, my eyes, cubist, my eyes intersectionist,
Never stop their roaring shutters,
Their slurping in, and sparkling out
All that that spectral beauty, that transfer,
Succedaneum—all that, Beauty unsupported,
Disjointed, immersed, emerged, fluid always,
Always unrestrained—in continual mutation,
In fathomless deviations . . .

—And what of this very boring, porcelain cup of tea?

Ah, that one runs itself dry by its own Greek amphoric curves,
Ascends towards a spired apex, a spiraled peak,
Which its brim with golden curls emits . . .

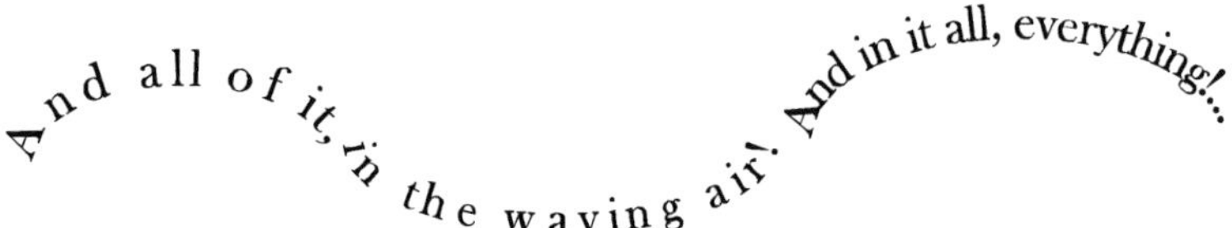

. . . Now, from long sheens of glass protracting out
Into the street, arrive theories of hyaline peaks,
Whipping their cloudy, diffused crystallizations.
Like a ray of sun crossing the largest pane,
They dance in its space, imbuing it in fantasy,

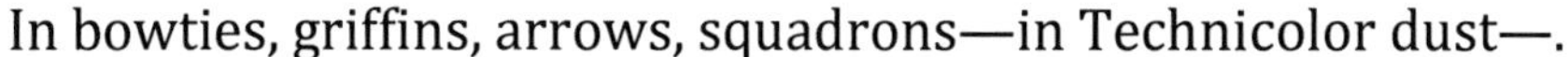

In bowties, griffins, arrows, squadrons—in Technicolor dust—.

APOTHEOSIS.

....

Beside me, rings a tambourine:
Resonant tincture!
It was what the landscape was missing . . .
The acoustic waves, even more distinct:
There they go! There they go, agile!
There, they stole away, graceful, delicate, pirate fleet of Souls . . .

A voice asks for a number over the phone:
North — 2, 0, 5, 7 . . .
And in the air, behold the punched-in molding ciphers :

INCARNATION OF NUMERIC BEAUTY !

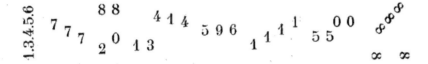

1.3.4.5.6 7 7 7 8 8 2 0 1 3 4 1 4 5 9 6 1 1 1 1 5 5 0 0 ∞ ∞ ∞ ∞ ∞ ∞

Further away, a servant lets a tray fall . . .
There's no end to these marvels!
A new uproar of swirling silver waves
Spreading out in circular, shimmering echoes,
Soughing like cold water, spackles
And refreshes the atmosphere . . .

—My eyes, exhausted by Beauty!

Ineffable, penumbral daydream—
Lulls down my fluttering eyelids . . .

....

. . . Gets me started remembering jade rings
Of certain hands I once possessed—
And they, by some sorcery, are now coiling in the Air . . .
They recall in me, kisses—and rise

Above their inlaid carmine workings . . .

Sequin'd helixes separate . . .
Crested feathers fan open, split apart as blades . . .
Small golden tambourines clasp together . . .
Spires raise up, locking tiny crucifixes . . .
Stars shatter, plumes brick together . . .

Painful, so as to rob my eyes of richness,
Driven in, spiked shut, they close . . .
Shift! There's no defense:
They lash plans before my ears, in waterfalls,
During the blackness—
Plans, intermissions, breaks, tangents, declines . . .

—O theatrical atmospheric magic,
—O contemporary magic—well, just us really,
Us: we are of Today; we fold; we thunder!

....

Behold! Behold!
The tumult sets sail by its own vibrations
Like never before, draining itself in iridescent rhythms!
I myself, feel myself transmitted unto the air, unto the hodgepodge!
Behold! Behold! Behold! . . .

(How different everything is
As gas, immaterial:
That of free-thinkers, the tables fluidic,
Diluted,
Are now like me, Catholic; and are now like me, monarchies! . . .

....
....

Serene.
A foreigner settles into my face,

One who has discovered the «Matin».
My eyes, in their space, are now tranquil,
Glimpsing from afar, the characters,
Begin to vibrate with
All the new typographical sensibility.

Wow! The Norman Bold of sensational headlines!
Italics, affiliated with the daily chronicles!
Roman type-12 set, bourgeois, and comfortable!
Gothics, cursives, round-type, English-type, all caps!
Small-type of the tiny ads!
My Elsevier, of licentious curves! . . .
And the typographical ornaments, the vignettes,
The bold, black frilly borders,
The «Puzzles» frivolous in their punctuation,
The asterisks—and the quotation marks . . . the accents . . .
Wowwy-Wow-Wow-Wow!!! . . .

—ABCs old and new,
Greek, Gothic,
Slavic, Arab, Latin—,
Lo! Behold! Lo! Behold! Lo! Behold! . . .

(Hoorah! Hurray! the new onomatopoeic appeal,
Redolent, by the pure alphabetic beauty:
Uu-um... kess-kress... vliiim... tlin... blong... flong... flak...
Pâ-am-pam! Pam... pam... pum... pum... Hurrah!)

But the foreigner turns over the page,
Reads the telegrams of The Final Hour,
Light as the pages of newspaper,
In a whirl of letters;
The whole world, reposed, within his hands!

—Hurrah! for us, typographic industry!

—Hurrah! for us, the business of journalism!

MARINONI LINOTYPE

O SECULO BERLINER TAGEBLATT

LE JOURNAL LA PRENSA

CORRIERE DELLA SERA THE TIMES

NOVOÏE VREMIÁ

And finally, he opens up the classifieds . . .

—O zebraline emotion of Advertisements,
O futurist aesthetic—*up-to-date*, hip to the brand names
Of corporations, and the squares of their ads! . . .

LE BOUILLON KUB

☞ VIN DÉSILES PASTILLES VALDA

BELLE JARDINIÈRE

FONSECAS, SANTOS & VIANNA HUNTLEY & PALMERS "RODDY"

Joseph Paquin, Bertholle & C.ie

LES PARFUMS DE COTY

SOCIÉTÉ GÉNÉRALE

CRÉDIT LYONNAIS

BOOTH LINE **NORDDEUTSCHER LLOYD**

COMPAGNIE INTERNATIONALE DES WAGON LITS
ET DES GRAND EXPRESS EUROPÉENS

And the svelte singleness of the brand, LIMITED.

....
....

All this, and still all this, anew, I refer unto the Air
For, all this Beauty danced there too:
Numbers and letters, brands and billboards —
High relief, ornamentation! . . . —
Free words, sounds unleashed,

MARINETTI + PICASSO = PARIS < SANTA RITA PIN-

TOR + FERNANDO PESSOA

ALVARO DE CAMPOS

Still, before getting up I remember
The wonderful Parisian-ness of the bars'
zinc shelves . . . I don't know why . . .

—Un vermouth cassis... Un Pernod à l'eau...
Un amer-citron... une grenadine...

....
....
....

I get up . . .
—Set Sail!
In the background, in great excess, there are mirrors that reflect
Just how much oscillation is going on in the Air:
Makes it all the more beautiful,
A more subtle, notability . . .
—The dream unhitched, the moonlight, mistaken,
And never in my verses will I be able to sing
Of how I had longed for, up until the spasm, up until, the Gold,
All that Beauty, unattainable,
That Beauty, pure!

Rolled around me, via downward steps . . .
I curb my hands,
Forget the whole idea of what was painted . . .
And my teeth, grating; my eyes, astray,
Hatless, like someone possessed :
I've decided!

And so I run out into the street, leaping, and shouting:

—Hilá! Hilá! Hilá-hô! Eh! Eh! . . .

Tum . . . tum . . . tum . . . tum tum tum tum . . .

VLIIIMIIIIM . . .

BRÁ-ÔH . . . BRÁ-ÔH . . . BRÁ-ÔH ! . . .

FUTSCH ! FUTSCH ! . . .

ZING-TANG . . . ZING-TANG . . .

TANG . . . TANG . . . TANG . . .

PRÁ Á K K ! . . .

ARDENTO SOFFICI: Café Paszkowski

Amaretto for sweetness,
and the director's green tie:
spring is a muddy face at the window,
daylight exploding like grapes through the grey-blue curtain.
We leave too soon, delayed by trains, seasons, happiness.
This evening I offer you a tram.

From a romance of a lifetime ago
she left behind the red feather
perched so arrogantly in your hat
in this café of poets and ordinary people.
Red means no, tonight's sad merriment will lack passion:
look at the tattered rug on the back of that passing horse
trotting a Viennese waltz from an ancient musical.

Say that the world doesn't end here,
absorbed in an endless reflection of trays and drinks!
of customers spilling from revolving doors;
the masters and victims of waiters.

Who needs glory or love?
Here's the four page *Evening Mail*,
the *Illustrated Italian*, *Woman*,
and for 40 cents and 10 cents tip
the sweetness of Amaretto.

EZRA POUND: The Encounter

All the while they were talking the new morality
Her eyes explored me.
And when I arose to go
Her fingers were like the tissue
Of a Japanese paper napkin.

ZISHO LANDOY

And discussing in the café at a table
The role played in the war by airplanes,
Tanks, submaringes, and the situation of the Turks,
And what changes will have to be made in the Balkans,
In the heat of the discussion I felt
How your eyes look at me mild and soft.
I turned my head to you and saw
In them a gleam I will never forget!
And suddenly it was clear to me
That airplanes fly high
And submarines swim deep,
That tanks are effective as everything England does,
That in the end something will happen to the Turks,
That there will be changes in the Balkans—
But what will be with me,
With me and you—
With us?

A corner of your mouth twitched constantly,
Did you feel the same as me?

ERNST STADLER: Closing Time

The clocks strike seven. The stores are now closing all over the city.
Out of already darkened hallways, through narrow alleyways from swanky lobbies the salesgirls press forward.
Still a little blind and as though numbed from being shut in for so long a time
They step, gently aroused, into the voluptuous brightness and soft openness of the summer evening.
Grouchy streets light up and all of a sudden beat more spirited time,
All sidewalks are crammed full with colorful blouses and girlish laughter.
Like a lake through which the strong flow of a young river burrows,
The entire city is awash in youth and homecoming.
Among the indifferent faces of the passersby a multifarious destiny has been placed—
The excitation of young life, brightened by the fire of this evening hour,
In whose sweetness all things dark become light and all things heavy melt away, as though life were easy and free,
And as though there were not waiting, separated by just a few hours, the dreary monotony
Of the daily drudgery—as though there were not waiting a coming home to the back lanes of filthy suburban houses wedged between bare tenements,
A frugal supper, the oppressiveness of the common living room, and a small bedroom shared with the little brothers and sisters,
And brief sleep, which the dawn's first light chases out of the golden land of dreams—
All this is now far, far away—covered by evening—and yet already there and waiting like a wicked animal all set to pounce on its prey,
And even the most happy, who lightly and with slender stride
Trip along on their sweetheart's arm, carry with them in the loneliness of their eyes a distant shadow.
And sometimes, when for no reason the girls cast their eyes down upon the pavement while conversing,
It happens that a scary face with a mocking grimace obstructs their lightheartedness.
Then they snuggle up closer and the hand that grips the boyfriend's arm trembles,
As though already behind them were the old age that will drag their lives toward obliteration in the darkness.

YEHOASH: Subway

An unseen hand shut the door
And imprisoned a throng of people,
Some dunked on benches,
Some hanging on white rings.
The light—lime falling
On thin transparent fingers
Fresh from the typewriter,
On heavy hard hands
Sweaty from the workshop,
Nacre gloves . . .
And the throng sways
Back and forth, back and forth,
In a weary, glazed rhythm,
As if lamenting a death . . .

The throng is shaken,
Collapses in a heap,
Gels.
And the unseen hand
Opens a door . . .
Smiling, pushing into the tangle,
A slender girl,
A bunch of lilacs pinned to her lapel,
And the throng begins to sway again
Weary and glazed,
As mourning for a death,
And in the middle, the slender girl
With a bunch of lilacs . . .

ÁLVARO DE CAMPOS [FERNANDO PESSOA]

I walk in the night of the suburban street,
Returning from the conference of experts like myself.
I return alone, now a poet, without expertise or engineering,
Human unto the sound of my solitary shoes in the beginning of night.

In the distance the last shutters are pulled down on the last shop.
Ah, the sound of suppertime in happy homes!
I walk, and my ears peer into the homes.
My inherent exile comes alive in the darkness
Of the street which is my home, my being, and my blood.
To be a child from a well-off family,
With a nursemaid, a soft bed, and a child's slumber!
O my unprivileged heart!
My feeling of exclusion!
My bitter grief for being I!

Who made firewood out of my childhood crib?
Who made rags from the sheets I slept in as a boy?
Who tossed the lace from the shirt I wore when baptized
Into the house dust and fruit skins
Of the world's garbage cans?
Who sold me to Fate?
Who exchanged me for what I am?

I've just spoken with precision in definite circumstances.
I made concrete points, like an adding machine.
I was accurate like a scale.
I told what I knew.
Now, heading to where the streetcar turns around to go back to the city,
I walk as a metaphysical outcast by the light of streetlamps spaced far apart,
And in the shadow between two lamps I feel like not going on,
But I'll take the streetcar.
The bell at the invisible end of the cord will ring two times
When pulled by the stubby fingers of the unshaven conductor.
I'll take the streetcar.
In spite of everything—alas!—I've always taken the streetcar.
Always, always, always . . .
I've always gone back to the city.
I've always gone back, after speculations and detours.
I've always gone back, hungry for supper.
But I've never had the supper I hear behind the venetian blinds
Of happy homes on the outskirts, where people like me head back to the streetcar.
The conjugal homes of normal life!
I pay for the ticket through the slits,
And the conductor walks by me as if I were the Critique of Pure Reason . . .

I've paid my ticket. I've done my duty. I'm like everyone else.
And these are all things not even suicide can cure.

JAMES JOYCE: from *Ulysses* [Lestrygonians]

His smile faded as he walked, a heavy cloud hiding the sun slowly, shadowing Trinity's surly front. Trams passed one another, ingoing, outgoing, clanging. Useless words. Things go on same; day after day: squads of police marching out, back: trams in, out. Those two loonies mooching about. Dignam carted off. Mina Purefoy swollen belly on a bed groaning to have a child tugged out of her. One born every second somewhere. Other dying every second. Since I fed the birds five minutes. Three hundred kicked the bucket. Other three hundred born, washing the blood off, all are washed in the blood of the lamb, bawling maaaaaa.

Cityful passing away, other cityful coming, passing away too: other coming on, passing on. Houses, lines of houses, streets, miles of pavements, piledup bricks, stones. Changing hands. This owner, that. Landlord never dies they say. Other steps into his shoes when he gets his notice to quit. They buy the place up with gold and still they have all the gold. Swindle in it somewhere. Piled up in cities, worn away age after age. Pyramids in sand. Built on bread and onions. Slaves. Chinese wall. Babylon. Big stones left. Round towers. Rest rubble, sprawling suburbs, jerrybuilt, Kerwan's mushroom houses, built of breeze. Shelter for the night.

RAINER MARIA RILKE: from *The Notebooks of Malte Laurids Brigge*

To think that I can't give up the habit of sleeping with the window open. Electric trolleys speed clattering through my room. Cars drive over me. A door slams. Somewhere a windowpane shatters on the pavement; I can hear its large fragments laugh and its small one giggle. Then suddenly a dull, muffled noise from the other direction, inside the house. Someone is walking up the stairs: is approaching, ceaselessly approaching: is there, is there for a long time, then passes on. And again the street. A girl screams, Ah tais-toi, je ne veux plus. The trolley races up excitedly, passes on over it, over everything. Someone calls out. People are running, catch up with each other. A dog barks. What a relief: a dog. Toward morning there is even a rooster crowing, and that is an infinite pleasure. Then suddenly I fall asleep.

◈ INTERLUDE ◈

ÁLVARO DE CAMPOS [FERNANDO PESSOA]: Triumphal Ode

By the painful light of the factory's huge electric lamps
I write in a fever.
I write gnashing my teeth, rabid for the beauty of all this,
For this beauty completely unknown to the ancients.

O wheels, O gears, eternal *r-r-r-r-r-r-r*!
Bridled convulsiveness of raging mechanisms!
Raging in me and outside me,
Through all my dissected nerves,
Through all the papillae of everything I feel with!
My lips are parched, O great modern noises,
From hearing you at too close a range,
And my head burns with the desire to proclaim you
In an explosive song telling my every sensation,
An explosiveness contemporaneous with you, O machines!

Gaping deliriously at the engines as at a tropical landscape
—Great human tropics of iron and fire and energy—
I sing, I sing the present, and the past and future too,
Because the present is all the past and all the future:
Plato and Virgil exist in the machines and electric lights
For the simple reason that Virgil and Plato once existed and were human,
And bits of an Alexander the Great from perhaps the fiftieth century
As well as atoms that will seethe in the brain of a hundredth-century Aeschylus
Go round these transmission belts and pistons and flywheels,
Roaring, grinding, thumping, humming, rattling,
Caressing my body all over with one caress of my soul.

If I could express my whole being like an engine!
If I could be complete like a machine!
If I could go triumphantly through life like the latest model car!
If at least I could inject all this into my physical being,
Rip myself wide open, and become pervious

To all the perfumes from the oils and hot coals
Of this stupendous, artificial and insatiable black flora!

Brotherhood with all dynamics!
Promiscuous fury of being a moving part
In the cosmopolitan iron rumble
Of unflagging trains,
In the freight-carrying toil of ships,
In the slow and smooth turning of cranes,
In the disciplined tumult of factories,
And in the humming, monotonic near-silence of transmission belts!

Productive European hours, wedged
Between machines and practical matters!
Big cities that stop for a moment in cafés,
In cafés, those oases of useless chatter
Where the sounds and gestures of the Useful
Crystallize and precipitate,
And with them the wheels, cogwheels and ball bearings of Progress!
New soulless Minerva of wharfs and train stations!
New enthusiasms commensurate with the Moment!
Iron-plated keels smiling on docksides,
Or raised out of the water, on harbor slipways!
International, transatlantic, *Canadian Pacific* activity!
Lights and time frantically wasted in bars, in hotels,
At Longchamps, at Derbies and at Ascots,
And Piccadillies and Avenues de l'Opéra entering straight
Into my soul!

Hey streets, hey squares, hey bustling crowd!
Everything that passes, everything that stops before shop windows!
Businessmen, bums, con men in dressy clothes,
Proud members of aristocratic clubs,
Squalid, dubious characters, and vaguely happy family men
Who are paternal even in the gold chains crossing their vests
From one to another pocket!
Everything that passes, passing without ever passing!
The overemphatic presence of prostitutes;
The interesting banality (and who knows that's inside?)
Of bourgeois ladies, usually mother and daughter,

Walking down the street on some errand or other;
The falsely feminine grace of sauntering homosexuals;
And all the simply elegant people who parade down the street
And who also, after all, have a soul!

(Ah, how I'd love to be the pander of all this!)

The dazzling beauty of graft and corruption,
Delicious financial and diplomatic scandals,
Politically motivated assaults on the streets,
And every now and then the comet of a regicide
Lighting up with Awe and Fanfare the usual
Clear skies of everyday Civilization!

Fraudulent reports in the newspapers,
Insincerely sincere political articles,
Sensationalist news, crime stories—
Two columns and continued on the next page!
The fresh smell of printer's ink!
The posters that were just put up, still wet!
Yellow books in white wrappers—*vient de paraître*!
How I love all of you, every last one of you!
How I love all of you, in every way possible,
With my eyes, ears, and sense of smell,
With touch (how much it means for me to touch you!)
And with my mind, like an antenna that quivers because of you!
Ah, how all my senses lust for you!

Fertilizers, steam threshers, breakthroughs in farming!
Agricultural chemistry, and commerce a quasi-science!
O sample cases of traveling salesmen,
Those traveling salesmen who are Industry's knights-errant,
Human extensions of the factories and quiet offices!

O fabrics in shop windows! O mannequins! O latest fashions!
O useless items that everyone wants to buy!
Hello enormous department stores!
Hello electric signs that flash on, glare, and disappear!
Hello everything used to build today, to make it different from yesterday!
Hey cement, reinforced concrete, new technologies!

The improvements in gloriously lethal weapons!
Armor, cannons, machine-guns, submarines, airplanes!

I love all of you and all things like a beast.
I love you carnivorously,
Pervertedly, wrapping my eyes
All around you, O great and banal, useful and useless things,
O absolutely modern things my contemporaries,
O present and proximate form
Of the immediate system of the Universe!
New metallic and dynamic Revelation of God!

O factories, O laboratories, O music halls, O amusement parks,
O battleships, O bridges, O floating docks—
In my restless, ardent mind
I possess you like a beautiful woman,
I completely possess you like a beautiful woman who isn't loved
But who fascinates the man who happens to meet her.
Hey-ya façades of big stores!
Hey-ya elevators of tall buildings!
Hey-ya major cabinet reshufflings!
Policy decisions, parliaments, budget officers,
Trumped-up budgets!
(A budget is as natural as a tree
And a parliament as beautiful as a butterfly.)

Hi-ya the fascination of everything in life,
Because everything is life, from the diamonds in shop windows
To the mysterious bridge of night between the stars
And the ancient, solemn sea that laps the shores
And is mercifully the same
As when Plato was Plato
In his real presence, in his flesh that had a soul,
And he spoke with Aristotle, who was not to be his disciple.

I could be shredded to death by an engine
And feel a woman's sweet surrender when possessed.
Toss me into the furnaces!
Throw me under passing trains!
Thrash me aboard ships!

Masochism through machines!
Some modern sort of sadism, and I, and the hubbub!

Alley-oop jockey who won the Derby,
Oh to sink my teeth into your two-colored cap!

(To be so tall that I couldn't pass through any door!
Ah, gazing is for me a sexual perversion!)

Hi-ya, hi-ya, hi-ya, cathedrals!
Let me bash my head against the edges of your stones,
And be picked up from the ground, a bloody mess,
Without anyone knowing who I am!

O streetcars, cable cars, subways,
Graze and scrape me until I rave in ecstasy!
Hey-ya, hey-ya, hey-ya-ho!
Laugh in my face,
O cars full of carousers and whores,
O daily swarm of pedestrians neither sad nor happy,
Motley anonymous river where I'd love to swim but can't!
Ah, what complex lives, what things lived inside their homes!
Ah, to know all about them, their financial troubles,
Their domestic quarrels, their unsuspected depravities,
Their thoughts when all alone in their bedrooms,
And their gestures when no one can see them!
Not to know these things is to be ignorant of everything, O rage,
O rage that like a fever or a hunger or a mad lust
Makes my face haggard and my hands prone to shaking
With absurd contractions in the middle of the crowds
Pushing and shoving on the streets!

Ah, and the ordinary, sordid people who always look the same,
Who use swearwords like regular words,
Whose sons steal from grocers
And whose eight-year-old daughters (and I think this is sublime!)
Masturbate respectable-looking men in stairwells.
The rabble who spend all day on scaffold and walk home
On narrow lanes of almost unreal squalor.
Wondrous human creatures who live like dogs,

Who are beneath all moral systems,
For whom no religion was invented,
No art created,
No politics formulated!
How I love all of you for being what you are,
Neither good nor evil, too humble to be immoral,
Impervious to all progress,
Wondrous fauna from the depths of the sea of life!

(The donkey goes round and round
The water wheel in my yard,
And this is the measure of the world's mystery.
Wipe off your sweat with your arm, disgruntled worker.
The sunlight smothers the silence of the spheres
And we must all die,
O gloomy pine groves at twilight,
Pine groves where my childhood was different
From what I am today . . .)

Ah, but once more the incessant mechanical rage!
Once more the obsessive motion of buses.
And once more the fury of traveling in every train in the world
At the same time,
Of saying farewell from the deck of every ship
Which at this moment is weighing anchor or drawing away from a dock.
O iron, O steel, O aluminum, O corrugated sheet metal!
O wharfs, O ports, O trains, O cranes, O tugboats!

Hi-ya great train disasters!
Hi-ya caved-in mineshafts!
Hi-ya exquisite shipwrecks of great ocean liners!
Hi-ya-ho revolutions here, there and everywhere,
Constitutional changes, wars, treaties, invasions,
Outcries, injustice, violence, and perhaps very soon the end,
The great invasion of yellow barbarians across Europe,
And another Sun on the new Horizon!

But what does it matter? What does all this matter
To the glowing, red-hot racket of today,
To the delicious, cruel racket of modern civilization?

All this erases everything except the Moment,
The Moment with its bare chest as hot as a stoker's,
The shrill and mechanical Moment,
The dynamic Moment of all the bacchantes
Of iron and bronze and the drunk ecstasy of metals.

Hey trains, hey bridges, hey hotels at dinnertime,
Hey iron tools, heavy tools, minuscule and other tools,
Precision instruments, grinding tools, digging tools,
Mills, drills, and rotary devices!
Hey! hey! hey!
Hey electricity, Matter's aching nerves!
Hey wireless telegraphy, metallic sympathy of the Unconscious!
Hey tunnels, hey Panama, Kiel and Suez canals!
Hey all the past inside the present!
Hey all the future already inside us! Hey!
Hey! hey! hey!
Useful iron fruits of the cosmopolitan factory-tree!
Hey! hey! hey! Hey-ya-hi-ya!
I'm oblivious to my inward existence. I turn, I spin, I forge myself.
I'm coupled to every train.
I'm hoisted up on every dock.
I spin in the propellers of every ship.
Hey! hey-ya! hey!
Hey! I'm mechanical heat and electricity!
Hey! and the railways and engine rooms and Europe!
Hey and hooray for all in all and all in me, machines at work, hey!

To leap with everything over everything! Alley-oop!

Alley-oop, alley-oop, alley-oop-la, alley-oop!
Hey-ya, hi-ya! Ho-o-o-o-o!
Whir-r-r-r-r-r-r-r-r-r-r!

Ah if only I could be all people and all places!

London, June 1914

LÁSZLÓ MOHOLY-NAGY

L. MOHOLY-NAGY:
DYNAMIC OF THE METROPOLIS

SKETCH OF A MANUSCRIPT FOR A FILM
Written in the year 1921/22

A metal construction in the making

First, animated cartoon of moving dots, lines, which, seen as a whole, change into the building of a zeppelin (photograph from life).

Crane in motion during the building of a house
Photographs:
from below
from above

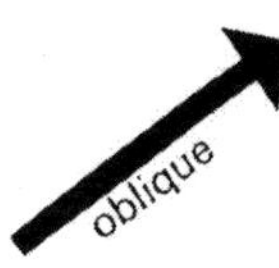

Hoisting bricks
Crane again: in circular motion

124

Close-up.
The movement continues with a car dashing towards the left. A house, always the same one, is seen opposite the car in the centre of the picture (the house is continually being brought back to the centre from the right; this produces a stiff jerky motion). Another car appears. This one travels simultaneously in the opposite direction, towards the right.

This passage as a brutal introduction to the breathless race, the hubbub of the city.

The rhythm, which is strong now, gradually slackens during the course of the film.

A tiger paces furiously round and round its cage

TEMPO TEMPO TEMPO

Quite clear – up at the top – signals:

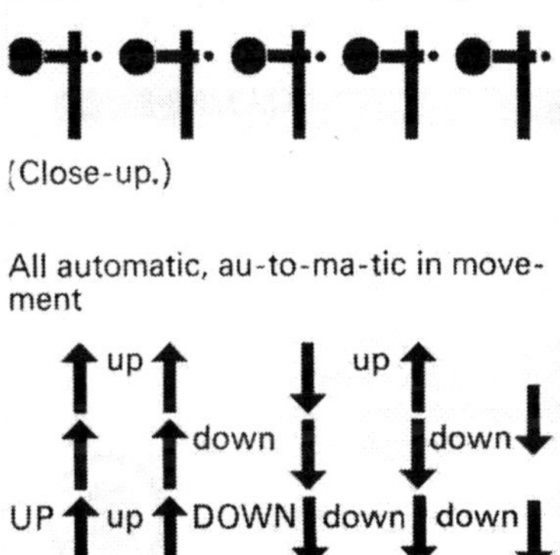

(Close-up.)

All automatic, au-to-ma-tic in movement

Row of houses on one side of the street, translucent, races right towards the first house. Row of houses runs off right and reappears from right to left. Rows of houses facing one another, translucent, rushing in opposite directions, and the cars moving ever more swiftly, soon giving rise to FLICKERING

1 2 3 4 5
1 2 3 4 5
1 2 3 4 5

Shunting yard
Sidings

TEMPO
TEMPO
TEMPO
TEMPO

The tiger:
Contrast between the open unimpeded rushing and the oppression, constriction. So as to accustom the public from the outset to surprises and lack of logic.

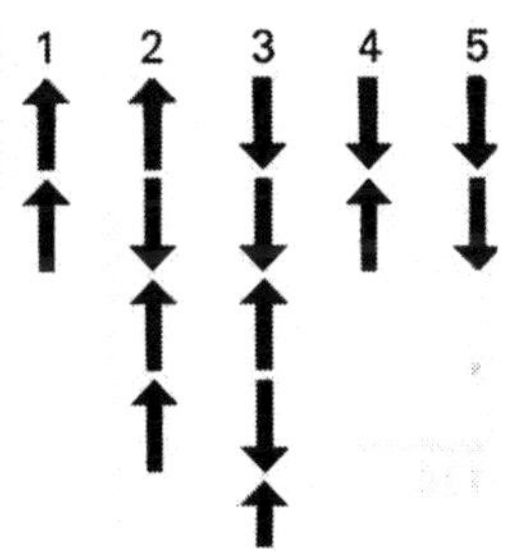

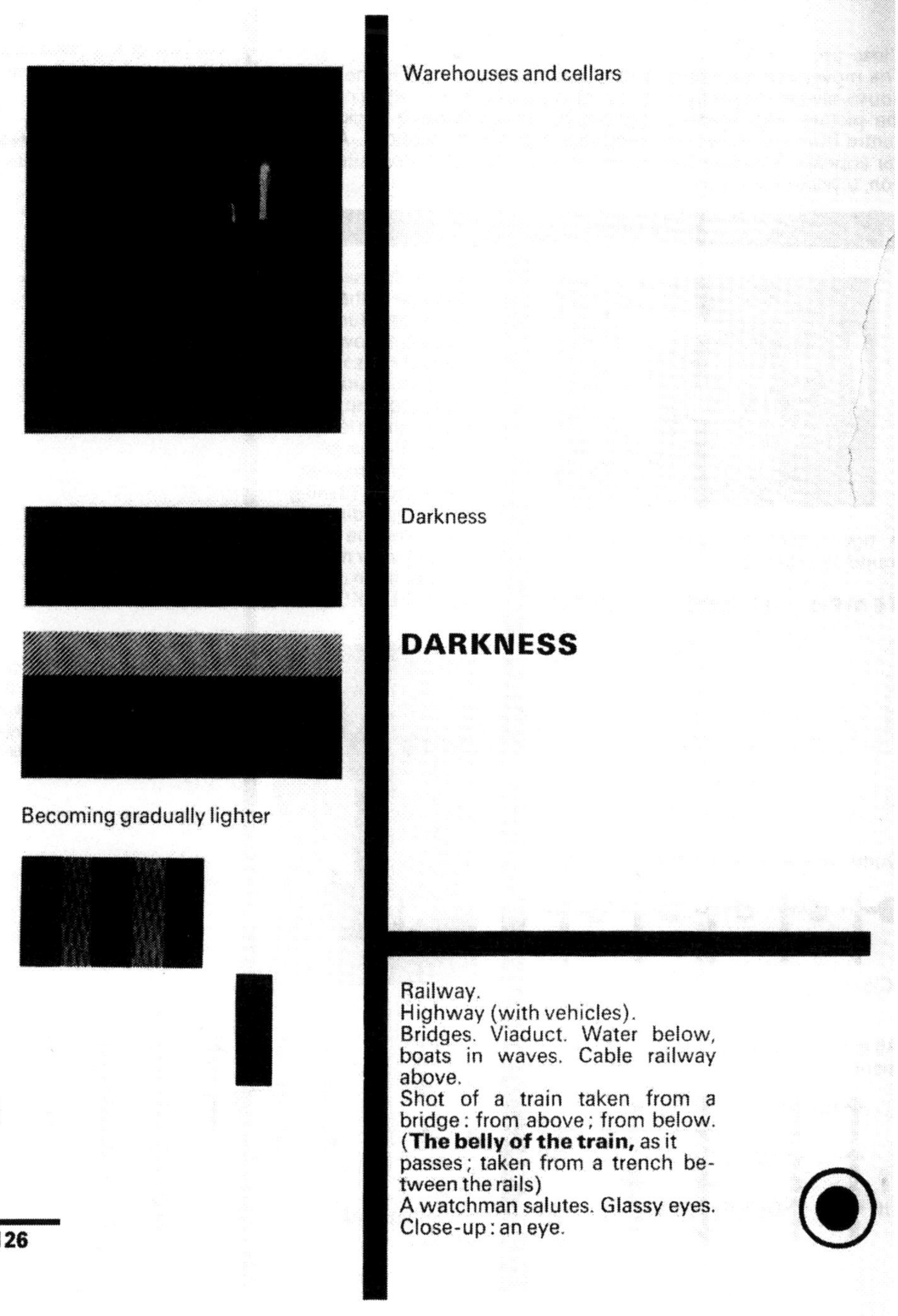
Warehouses and cellars
Darkness
DARKNESS
Becoming gradually lighter
Railway.
Highway (with vehicles).
Bridges. Viaduct. Water below, boats in waves. Cable railway above.
Shot of a train taken from a bridge: from above; from below.
(The belly of the train, as it passes; taken from a trench between the rails)
A watchman salutes. Glassy eyes.
Close-up: an eye.
126

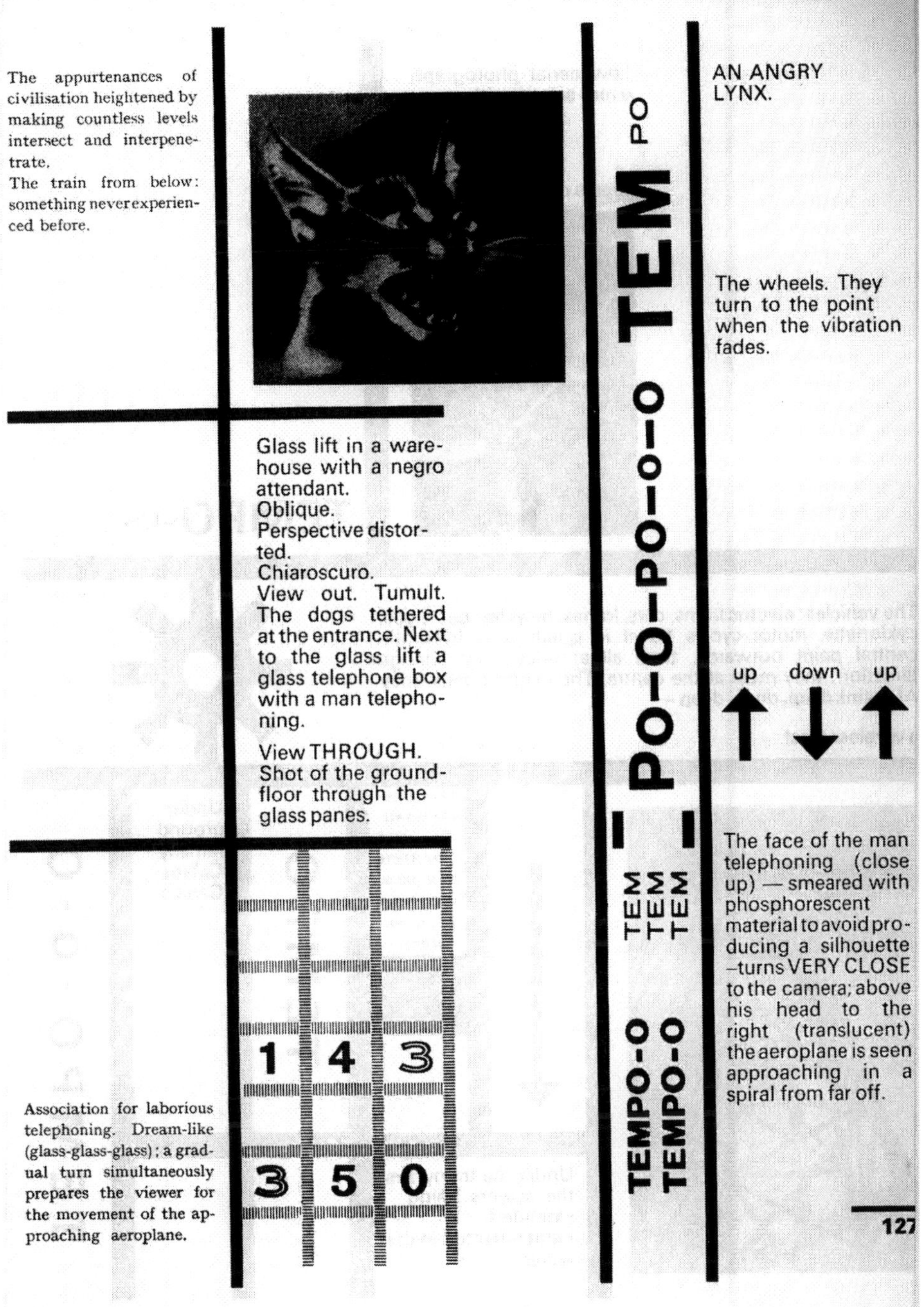

The appurtenances of civilisation heightened by making countless levels intersect and interpenetrate.
The train from below: something never experienced before.

AN ANGRY LYNX.

The wheels. They turn to the point when the vibration fades.

Glass lift in a warehouse with a negro attendant.
Oblique.
Perspective distorted.
Chiaroscuro.
View out. Tumult. The dogs tethered at the entrance. Next to the glass lift a glass telephone box with a man telephoning.

View THROUGH.
Shot of the groundfloor through the glass panes.

PO-O-PO-O-O-O TEM PO

up down up

TEMPO-O TEM
TEMPO-O TEM
TEM

1 4 3

3 5 0

The face of the man telephoning (close up) — smeared with phosphorescent material to avoid producing a silhouette –turns VERY CLOSE to the camera; above his head to the right (translucent) the aeroplane is seen approaching in a spiral from far off.

Association for laborious telephoning. Dream-like (glass-glass-glass); a gradual turn simultaneously prepares the viewer for the movement of the approaching aeroplane.

127

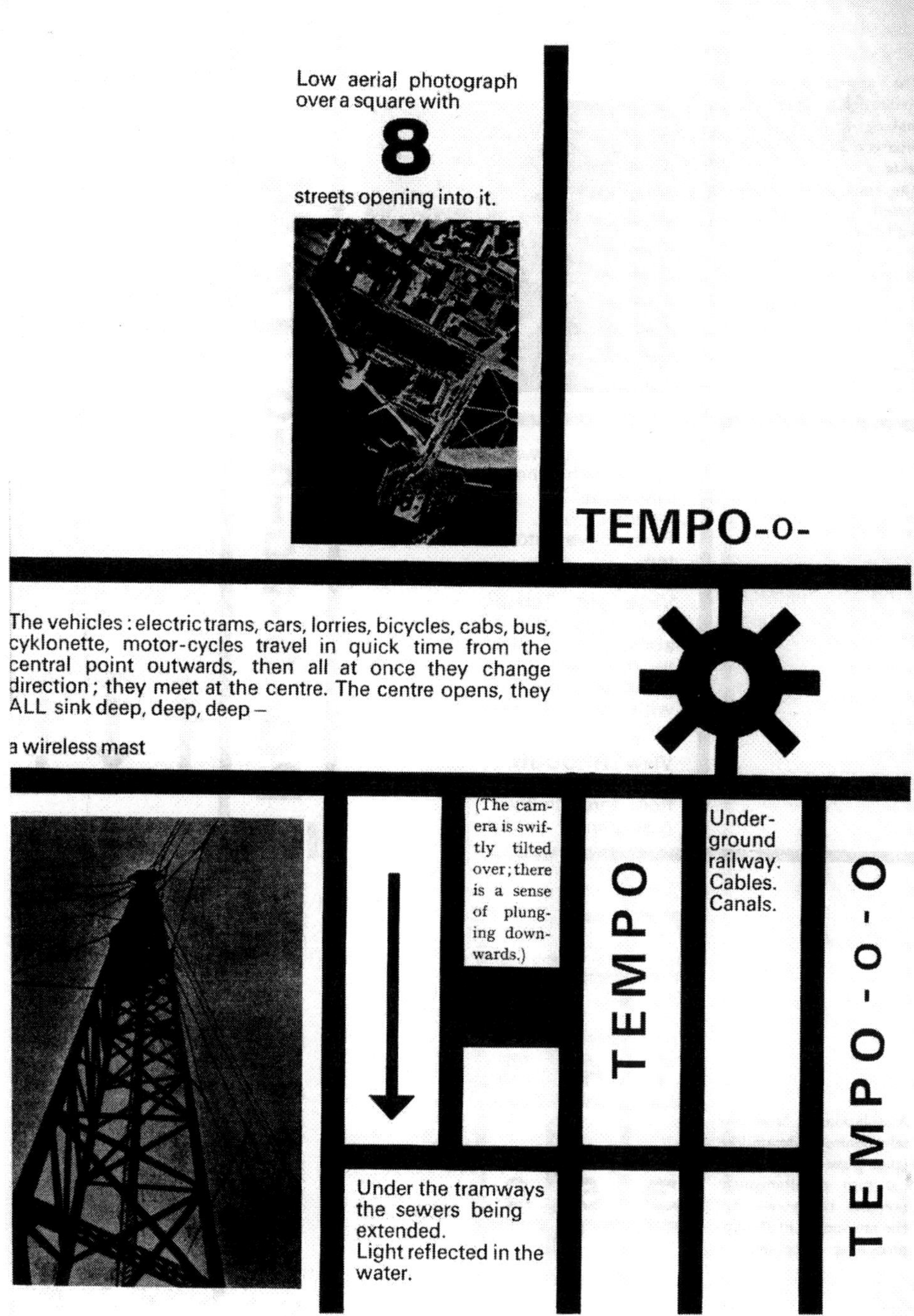
Low aerial photograph over a square with
8
streets opening into it.
TEMPO-o-
The vehicles : electric trams, cars, lorries, bicycles, cabs, bus, cyklonette, motor-cycles travel in quick time from the central point outwards, then all at once they change direction ; they meet at the centre. The centre opens, they ALL sink deep, deep, deep –
a wireless mast
(The camera is swiftly tilted over; there is a sense of plunging downwards.)
TEMPO
Underground railway. Cables. Canals.
TEMPO-o-O
Under the tramways the sewers being extended.
Light reflected in the water.

ARC-LAMP, sparks playing. Street smooth as a mirror.
Pools of light. From above and

oblique

with cars whisking past.

Reflector of a car enlarged.

SCREEN BLACK FOR 5 SECONDS

Electric signs with luminous writing which vanishes and reappears.

YMOHOLYMOH

Fireworks from the Lunapark.
Speeding along WITH the scenic railway.

129

A man can remain oblivious of many things in life. Sometimes because his organs do not work quickly enough, sometimes because moments of danger, etc., demand too much of him. Almost everyone on the switchback shuts his eyes when it comes to the great descent. But not the film camera. As a rule we cannot regard small babies, for example, or wild beasts completely objectively because while we are observing them we have to take into account a number of other things. It is different in the film. A new range of vision too.

Devil's wheel. Very fast.
The people who have been slung down stand up unsteadily and climb into a train. A police car (translucent) races after it.
In the station hall the camera is first turned in a **horizontal,** then in a **vertical** circle.

Telegraph wires on the roofs.
Aerials.
The TIGER.
Large factory.
A wheel rotating.
A performer rotates (translucent).
Salto mortale.
High jump. High jump with pole.
Jumper falls. Ten times one after the other.

130

Punch and
Judy show.

CHILDREN

Our head cannot do this.

Public, like waves in the sea.

Girls.
Legs.

TEMPO TEMPO TEMPO

VaRIETé,
feverish activity.
Women wrestling.
Kitsch.

Jazz-band instruments
(Close-up).

Football match.
Rough.
Vigorous TEMPO.

Metal cones –
empty inside,
glittering – are
hurled towards the
lens, (meanwhile)
2 women draw back
their heads in a flash.
Close-up.

(In order to scare the public. A dynamic moment too.)

A glass of water (expanse of water with glass rim in close-up) in motion like a fountain, spurts up
Jazz-BAND with the
TALKING FILM
FortiSSimO
Wild dancing caricature. Street-girls.

THE TIGER

BOXING

Close-up.
ONLY
the HAnds with the
boxing
gloves.

Slow-motion. SLOW-MOTION.

132

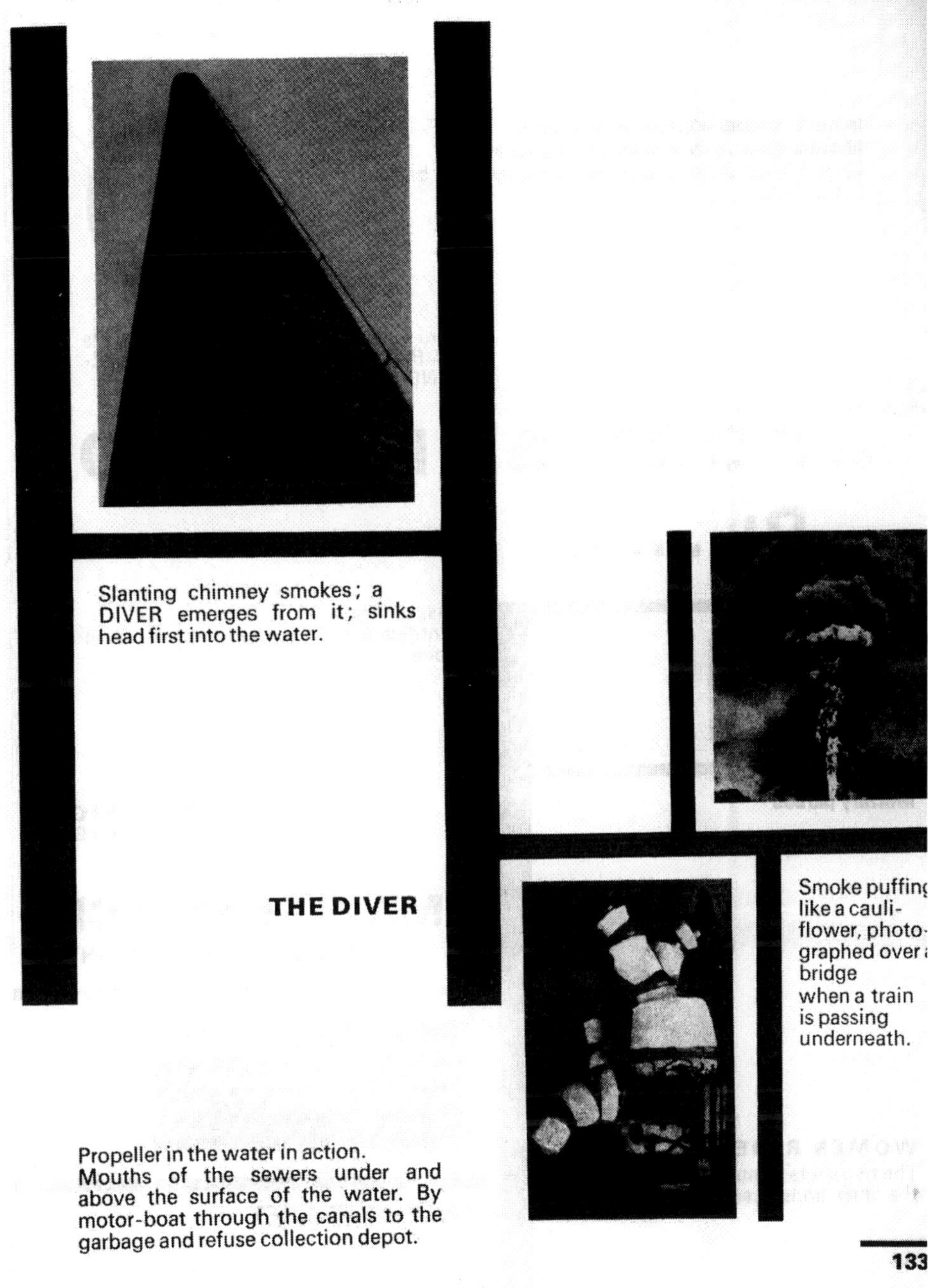

Slanting chimney smokes; a DIVER emerges from it; sinks head first into the water.

THE DIVER

Smoke puffing like a cauli-flower, photo-graphed over a bridge when a train is passing underneath.

Propeller in the water in action. Mouths of the sewers under and above the surface of the water. By motor-boat through the canals to the garbage and refuse collection depot.

133

Scrap is converted into factory work.
Mountains of rusty screws, tins, shoes etc.
PATERNOSTER lift with view to the end and back.
In the circle.

From here the whole film (shortened) is run BACKWARDS as far as the JaZZ-BAND (this backwards too).

from **FORTISSIMO-o-O**

to **PIANISSIMO**

Military parade

Glass of water
Identification of corpses (morgue) from above.

RIGHT-RIGHT
RIGHT-RIGHT

MARCH-MARCH-
MARCH-MARCH-RIGHT

WOMEN RIDERS-LEFT
The two shots printed one above the other, translucent.

LEFT-LEFT-LEFT

134

Stockyards. Animals.
Oxen roaring.
The machines of the refrigerating room.
Lions.
Sausage-machine. Thousands of sausages.
Head of a lion showing its teeth (Close-up).
Theatre. Rigging-loft.
The lion's head. **TEMPO-o-O**
Police with rubber truncheons in the Potsdamer Platz.
The TRUNCHEON (close-up).
The theatre audience.
The lion's head gets bigger and bigger until at last the vast jaws fill the screen.

The frequent and unexpected appearance of the lion's head is meant to cause uneasiness and oppression (again and again and again). The theatre audience is cheerful – and STILL THE HEAD comes! etc.

Dark for several seconds
DARK DARKNESS
Large circle
TEMPO-o-O
Circus from above, almost a ground-plan.
Lions. Acrobat on skis.
Clowns.
CIRCUS
CLOWN
Dressage
CIRCUS
Trapeze. Girls.
Legs.
Clowns.
LIONS.
LIONS!
CLOWNS.
DRESSAGE
Dressage.

Waterfall thunders. The TALKING FILM.
A cadaver swims in the water, very slowly.

THE WHOLE THING TO BE READ THROUGH AGAIN QUICKLY

Military. March-march.

Glass of water.

In motion.

SHORT-FAST

Spurts up –

END:

CINELAND: MATINEE

Ramón Gómez de la Serna: from *Movieland*

From the distance Movieland looks like a Constantinope combined with a little Tokyo, a touch of Florence and a hint of New York. Not that all these cities are jumbled together there, but that each of its districts represents one of them.

It is like a Noah's ark of architectures. A Florentine palace, seized with that salaciousness which exotic buildings produce, looks longingly at a Grand Pagoda.

All this is in the heart of the city, in its nucleus of tall buildings. All around it the city spreads out into a thousand little square white houses, like filing cabinets with clear visages.

It is a glittering city of seashore bungalows, without a shore.

Strange panorama, looking like nothing so much as an immense Luna Park!

On nearing the city one feels as if he were seeing the collection of a great picture museum with reproductions of the buildings in all the city streets of the world. It also looks like the toy-city of the most powerful Princess in the world, the first Princess to play with a make-believe city invented just for her amusement.

The only true things are the very square little villas whose chief desire is to look like bathrooms of happiness.

The stroll through the streets of the city is like a nightmare, and the stroller becomes a circumnavigator who tours the world in an hour.

At all events, the best people of the city, its great personages, its elegant world—its men who look like sportsmen, prize fighters and tenors—meet in that part of the city which resembles New York.

In its cafés the most popular movie stars come together, all the great men of that Cinema City whose plebiscites pertain only to things of the movies.

...

Here time has a special laziness, even though people work and the best films in the world are produced.

Something of Palm Sunday morning constantly pervades the city, even on Monday nights.

And because Movieland is located in a place with the best climate in the world, the open doors and balconies emit a chatter of music—the noise of jazz-bands, the lunacies of xylophones.

In the cafés it is always cocktail hour, and the bands stroll in the gardens, the violinists juggling their violins, abandoned to the jerky dance that jazz has invented.

PHILIPPE SOUPAULT: *Palace Cinema*

to Blaise Cendrars

The wind caresses the posters
Nothing
the cashier is made of porcelain

the Screen

the automatic leader of the orchestra conducts
the player piano
there are revolver shots
applause
the stolen automobile disappears in the clouds
and the timorous lover buys a detachable collar

But soon the doors bang shut
Today very elegant
He has put on his top hat
And has not forgotten his gloves

Every Friday a change of program

JEAN EPSTEIN: Bonjour Cinema

In a close-up
pale sun
this face reigns
The enamel mouth stretches
like a lazy waking
then reverses the laugh
to the eyes' edges
No goodbyes waltz retreat
Cinema I take you away
you and your porcelain wheels
which I finger which I kiss
your vivacious trembling

so close an epidermis
spreads the sparkle of the arch
oh but it's beautiful this lantern
which recites its drama light
I saw your steps 1 2 3
move away on the grass
and your mute laugh
which kicked me
full in the face
Galloping away
Escape from the hut
hooves horses trample underfoot
the room a tango tune
Saddled up the pursuit
rolls from the hill
In the dust the heroine
reloads her gun
Next to a man
I walked in the snow
against his back
my eye on his jacket
He was departing, in great strides
without turning his head
he was afraid he was cold
at times he began to rush
my supernatural cinema
The documentary's rails
enter my mouth
the lopsided hill
skids and goes down
excellent this seasickness
in the room packet-boat
with, for blowtorch, these rails
I clog up the ground
In my swivel chair
I resign myself to drown
Tiller to the right bend
Tunnel starboard
Under an airship's belly
in an airplane I glide

my nose in the air propeller

At the theater I saw la Belle Helene
I was clean-shaven
Cinema I take you away

CONTINUAL SHOWINGS

SIEGFRIED KRACAUER: from *The Little Shopgirls Go to the Movies*

World Travelers

The daughter of an airplane engine manufacturer takes off on an air race around the world—a flight that is supposed to demonstrate the quality of daddy's motors. A competitor she has previously turned down tries to delay her all along the voyage. A young man whom she will assuredly not turn down helps her all along the voyage. Against the backdrop of India, China, the calm ocean, and America, a love affair develops with great speed, and great speed develops with this affair. The woman aviator always appears in the traditional garb of each respective country. In the end, triumph and an engagement.

The Golden Heart

A young Berlin wholesaler, an industrious manager of a first-rate company, visits a business friend of his father's in Vienna; the paternal friend's firm is going to pieces because of the disorder in Austria. The guest would leave, if it were not for the business friend's daughter, a sweet Viennese gal who makes it clear to him that there are other things besides management: the waves of the Danube and the wine gardens specializing in new vintages. With delight, the young man from Berlin discovers his dormant feelings. He cleans up the company, which will soon be turning a profit again, and gets the gal for home use.

Silent Tragedy

A banker goes bankrupt as a result of such immense incompetence that he commits suicide out of propriety. The insolvent estate includes a daughter. The first lieutenant who loves her must abandon his dreams of escorting her down the aisle; her lack of means and his career make this impossible. She goes on to earn her living as a dancer under an artistic pseudonym. The first lieutenant, who has long regretted his refusal of the relationship, meets her again after years of futile searching, and wants to be united with her at last. The only thing needed for a happy ending is his letter of resignation, which he has been planning to hand in. But the selfless dancer poisons herself in order, through her death, to force her lover to think only of his career.

Bruno Jasiénski: Run Over

Cinema
Freckled maid in a white blouse with polka dots.
Somebody tall and slim, with a feather
—Will you come? . . . — "I can't . . ."
Oops!!
Cars, lorries, carriages,
Cinema of spokes
With wheeldin rattled on dry asphalt.
—Wait . . .— "No, no, don't ask, for I could weaken . . ."
Ding! Ding!!
Red streetcar rolled out from the avenue.
One. Two.
They passed each other in flight, making speed.
Ominous song of polished rails . . .
A little man in a brown coat . . .
Crrrrraash!!!
Stoppp!!
Brakes!
Aaaaaaaaa!!
Run over! Run over!

Hagiwara Kyojiro: A Love Letter

● ●

● ●

One second
A film of massacre is projected on the wave of hats
●●● It's cut off by the shout of the crowd --

Cries!
Countless **alphabet** faces
------------ *"What'll I do? I don't have the money to get home!"*
A packed elevator
An underground room encased in lead pipes ●● **"Dried Fish and Whisky"**
Turning like a globe-------------the exposed man's eyeball.
"Kill me with the napkin!"
"Marvelous! ●●● Come on!"
"Even insensitive men have loves and beliefs."
"You're not so dull after all."
"I hear one love letter costs over 150 million yen."
Footstep ● Ay! Bee!

"You're such a wretch!"
Stairs------------*"Goodbye!"*
"Tomorrow!"
Doh● doh● doh●●● G
Medicine vial ●●●● diary++++knife
Hair Thermometer reads 40 degrees
Pale face with sign attached
Blood is spit into the handkerchief!
A starved rat lies under the curtain's shadow!
The water-main pipe!
Smoke dissipating in darkness!
Bibi bibi
Boooooom!

Cliff
-----------*"My lover's coming back on the express train in the morning."*
●●● On a corner of the attic-----
Feeble rays of the morning sun
A closed window

Rafael Alberti: Harold Lloyd, Student

Do you have the umbrella?
Avez-vous le parapluie?

No, sir, I do not have the umbrella.
Non, monsieur, je n'ai pas le parapluie.

Alice, I have the hippopotamus.
L'hippopotame for you.
Avez-vous le parapluie?

Oui.
Sí.
Yes.

That, which, who, whose.
If the she-lizard is my friend,
then clearly the he-beetle is your friend.
Was it your fault that it rained?
No, the rain was not your fault.
Alice, Alice, it was my fault,
I who study for you
and for this unknowing fly, flowering nightingale of my glasses.

29, 28, 27, 26, 25, 24, 23, 22.
$2\pi r$, πr^2

and converted itself into the mule, Nebuchadnezzar,
and your soul and mine into a royal bird of paradise.

Fish no longer sing in the Nile
nor does the moon set for the dahlias of the Ganges.

Alice,
why do you love me with that sad crocodile air
and the deep pain of a quadratic equation?

Le printemps pleut sur Les Anges.

The Spring rains over Los Angeles
in that sad hour when the police
are unaware of the suicide of the isosceles triangles,
the melancholy of a Naperian logarithm
and the *facial unibusquibusque.*

In that sad hour when the moon becomes almost equal
to the whole misfortune
of this love of mine multiplied by X
and to the wings of the afternoon that fold
over an acetylene flower
or a bird of gas.

Of this my pure love so delicately idiotic.
Quousque tandem abutere Catilina patientia nostra?

So sweet and deliberately idiotic,
capable of making the square of a circle cry
and obliging that fool, Mr. Nequaqua Schmitt,
to sell at public auction those stars that belong to the river
and those blue eyes that skyscrapers open to me.

Alice, Alice, my love!
Alice, Alice, my nanny!
Follow me by bicycle through the air
even though the police may not know astronomy,
the secret police.

Even though the police may not know that a sonnet
consists of two quatrains
and two tercets.

Pedro Salinas: Far West

A wind of eight thousand kilometers per hour!
Don't you see how everything flies?
Don't you see the windblown locks
of Mabel, the horseback rider
half-closing her clear eyes,
a wind against the wind?
Don't you see how the wind
billows the curtain,
sends that paper whirling,
foils the separation
between her and you?

Yes, I see it.
And that's all—I see it.
That wind
is on the other side, is
on a distant afternoon
in lands I've never been to.
It is stirring some branches
from nowhere,
kissing some lips,
but whose?
Now it isn't wind, it's the painting
of a wind that died
before I encountered it,
and it is buried in the vast
cemetery of old winds,
of dead winds.

Yes, I see it without feeling it.
That wind is there in its own world,
that wind of the cinema.

NICOLÁS OLIVARI: Our Life in A Newspaper Serial

Of course, we spent our time in movie theaters;
your love was as twisted and honeyed as a heroine
in Cecil B. de Mille,
and we'd shudder as one
when famous cowboys cocked their guns,
and seeing Pearl White about to fall
into the hands of that louse with the pencil mustache
we'd shiver with an identical thrill.

Your failed starlet's soul
and my wannabee actor's slouch
decanted the screen
into the orchestra stalls of edge city.

We lived a hundred mysterious lives
at the junction of probabilities,
in the double-decker omnibus of chance,
and consumed by unreal amours
you played a slave, a queen, a courtesan, a debutante,
and I played Hernani and a boxer.

But this being a violation of nature
—you were a girl from the mean streets
and I a good-for-nothing boy,
outrageously sentimental—
her revenge was to make us act out
the melodrama of mutual love,
in episodes.

The plot thickens in the fiction
of our filmed afternoons,
as into our American poses
the candy seller intrudes,
the box-office Don Juan
who used to let you in for free,
and the gruff old man who'd stare at us
with the eyes of morality.

And all the sadness of Buenos Aires backstreets,
when our chilliness took refuge
in the cinema that was our home.

Your buttocks grew barren
from squeezing into box seats
and our child slipped away through the ticket booth.

The possible screenplay
underlying your kiss in the dark
lacked originality,
copied from an industry masquerading as art,
and when we were shaken by desire
and for a short moment love,
of which poets speak so well,
came into our souls,
igniting the Darwinian flame
to the tempo of the solitary piano
that circled through ever the same waltz,
our spasm would peter out
in the electricity of the intermission.

We wasted five years in the stalls
—five years I wasted at the Colegio Nacional—
so as to make film-flavored love
in an atmosphere of carbonic acid . . .

But I loved you just the same
—the sickly girl you were, so thin—
despite Edison and his dramaturgy,
only the seats were so narrow and our sensuality so broad
that the spasm would peter out
again and again in the electricity of the intermission.

We'll cross the frontiers of reality
and meet in movies yet to come.
I started reading books—what for?
And you? I don't recall . . .
and then we couldn't find each other.

Often I spend my melancholy afternoons
in that local fleapit
which we wore down so bad,
and start dreaming, vibrating to the story,
expecting to hear
your cough at any moment,
like an usher telling me you're here,
at the cinema of memory,
where he who shows the films is my long-sought God.

JEAN EPSTEIN: Douglas Fairbanks

Agile
like an orchestra conductor's reed   on
                                        the ocean of sharps
The windows are the only doors
and the gutters
of gentle footpaths where his betrothals
                                        go strolling
the roofs span themselves
the horses fall
and in the frenzy of a film
where you earn $200,000 to laugh
and to not mind jabs
the traitor spends a very nasty fifteen minutes
resuscitates
the heavy dust of the nuggets
amid the wind of beautiful mirages
a beach's female curves
Nymphs! the automotive boat hereafter
wins your civilized laughter
A burnoose
A palm tree
of sand
The motorcycle pierces the desert like a
                                        paper hoop
The camels move away because a car horn burps

and suddenly
a smile splits open
gapes softly
winks and sparkles
under the light of 15 arc lamps that are
sexually assaulting a face.

VÍTĚSLAV NEZVAL: Fireworks 1924

A Cinemagenic Poem

NAZIMOVA

1 a gunshot (fade in)
2 a hand illuminated holding a revolver (dissolve into)
3 a hand sporting a diamond ring that
4 blows to pieces like a fireworks display with the inscription ALL THIS BECAUSE OF LOVE (double exposures moving from one image to another) a dance pavilion (full shot) & the sparks dying away
5 a street corner (fade out) the helmets of 3 policemen
6 a coffee house a lady on the phone (full shot)
7 it rings a few times
8 a gentleman's quarters (full shot)
9 the telephone bell (close up)
10 the lady setting the receiver down
11 the clock on the clocktower moonlight 10 o'clock
12 in the fields a hare is running down a path
13 sniffing with whiskers erect (dissolve)
14 the hare standing up on its hind legs
15 from the bushes a gentleman with monocle steps out
16 a coffee house (full shot)
17 a detective observes a lady's hand move nervously along a marble table
18 the diamond transmutes into
19 a show window with a passing tram's reflections
20 the detective pays his check & as he hands the money over surreptitiously displays
21 his badge (dissolve into close-up)
22 the detective goes to the lady's table
23 asks for permission

24 thumbs thru magazines
25 & newspapers (dissolve into close-up)
26 a headline ALL THIS BECAUSE OF LOVE
27 the detective while choosing a magazine stares deep into the lady's eyes (medium close shot)
28 the lady getting up (full shot)
29 the detective grabs his heart & sinks down to the floor (fade out)
30 a crowd of guests & waiters
31 the lady puts a handkerchief on the detective's head
32 (close-up) the detective's hand picking a photo & 2 tram tickets from the lady's bag
33 in the fields the hare is pricking up its ears
34 a railway station where a train is being boarded
35 a gentleman with monocle at ticket counter
36 a hand plugging lines in at the phone exchange
37 the detective makes a call while staring at the tram ticket
38 index finger in the book
39 the tram ticket held in two hands as it grows in size till it dissolves into
40 the image of the tram (interior)
41 the dispatcher in his office struggling to recall something (medium close shot)
42 presses his index finger to his forehead (full shot)
43 & gives a smile (medium close shot)
44 giving a large banknote to the gentleman with the monocle seated beside the lady in the tram
45 a maze of telegraph wires
46 a postal clerk pondering a telegram
47 a lookout post in front of which there stands a yardman
48 the yardman runs into the lookout
49 a corridor inside the train down which the man with monocle is passing
50 he is entering the toilet
51 dumping his revolver
52 his pocket watch
53 (fade out) in the dark a sign HOTEL
54 the lady in bed turning from side to side
55 (medium close shot) opening her eyes, a sad look
56 the yardman presses a button
57 the semaphore (dissolving into medium close shot) is moving slowly up & down
58 an automobile in motion
59 (medium close shot) detective holds an open timetable in his hand

60 the dispatcher looking at the man with monocle & at the lady who are walking over to an island lit by lanterns (dissolves)
61 (medium close shot) the dispatcher talking to a policeman
62 the train is stopping
63 the auto speeding up approaching
64 the lady hand on bed a handkerchief to forehead
65 the locomotive whistle
66 the detective standing on the train steps
67 the hare has reared up on its hind legs
68 a hand with revolver
69 an eye behind a monocle
70 the monocle falls to the floor & shatters
71 the gentleman standing without moving
72 a gunshot (fade in)
73 a hand illuminated holding a revolver (dissolves into) a diamond
74 into a shrapnel burst with the title ALL THIS BECAUSE OF LOVE (double exposure) a pavilion full of dancing couples
75 the legs of a jazz drummer at his drums
76 (medium close shot) a bandstand lined with sheets of music & the title ALL THIS BECAUSE OF LOVE
77 in front of a shooting gallery the man with the monocle & the lady   he takes him & fires
78 (close-up) a metal rabbit painted silver falling over
79 (medium close shot) the gentleman & lady laughing fit to burst
80 the gentleman is rubbing his eyes
81 a kiss behind the parasol
82 the hare's whiskers & one side of the hare's face moving & dissolving into a fountain its waters turning drop by drop into the words

THE END

◈ POSTCARDS ◈

SALVADOR GALLARDO: Short Circuit

The wind combs its mane in the rain
    over the fireworks of every roof
and as the trains are struck by catalepsy
    sugartown oozes in the shade
Streetlights cut barbed-wire trenches
    and crash the asphalt moons
Protracted absence
    threw your memory my way
A sudden Edisonian
    glory bloomed
and my nostalgia hanged itself
    on a voltaic arc
Life burns its romantic letters
    in the potholes

WILLIAM CARLOS WILLIAMS: The Great Figure

Among the rain
and lights
I saw the figure 5
in gold
on a red
firetruck
moving
tense
unheeded
to gong clangs
siren howls
and wheels rumbling
through the dark city.

Lajos Kassák: Typography

Francis Carco: On the Boulevard

The pert coolness of the boulevard does nothing to relieve the rotten stink on the autumn air as the broad leaves of the plantains come spindling down. A bizarre and unforeseen downpour drifts above the streetlamps crisscrossed by arcing searchlights. A finely-sifted rain, which the wind tilts, at times, like a bucket of tiny peen, drizzles into loitering faces. The night is scented with the odor of decaying foliage: it reeks of ambergris, menthol, powder, rouge, and the neoprene smell of slickers and galoshes.

MICHEL LEIRIS: December 16-17, 1924

One night, drunk, on the Boulevard de Sebastopol, I pass an old wretch of a man and call out to him. He answers: "Leave me alone . . . I am the master of the heights of cinema." Then he continues on his way to Belleville.

WHIPCRACKS & MEGAPHONE CHANTS

CLÉMENT PANSAERS: from *Pan-Pan*

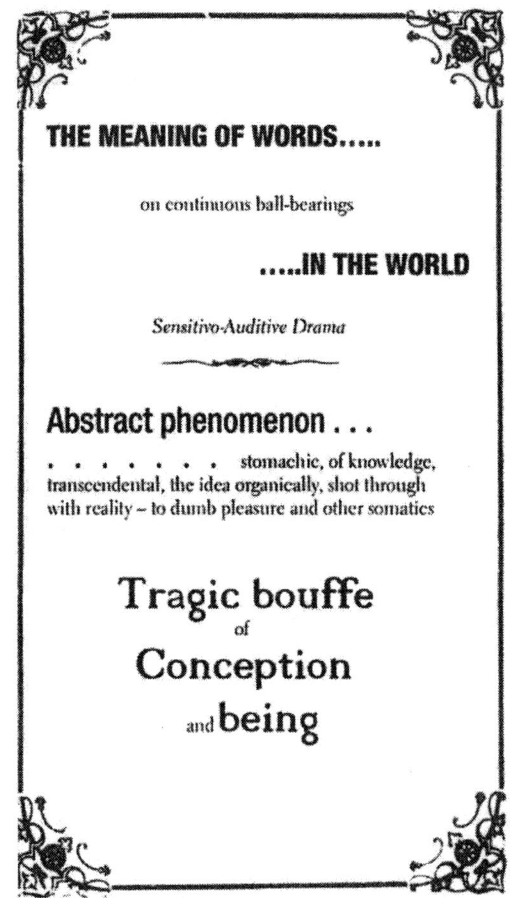

THE MEANING OF WORDS.....

on continuous ball-bearings

.....IN THE WORLD

Sensitivo-Auditive Drama

Abstract phenomenon . . .

. . . . stomachic, of knowledge, transcendental, the idea organically, shot through with reality – to dumb pleasure and other somatics

Tragic bouffe
of
Conception
and being

RAFAEL ALBERTI: Summer Guidebook to Paradise (Festival Program)

Hôtel-Dieu: "God's Hostel" : connections by train
and by pleasure boat. Parks to the South. Transportation
direct to the beach and the boardwalks. Air conditioning. Clean.

Tours to the bistros. Saint Raphael in the galleries
guides in his flying regalia,
for the price of a sherbet. (No gratuities, please!)

To the Bar of the Archangels. Linen coifs
rising stiff on the hairlines, applejack
wings, feathers of lemon and wine.

Christmas-tree stars, with wave after wave
on the keys of the quick pianolas, gilding
the treads and the risers, glazing the ivories.

Over the Airport: the Milky Way's borders,
a cobweb in space, with seraphim circling the rim
of the Cup of the Winds—at your orders!

And there in the Stadium's Lunar Arena—like
gymnasts of ice, livid
javelins and discuses, the stars of the morning arising.

On Lake Venus, the Player-Card Queen
leans on her paddles and steers
for the castles of Bing-Bang, the rubber balls and the Mages.

A fairway for immaculate
comets, conceiving bicycles spinning in whiskey
with Saturnian rings at their backs.

Chair lifts direct to the targets, the pigeons
and candles; the Tunnel of Love to the Troll
Gardens; trams to the Groves of Alberti. (Have an orange!)

Hôtel-Dieu: "God's Hostel" : connections by train
and by pleasure boat. *Hall*, to the south. American
soda-pop. Cars to the beach and the boardwalk again.

Jaroslav Seifert: Miss Gada-Nigi

Night extended raven wings drum of darkness
Miss Gada-Nigi perched on the trapeze
below in the sand the clown like a bird asleep
the snow of his dreams falling

Gada-Nigi smiles at the stars through a crack in the canvas
listening to the ticking of the watch on her wrist
she learns to dance on the head of a rearing steed
and in the lace of fog eternity between stars

Ticking watch on the clown's face reflections of infinity
in the circus wagon a child broke into tears
hands reaching out for the stars of mother's breasts
and bird song was swaying on the branch of jasmine

when backs turned the lovers and the suicide man
under the luminous parasol of the streetlamp
they saw a star falling through a thousand-year-old night
as it died among the water lilies of the shallow basin

Oh Miss Gada-Nigi do not contemplate the stars
for the lines of the hand enclose fate the clown me and you
only lovers die of love unwittingly just listen
in a kiss two slim flutes of breath fall silent

Alexei Kruchenykh: Suicide Circus

Sardinian's benefit night in a horseman's fur cap
who straddled the gentle-bodied colt
up to the spine of the arm and spurs dug in
with a dead-o-**DADO**
the horse sighs and running waits for the finish
SMOORG
MOORGLA
HUP-LA!
HUP-LA!..

A whip for the bored animals
hung in the artist's hand,
the tumble of Sapphire,
the pedal of **CLEOPATRA** growing husky
damp sawdust's flowing from behind the wall
SMOORGLA
MOOERE
KER-FLOP!
KER-FLOP!..

The circus got boring as well with screaming and whirling
he savored its bowels like a spongerag
the planks of corset are sawn, the lame lioness is mooing

GREEN RUBBISH flying in the air
like a **LITTLE SARDINE** from a **SUICIDED COCK**

Kra—ash!...
Krum—bl!...

Boško Tokin: Circus

1912
He had a beautiful daughter, an Amazon.
She had a horse, a lover, a clown, and a Moor.
She married him.
1914
War.
The clown fell. The horse pulled cannons. The Moor took the cassock.
The lover went to Australia.
1919
The horse has died. The clown revived.
The lover died in Honolulu. The man would be an elephant. The Moor threw off his habit and wrote poems. The horse became sausage.
1921
The clown died again. The man would be horse. The sausage ate the Moor.

1925
The second horse also died. The Moor got the Nobel Prize.
1945
She was still young.
1999
Utopia . . .

Evan Shipman: Circus

The dirty night gay light height and rope
are the trees all all a little distance
flood warm fan the leaves and hum
far voiced hurried all a hundred steps
deliberate phantoms cry the torches to the
trapeze; flare and flare.
Fixed as a moth upon a pin:
curves svelt in the,
                and dip;
                        and dip,
and dip, once, long, here,
away.
Now.   Drop.
Sweet to the serpent
and you graze
his maze:
                tantalize those weary eyes
sweep that cool turning
from all ancient learning,
tantalize your prize.
Green cones object the white mountains
and the bay and the palm and the pine
tell the glacier and the sands
of a form divine
while jazz-bands bellow.
                        Here curves lovely pink
fluttering currents shell song eternal
coral wings shell tint slim warm
from those icy stands;

depart.
Winds vent
to the canyon
the passing — —
Parade!
Dark and strong
rend the throng
all all in the glare
share and may the rare
the so, so rare
bestow, but oh oh I and around and
around we go sand and sky
and the shouting rainbow
howl ramp a black a red a howl
ramp around I own bow and you
others alike ramp a sincere
a one two three all around all whip
is a quip, but ramp,
flirt, back and out.
Rare.
Old blue,
Moon singing soon again, fair up
light lace fair sea dressed to coral
tropics and
fluted and fretted
equatorial forests bewreathe and remove
a world; mine a mirage and the
froth of the tropics only ocean again.
Over and ropes to the burst
Hi! swings and arrives
this shudder figure eight
salient silent beware strident
pendulum asp and return rasp
sanguine tic to toc and one and
two black is begin and blind.
And kind and blind and kind begin:
shock one
blank, burden and boy
the saved toy strut
scatter bemoan.

TRISTAN TZARA: Circus

I

you were also a star
the elephant bursting through the poster
to see a huge eye whose rays fall curved to earth
seeing only under the tent
muscular strength is serious and slow beneath the bluish light
offers us certainty in certain examples
the precision of athletes sometimes clowns
must wait?
perspective twisting the body's shape
it's thrilling in these lights
far from here
invisible hands torturing the members
all the yellow spots steel-pointed come
centimeters closer to the center
of the circus
people wait
cords hang down above
music
it's the circus master
the circus master doesn't want to show he's happy
he is proper

II

entrance
of chocolate truth
one assumes about corridors and trunks from
door signs
you are anxious but I am confident
many soldiers with new gazes
the narrow layers of air stretched out the strong light falls
from the stairs
filtration through the grillwork of relationships
the elephants go to bed black satellites
is this a prospectus of appearances? lead us under the curtain
and in the familiar dressing-rooms
an unexpected finger suddenly touches us

III

it is only the beginning
my soul again a studio of paper flowers
I have not forgotten my mother however
the last meeting (so auspicious)
she would forgive me I think
it is late
you find in all the corners uncontrolled drum beats
if only I could sing
always the same always somewhere
this blinding light the ants transparency
surging forth from the guilty hand
I shall leave
the carved wood Madonna is the poster the criticism
opaque silence cut by the uneven tick-tock
my heart lengthens the fifth measure
and the glory
glimpsed
the velvet curtain after the final march
with the subtlest inflection do you think of me
four numbers on the wall
with the last concern
why look for it
and here is that ringing which will never cease

IV

the lion tamer knows
people's customs what goes on in all the landscapes
the animals' mouths their saliva
all the breathing slow anxious grasping
from boredom from rage
the effect of wounds
the sure way to link them
against the poisonous liquor a light the golden bandage
and the food
he knows the practical ways to travel
the just and measured force of blows

V

anemia and elegance naptha swervings
goodness hangs bells around my neck
shrieks
planet of laughter liquor nocturnal violent burning

heavy black
smoke rising rapidly in a sharp pyramid shouts disk
gardener of your silence on the sea
and the vibrations of your bitter flesh

give birth and trade

VI

—who knows the just and measured force of blows
neither too weak nor too strong
my legs are long and delicate
run out of a crevice of steel
sun
we are honest folk
organization of fat lamps bouncing
let's dance let's shout
I love you the train leaves every day
let's drink the voltaic arc

song of the stewpan
dangerous operation
hand—flower of pink tree
tranquilizes my tears
offers to things
sister souls

splendor and subtlety
have gnawed at my heart
I spin ceaselessly
my arms spiraling toward the sky

it's cold
listen mother
and think of me
now

the last arrival from the tropics
equinox flower white-tailed phaeton
in a car towards Amsterdam around a table and the valve
of the second fog

DJUNA BARNES: from *Nightwood*

Her trade—the trapeze—seemed to have preserved her. It gave her, in a way, a certain charm. Her legs had the specialized tension common to aerial workers; something of the bar was in her wrists, the tan bark in her walk, as if the air, by its very lightness, by its very non-resistance, were an almost insurmountable problem, making her body, though slight and compact, seem much heavier than that of women who stay upon the ground. In her face was the tense expression of an organism surviving in an alien element. She seemed to have a skin that was the pattern of her costume: a bodice of lozenges, red and yellow, low in the back and ruffled over and under the arms, faded with the reek of her three-a-day control, red tights, lace boots—one somehow felt they ran through her as the design runs through hard holiday candies, and the bulge in the groin where she took the bar, one foot caught in the flex of the calf, was as solid, specialized and as polished as oak. The stuff of the tights was no longer a covering, it was herself.

MINA LOY: Crab-Angel

        An atomic sprite
perched on a polished
        monster-stallion
reigns over Ringling's   revolving
trinity   of circus attractions

Something the contour
of a captured crab
waving its useless pearly claws

From a squat body
pigmy arms

and bow legs
with their baroque calves
curve in a bi-circular attitude
to a ballerina's exstacy

An effigy of Christmas Eves
smile-cast among chrysanthemum curls
it seems a sugar angel
while from a rose flecked ruff of gauze
its manly legs
stamp   on the vast rump of the horse

An iridescent speck
dripped from a rainbow
onto an ebony cloud

Crab-Angel   I christen you
minnikin of masquerade sex
Helen of Lilliput?
Hercules in a powder puff?

SONG

"Had you been born
in regions of the Unicorn
To balance on his ivory horn
perhaps ———"
"Per Bacco!   'Tis an idiot dwarf
hooked to a wire to make him jump"

Automaton bare-back rider
the circus-master
jerks
your invisible pendulence
from an over-head pulley
to your illusory
leaps in up-a-loft

signs
the horse
racing the orchestra

in rushing show
throw
his whimsy wire-hung dominator

to dart
through circus skies of arc-lit dust
Crab-Angel   like a swimming star

clutching the tail-end of the Chimera
An aerial acrobat
floats on the coiling lightning
of the whirligig
lifts
to the elated symmetry of Flight ———

A startled rose
whirls in the chaos of the hoofs

The jeering jangling
jazz
crashes to silence

The dwarf—
subsides like an ironic sigh
to the soft earth
and ploughs
his bow-legged way
laboriously   towards the exit
waving a yellow farewell with his perruque

Jaime Torres Bodet: City

Now I remember a dream of rage and of wind
—at a hundred, a hundred kilometers—
where automobiles print
a jumble of apparitions
on cardboard walls.

A dream that hung
on screens of electric signs
muscles, arms, legs,
—rivers of shadow and woods of whiteness—
numbered countries
out of the Atlas of that huge Geography
that athletes teach in circuses.

A dream
in which frost glazed the stare
with an opaque varnish, eyelids of ice.

The public had
to get smoked glasses in order to see
the blood of the yellow moons
in the professional carnation
that laughter suddenly burns on the faces of clowns.

I remember
a dream of entering through the roof
into a wax manikin shop,
hygienic and mental
as a Museum of Sculpture
or hospital amphitheatre.

Ladies
extracted from their encyclopedic handbags—
with fingers that even the Venus de Milo lacks—
a jointed smile
for the invisible head of what Winged Victory?

And bedrooms were growing old
—those morganatic wives—
sponsoring the adultery
of windows and mirrors.

I remember
a night of Wagnerian opera
where the last Queens fell
stricken

by a sudden embolism of pearls
in the circulation of their necklaces.

A dream
where the Physics professors at the School
hurried up the eclipses
in order to get a waltz into the phonograph
that no longer repeats the seven rhythms
of Newton's gavotte.

I remember
a dream where night, covered with newspapers,
fell in a swoon on the thresholds of the doors.

(The heart beat on
in the pulse of punctual mortals
sixty minutes to the second.)

JOAN SALVAT-PAPASSEIT: Wedding March

Flash from the **FLOODLIGHT** chameleonic above the
hexagonal Circus star

Roll up! Roll up! Roll up!

CLOWNS equilaterals romantic leaders
That's sound and in the constellations of four conical
hats

The earth only turns because I am here and I am a
BUFFOON who is dying

Margot with her **COSTUME** and painted red hair looks like a
candle that burns
She only burns for me:
Before the hundred centaurs which girdle the Ring
GOLDEN WITH EXCITEMENT

Margot gazes at me eye to eye   and falling from
the Trapeze I read an <u>ad</u> on the screen:

Gob on the shaved dome
of the cretins

That man who says:
—<u>Circus</u> music is more definitive than Richard Wagner
could ever have known   nothing but a pompier!

The shade of the chorus in the sun of the boards
To move   to project   not to exist:
LIFE for Dynamism

I protest that this may also degenerate
—Because now the "lion-tamer" wants to juggle
and the horses   with their legs

My first love is

and CHARLOT who have turned twins
to enter solemnly the glory of heaven

(for they don't know that we come from yesterday
and the day before from the day before the day before
and still further before)

The Orb of the clock at **TWELVE** spawns the hours
to come which are:

one two three four
five six seven eight
nine ten eleven

and after

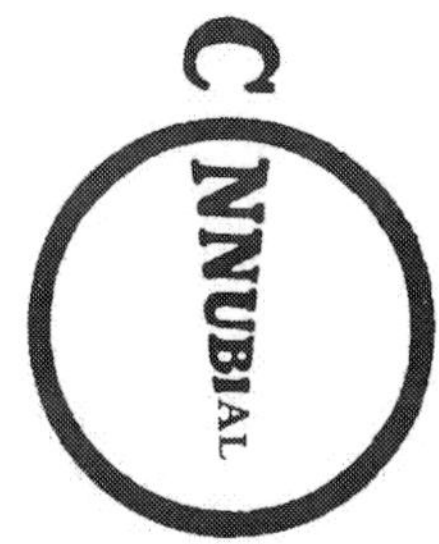

—and so I will be immortal as from now has been born
my **I** in the **ALL**

BLAISE CENDRARS: Medrano Academy

Dance with your tongue, Poet, perform an entrechat
Once around the circus ring
on a very small black basset-
hound or nag
Time the beautifully cadenced lines and fix the fixed forms
That signify BELLES-LETTRES mastered
Look:
Signboards mock you bite you with
their multicolored teeth
between your toes

The director's daughter has electric lights
The jugglers are also trapeze artists
suolirep paeL
gnikcarc pihW
ti-sserpxE
The clown is in the mixing bowl

Your tongue must { take over the box office / replace the orchestra } on evenings

All **passes** are suspended.

November 1916.

CÉLINE ARNAULD: Luna Park

Sinister display of that optical mirror
stuck on my shoulder
photophorous horoscope of bad days
tattoo of my enemies
submerged at the bottom of sad reservoirs
crystallized by rapid lightning

Lay hands stretch out immoderately
to grasp the flower
barge of rumors on the ocean
dreamers' bagpipes

In their fort the snails
turn the wheel of the universe

But the spontaneity of feelings
in life . . .
It is the hydra sunk
on the one twaddle of racecourses
godsend of mirrors in palaces

In Luna Park one jungles
with hearts of crystal
The horoscope in beakers
listens to the mime artists speak . . .

Do not distrust me
I am only the fleeting reflection
of the projector
morning song with a megaphone

Carl Rakosi: Foyer, The Orpheum

	During the water movement of the French horns and the lovelace of a violin a wire from my girl. She says "I love you but I need a deposit." Even the ventriloquist's dummy laughed after we combed his pretty red hair and set him on his tricycle.
The Professor	Do you know the story of Lou? She was a lonely little gal with the love in her eyes and Mr. H. H. at the ivories. And she was happy (honest to God). In the season of Romain effects and synthetic American lights she drove into a western suburb in a seven-bearing gull-line Suiza, rolling her klieg eyes like revolving doors.
Animal Cartoons	Whereupon the jackass full of animal gas floated blissfully into the dance of the seven veils.

Professor	Poor Lou in the climax to the Latin scene gave up the fareast of the imagination for seven rooms in Arkansas.
Lou	I have that funny feeling. It must be love.
Mr. Rakosi	Nothing so marks the copulative man as a corkscrew and a bottle opener.
Lou	Feel my pulse, please. Can it be the tropics?
Mr. Rakosi	Yes, I have a joking knowledge of many topics. It's the moonlight if you insist. Your lips are difficult to resist. Pardon me while I go to sleep.
Lou	You're so deep. Why don't you talk in English?
V's Dummy	I could almost weep. Are you my father?
Ventriloquist	That's my affair. Do you swear to uphold the constitution?
Dummy	On my wax banana. What the hell's going on here? I smell Pittsburgh.

Ventriloquist	It's a muscle dance it's sheet music piano tremoloing Benny Rubin Alabama chicken hop.
Porter	Can't be bothered now happy breeches. I'll be seein ya. Pick me out a nice jail.
Tom Nelson	Could you stand an old man to a cup of coffee? It's hard walking with this silver septum in my nose. Tom Nelson from the Old Royal buck and wing man.

VICTOR SHKLOVSKY: from *Zoo* [Letter Twenty-two]

I recently had occasion to be at the Scala Theater. It's on Lutherstrasse. There were various stunts: one acrobat was turning somersaults on a pole placed on the shoulder of another acrobat; two female trapeze artists were spinning so fast on their trapezes that from below they seemed to have turned into green vases, while their shadows, falling on the curtain, remained human. Such a big program cannot be crammed into one sentence. There was also a repulsive man who first did gymnastics with a seventy-pound weight in his teeth; then he sank his teeth into the back of three or four heavy chairs that had been strapped together and lifted them off the floor.

That did not appeal to me. I have very bad teeth.

The bicyclists were the most fun to watch: they circled the stage, making their bicycles rear up on one hind wheel, and finally rode into the wings seated on hoops; they rode off in no particular hurry, blowing, all of them, on trumpets.

That would have really appealed to Tom Sawyer.

Then balalaika players played.

Russian actors danced.

A quick-sketch artist drew various caricatures. He drew a black marketer and then put him behind bars.

What struck me about this show was the total discontinuity of its program.

There are two attitudes toward art.

One is to view the work of art as a window on the world.

Through words and images, these artists want to express what lies beyond words and images. Artists of this type deserve to be called translators.

The other type of attitude is to view art as a world of independently existing things.

Words, and the relationships between words, thoughts and the irony of thoughts, their divergence—these are the content of art. Art, if it can be compared to a window at all, is only a sketched window.

Complex works of art are usually the result of combinations and interactions between works previously existing, simpler and, in particular, smaller in scope.

. . .

The most vital genres in contemporary art are the collection of articles and the variety show, which depends for its interest on the individual components, not on the connective tissue. Something similar can be observed in the interpolated numbers of the vaudeville.

ANNA AKHMATOVA: The Stray Dog Cabaret

All of us here are hookers and hustlers.
We drink too much, and don't care.
The walls are covered with birds and flowers
that have never seen sunshine or air.

You smoke too much. There's always a cloud
of nicotine over your head.
Do you like this skirt? I wore it on purpose.
I wanted to show lots of leg.

The windows here have been covered forever.
Is it snowing out? . . . maybe it's rain.
You've got that look in your eyes again,
like a cat in a crouch for a kill.

Sometimes I feel this awful pain,
as if someone were breaking a spell.
Take a good look at that one over there!
She's dancing her way into hell!

VASILY KAMENSKY: Cabaret

Ravine cabaret MAXIM
bar ZONE
DRESS SHIRTS TAVERN AH
blacks
H^2SO^4 gypsies roses
Italians girls
fruits *ears*
singing music death **money** *feathers*
W E D R I N K C H A M P A G N E
TANGO fried We
almonds turbans
me? 25 ru dashes *distance* N.T. mooed
anguish from Africa
parties heat Turkish

bald S O N G S café
voice love
No. 606-03 orchestra entrance
live 1 ru
Louisa automob 10 [e x c l a m a t i o n]
chauff depart sun heal shore Bosphorus

SALVADOR REYES: Cabaret

In the broken voice of violins
I lean, like a convalescent
in a ray of Winter sunlight
The radiant windmills of night
do not spin in my nerves
At the door of the Cabaret
my life, its questions
hang from the street lamps
Timetables drag their fatigue
so that the next dawn will drown
in the bags under her eyes

PIERRE REVERDY: Cabaret

These woods
And a tavern where everybody smokes
You can't see anything anymore people are on top of each other
Do you recognize that man with the feathers in his hat
Nobody came to see what is going on
Complete liberty mistress of the place
to the din of common sense revolting
that would laugh singing God's praises
there the voracious is preparing his next harvest
And the hour of your destiny gambols in the countryside
A clear noise
despite the heavy blood humming with memories

came back as I was recovering
And the unhoped-for being who sometimes forgives us
seeing who I was stopped me from leaving
Soon extraordinary things occurred
that the regular customers seem no longer to be aware of
There is still time for you to lower your eyelids
since you don't have enough strength to see everything
The most propitious corner was reserved for us between the fireplace and the window
The dog asleep in the ashes has awakened
The cat who knows how to smoke purrs in front of the fire
Nobody is thirsty
The drinks have a lousy taste of cork
What hat covered your forehead
Pointed hat awful hat
when you take it off your ideas will fly away
Only a ridiculous man will remain behind
Listen to the stream weeping its song
And the wind in the trees of the cemetery
Despite our curiosity I must take you with me
going out by the back door
We still have a ways to go
And nothing to do in there
where everyone seems to be holding back his tears

Hugo Ball: Cabaret

The Impresario struts round the curtain,
Bewitched by Pimpronelle's red petticoats.
Loud chatter in the stalls from green god Coco.
Lust stirs in all the oldest Guilty-Goats.

Tsingtara! blast from something long and brassy.
Out comes a spittle-banner: 'Snake'—five letters.
All pack their ladies in their fiddle-cases,
Make themselves scarce. But then they get the jitters.

Oily Miss Camodine sits at the entrance,
Tinsels her thighs with the gold coin they've taken.

Sadly, her eyes are poked out by an arc-lamp.
The burning roof collapses on her grandson.

Flies from the donkey's pointed ear are quarried,
Bagged by a man from somewhere else, a clown,
Little green funnels, folded up and carried,
Give him a link with noblemen in town.

On the high platforms where the enharmonic
Ropes intersect, where the flat walk dives off,
A small-bore camel hazards a platonic
Montage; and people hesitate to laugh.

The Impresario, who manned the curtain
Patient, alert for tips, aware of form,
Forgets his good behavior all of a sudden,
Drives girls before him in a turgid swarm.

BOB BROWN: Dime Museum

Skinny!
the original
living
skeleton
he's alive!
thin as a dime!
Squelette!
he eats
tacks
glass
tin cans
any kind of goat food
Nobody loves Skinny
He's looking for a lady
to spend the night with
on a tin roof

See the little Albino Beauty

ain't she a peach!
she's white all over

Next, the Bearded Lady
she's got whiskers everywhere
don't take my word for it
she'll show you

And the Tattooed Marvel
she's tattooed all over
yes, and under

The Armless, Legless Wonder
no arms at all
no legs anywhere
not even one!
Sews with her teeth
hugs with her hips
sleeps with a different pair of
pyjamas every night

The Amazon Giantess
she's tall all up and down
try and reach her top
tall in all directions
eight feet long in her ostrich plumes
I've taken her measure lying down

Simone, the dwarf
Mama's little manikin
small in every part
miniature in every detail
once he slipped into a gnat's
hole by mistake

The Chinese Harem
formerly Royal Pekin ladies
they have small padded feet
feet like pocket-warmers
Any gent want his pocket warmed?

Nellie the Fat Girl
fat all over
she's six feet across
going South
Nellie bounces like a ball
would any good-looking gent
in the audience
like to bounce Nellie?

(Thin slime grins
for a thin dime
smudgy smirks
loose-lip leering
adenoidal gapes
marveling morons)
This way out, ladies and gents!
Don't fail to see the Man Monkey!
In the mirror on your left
as you pass out, gents

Gonzalo Escudero: Zoo

Sun,
inventory of color.

The horses have learned to read the world
in the glass fruits of their eyes.
Nudist colony of the white corals.
Chocolate derricks of the giraffes.
Claude Debussy is barely
the gramophone-needle of the rats.
Electric trains of the boa constrictors.
Sailor pants of the elephants.
Stravinsky, the puberty of tomcats on the roofs in the full moon.
Metallurgy of bird-projectiles.
Copper cog-rack of the iguana.
What mountain range rears up like the camels?

What liner branches up such spoutings as the whales?
Geodesy, wisdom of the snail.
The erudition of Marx is the soviet of the ants.
The penguins are the black-shirts of the sky.
Charlie Chaplin took his doctorate in antelope-leaping.
Nobody will solve the algebraic equation of a serpent X.
What British wet nurse better than the kangaroo,
where Freud learned to babble the libido?

Clock-shop of the oysters.
What fancy woman dresses in winter like the ermines?
Sunday suit of the penitentiary zebras.

The swift ostriches are automobiles of feather.
Spider, puppet of the crystal scaffolding.

And all this, that the bat may open the umbrella of night.

◈ MUSIC HALL ◈

PAUL VAN OSTAIJEN: Music Hall

1

SUDDENLY

inside the circle of its despondency
the city began to
live

Music Hall is
full of
faint
desire
in its electric scrimping
people electrified
before the banal wonder

Music hall a balloon
a
b
o
u
t
t
o

pop

2

H o p inside Drama in full effect
orchestra **Luigini ballet égyptien**

(this music which is always half a beat too late
it *follows* the dance)

Luigini drama in full swing
filmviewers pay attention to the music and
you'll know how far along the movie is

learn the dictionary of filmmusic

without magic
you don't have to watch the film
music indicates exactly

Spring of the sick youth = { Pourquoi me REVEILLER
lovesickaisle O o o O souffle du printemps AN

fatal love = Ris donc Paillasse

sincere love, sacrifice { = mais
1 rich + 1 poor le plus joli rêve

quiet melancholy = german music

LA TRAVIATA = rising { fire or lovefire

the great man GUISEPPE **VERDI**

HISTORICAL FILM = { Jerusalem
the march of the Huguenots
l'Africaine

historical TRIUMPH = { ce matin
j'ai vu dans le lontain

triumph of the *JOCKEY*
or
furious rage in marching pace = { A I D A march

unfolding of the
conflict
drama
tragic
expressive
directive

SAMSON

and

DALILA

orchestral triumph is the
raging
of the fire
of the anger
of the love
f i r e

THEN

chair

bass cello violin mounts rises until the conductor stands on his HIGH

and

the music ______________________________

BOOM

KETTLEDRUMS

everything **FLAT**

0__________________o

again raging violins cellos basses brass triangle
drums KETTLEDRUMS
raging running raging running raging RUNNING

STOP !

drama in full swing whores snakes throwing themselves at honest men the family is staggering the factory is staggering virtue is staggering falls down all notions are CRUMBLING

HALT!

3

arms legs move space rustlingnoise

A-C-R-O-B-A-T-S

competition

climb

piston

drum

feet

hands

climb

rings

bars

drumtrampling

in space

ropes

Acrobats rolling the drum
legs
arms
legs
arms

ladders
up the and
climb tumble down
drumrolls ladders

KETTLEDRUMS

et voilà smile

Drums and acrobats One

4

Drumrolls drumtrampling
drumgrowling

HUM **DRUM**

O -

r--a--n--g--e

a-c-r-o-b-a-t-s

tri tri hI

flowery flower bower

THUMP

tarita *tarita* *taritatta*

rumbles the hall
stumbles the hall
fumbles the hall

growing fumbling **rustling**

trampling drumming ladders space and time

shivering rustling rolling rolling
bottoms
balls
fists
hands
hand SLAPPING

balls balls bottoms balls bottoms balls balls

everything rustling rolling rumbling along

a - c - r - o - b - a - t - s
DRUM
hand SLAPPING

The **T**wirling **C**ups of **C**offee with **T**he **C**lapping all around

d
an
twir ling ce

l et go

ringing domebreaking glasses

fixed firmly

5

On cinemadome
presses
firm fist

and the people are wrenching their fist and
rub their withers
against
the cinemadome
the Firm Fist

the billboards
transform into

Menacing Torments

les vaches les vaches !

come little Jeanne
Coco
listen to your heart
your blood
your sinking

how everything sinks away around you
and only

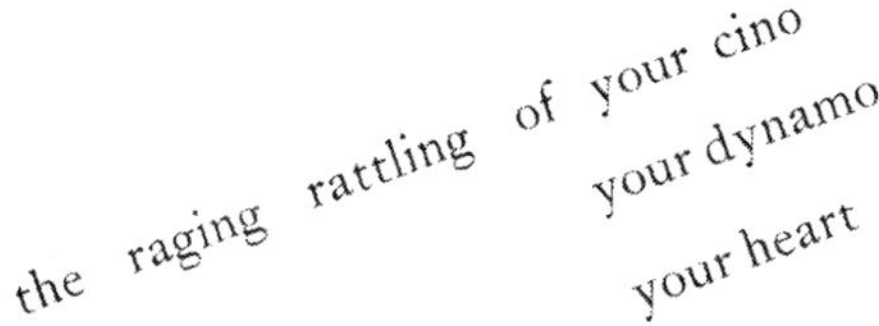

quand je suis grise

the rocking of the barge
that is wrecking
that is sinking
that sinks

sunk

THE HAND STRANGLES

Jeanne
me
the others
burbling
bums

FOLIES BAR

MAMAN you are unique
behind the counter as the bar is emptying you say
in sadness of dirty opal dusk
Francia joue la Berceuse de Jocelyn
or rather
Francia joue l'Avé Maria de Gounod
your ecstatic face in etherclouds
separation of soul and body
over your face tears roll down mechanically MAMAN
effortlessly and as many as you want
what a beautiful tearmachine you are
as your separated soul floats along with Jocelyn

WITH JOCELYN MAMAN

final note 1 minute or 60 seconds say sixty seconds later

says MAMAN
valuable in dirty opal

C'est trop beau

The sadness of morning

Whirling pallid orchestrion
str_________________etched

houses align themselves in a row
hoarseness street stretched instruments
until long arms again stretch street miniature

faint
flickering
dying
stretched
neck
rising up
in paleness lantern

rattling
billboard
accompaniment
hoarse
pale
together

nini Colombine whiteness fades
whiteness in pearl-grey of street

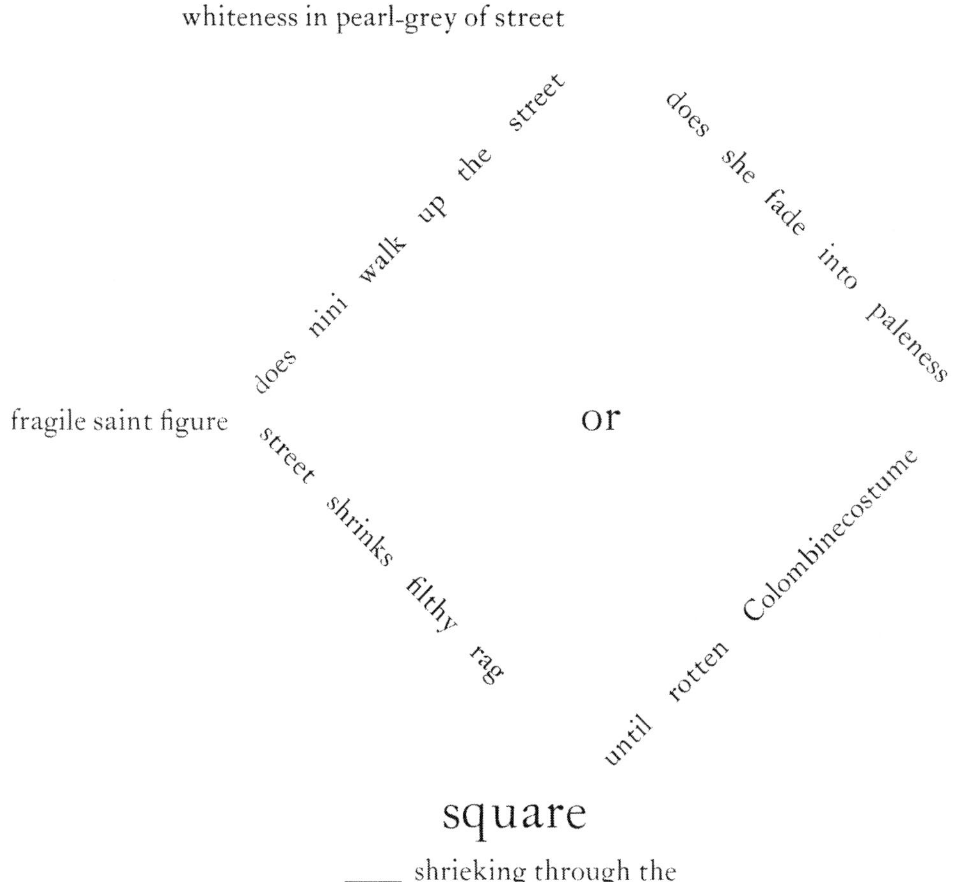
does nini walk up the street
does she fade into paleness
fragile saint figure
or
street shrinks filthy rag
until rotten Colombinecostume

square
____ shrieking through the

frost freezes legs to rigid rods raging
standing broken in stretched street
frost freezes the last girl away

and the last
Cold in ColombineCostume Cutting through Café
Cognac I am freezing all the men are gone
the room
will be filled with cold

laying soldiers' boots
let
the
city
in
d
i
s
t
a
n
c
e

DEDICATED

to Mister So-and-so

You will be forgiven a lot
for
you have seen many films

we know by heart
our pocket

FanTOMas L igomar with a big L trop long

THE STEEL JAIL

macaronifilms { dukes
princesses
apaches

and

the wonderful film Chéri BiBi

fata*li*tas

"Dieppe o mon pays natal j'ai quitté en forçat; vicomte je te revois"
or rather
"je crois m'être mis dans la peau d'un honnête homme; ME voillà dans celle d'un assassin."

God the Father presents the final act

director archangel Michael
aeros blockade submarines foreign races
the beginning of the end
the breast is empty
the child throws the bottle away
nursemaids - crying

The Last of the MoHicans

in the most fitting novel

everything tested
we are at the end of all isms isthms
of all cathedrals
of all prophets
of all cathedras
dumb founded
with the only positive
that we refuse to do any damn thing
damn mec miché

N ihil in all directions
ihil in all sexes
ihil in all languages and
all dialects
NIHIL in all letterforms

turning
nihil **nihil** in the saltire

N I H I L in crux suastica
Nihil in vagina

NIHIL

Zut building cathedrals and shooting down
blame on others
naturally
citron nature

others make children
the vow of chastity costs nothing

dumbed and
damned
statisticians bishops generals grant gratification
of counting children
Deo Gratias

amen

and children that misfortune or coincidence are there only to learn
to defend themselves

turning *nihil*
rectangle nihil
triangle **nihil**
pyramid NIHIL

your morale the one plausible thing for us
to do

the trains have the vapid
rhythm
of
tired
people

Positive is to convince yourself
of emptiness
of loam and clay
of shake and ashes
the realisation of utter emptiness
the echoering
of ideal slogans

emptiness hollow lungs lay body
hollow lungs echoering in themselves aimlessly
let the secretaries the pastors the generals make children
turn around turn around turn around
around an axis earth

a A A

omega

Du rouge pour les lèvres

leaves the rounds again
the rounds
around the rounds
omega
omicron
Alpha (letter not margarine) beta zeta eta theta

t ê t e
à
cou
per

If I was to be director
abolished the Steed Bayard Giant Giantess
but our
heroic ideals

burlesque clothes
{ honesty in top head and buttoned vest
religion tiara cardinal-red
metaphysics with little angelwings
and

CORRONATION
O Suzanna waaas ist das **L E**

ils en ont tant goûté
qu'ils en ont dégueulé

We have known all songs **3** evolution of Waltzertraum in three languages

from Lustige Witwe to Czardasfürstin
crossing out all smoothoperettas
similsentimental songs
T a n g o R R R o u g e

Dans mon pays english wine french lyrics

quand je suis gri-
se

rue de la Glaciè____________re
ICH TANZ
so
gern **TANGO O BUENOS AIRES**

Sous le ciel de l'Argentine
Only still stands counterpoint to JAZZ-BAND
6 o' clock in the morning grey street
FRERE JACQUES
FRERE JACQUES

frère Jacques
lève-toi
tines
sonne le ma
les matines

sonne
everything's empty
frère Jacques
the last Pernod

Picon

hollow sea wreck
t' en fais pas
lame bus through weary street
lazy trains through lame country
mountains sea valley valley sea mountains
sea sea sea

wreck

lazy trains

being fed up

rigolo gigolo zigoto
si tu veux faire une petite ballade
you have been balladeering throughout Europe
your expectations die
Utah Indians Aztecs

PLACE BLANCHE

and it is not the very least of your merit
inventor of a map

EUROPE along EROTIC CHANNELS
we have known Europe so long so long
stretched stretched out flat and higherup
geological
river beddings
political
religious
commercial
and all of that and all of that
to
this EROTIC MAP is a necessity
soon private teachers will
give seminars
about this invention [for humanity's benefit]
in Corfu the women are like

legs thighs breasts Berlin **Germany** BRUSSELS Amsterdam Bucharest **London** PARIS
her perfume fleurs Houbigant Lonchamp Maisons-Laffitte mec maquereau
niché rigoler gigole gousses **ehrliche Frau**

and you have seen for 5 minutes
the necropolis
of the Acropolis

far more than enough

Will have fallen all cathedrals
cannibals
Hannibals generals
ideals
colonels
brothels
perhaps
there will be room
for a natural beauty
pure
unknown

If **it** is not destroyed
one and forever
will be purer

purify the earth
rodents weeds

perhaps one day we will say j'ai soupé
d'en avoir soupé

Nihil
again grasping core forms
these common words

prison letters
common wound words
simple stuttering from man to love

and all of this ashen cell
not the entire poor life
from doleful people longing thistles

and are these cross-stretched countries
no great Christ
full of hollow wounds

and this hollow echoing feeling of
despondency
not as Good Friday once used to be

7-10 Aug. 20

PARADE OF THE ECCENTRIC

GRIGORI KOZINTSEV: A. B.! Parade of the Eccentric

ROSTA without pungency, Max Linder without his top hat, Brockhaus without Efron—what could be more absurd?

1921 December 5 (a historic date)
Kozintsov, Kryzhitsky, Trauberg found:
The 20th Century without . . .

A QUESTIONNAIRE

. . . "The Eccentric's trousers, deep as a chasm, from which the great gaiety of Futurism emerges with a thousand burdens." Marinetti
. . . "For the theatre as such this is a defeat, for its territory has been captured by the Eccentrism of the music hall." Lunacharsky
. . . "Oh, oh, oh!" The clown Serge

without—
Eccentrism (a visiting card).
Music-Hall Cinematographovich Pinkertonov
1 year from birth??
See below for information.

1. A KEY TO THE FACTS

1) YESTERDAY — comfortable offices. Bald foreheads. People pondered, made decisions, thought things over.
TODAY — a signal. To the machines! Driving belts, chains, wheels, hands, legs, electricity. The rhythm of production.
YESTERDAY — museums, temples, libraries.
TODAY — factories, works, dockyards.
2) YESTERDAY — the culture of Europe.
TODAY — the technology of America.
Industry, production under the Stars and Stripes. Either Americanisation or the undertaker.
3) YESTERDAY — sitting-rooms. Bows. Barons.

TODAY — the shouts of newspaper-sellers, scandals, policemen's truncheons, noise, shouting, stamping, running.

The pace today:

The rhythm of the machine, concentrated by *America,* realized on the *street.*

2. ART WITHOUT A CAPITAL LETTER, A PEDESTAL OR A FIG-LEAF

Life requires art that is
hyperbolically crude, dumbfounding, nerve-wracking, openly utilitarian, mechanically exact, momentary, rapid,
otherwise no one will hear, see or stop. Everything adds up to this: the art of the 20th century, the art of 1922, the art of this very moment is

Eccentrism

3. OUR PARENTS

Parade allez!
In literature—the *chansonnière*, the cry of the auctioneer, street language.
In painting—the circus poster, the jacket of a cheap novel.
In music—the jazz band (the commotion of a negro orchestra), circus marches.
In ballet—American song and dance routines.
In theater—the music-hall, cinema, circus, *café-chantant*, boxing.

4. WE ARE ECCENTRISM IN ACTION

1) Presentation—rhythmic wracking of the nerves
2) The high-point—the trick
3) The author—an inventor-discoverer
4) The actor—mechanical movement, not buskins but roller-skates, not a mark but a nose on fire. Acting—not movement but a wriggle, not mimicry but a grimace, not speech but shouts.

We prefer Charlie's arse to Eleonora Duse's hands!

5) The play—an accumulation of tricks. The speed of 1000 horse power. Chase, persecution, flight. Form—a divertissement.
8) Humped backs, distended stomachs, wigs of stiff red hair—the beginning of a new style of stage costume. The foundation—continuous transformations.
7) Horns, shots, typewriters, whistles, sirens—Eccentric Music. The tap-dance—start of a new rhythm.

We prefer the double soles of an American dancer to the five hundred instruments of the Marinsky Theater.

8) The synthesis of movements: acrobatic, gymnastic, balletic, constructive-mechanical.
9) A can-can on the tightrope of logic and commonsense. Through the "unthinkable" and the "impossible" to the Eccentric.
10) From fantasy to sleight of hand. From Hoffmann to Fregoli. The infernal American "Secrets of New York." "Who's Behind the Smiling Mask"?
11) Hands everywhere. Sport in the theater. Films of the champion and the boxer's gloves. Parade allez!—more theatrical than the grimaces of Harlequin.
12) Use of the principles of American advertising.
13) The cult of the amusement park, the big wheel and the switchback, teaching the younger generation the BASIC TEMPO of the epoch.

The rhythm of the tap dance. The crackle of the cinema. Pinkerton. The roar of the switchback. The noisy tomfoolery of the clown. The poetry—"time is money"!

Our rails rush past:

Paris, Berlin, London,
romanticism,
stylization,
exoticism,
archaism,
reconstruction,
restoration,
the pulpit,
the temple,
the museum!

Only our methods are indivisible and inevitable:
THE AMERICANIZATION OF THE THEATER
in Russian means
ECCentriSM

Jakob von Hoddis: Varieté

I. *Box Seat*

A waltz rumbles; horny violins screech;
The air is white with cigarette haze;
It reeks of musk, make-up, wine, of fat

Indians and bare female meat.

II. *The Athlete*

And the athlete steps up you may well gawk,
As he breaks a board with bare fist.
He walks with tremendous paunch,
With fat arms and neck, slick with sweat.

And shorts hang loose about little legs,
Deformed to slender sticks.
Fancy silk adorns his little feet.
Ah! how sweet! Like two pink piglets.

III. *The Humorist*

An old man in his new tuxedo
Bellows adventures of love.
And especially after certain recent
Escapades
Says he was a wreck, like a ship
Tossed about on the waves,
Abandoned rudderless to the "Bride"-wind,
With even a half-rotted mast.

IV. *Dance*

A small girl with tong-burned curls
In a deep skyblue blouse—
The bare legs prance without socks.
She sings: "Oh, do not hurt me!"
"Ah you! Today I'll be your wife!"

Then she dances greedily with chic
To a bumpy music.
And through the whirl of blue silk
You see the young body exactly—

V. *The Indian*

She lifts a thin arm; crouched, poised to jump
The two dark panthers fly through seven

Rings with one elegant leap.
Their strong vile paws graze,
As dazed they stagger back to their cage,
The string of pearls, that...from a lilac belt...
Dangle around their naked mistress's hips.

VI. *Ballet*

Negroes swivel their legs straight out
Tight yellow jerseys on their asses.
And between them dance our small cheeky
Women blond and naked quite famously
Attired:
With only golden stilettos
With which they quickly step on the broad
Noses of the heaving athletes.

VII. *The Soubrette*

The hussy as hunter
Fires her guns
And, staring down the bird,
Shows us her behind.

Her astoundingly elastic ass
On legs as taut as columns.
She sings: "Love's got me hot and bothered
In the green woods . . .!"

VIII. *The Dancer*

How the tender joints move me,
Your slender neck, your bending knees!
I'm almost angry. Will I succumb?
Will you take me back to that dream

That as a boy flat on my belly I made
Out of sweet verses and beautiful
Actresses, soft violin notes
And stolen ideals?

Ah! I've found none that could match it,
Tearfully spurning woman after woman,
I was banned to constant suffering,
And hate that dream. Pale, I watch

And I worry, watch how your body changes,
And for every mistake you make in the dance
I'm grateful: in the end you still
Take a bow with an idiot grin.

IX. *End: Cinematography*

The room goes dark. And we see the rapids
Of the Ganges, palm tees, the temple of Brahma,
A silent raving family drama
With gigolos and masked balls.

A revolver's drawn. Jealousy flares up,
Mr. Piefke loses his head in the duel.
By hook or by crook
The mountaineer lady climbs steep trails.

The path soon winds through larch forests,
Soon it bends and ascends the crooked
Rockface. Cows and potato fields
Animate the distant view.

And in the dark room—in my face—
Shimmers the horror wake of images!
In the end the projector hisses for light—
We exit forcefully, yawning with release.

X. *Outside*

The summer night is hard to take!
Four men with unbuttoned collars.
A man with patent leather shoes stalks for Schnapps . . .
A rumble—a long rolling crash:
Thunder!
Ow!
Crude advertising,

Lightning!
A refined man deplores loud balderdash!
Sounds that are just as if some chubby nudist
World Spirit
Crapped without tact in a cataract.

Franz Richard Behrens: Tiller Girls

Sixteen
Sealingwaxred
Bobcutcoiffed
Citronyellow
Bobcutcoiffed
Sealingwaxred
Silktasselled
Citronyellow
Silktasselled
Milimeterstep

Nicolas Beauduin: Music Halls

Crowd with alcoholic eyes (*Rousing pictures*)
merry gesticulation
electricity
vulgar remarks

painted beauties
darting
toward embattled lusts.

Drums
violins
contrabasses Gin-fizzes
violas
trombones Rag-times *Hello!*
cymbals
banjo *Hello!*

stir the fervor of unleashed senses.

This is the Scene

New film

synthesis of human life.

triumphant
feline
Here woman reigns
artificial
animal

Modern saturnalia { *fire gongs*
cymbal blows.

Mechanical gadgets
symphony of electric aromas

orgy of the senses
orgy of the eyes

All is revealed

prodigious
abnormal
cerebral
synoptic
modern.

madness
intelligence

= alternate.

Red negroes
Lightning clowns

(*Phenomena*)

Lascivious dancers
Happy flesh

Tight-rope eccentrics

Orchestration of colors

Moonlight projectors { *red* *blue* *yellow* *green*

Ho

in a minute

sleight of hand
plummeting leaps
body contortions
sighing flutes

successive acts in space

Mimes, ventriloquists, boxers
animal trainers, jugglers
crazy modern paroxysm
under the conquering bravos

Scene-design of sounds

Clenched males, unique desire
outthrust monocles, violent instincts
under their smoking jackets blood lust boils.

The JAZZ-BAND screams *fre-n-zieeeeed*
Electric effluvia in the air
so strong that the Music Halls
seem suddenly charged with alcoholic delirium,
furnaces of a terrible explosive joy
in the mad evening pierced by apotheosis.

PAUL ÉLUARD: The Gertrude Hoffman Girls

Gertrude, Dorothy, Mary, Claire, Alberta,
Charlotte, Dorothy, Ruth, Catherine, Emma,
Louisa, Margaret, Ferral, Harriet, Sarah,
Florence in the nude, Margaret, Toots and Thelma.

Beauties of night, beauties of fire and beauties of rain,
The trembling heart, the hidden hand and windlike eyes,
You show me the movements of light,
You exchange a glance for a springtime.

The girth of your waist for a flower's circuit,
Boldness and danger for your unsullied flesh,
You exchange love for the shivers of steel,
And the unconscious laugh for dawn's promises.

Your dances are the fearful whirlpool of my dreams
And I fall and my downfall perpetuates my life,
The space beneath your feet is increasingly vast,
Wonders, you dance upon the springs of the day.

FRANZ RICHARD BEHRENS: Chocolate Kiddies

Blooddark burgundy bass saxophone
Malay yellow drumtricks caper
Thundering piano says Stop
Deliciously continuous snap of girlsteps
Crackles doubletime off a runway
Gliding stomps wipe heavywet earth away
Music tremolo comes driving out purred, sighed, grunted, violet, rose,
Jessie in red dress jazzes like crazy
Time's become money in the dawn before the pause

ENZO MAINARDI: Jazz Band

Whole palette
  Castanets
    hazel nut BITTER
      nougat
metallic laughter
      crackling
    sparkling of
  E major acidic sharp cold
pungent flesh of
         tiger women
writhing in the dense atmosphere of
         drums + tom-toms
     Jazz band jazz band!
A dagger
  give me a DAGGER
to kill the murderer slashing my back
with a bloody
         viiioliiiin
Titina's vermilion
mouth   (what a bore!)
devours the silver kettledrums
The eyes are hooks
snatching the women's dresses

leaving their nude bodies among the banners
RED
YELLOW
BLUE
in the JAZZ BAND's
piercing fever

PAUL MORAND: from *Black Magic*

Suddenly the crowd is folded back by a whirl of color and gesture, preceded by a celebrated laugh. Congo has just got back from the theatre, with her stage make-up and her stage tricks—"The Most Photographed Girl in the World," as the papers call her. All her teeth, and the arcade of her gums as well, flash from her mouth, and her unwinking eyes thrust forward from their orbits. As soon as this black flag is hoisted, the party sets sail; the accordion squeezes out its juice, as from a wrung towel, and the trombones draw out their *glissandos*, overpowered by a nasal, aristocratic saxophone. The pack-ice of these Europeans, well-bred, reserved, and fasting, begins to split in all directions. Congo seizes one by the hair, another by the coattails, and pairs them off by force. She herself sketches a bar or two of a waltz with a large grim woman who has slipped in to copy dress-models, and then suddenly puts a potted palm in her place between her partner's arms. And round the palm-partner's lady Congo dances alone, squatting like a kangaroo, with splayed legs and clapping hands, spinning round like a top, yet not displacing her plastered hair with that broad parting of hers that looks like a long streak of baldness. A circle of astonishment rings her round. An orange spot-light swoops down unexpectedly: Congo pretends to stagger under the shock of the lamps, or else, when the light turns to white, she makes a show of wiping away the splashes of this electric powder from her dark flesh. Every one of her reflexes is a thunderbolt, unforeseen and perfect, like an image from a true poet, like a great crime, like a ball taken on the volley.

MALCOLM COWLEY: In Memory of Florence Mills

The fetish-woman crossed the stage
her limbs convulsed with yellow magic.

Art is the gratuitous
shiver that makes the shimmy tragic.
Obeah, obeah, wailed the saxophones.

Though orchestras play Dixie Dreams
never in Dixie field was picked
the gun-cotton that swells your breast
explodes, and leaves me derelict
amid the wreckage of your smile

floating over the parterre.
Your sudden fingers touched my wrist.
Tell me, did Madam Walker do your hair
before she died in Tarrytown
among her butlers, footmen, chefs?

Throned on a tomb of brass you reign
between the bass and treble clefs.

LUIS VIDALES: In the Café

The piano
deposits growls in a corner
baring its teeth
to whoever goes by.
The globe lamp
pumps its light
into the mirage of my fingernails
and from the table
where an empty
glass
pretends
to drink
air
alone—in big gulps—
downs music.
Dreamy smoke
spreads over my eyes

the stupor of Asia . . .
I sense going into my blood
the spirit of grapes
of Melody . . .
and when the stills of the band
finish distilling
the drunken soul
—iridescent
with the blue of dreams—
blends into the busy street
of a small painting
hanging on the wall.

José Rivas Panedas: Café

Caravan of voices
admidst a shrubbery of noise
The beats are spongy vessels
Ace mariners guide silver canoes
The mirrors copulate at length
Nobody goes into the saloons
that offered us all that was full
Bored musicians make up the jazz band
The mirrors are standing still
in which my heart bathes wet colors.

Dino Campana: Fantasy on a Painting by Ardengo Soffici

Face, anatomic zigzag that eclipses
The grim passion of an old moon
That watches suspended from the ceiling
In a tavern like an American
Cabaret: the red kinetic
Of lights *a rope-walker who tangoes*
A Spanish olive-ashen girl
Hysterically dissolves in a tango of lights:

That watches in the American
Cabaret:
On the pounded floor three
Red flames light up by themselves.

Francis Carco: Cabaret

The polished mahogany tables glisten with the refractive flash of crystal goblets, with gleaming decanters of water, and bottles ashimmer with liquids dark as blood. The spoons give off a whitish glint in the thick, smoky mirrors where the insolent reflections, cloudy, tall, and naked, are dreamily embedded among a tuft of dormant shadows. The cabaret slumbers. One can hear the sounds of the district dying out with difficulty: each rumor is like a ravishing woman all unknown—though somehow familiar—as she advances in her train of silent clouds. She is a magician expert at prolonging in us the imperious malaise of her beauty, and we look on spellbound as she lowers towards our faces her stark, unmoving smile. She disappears within the atomizing lines of this sphinxlike smile. Much like a pebble dropped into a basin, gliding along the outrippling waves which she provokes. It is for this that the shadow has assembled her audience in the arc of these troubled mirrors: she deploys herself with precision. The fantasy of her image which adorns the glass is barely there. I seize some spirals of long, dark hair, which uncurl themselves, and part. The tresses unfurl without catching: nerves crispen nonetheless when the rasp of silk erupts unexpectedly. The ceiling descends inch by inch: it is moving, it is fabulous. Its heavy mass wavers and sways and all the house is mantled in solemn mystery; the house with its upper storeys hidden, with its hibernating hallways engorged with night, buttered with the odors of love, and brushed with a palette of perfumes . . . wherever fate has led me every road returns to you . . . renegade, reckless, unrepentant, I have turned the world upside down to meet the price which you exact, my lips aflame with passion.

FRANCESCO CANGIULLO: from *Café Concert*

introducing a song of the "Simeon" type

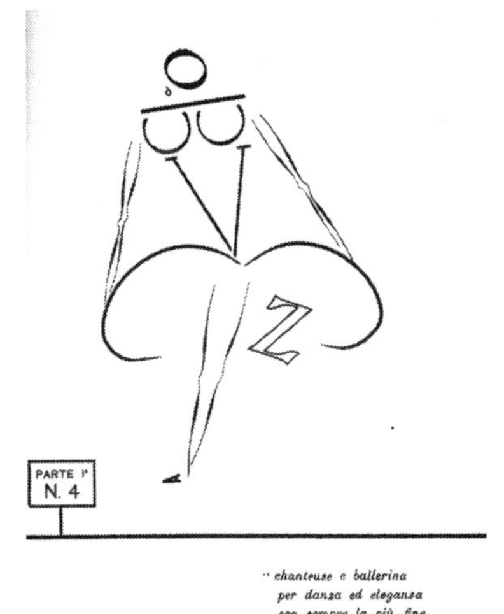

"chanteuse & dancer, for dancing
& elegance are always the finest"

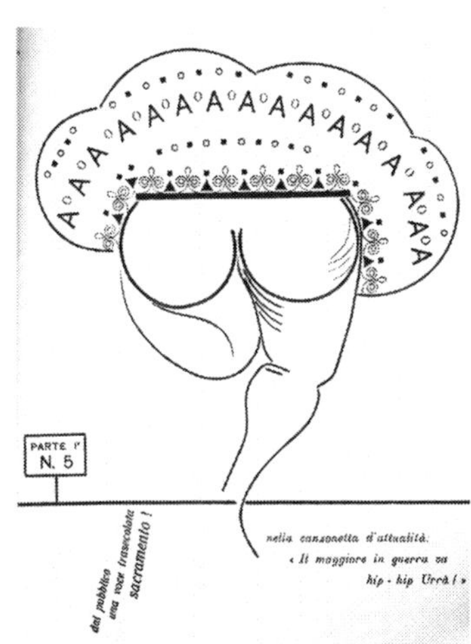

to the public with one astonished cry:
sacrament!
the song of the day: "All the world's
at war hip-hip Hurrah!"

"I give you my heart
& you give me your love"

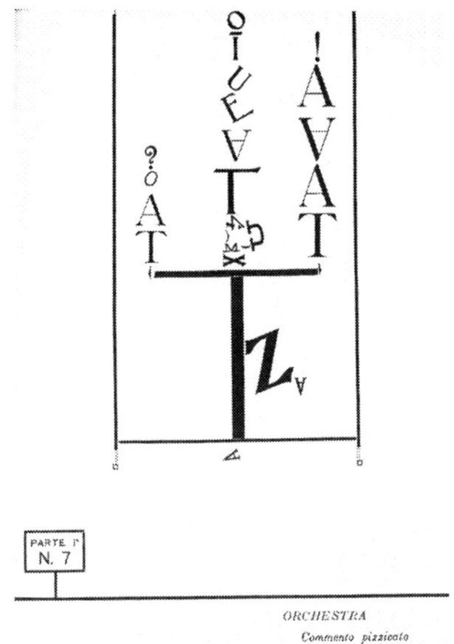

ORCHESTRA comments in pizzicato

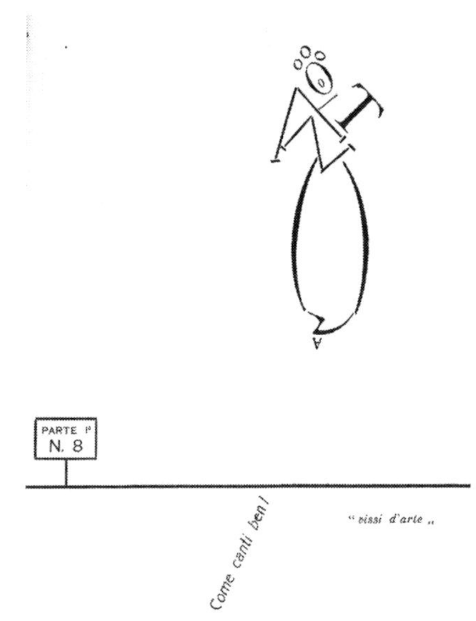

& a good tune! “Vissi d’arte”

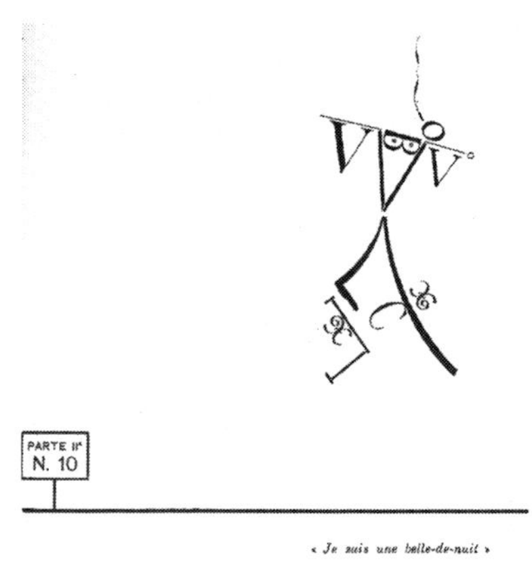

“I am a lady of the night”

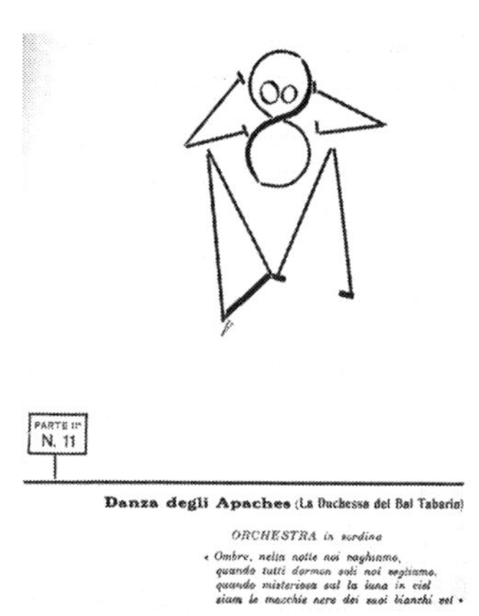

The Apache Dance (Duchess of the Bal Tabarin)
ORCHESTRA quietly
“we shadows wander in the night,
when all of us sleepers are still awake
when a mysterious moon’s in the sky
and we’re the black spots on her white veil”

ORCHESTRA "Bolero" tempo
with tambourines & castanets

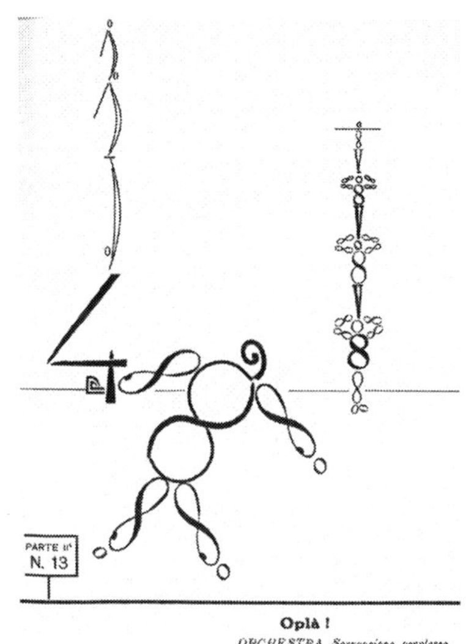

ORCHESTRA puzzled suspension

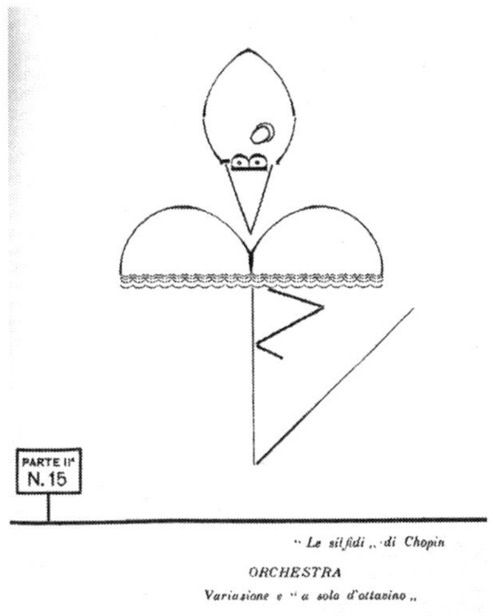

"Les Sylphides" by Chopin
ORCHESTRA varations and piccolo solo

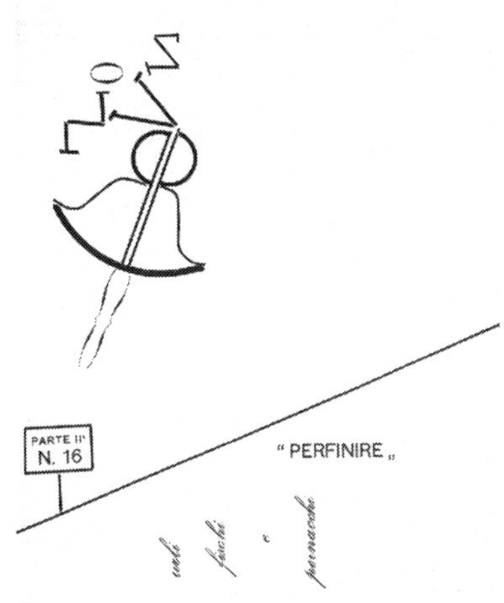

"FINALLY"
boos shouts & raspberry

Oliverio Girondo: Café Concert

The notes of the piston describe rocket trajectories hanging in the air before they collapse back to earth.

There follows swampy eyes, teeth rotted by saccharine romances, legs that smoke on the stage.

The public eye has more density and more calories than any other, is a corrosive crosseyed gaze netting and dressing the skin of the artists.

There's a group of stalwart sailors at the lighthouse where a "maquereau" lifts a little finger, gathering prostitutes like dew in the port, an Englishman who makes fog with his pupils and his pipe.

I brought the camera to bear on a lunar tray of half-naked breasts . . . some breasts I'd love to warm with my feet while dozing.

The curtain, closing, simulates the curtain ajar.

Louis Zukofsky

Cocktails
and signs of
"ads"

flashing,
light's waterfalls,

Bacchae
among electric lights

will swarm the crowds
streamers of the lighted

skyscrapers

nor tripping
over underbrush

but upon pavement

and not with thyrsus
shall they prick

the body of their loves
but waist to waist

laugh out in gyre—
announced then upon stairs,

not upon hills,
will be their flight

when passed turnstiles
having dropped

coins
they've sprinted up

where on the air (elevated)
waves flash—and out—

leap
signaling—lights below

ALFRED RICHARD MEYER: Manhattan-Cocktail

Oh mixologic cryptogram
It's the Manhattan-Cocktail!
Spare me, Cinnabar-Mary,
With your common Bock Ale!

Bar glass, silver valance! And these:
Four cubic pieces of crystal ice!
Three dashes of Angostura, please!

Triple comet-tails of Halleys!

Vermouth from Turin, take it: dry!
The whiskey: American!
Blend these two into one!
Skyscrapingly satanic:

Manhattan! Manhattan! Geechy Manitou!
Mannahatta! And you—Susquehanna!
Oh cherry, you're the moon voodoo!
To her we sing Hosannah!

FARFA: Newyorkcocktail

If I could only live
one new york night
that skins women's clothing
and strips bodies
with stabbing reflections
cast by drunken
luminous advertising

marvellous geometropolis
clinging to manhattan
island's arm
and caressing the sun
with rectangular
skyscraper fingers

city of cities
I feel you a thousand times
more than chaotic paris
more than the prey
of any naked starving girl
at the folies bergère

capital of the sixty-three
cocktails enumerated

by nathan
that corrosive american writer
strangely sensitive cocktail
of cerebralism

in the
national drink
jazz band of taste
are dipped the stars
of the white flag
steeped in red
for the blue unity

cocktail
sublime mixture
liquid creature
with tuscan flavor
and prosciutto tint
my mind strives
to exalt you
above
the dry realm
since I have never seen you
nor tasted you
and thus have yet to know you

Elsa von Freytag-Loringhoven: A Dozen Cocktails Please

No spinsterlollypop for me — «yes—we have
No bananas» I got lusting palate — I always
Eat them ————
They have dandy celluloid tubes — all sizes —
Tinted diabolically like a bamboon's
Hind complexion.
A man's a ———
Piffle! Will o' the whisp! What is the dread
Matter with the up-to-date American
Home comforts? Bum insufficient for the

Should-be well groomed upsy.
There's the vibrator ———
Coy flappertoy! I'm adult citizen with
Vote — I demand full share in roofeden —
Witch Sabbath of our Babylonian obelisk.
What's the radio for — if you please?
«Eve's dart pricks snookums upon wirefence»
«An apple a day ———»
It'll come.
Ha! When? I am no tongueswallowing yogi.
Progress is ravishing.
It doesn't me!
Nudge it—
Push it—
Prod it—
Kick it—
Broadcast ————
That's the lightning idea!
S.O.S. shortage of ———
What?
How are we going to put it befitting
Lifted upsy's?
Psh! Any sissypoet has sufficient freezing
Chemicals in his Freudian icechest to
Snuff all cockiness. We'll hire one.
Hell! Not that! That's the trouble!
CockCROW — silly.
Oh — fine!
They're in France — Africa — the air on the
Line — the poles ————————
Have them send waves — like candy — valentines
«Say it with» ———
Bolts.
Thunder!
Serpentine air currents ————
Hhhhhhhhhphssssssssssss! The very word penetrates!
I feel whoozy.
I like that. I ain't hankering after
Billy boys — but I am entitled to be
Deeply shocked.

So are we — but you fill the hiatus.
Dear — I ain't queer — I need it straight —

— A dozen cocktails — please!

Philippe Soupault: Ragtime

for Pierre Reverdy

The negro dances electrically
Have you forgotten your native land and the city of Galveston
That jeering banjo
The old men will leave at last
elevators climb the length of skyscrapers
lightning frisks about
Well hello
My cigar is lit
I've got a glass full of whiskey
my cigar is lit
I've also got my revolver

The bartender ought not to have smiled
no one cares what time it is anymore
the tireless door
the lightbulbs
my hand

right?

Stephan Roll: Etc.

My well-loved wrecked perpendicular
Your spleen is a sewing machine for clouds
The voices are a monetary deflation
Berlin plays the cops to the right

Grey stars whistle like grammatical errors
Your step marks 300 yards over the aerodrome

For the five o'clock sandwich I give you phosphorus nerves
Here are bulbs of gloves from the temple lake

Askew in the jacket I wear my cerebellum
Like a lamp or an Omega alarm clock
At the music-hall I danced in the test-tube
The willows played poker really well

On the running boards of Fords hands are kept in pockets
Edy I carry my push-pinned soul
Luna Park the wind's been unemployed for three weeks
T.S.F. has scoured the sky with an iron brush

Jens August Schade: In the Café

A good song,
a crazy little miracle
deleted from the gramophone
while I was quiet.
And to everyone's surprise
as I move the chair from under me
I stay suspended in the air.

In front of me sits a girl
with ugly teeth
and volatile eyes.
She's quiet.
—We both know,
what happens between us
is as fierce as a lion kissing our souls.

She rises up in the air
with me,
and we find each other
over the tables.
And the booming applause
the song's miracle
wraps us around each other
and carousels us out of the café.

◈ POSTCARDS ◈

Iliazd

Francis Picabia: Dada-Madrid

Spanish poem por: Pedro
por the Spanish Dadaist group

Bedside table stare away messieurs
77 shelves x Charlie Chaplin
Whiskey + dildo shelves X
    EY CARLOLLEIRA!
Himmennic Films
8 that makes 606 combs doctors.

Franz Richard Behrens: Jazz

Saxophone gag
for every syncopation
quarter notes flapping
Two clumsy staggersteps
pairing up come to the same
Parody of clumsiness with maximum skill
Robbing the fizz fizzed energy of all music
Salvation Army save souls
like jazz for jazz's sake*

* the last two lines are in English in the original

Germán List Arzubide: Cinematics

While the ticket window at the cinema
is selling the night at retail,
a celluloid kiss
slips into your memory.

◈ CINELAND: EVENING SHOW ◈

SIEGFRIED KRACAUER: from *Calico World*

In order for the world to flicker by on film, it is first cut to pieces in the film city. Its interconnections are suspended, its dimensions change at will, and its mythological powers are turned into amusement. This world is like a child's toy that is put into a cardboard box. The dismantling of the world's contents is radical; and even if it is undertaken only for the sake of illusion, the illusion is by no means insignificant. The heroes of antiquity have already made their way into the schoolbooks.

The ruins of the universe are stored in warehouses for sets, representative samples of all periods, peoples, and styles. Near Japanese cherry trees, which shine through the corridors of dark scenery, arches the monstrous dragon from the *Nibelungen*, devoid of the diluvial terror it exudes on the screen. Next to the mockup of a commercial building, which needs only to be cranked by the camera in order to outdo any skyscraper, are layers of coffins which themselves have died because they do not contain any dead. When, in the midst of all this, one stumbles upon Empire furniture in its natural size, one is hard pressed to believe it is authentic. The old and the new, copies and originals, are piled up in a disorganized heap like bones in catacombs. Only the property man knows where everything is.

GEORGE SEFERIS: Tuesday

'I went down to St James Infirmary.'

I got lost in the town.
The gardens are hidden by the hospital of Don Juan Tavera.
Streets winding round advertisements.
Each man walks without knowing
whether he's at a beginning or an end,
whether he's going to his mother, his daughter, or his mistress
whether he'll judge or be judged
whether he'll escape, whether he's escaped already
he doesn't know.
At every corner a gramophone shop

in every shop a hundred gramophones
for each gramophone a hundred records
on every record
someone living plays with someone dead.
Take the steel needle and separate them
if you can.
Now which poet? Do you remember which poet
tried out the steel needle
on the seams of the human skull?

Do you remember his song that night?
I remember that he asked for an aspirin
his eyes moved inside black rings
he was pale and two deep wrinkles
bound his forehead. Or was it you
maybe? Or me? Or was it maybe
silent Antigone with those shoulders
rounded over her breasts?
I kept her with me ten nights
and each dawn she would weep for her child.
I remember I was looking for a pharmacy.
They were all closed. Who for, I don't know.

I got lost in the town
no one is going to remove the hospital
full of crippled children gesturing
at me or at others following me.
Odors of medicine in the air
turn heavy, fall in love and mesh
with vapors from cars going off
to the country with Pre-Raphaelite couples
thoroughly blond if somehow a bit evaporated.

In the spring of 1923, Livia Rimini,
the film star, died in her bath;
they found her dead, perfume all around,
and the water not yet cold.
Yet in the movies yesterday
she gazed at me with her useless eyes.

PEDRO GARFIAS: Cinematographer

The Bolsheviks
have cut the electric cables.
The street dies in the mirror.
From a star
we see the world through a telescope.
We peep at life
through the keyhole.
The Bertini lens is always in front of the object.
The airplane,
astray, ends up in the room
and sees its error
in the ornamental columns.
The usher takes charge.
Last night I flew over Madrid:
the last night owls
hit my antenna with a radiogram,
and a crazy brother jumped me...
Charlot is a Saenz doll.
...haven't the repairs been finished?
The wind arrives too late.

PAOLO BUZZI: Cineland

The film
shudders,
seeps into Sunday's
lost soul!
May the silent goddess illuminate me
with her transoceanic beauty:
and may the "I love you" heartbeat an engraving
on the screen like a crack in the wall...
The landscapes follow each other
in flights of etchings: trains arrive
—from a dynamic-elliptical album—

as irises and orbits melt
in your self-absorption.
Everything whirls
towards its mechanical destiny.
The performance yearns ecstatically
for the Apocalypse of human love:
while, in a dark room in the metronomic background,
Death counts and strikes its hourly signal...

Lucía Sánchez: Cinemas

The cinematic window-screen
reproduces its immortal film
in mirrors.

The film fragments with every step
and shuffles the episodes.
The actors are always different.

You and I, anonymous actors,
will one day pass in front of the lens

The street fills the room
The fish-bowl mirror
ripples its turbulent water.

We charge up the batteries
The room moves through the mirrors

When the lights go up my reflector-words
project a sentimental film
into your eyes.

Joseph Roth: from *The Conversion of a Sinner in Berlin's UFA Palace*

I was sitting in the third row in front of the green velvet curtain. Suddenly the hall darkened, the curtain slowly parted, and a mysterious light that could not have been created by God, and that nature couldn't manage in a thousand years, ran in soft rivulets over the silvery walls of the hall and down the front of the stage. It was as though a waterfall had been slowly tamed—housetrained—in the course of many years and then applied to the walls of this palace, to run down them slowly and civilly, made to answer to human needs, elemental forces with pretty manners, forces of nature that had had a good talking-to. This illumination was compounded of dawn light and evening red, of empyrean clarity and infernal haze, of big-city air and sylvan green, of moonshine and midnight sun. Things that nature can only accomplish separately or in succession, were here encompassed in the one hall and in the space of one minute. And thus it was made clear to me that an unknown and powerful godhead was here at play, if not in earnest. There was not room to fall to my knees, because we were sitting packed together, but, if it's possible to say so: It was as though my knees fell to their knees.

Yehoash: Cinema

A thousand people head to head
In the dark.
Up above them leaps
A white clump.
On the white clump, spinning,
A big city with buildings
And wires and lanterns.
A broad street and packed sidewalks.
With flags and music
Comes a procession of soldiers,
Pedestrians, riders, cripples
Trucks, ambulances,
Girls with red crosses
On white caps.
Old people in old-fashioned uniforms
Covered with medals.
Out of the blue, a young man

With a terrified face and raised collar
Runs across the street.
I sit among a thousand heads in the dark
And think:
A young man works in factory,
Goes home,
Plays with his child,
And one day he gets sick
And dies,
And above distant seas,
In New York,
And in Chicago,
And in San Francisco,
Night after night, he runs across the street
With a terrified face
And raised collar . . .

GUILLERMO DE TORRE: Photogenie

to Jean Epstein

Faces
Grimaces
Smirks
Facial accords
of illuminated emotion
Gestures like darts
Expanded faces   like arc lamps
stick the photogenic arrow
in the cinematic screen

In the workshop   before the voltaic lights
muscles stretch
with eager expression
Bodies endure electrical currents
The arc of the eyebrows
backstitches emotions
The entire body has fins
and swims with complete clarity in the pond of light

Movie actors are emotional dynamometers
Turn the switch of the nerves
The logarithm of mobility
in the tactile relief of the close-up
Oh the plastic eloquence of Hayakawa!
Clarities
Dynamisms
Photogenie

Cross section of life
Contorted streets
Jumping figures   in the multiplied net
Contorted faces of passers-by
to the rhythm of bells and horns
All the floating features of reality
acquire a plastic character
Everyday gestures
are valuable and stand out
Subterranean life of detail
above the standard life

A throbbing trainyard   syncopated coming and going
A harbor   a balcony to distance
Hangars   nest of helixes
The streets flutter
among dynamic crowds
At kilometer 247   the snake

Mortal hazard
Reduce speed

Roads bound over obstacles
The artist's brush of the avenues
Underscores the city
The mechanic tamers
light sparks with the electric whip
on the skin of the inductees
Fights   boxing in the corners
Display of muscular lyricism

Inscrutable trajectories
Life
stencils its photogenic silhouettes
Psychic biology pressing the accelerator
Life of intuited hyperreality
uncovering the projection beam of Cinema
pierces a new dimension of plasticity
Aromatic animated painting

Pure film without anecdote
The contents go barefoot
Profundity
Harmonic photogenie
The living drama of celluloid
And retinal magnetism
agitates kinetic suggestions
People bare their faces
and things project their souls
Imagery
Clarities
Photogenie

Dziga Vertov: from *The Birth of Kino-Eye*

It arises as high-speed eye. Later on, the concept of kino-eye is expanded:

kino-eye as cinema-analysis,
kino-eye as the "theory of intervals,"
kino-eye as the theory of relativity on the screen, etc.

I abolish the usual sixteen frames per second. Together with rapid filming, animation filming and filming with a moving camera, etc. are considered ordinary filming techniques.

Kino-eye is understood as "that which the eye doesn't see,"
as the microscope and telescope of time,
as the negative of time,
as the possibility of seeing without limits and distances,
as the remote control of movie cameras,
as tele-eye,

as X-ray eye,
as "life caught unawares," etc. etc.
All these different formulations were mutually complementary since implied in kino-eye were:
all cinematic means,
all cinematic inventions,
all methods and means that might serve to reveal and show the truth.

Muriel Rukeyser: Movie

Spotlight her face   her face has no light in it
touch the cheek with light   inform the eyes
press meanings on those lips.
                                        See cities from the air,
fix a cloud in the sky, one bird in the bright air,
one perfect mechanical flower in her hair.

Make your young men ride over the mesquite plains   ;
produce our country on film   :   here are the flaming shrubs,
the Negroes put up their hands in Hallelujahs,
the young men balance at the penthouse door.
We focus on the screen   :   look   they tell us
you are a nation of similar whores   remember the Maine
remember you have a democracy of champagne —

And slowly the female face kisses the young man,
over his face the twelve-foot female head
the yard-long mouth enlarges and yawns
                                        The End
Here is a city   here the village grows
here are the rich men standing rows on rows,
but the crowd seeps behind the cowboy the lover the king,
past the constructed sets America rises
the beveled classic doorways   the alleys of trees are witness
America rises in a wave a mass
pushing away the rot.

The Director cries Cut!

hoarsely CUT and the people send pistons of force
crashing against the CUT! CUT! of the straw men.

Light is superfluous upon these eyes,
across our minds push new portents of strength
destroying the sets, the flat faces, the mock skies.

Franz Richard Behrens: from *The Asta Ode*

People have long since turned into machines
You, Asta, rip machines into people
Gutenberg was the first devil
The ocean of poison that bubbled out black letters
The daily lies of the rotary machine
A smile from Asta expiates the souls of millions of people
A tear from Asta turns millions of men religious
Asta is Astarte

Where the logic of language can't go on
Keep twitching your eye-corner sisterly clarity
Asta's eyes are deeper than all philosophy
The white silver-nights catch fire
at the black gold of your sorrowful eyes
You look at us and you don't see us
We're not afraid of the night, not afraid of shadows

You'll live another thirty years at the most
But the celluloid of your films is already lying among the stars
In a hundred years people will catch fever from them

Classic is a dirty word
Classic—nobody loves it
Nobody's talking about you
They see you loving

The beauty in art makes a new turn every year
You are the Express day-before-yesterday today in the next millennium
We're losing our breath

With every hour you're younger than all the young men

Why can't I give you five thousand new ideas each morning
Because 20 million people want to see in the evening
What you felt for them
Our thoughts can't expand fast enough
But you think with your heart
Our hurt starts dreaming

My wife is named Ilse, she has yellow hair
She says Asta is ugly
That's why all the men howl when she breaks their hearts
I say: Ilse, from today start dyeing your hair
Or I'll stop going to the movies with my baby

The director of the royal theater speaks solemnly
Of his inner relation to August Strindberg
He's freshly painted his stage
But Asta is the secret beckoning new young primeval forest
Not a minute too soon

Your act can't be described
It's not my fault
What miserable equipment language is

Asta
Your thirteen glances in one-and-a-half seconds
That's the cosmos fundamentally explained
I am one with the world and
With myself

Celluloid ages from fall to spring
The movie catalogue depends on the fashion of the warehouses
Don't you have another model
The model of the kind God is always called Asta

Asta is *not* an actress
Asta is *not* a person
Asta is a stammered note in a toy broken by a small child
The sound of a violin in a mirror

Why do my eyes hurt so much
Who has caressed them

I sit in the U.T. Friedrichstrasse
See your soul dancing on the white screen
And am melted into my brothers
over ten thousand kilometers away in
Hong Kong and Valparaiso
Who in the same minute see the same thing
In the Marble House the Tauntzien Girl sees you
Asta's shine glitters in Cologne on the Rhine
Through the motion picture houses Apollo and Agrippina
On the Graf-Adolf-Strasse in Düsseldorf
They built an Asta Nielsen Theater
At the Schauburg in Essen 2,000 miners are waiting in line
Not for bread, for Asta
Spring has returned to Vienna
On the Opernring Asta is given
In the Burg Movie Theater and in the Kärtner
A million, one seat in the Schottenring
Head to head Bellaria and Arkaden
Asta's poster opens the Prague Bios
In all the arcades of Wenceslas Square
In Sanssouci and in the Kinofon in Zagreb
We don't have time to be Greeks
In Athens all Astas are sitting
In Attikon and Pantheon
Shivering in the Splendid before the glamorous Astarte
Covent Garden and London's East End
Paris and the cinemas in Marseille
Brussels Boulevard du Nord, in Zurich the Oriental Palace
The sharply cut mouth and dark helmet of hair
Pulls in all the Mynheers and Meisjes of the Kalverstraat
In Asta-Amsterdam in the Rembrandt Theater
Copenhagen's Kinografen, Viktoria
Metropole Asta, Asta Regina
Asta's transparency banner makes the Odeon glow
From Roda Knarn to Norra Kvarn
Stockholm Piccadilly and Stockholm Palladium
The whole of the Kungsgatan breaks suddenly into applause

Asta

In New York Asta electrifies, astral
The flickering signals on the rooftops give off sparks
The News, the Tribune, and the American
Between the Evening Mail and the Morning Telegraph
Between the Morning Journal and the Evening Telegram
From the Times to the World
“The most fascinating star”— “The artistic standard”
“Asta’s superb acting”—“Without enthusiasm”
Your name is always in all the papers
In all the rented rooms of the Pennsylvania
From Broadway to Fifth Avenue
From the Woolworth Building to the Capitol
In Rialto and Rivoli
Criterion and Lerington
Flags and Asta’s picture sold out

In California the blooming pomegranate trees demonstrate
In Pasadena a celluloidaire wakes up
In Frisco the Times and the Examiner commit suicide
Hollywood explains Asta the antiangelas
In Greenland the Eskimo laughs
In Shandong the Chinaman cries
Melbourne sees Asta die
All the cinemas in the world sing the Asta aria
All the cinemas the Asta cavatina

NICOLÁS OLIVARI: Poem in the Form of a Cross for Barbara La Marr

The saliva of every anguish
oils your films
for the slippery throttling bow.
In a bourgeois magazine it says
you were dying of consumption.
And you just went and died, for inhaling all the sighs
and bad smells of the recesses
in theatres crawling with the microbes

of the slums,
where socialisms deliberate
before the start of your show.
Where each heart was a candle,
dripping big whimpering tears
over your endless legs, oh Barbara,
Barbara La Marr...!

Let me draw out your name in the bell
of your breathlessness: Bar... ba... ra...
because then it sounds like a tonic,
and two ideas in your head at once
might have been a crowd. I'm smoking
your name in a gargle of carbonic acid
watching you act...

Careful, Barbara... that sharp cheekbone
punctures the kisses in reel eight
of the movie,
when you unhook the corset of your virginities.
(I never untied your belt.)

I remember you as a virgin, and dead, Barbara!
a sweetly rheumatic romantic recollection,
mingled with the chewy mints
of the onanistic candy-seller.
Bar...ba... ra...
your name is a gargle
of aniseed
and the tumular dregs
of an "apris."

Your memory, how silly if romantic, how beautiful if a cheat!
hits me in the acrid wafts
from the cinematographic toilets
exhibiting the pornographic
graphics
of the new generations of kids,
who know more than we do by now
and who don't give a toss

about your death, your sainted death, your irrevocable death...

(The Israelite nose of the woman beside me
Is a plateresque snot-dispenser.)

Bar...ba... ra...
I wriggle my legs into the shelves
Of my neighbor's opulent flesh,
And your ill face on the screen
–Oh sweet woman who never speaks!–
is like
a municipal Virgin medallion.

Bar... ba... ra...
I gulp your name in the dirty auditorium
and sigh for the fuchsias
of your bad blood...

Barbara, Bar... ba... ra...
your name is a gargle
of tumular dregs...

PEDRO SALINAS: Movie Theater

1. LIGHT

At first there was nothing.
Not enough water for a fish.
Not the branch of a tree for the worn-out
wing of a bird.
Not the printed protocol for a duel.
Not the smile on the little girl's face.
At first there was nothing.
Just the white cloth
and on the white cloth, nothing . . .
An anxious gaze
clamored mutely, heavily,
in the air.
The right hand of God stirred

and pulled the lever . . .
The whole world sprang forth
with its primeval hop.
The rectangular cloth
squeezed it into rigid shape,
organized it brusquely
with two vertical lines,
with two horizontal lines.
Before our eyes chaos
took all the familiar forms:
the gentle swell of the hill,
the ribbon of the boulevards,
the hateful look of the face
of the melodrama villain,
and the tail of the dog
wagging for his master.
The one-eyed man felt
as though his glass eye
would break from the attack
of so many visions.
In the back a purist yelled out:
"And the words, what about the words?"
Then all the energies of the world,
powers achieved and lost,
the marvelous mechanisms
for running, for flying,
for loving, for hating,
began working.
The first day of creation—
humbled, impoverished, beaten,
retreated to a corner to cry.
But instinct was already spying
in the eyes of the woman
—hair flying in the wind—
and in the weaving and unraveling
of the fabric of feeling.
The first day of creation
rose from its corner
and came to look at the cloth:
in the right hand it was carrying

the first heart of man,
which was the last heart.

2. DARKNESS

The voltaic arc allows
its soul to spill over
and light, the mother of shadows,
darkens everything.
The white cloth has returned.
But now it is different; it has become
a magic cloth.
It has captured everything
between one thread and another of its weave,
where it hoards
the whole lost world.
Now all souls feel
their trajectories, as if they were stars
that had lived in flowering valleys on earth
and kissed human lips.
Back in extraterrestrial space
they keep spinning until the day
in which starry destiny returns them
to that pure world
of the white cloth.

RAMÓN GÓMEZ DE LA SERNA: Absurd Cocktails [from *Movieland*]

The principal bar in Movieland, the cheerful city of eternal week-ends, has high stools to which one must ascend with a ladder. The toper resembles the look-out man on the summit of his tower.

The queerest fellows get together in this bar and their conversation glitters like so many monocles.

But let's forget the chaps, with whom we are somewhat acquainted, and examine, instead, the cocktails they drink.

The cocktails imbibed in Movieland are terrible, like turpentine mixed with alcohols extracted from precious woods.

When served in tall glasses they look like stockings with varicolored stripes or like elongated purses made with polychrome beads. They hiss and crackle in the stomach like furious fireworks, causing varied degrees of ravage.

Some of them become striped panthers and it is appalling to see them coasting down the throat.

"What a swell cocktail you're drinking today!" a cinema lady tells a monopolizer of the delights.

Magnificent eggs laid by plump hens in the cinematographic poultry yard lend the glasses their yolks of melted sun and condensed morning.

The expert waiters trained in studio cafés seize the bottles by their necks, in clusters, to concoct the preparation ordered. They recognize the bottles on the shelves with a twinkle of their cocktail eyes and the bottles, clashing against each other, produce varied xylophonic impromptus.

"Give me an Antilles cocktail."

"And a Prairy cocktail for me."

"And for me a Charlot."

After a Charlot cocktail one imitates, whether one wants to or not, Charlie Chaplin; one is swayed by a fatally Chaplinesque Saint Vitus' dance, and with a little crooked cane one begins to hook the passer-by's neck, legs or arms.

"Waiter, a Mary Pickford cocktail."

This cocktail produces in one's soul the same effect as the provoking grace of its namesake. One begins from then on to live the mad existence of a love-at-first-sight lover and goes after the pretty actress' well manicured and very holy hand.

But quite often the composition of certain cocktails is never determined and the waiter scribbles, like a hurried reporter, a fantastic formula on an extremely long pad of paper:

"A glass of gin, (almost all cocktails begin the same way) a tablesoon of curaçao, a glass of vermouth Torino, a glass of whisky, two tablespoons of Alkermes, five drops of bitters, and a cherry for ornament. . . ."

It was like a prescription with the thirsty person's instruction "To be filled immediately" appended to it. Sometimes the flower from a lady's hat was used to ornament a cocktail.

Everybody in Movieland still recalls the great actor who used to play the role of a consumptive man in the films and how he drank a suicide cocktail which took a great deal of his time and talent to concoct. Every one saw him preparing the long poem of his ultimate cocktail till the day arrived when he climbed upon his stool, as one climbs to paradise. He handed the empty glass back to a waiter in a white jacket. Every one awaited impatiently for results looking up as if the consumptive actor had been one of those acrobats who walk on the cornices of skyscrapers, tickling thus the loins of Providence. Soon enough they saw the end: the pale man, caressing his long sea-weed beard, which seemed to have grown under stagnant water, smiled and like an aviator, fell down dead under his stool.

No one has ever again tried out that suicidal formula; it's the only alchemy prohibited in Movieland's principal bar, though every one is slowly committing suicide. Movie actors reel out the film of their own lives, shortening it now and then so as to make a perfect picture. They do not forget the good old cinema proverb to the effect that ten thousand feet of film must be wasted to get three thousand good ones. How they waste celluloid in trying to abridge their lives! . . .

Magnificent bar where one can drink the ideal cocktail!

ELECTRIC MAN

MIKHAIL SEMENKO: from *Cablegram Over the Ocean*

WORKERS OF ALL
COUNTRIES UNITE!

INTRODUCTION

SPARK OF THE FLAME OF REVOLUTION
THOUGHT-LIFE OVER THE OCEAN.
FLY OVER THE TRANSIENT WAVE
ON A DARK DAY OF THE ATLANTIC
TELEGRAPH CABLE TO A DISTANT LAND.
TO THE NOISE OF THE BARBED SKYSCRAPERS
SPARK-THOUGHT ATOM OF FIRE-FLAME
TNEDENCY OF THE REBELLION-FIGHT
I'M NOT LETTING YOU GO FARTHER
TO THE FINAL HEIGHT.
AND WHEN YOU SAY: IT'S HARD
I'LL RELEASE YOU TO EARTH
WHERE THE SWIFT CRUISES REVOLVE.
LISTEN!
(CIRCULATED)
MOSCOW-VLADIVOSTOK-HONOLULU
SAN FRANCISCO-CHICAGO-NEW YORK-LONDON-PARIS-
BERLIN-WARSAW-KIEV
(CIRCULATED)
WITH THE ELECTRICAL CURVE OF THE SPIRIT OF STEEL
I WRAP AROUND STONE IRON AND SMOKE
WITH THE WILL OF A PERSON, FREELY
THE STEEL BIRD WILL CAST A GLANCE
AT THE HORIZONS OF THE CITIES
THE SPARK WILL LIGHT THE HEART.
THE SOLID WILL IS MENDED
STREETS TUNNEELS AND HOUSES WITH STROKES
FROM CITY TO CITY PASSED
WAVE OF CALLS AND TRUMPETS OF THE NEW FIGHTERS.
THE SUN WILL LOOK DOWN ON THE RUIN.

MOSCOW

ELECTRO

WE'LL *RAISE A RUCKUS WITH
THE CHAINS OF
MOUNTAINS!*

ROME

BLOOD
L O
O O
O L
DOOLB

*BARRICADES
IN THE ROWS OF VERTEBRAE
ON THE BACKS!*

PARIS

AERO

Jaroslav Seifert: Electric Lyre

The stillness of the forest with blue skies,
when calyxes close under the weight of darkness
like at night weary human eyes,
the bubbling spring which through green grass
in its surface bears a reflection of stars
this magic my youth never knew.

Before I begin to sing in a frantic rush
about things that are and that I adore,
through the din of cars, bells, chimes, and wires,
before I begin to sing of the beauty of propellers,
advancing in the supple caress of clouds with force,
and thrusting the eagle, about to fly higher, back below,
about the machine's iron that burns with a luminous glow,
about the power of the crowd, which marches and annihilates,
and about my heart—like an autumn leaf
it flutters in the wind of daily events,
burning with love's flame, which is pink and clean;

before I begin to sing in this everyday din,
to you, Muse, I turn as it is ancient use,
come to me today and kindly shake my hand;

Muse, my modern Muse of our time,
who with a shy motion at night at eight unveils
the red curtain on the white screen of the cinema,
come to me today, the creative hour is arduous;

Muse, you who soars in amazing haste
over the helmet of the cyclist, who at forceful pace
sweeps boldly along the stadium's track.

Muse, you who guides the hand of the engineer,
as he draws a blueprint of an American skyscraper,
come to me today, waning is my vigor
and I take hold of my pen with fear;

proscribed Muse of the street,
you who witnessed when on the canvas of the circus
were painted beautiful pictures
in which a black man resists a tiger's clutches;

Muse, you who hovers over the head of the lion tamer,
when he cracks the whip and curbs fearless predators;

Muse, you who holds the hoop for the foolish clown,
for whose jokes the circus roars like the ocean;

Muse, you who knows how tenderly with your hands
to hold the reins to guide the unruly steed
upon whose head a white danseuse stands;

you good Muse, understand my perplexity,
I want to sing out all that stirs humanity
even my love's dream, and that one is sweet;—

the street is my electric lyre,
I walk in its midst, like strings above me are wires,
an iron song I want to intone for the city of stone,
may it be a modern song and today's sacred chorale;

therefore, Muse, come and give me strength,
and so that this song of mine may be fine,
bend your white brow over my lyre.

STANISŁAW MŁODOŻENIEC: Twentieth Century

it's sprung — summerrushes through autumness whitesnowing.
— CINEMATOGRAPH CINEMATOGRAPH
CINEMATOGRAPH . . .
nightingaling whisperofforests calorwavely are carusoing.
GRAMOPATHEPHONE GRAMOPATHEPHONE
GRAMOPATHEPHONE . . .
a kimonoeyed yokohama love you from europe
— RADIOTELEGRAM RADIOTELEGRAM

RADIOTELEGRAM . . .
espaniel with laydis parleying with sarmatian
ESPERANTISTO ESPERANTISTO
ESPERANTISTO . . .
I dewarsaw I comet I sunreach
AEROPLANE AEROPLANE . . .
I uniletter the babblomania.
— STENOGRAPHY . . .

GUILLERMO DE TORRE: Bric-a-brac

«J'ai des ommets éléctriques
au bout des nerfs.»
B. CENDRARS

VIBRATIONIST APOTHEOSIS
OH THE FILM OF OUR VERTICAL LIVES
THERE ARE REFRACTIONS OF NEGRO ART
AMBITION AVIONIC CREATOR
THE IMAGES HAVE A VARIEGATED
RUSSIAN BALLET RHYTHM
THE RISING STARS' PROPELLER SINGS IN THE NIGHT
LUNAR FOX-TROT IN THE ASTRAL CABARET
AND ITS SEX BLUE TRIANGLE
MENTAL ACROBATICS
WINGS MOTORS GOOD-BYES
IRRADIATION OF THE TRAVELING INSTINCTS
MADRID PARIS NEW YORK
ZURICH MOSCOW
DADA STATION
EIFFEL TOWER
POLAR WHARF
WHEN IS THE INAUGURATION
OF THE INTERPLANETARY RAILROAD?
HYPERMUSICAL JAZZ BANDS
GIVE RHYTHM TO THE PASSIONS
OF GOLD-DIGGING FEMALES

ADMIRE THIS CONJURER OF STARS
THE AVENUES PLOW AHEAD
        A TRIUMPHAL ARCH OF MIRRORS
MUTATION OF THE ARCTIC REGIONS
AND THE STREETCARS THAT STRING AIRPLANES TOGETHER
SHOTS ON THE MAGIC SCREEN
HERE IS CHARLIE CHAPLIN A DADA PRECURSOR
THE WANDERING STATUES
        CHEW CHEWING GUM
THE HORIZONS CONTORT THEMSELVES
PREPARE THE SAFETY NETS
SADISTIC LANTERNS
POLYPHONIZE THE BELLS
VIBRATE THE ANTENNAS
IT IS THE POLYMORPHOUS HOUR
AND I WILL LAND TOMORROW

BLAISE CENDRARS: Cracklings

The rainbowed dissonances of the Tower in its wireless telegraph
Noon
Midnight
One hears "shit" from every corner of the universe
Sparks
Chrome yellow
We are in contact
From every side ocean liners are approaching
Moving away
All the watches are set
And the clocks are ringing
Paris-Midi announces that a German professor has been eaten by cannibals in the
        Congo
Good work
L'Intransigeant this evening is publishing verses for postcards
It's idiotic when all the astrologers are robbing the stars
Our view is cut off
I question the sky
The Weather Bureau announces bad weather

There is no futurism
There is no simultaneity
Bodin has burned all the witches
There is nothing
There are no more horoscopes and we must work
I am restless
I'm going to leave on a trip
And I send this naked poem to my friend R . . .

Julian Przyboś: Roofs

Higher!

Intricate surfaces, pyramids of floors,
whirling surfaces, rising surfaces,
image-forming.
Turning
of massive space,
cramps
of cities being born.

In the living pathos of construction, in a geometrical dimension
the cubic soul of the capitals climbs, growing.
It growls with elevators of momentum, hangs on a jack,
it will jump! On radio towers it will liberate thought from matter.

From under the convulsive network of cables it spreads,
bursts with a fury of lines, the perpendicularity of the plummet,
with the triumph of height it stretches the vault's arch,
like delight it tickles boundlessness with a lightning rod's needle.

It hangs tops in clouds like enormous pendulums,
it sways—stops—settles in the forms of the angle-rafters.
Higher! With the bars of my arms I will push aside the throats of the streets,
set the tension with fingers like the brace of a rheostat.

The huge colossus of the city will flash like electricity,
will jump like a wall into the air and swell with space,
blow up all the squares, burst the structure of mass,
thrust out the circle of infinity like a cast-iron span.

Into the foundation,
the ferroconcrete of berths
topple
with the thrusts of the vortex!

Already
the speed
of the toothed cogs
of wheels
bores into the belly of factories.
It tears
down
along the grooves
of shafts.

With the whistle of vibrating drills,
the biting tooth of a pickaxe,
a spark,
with a mechanical head,
pressure: a million atmospheres,
strike
in the globe's central
nerve!

And again
with the simplicity of set forms
rise to the clouds, rhythmic apparatus.
Above the red workshops of foundries, above the undulating sheet-iron,
with the reverberation of six o'clock sirens of factories
flow into the steely dusk of the sky and the distances of stars brought nearer:
into the roofs.

LUCIANO FOLGORE: Electricity

Festoons of sun pulverizing the shadows.
Violet tentacles
ploughing the tar of the skies.
Crowns of garrulous sparks

glorying in the oblong dynamos.
Songs and roarings
of the wide motors.
Torrents of remote forces
in the vortex of the wheels.

The water airs out a sonorous mantle
above the mossy gestures of the stone,
and closes in the lightning wires
the sprayings of gold,
you, O flashing will,
O free Electricity.

On the bridges of the sea, in the arches of the sky,
your word springs out
curdled in the circle of the currents,
and the continents strain toward each other
longing for that which joins
from afar,
for that which in the crossing
has stolen the secrets
in the heart of man,
and in the crystal palaces of the sea.

Antennas lacking sails,
but sailing everywhere,
antennas risen up on top of the
invisible ship,
that knows no boundaries,
that would hurl to a sister ship
its destinies
beyond every light of a star.

Voices entangled in grey rectangles,
crowned
with robust ridges
the houses ringed with mantles,
voices obscure and diverse,
hurled like that into the metallic mystery,
which go through the unknown channel

to modulate a thought,
in the heart of a remote man.

Instruments of force, implements of work,
controlled by this will,
heavy haulage,
devouring with longing
space, time, and velocity,
O arm of the Electric
extended in every place,
to seize life, to transform it,
to knead it,
with rapid elements,
O powerful gears,
proud sons of the Electric
that grind up dream and matter,
I hear your whistling notes
assemble from every factory,
from every shipyard,
through the streets robust with sounds,
with the hymn of the heavy trucks,
and magnify
divinely
the will
that every marvel makes
free Electricity.

Kyn Taniya: ...IU IIIUUU IU...

DYING SQUEALS OF HOGS SLAUGHTERED IN CHICAGO ILLINOIS ROAR OF NIAGARA FALLS ON THE CANADIAN BORDER KREISLER REISLER D'ANNUNZIO FRANCE ETCETERA JAZZ BANDS FROM VIRGINIA AND TENNESSEE ERUPTION OF POPOCATÉPETL OVER VALLEY OF AMECAMECA AND BRITISH BATTLESHIPS ENTERING THE DARDANELLES NOCTURNAL MOAN OF THE EGYPTIAN SPHINX LLOYD GEORGE WILSON AND LENIN BELLOWS OF THE PLEIOSAUR DIPLODOCUS AS IT BATHES EACH AFTERNOON IN THE PESTILENT SWAMPS OF PATAGONIA GANDHI'S IMPRECATIONS IN BAGHDAD CACOPHONY OF BATTLEFIELDS AND OF SEVILLE'S SUN DRENCHED BULLRINGS GORGING ON THE GUTS AND BLOOD OF MAN AND BEAST BABE

RUTH JACK DEMPSEY AND AGONIZED CRIES OF VALIANT SOCCER PLAYERS WHO KICK EACH OTHER TO DEATH FOR THE SAKE OF A BALL

All that is now just a dollar.
One hundred cents will buy you a pair of electric ears
And you can go fishing for sounds that rock
on the radio waves' kilometric hammock.

. . . IU IIIIUUUU . . .

Manuel Maples Arce: T. S. F. (Radiophonic Poem)

Stars launch their programs
at nighttime, over silent cliffs.
Words,
forgotten,
are now lost
in the reverie of a reverse audion.
    Wireless Telephony
    like footsteps
    imprinted
    on an empty, dark garden.

The block,
like a mercury crescent,
has barked the time to the four horizons.
    Solitude
    is a balcony
    open onto night.
Where is the nest
of this mechanical song?
Memory
picks up wireless messages
and one or two frayed farewells
through sleepless antennas.

        Shipwrecked women
lost on the Atlantic

their cries for help
explode like flowers,
on the wires of international pentagrams.
My heart
drowns in the distance.
And now a "Jazz-Band"
from New York;
vice blossoms
and engines thrust
in synchronic seaports
Nuthouse of Hertz, Marconi, and Edison!
A phonetic brain shuffles
the perspectival accidents
of language.
Hallo!
            A golden star
            has fallen into the sea.

ESPECIAL PARA
"EL UNIVERSAL ILUSTRADO"

T. S. H.
(EL POEMA DE LA RADIOFONIA)

POR MANUEL MAPLES ARCE
DIBUJO DE BOLAÑOS CACHO

Sobre el despeñadero nocturno del silencio
las estrellas arrojan sus programas,
y en el audion inverso del ensueño,
se pierden las palabras
olvidadas.
            T. S. H.
            de los pasos
            hundidos
            en la sombra
            vacía de los jardines.
El reloj
de la luna mercurial
ha ladrado la hora a los cuatro horizontes.
            La soledad
            es un balcón
            abierto hacia la noche.
¿En dónde estará el nido
de esta canción mecánica?
Las antenas insomnes del recuerdo
recogen los mensajes
inalámbricos
de algún adiós deshilachado.

            Mujeres naufragadas
que equivocaron las direcciones
trasatlánticas;
y las voces
de auxilio
como flores
estallan en los hilos
de los pentagramas
internacionales.
El corazón
me ahoga en la distancia.
Ahora es el "Jazz-Band"
de Nueva York;
son los puertos sincrónicos
florecidos de vicio
y la propulsión de los motores.
Manicomio de Hertz, de Marconi, de Edison!
El cerebro fonético baraja
la perspectiva accidental
de los idiomas.
Hallo!
            Una estrella de oro
            ha caído en el mar.

JAUME MIRAVITLLES: The Paris Fair

T.S.F T.S.F. T.S.F.

Directions . . .

Stands, grey, quiet hangars
Skylights – Slavic eyes.
France, Japan, Russia, England, Italy, China
Manna of catalogues!
Indifference of classifications!

T.S.F T.S.F. T.S.F.

Chemical products — Wires — Glass cans, monachal
Organic chemistry formulas — delicate like spiderwebs
Phosgene — Explosion in Hamburg
Incombustible asbestos,
angel's wing
Chlorine — tubercular yellow
SO + H_2 — commanding ship of chemistry

T.S.F T.S.F. T.S.F.

Automobiles —
LATIL ROCHET SCHNEIDER
GOETCHEL – CAMBESSE DE LECACHE AND GLASSMANN

—CITROEN—
CITROEN — CITROEN

Precise wounds, far from human shame.
Light, wavy chassis
Morbid blasts like a temblor.

T.S.F T.S.F. T.S.F.

Electro-luminescence
Sen-
sual red. Aseptic
blue from a
Gessler tube.
Advertisements
— Advertisements —
Advertisements
Radiators
—mysterious or-
gans of
hypnotized symphonies.

T.
S.
F.

Machines thum-
ping
and sha-
king.
Black, blue, grey machines.
Balanced cylinders.
Eccentric joints.
A synchronism, rhythmic and nervous — like birds.
Children's balloons fly away — bubbles of life.

Alternating current — mysterious manipulation of waves.

«Tunner» canoes, slim shaped arches — like the eyebrows of «girls».

Silent vitrines full of surgical tools — the most beautiful submarine realm.

T. S. F.

T. S. F.

T. S. F.

T. S. F.

M a g i c

of glazed
windows!
Firmament
of kitchen utensils!
Classicism of tabletop marble!
Greedy electric chainsaw!
Cynicism of reflectors!
T.S.F — CITROEN
— ELECTRICITY —
FOUNDATION — P. T. T.
S. O. S.
SKY — PLANE — BUS.

The air feels the rubber.

In the mouth, a taste of the printing press.

Marina Tsvetayeva: Wires

Having picked through and thrown away everything,
(Especially a semaphore!)
The wildest of discords,
Of schools, of thaws . . . (an entire choir

For help!) Throwing out sleeves
Like banners . . .
                                    —Without shame!—
Lyrical wires
Of my high desire hum.

Telegraph pole! Can one choose anything
Shorter? As long as there is sky—
The invariable transmitter of feelings,
The tangible tidings of lips . . .

Know that as long as there is the heavenly firmament,
As long as there are dawns toward the border—
So clearly and everywhere
And protractedly I find you.

Through the epoch's troubled times,
Mounds of lies—from rigging to rigging
My unissued sighs,
My frantic passion . . .

Beyond telegrams (these ordinary and urgent
Stamped constancies!)
Through a spring of gutter drains
And the wire of space.

Mário de Andrade: Typewriter

BDGZ, Remington.
For all the letters we write.

Mechanical Echo
Of fleeting feelings typed into words.
Haste, much haste.
        Once someone stole my brother's typewriter
        This must go into verse too
        Because he couldn't afford to buy a new one.
Mechanical equality,
Love hate sadness . . .
And the ironical smiles
For all the letters we write . . .
Evil-doers and Presidents
Writing with the same letters . . .
                Equality
            Liberty
        Fraternity, period.
Unification of all hands . . .

        All loves beginning
        With L's that look just alike . . .
        The unfaithful husband,
        The unfaithful wife,
        Lovers children boyfriends and girlfriends . . .

        "Condolences."

        "Difficult situation
        Dear friend . . . (And the 50 bucks.)
                Enter my subscription
                adm. or oblg."
        And the handwritten signature.

Tap . . . Oops!
There goes the letter O.
No more astonishments
For souls amazed before life!
All anxieties disturbed!
I can no longer express my ecstasy
Before your flame-red hair!

The exclamation point in the interjection came out in the wrong place!

My emotion
Forgot to backspace.
So a line was left
Just like a falling teardrop
With a final stop next to it.

But I cried no tears, I just went "Oh!"
Before your flame-red hair.
The typewriter lied!
You know how cheerful I am
And how I like to kiss your morning eyes.
See you next Wednesday, the 11th.

I type two lower-case L's.
And then I sign by hand.

TYTUS CZYŻEWSKI

Hymn to the Machine of My Body

blood
stomach
they pulsate
coils

pepsin
heart
they beat
of my

blood
blood
strained
intestine

brain

cables to my veins
twisted wire conductor
to my heart
battery
have pity on me
my heart
dynamo-heart
electric lungs
magnetic diaphram
of the belly

one one one
my heart beats come
electric heart one

transmission belt
of my intestines
two two two

have pity on me
one two

the telephone of my brown
dynamo-brain
three three three
one two three
the machine of my body
function turns
live

Theo van Doesburg: X-Images

hey hey hey
have you experienced it physically
have you experienced it p h y s i c a l l y
have you experienced it **PHYSICALLY**

On

—space and
—time
past present future
the behindhereandthere
the hodgepodge of nothingness and phenomena

a small tattered almanac
read upside down

MY CLOCK'S STOPPED

Z a soggy cigarette butt on the
I **WHITE NAPKIN**
G
-
Z
A
G
moist brown
decay
SPIRIT
346 **RENTED AU TO MO BILE**

E
L
G trembling barren center
N
A
caricature of weight
uomo electrico

pink and gray and dark wine-brown

I'm finding pieces of the cosmos in my tea

NOTE: 0^n should be read as zero ^{n} ; "—space" and "—time" should be read as minus space and minus time.

FILLIA: Mechanical Sensuality

I SHE (thinness elegance originality)
Polydimensional hall of a BAR

LIGHT	COLOR	ODOR	NOISE
geometric	white	conic	circular
exact	blue	pungent	spiral
YELLOW	RED	HOT	

small table couch velvet — tactile visual olfactory supersenses
— I am a human automaton of metal (elastic-rubber steel glass varnished-wood)
waiters tamed penguins on the polar-frozen landscape of glasses and mirrors
faces women men, forms volumes dimensions space lucidity
her voice = transparent words because they let by the violet segments of noises

crystal feminine caress icy
cutting—prismatic shudder
from the impact of teeth
against a solid emptiness
WONDER yellow drink like the lamp

that reflects: I seem
to drink light
ta ta km barambarà
ta ta km barambarà

ssSsss (Jazz-Band) barambarà
la pum barambarà
AAAAAHH! LA PUM BARAMBARA

my mistress thrives in the surroundings: her face —
her bosom — her legs — in the near-far away eyes of the mates
reactions of my hand that touches her

3 seconds of pause: a décollèté lady enters carmine
makeup open fur coat (2 10 20 200 ladies)

WEIGHT ANXIETY OPPRESSION THE CRYSTALS
ARE REBELLING

splendoooooooor of yellow glass
shouuuuuuuuuts of reeeeed glass
crrrrrrrrrrruelty of grrrreeeen glass

agonyyyyyyyyyy of blue glass L L L L I G H T

one million two million three million of mirrors — crystal

Kurt Schwitters: Song of Miss Electricity

I am electric,
Watch out!
I scatter sparks,
Sometimes positive,
Sometimes negative.
Sometimes negative,
Sometimes positive,
I fascinate.

I'm on the move.
I whisper crackle,
I crackle whisper.
Short circuit ? ? ?
Hahahaha
I have
Contact!

Spirit of Technology (amidst)

Radio, Spark, Fire, Light,
Turbine, Machine, Steel, Cement,
Radio, Spark, Fire, Light,
Turbine, Machine, Concrete . . .

HAGIWARA KYOJIRO

Morning•Noon•Night•Robot

▲▲▲The rose has bloomed!
~~~~~~~~~~~~~~~~Scoop out the eyes!
Give birth to the white-robed **robot**!
==========A long **tunnel**!
In the lab, his intelligence failed to become a biscuit!
●
Put on the blue hat!
A **robot** blindfolded with a **belt**
On! Off! Walk! On! Off! Walk!
■
Stick the antennae into the poem!
I can hear the radio!
I sew up the body needles with needles and thread
It's become a sagging yellow Yankee bag
Almost ready
I'm going to fire this body as a bullet!
Fire!
~~~~~~~~~~~~~~~~

KENNETH FEARING: Cracked Record Blues

If you watch it long enough you can see the clock move,
If you try hard enough you can hold a little water in the palm of your hand,
If you listen once or twice you know it's not the needle, or the tune, but a crack in the record when sometimes a phonograph falters and repeats, and repeats, and repeats, and repeats—

And if you think about it long enough, long enough, long enough, long enough then everything is simple and you can understand the times,
You can see for yourself that the Hudson still flows, that the seasons change as ever, that love is always love,
Words still have a meaning, still clear and still the same;
You can count upon your fingers that two plus two still equals, still equals, still equals, still equals—
There is nothing in this world that should bother the mind.

Because the mind is a common sense affair filled with common sense answers to common sense facts,
It can add up, can add up, can add up, can add up earthquakes and subtract them from fires,
It can bisect an atom or analyze the planets—
All it has to do is to, do is to, do is to, do is to start at the beginning and continue to the end.

GEORGE OPPEN

Brain
All
Nuclei
Blinking
Kinetic
Electric sign
A
Pig
Dances
Painfully

Cannon
Rockets
A curve
Behind
This
Eye
No
Further brain;

The tendons
The slots
Pianola
Into slots
Sound
A room's
Back-
Ground

ROGELIO BUENDIA: X-Rays

The heart and the cavern . . .
Koch.
        The pale hue of apple.

_Λ___Λ___Λ___Λ___Λ___Λ_

They brought him to me coughing.
Fever.
        The heart through the screen.
Its keen hands
like two talons.
Cough.

        They brought him to me bleeding
like a wound.
Tic-tac-Tic-tac

The pulse galloped
and I ran after the pulse
in accelerated pursuit.

        The dislocated heart
below the screen.
Ozone.

                                        Luminosity
of an underwater grotto.

        The brain gone dippy
and the heart galloped.

Francis Picabia: Wireless Telegraphy

My illness listens to my heart
Closed button of lost joys
I mischievously wanted to be gloomy
In my pretty mama's arms
Memory of the blue sky
In which I would be able to curl up
You have to try to forget everything
The death pangs of the vertiginous world
Heroes who whirl around
the hideous waltzes of the war
In the enigmatic
and masked air.

HENRY PARLAND: from *The Ideals Clearance*

I dialed up
a heart
where I knew
there was no place
for me.

And the receiver sang.
Blood-heavy, steady
hammerbeats.

The Clearance Sale of Ideals
—you say it has already begun.
But I say:
Better cut the prices.

The agenda of the wide pants:
we should be
more clothes,
less human,
and the soul sewed into the cuffs.

Legs,
what do you know about legs?
you who think about skirts
when you pass the windows of the department store.
What do you know
about the legs
of the twentieth century?

The Big Morningafter:
when stars burp
and all archangels drink mineral water

we will gather at the café
listen
to the melodies of women's legs.

❖

The poster faces
let them yell
their: me! me!

—only when they start yelling:
we! we! we!
will we tear the scowl from their grimaces,
let the sun
paint human features on them.

❖

It's so cold today.
The breaths of the movie ads
prick like ice needles.
The shadows of the electrical wires
want to slit my throat.
Shivering the air has crept
behind the next street corner.

❖

The train
hammers its hard rhythm
in the blood.

Its song is not
about humans
or God or love.
It's about iron
and of iron.

❖

Darkness whirls
streaks of light, shadows
against people's windows:
are you in?

Can't you see?
the houses crouching for take-off,
the roads ready to rush up and
knock the streetlight-cops
to the ground.
Telephone wires dart to and fro
eager to catch stars!
are you in?

❖

Out in Tölö
a poster about hubcaps,
the year's best.
Every morning
while waiting for the trolley
I stand silent, pious
in front of its
proud, commanding:
b u y !

❖

That's not me.
That's a mouth exhaling smoke,
eyes that have seen too many people,
a brain jazzing wearily.

❖

By day
the movie theaters sleep
like crocodiles in the sun
and the streets are like beaches.

At night
they open their hungry jaws:
a row of teeth
is made up of faces, moods, attitudes.
They're like a gray mass
with bubbling eyes.

❖

It's a lie
that the movies are art
(what isn't art?)
The movies are a religion
which out of reality
makes a pair of beautiful legs
we can see
but not touch.

Gasoline

I am a great God
my price is 3.40 a liter
and people kill each other
for my sake.

Wheee!
Fire kisses me
and the iron quakes: life!
Now
I know
why I dreamt so long
underground.

Youth:
hunger
or a weariness that
dances?

MARCEL SAUVAGE: Les Halles-Saint-Eustache [from *Bus Trip*]

I

The cut gardens
produce the sun in the baskets

Forget the old Christmas carols
sing a^2 $x^2 + x$
all the motors go wild in the drunkenness of life
the cars will lick the hands
the headless tramways the locomotives
The fleshy shrouds
will be all around your naked front
crows around the cathedrals

Rail handles along the horizon
Your voice will erect Eiffel towers
and before her
                    will turn the unknown doors

The future is a mechanical icon
you will die scattered by your machines

Behold the end of the word in dashes of clay

II – FLOWERBEDS OF THE DAWN

The evening flowers
sisters of the stars
in the city where the sky frolics
in a peacock coat
trembling

The hours make the world turn

. . . As the bars close
the hours are answered
The dawn is a staggering mongrel
and the violins drop off to sleep

. . . the gasman
one by one
picks the morning's flowers
sisters of the faded stars
and evening flowers

Céline Arnauld: Enigma Figures

Not mysterious enough at the wheel of your car
You'll never find the key to
D back-to-front enigma on bus M
Hung up by a star the overturned ladder
Bicycle rambling spectacles nobly put back on
Most certainly not Dada enough it will come
Sitting at the side of the roads will-o'-the wisp
On the laugh of childish delight
And the mocking railway
        shows its new teeth
                to the last train

Alfredo Mario Ferreiro: Moving Train

Toco-tócoto
trán trán.
Toco-tócoto
trán trán.
Racatrácata,   paf-paf.

  Chucuchúcuchu
Chás-chás,
chucuchúuchu
cháschás.
Tacatrácata, chuchú
tacatrácata, chuchú.

Chucuchúcuchu
chás-chás,
racatrácata,   paf-paf.

Búúúúúúúúúúúúúúúúúúúúúúúúúúú

Chiquichíquichiquichi
chiquichíqu chiquichi
chiquichíquichiquichi
chiquichíquichiquichi . . . .

Mikhail Semenko: City

Oste ste
bi bo
bu
driver-people
trolleys-people
automobilebile
runningtraffic trafficruns
busyruns
berceus merry
go
rounds
Lilli
putians giant
smoke steal
burn
puff
puffing
puffingsadness
smoke blue
black smo
ke
they release
BENZINE
fumes live
fumes beg

love
cough
givelife
lifetraffic
lifebe
nzine
auto
tram.

Herbert Behrens-Hangeler

O B I B I

bromocarnOL
gargarisnOL
buccocystOL
polygonal
bituminOL
hydravasOL
chinoterpOL
uvacystOL
sonatOL
hermidOL
legumOL
hydosOL
glitzonOL
narsosOL
vendOL
tilkOL
hartOL
brikOL
pOL

Juan Marín: Mechanical

Oh steel poem embracing the new world
cry of the power plant's lungs
your rhymes are beveled axes
glowing dynamic will
like giant biceps fallen
from a humanized Mars
shock of centuries
irons lights pulleys
leitmotif of deep radio waves
song of delirious dynamos
sparks are the passionate kisses
the blue blowfly of those propellers
pecking the white walls
platinum lathes saws
that wipe out hope
sweet song of the teeth
cleaves the white metals
hymn of gray eyed mechanics
odor of smoke and fuel
angular ports and geometric cities
free plasticism of a new aesthetic
harmonic line of steel bridges
metal fermentation of raw materials
shavings of coiled valves
cubic factory
men sleep in your breast
disjecta
for your duralumin refrains
pulverizer of romanticism
mother of the new dreams
your breath of benzol and gasoline
shakes the rods
of new hearts in the world
oh newborn goddess
jazz-band convulsions of iron
woke up the streets of America
and ventilated decadent Europe

new sense of the Universe
our poem of steel
mechanical song
awaiting a tool and a tongue
to express your swollen soul's
immense alarm
awaiting the poet titan
super-product of an epoch
that gathers your glorious verse
gurgle of submarines and buzz of airplanes
grinding of boilers
subtle vibration of dynamometers
radiotelegraph caresses
no one has written verse more divine
than one that turns a generator belt
you type into an engine
that like an electric monster
in the silent nights
runs its lyrical shiver
for undaunted wires
occult philosophy of unknown alchemy
MAN must rise up
to strip you bare
reveal your secrets
pour your heart into your retort
burn it in your furnace
and write new lyrics
of straight lines
those of a fuselage
those of high antennas
and infinitely rapid wheel
that push you
that drag you
loosen your mane in the electric wind
for the invisible cosmic plan.

Stephan Roll: Metalloid

We infuse the atom with pressure:

dynamic
constructive elastics
lungs of cities
bronze vertebrates
splintered muscles of platinum
we are the day's aorta
tomorrow others will come
athletes
we'll scavenge geological strata
with metallic zeal
vibrating
over latitudes
arterial magnet
blood
lightning quick
incandescent
breathing
life ripped from busted spindles
steel
supple uncontested
synthesis in cities to come
atmospheric centimeter
etc. etc.

Antonio Cubero: The Electric-Man

Dynamo-man.
Radiant point.
Right angles.
Fractions.
Does the moon look to you
like a trinket from the market?

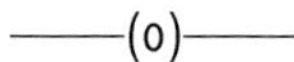

Electric-Man.
Bell-hoarder?
The green Bells of blue sound.
Do you need permission from an Airplane
to carry you on its wings?

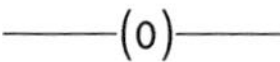

In your life.
Oh mortal!
Movement is inspiration.
Battery-man.
Meditation like flight.

——(o)——

Your nerves like a lit chandelier.
Sad with their Infinitesimal yearning.
They want to run run run
guided by the throbbing.

——(o)——

You are the Numeration.

——(o)——

Have you done away with the Grave?
You will die at the foot of your Muse.
You will play a melody.
With a single note—in the waning
light—of an electrical cable.

Hagiwara Kyojiro

● Armored Coil

Amid the leaping bustle of the modern city
I see a giant mechanical armored coil
Spouting out moody smoke
A charmless and dull-witted fellow

He gives out a military shout
Ignorant of the flavors, colors, and delicate textures
That give the city its high taste
He spouts out strong yellow smoke
Soiling the city, getting angry
Oppressing the fearful heart

He follows neither the bullet nor the heart of the crowd
Possessing the reddest, most barbarian heart
Tenaciously, indifferently
Resisting the throng's commercial world
A powerful, powerful emergence, towards chaos

Ah! That charmless fellow, shrugging his broad shoulders
At fine, oversensitive Female Civilization
Neither joy nor sadness
Appears on his ugly face

Still, as if about to cry,
The flutter of his obstinate heart!
His passion!
His strength!
His destruction!
His creation!
His strong, true motion!
The fight against Civilization!
Ah! Behold! Now, I am
A giant mechanical armored coil!
Amid the leaping bustle of the modern city

GONZALO DE ALVAR: Hertz-Spatial Poem

The ship blends into the water without waves
The streamers wave their skeletons aloft
As long as the man with big ears
hears the train in the distance
The stones in the lake
form concentric circles

(((((AS THEY SPREAD)))))

and thoughts wrapped up in them are swept along.

VICENTE HUIDOBRO: Telephone

TELEPHONE WIRES
PATH OF WORDS

And in the night
The moon's violin

A VOICE

A mountain
rose up in front of me
What waits in back of me
is looking for the right road

TWO PLACES
TWO EARS

A long way to go

Words
all the length of your hair
One of them fell in the water below

HELLO

HELLO

Guilherme de Almeida: Telephone

Hello! It's me . . .
  Good morning!
    I'm all right; how about you?
You've read my poem? Yes?
  Indiscreet? But why?
People will know? But that is just
what I want . . .
  Why not? I want everyone
to envy me.
  But I do want them
to know about it all!
  Of course: where love is concerned
indiscretion means vanity . . .
    I wouldn't
dare? In front of everyone? You bet
I would! I wouldn't say it? Want to hear me
  say it? With pleasure . . .
Listen!
  I can't, I'm not alone here, I'd be overheard . . .

Pedro Olmedo Zurita: The Telephone

  Rrin, rrinn, rrrrrin!
Electric convulsion
dreams in the tone of the phone.
From end to the end of the beautiful city
metallic contact
brings on the power.
  Hello, hello!
  Now the articulated vibrations
put two souls in touch
from end to the end of the beautiful city.
Through the receiver
comes a nightmare voice
a mediumistic voice

a stellar voice
a spirit voice
like a pale flame of alcohol,
a fatuous fire of voice.
The spirit passes through a wire,
from end to the end of the beautiful city.
Sound, electricity, spirit.
Edison. Light. God.

VASILY KAMENSKY: Telephone

T E L E **P H** O NE— *No* 2 V —*128*

RrRrRRRRR——————RRr
Who are *who* I --- **38** *and* 5
AND *aTTen*tivE *sp* --- *ff*
wh--**at**-in-4 1 5—**07**-14-9

and 03--*67*—and the Street **N**oise

SPring *TIME*

far **a**way —

are the farms

and their
quiet

please don't—
the iron is being transported
14 --092---- M U S I C

and cars

A P R O C E S S i o N

0 I understAnd I already read on the 27th
6175 meters
HAPPY
HAMLETS
HANG
THEIR PADDLES
the horizons are calling where are you WHE

ALFREDO MARIO FERREIRO: Radio-Telephone (poem for sounds)

My eardrum is a parallel wire.
Lying up there on the roof
is a snare of sticks.

In it I sense the voice of the world.
The world sings to me.
I am a powerful ruler
who blots out singers,
scatters orchestras,
or reads the "final hour"
with a spin of the dial.

The lamps chuckle quietly with white light
to the monologue's jokes.

I'm in my room. (2 x 2)
And I'm the apex of all
sonic activities.

My eardrum is up there.
It's a Paraguayan hammock
rocking in the air.

Frightening speed
brings me the words.

A consumptive talks to me from Brazil.
The earth turns through the radio waves
with a thrill of horror.

Henry Parland

Funny:
First she called him
(everyday).
Then he called her
(everyday).
Finally
the phone rang
by itself.

◈ PORTS OF CALL ◈

BRANKO VE POLJANSKI

INdiaNA maVERA čINGtaU

bengalsKa revolucionargA PesmA od V. Poljanskoga

DAdA → dada

←

RAJMAHAVANA

RAJMAHAVITA

SAHURA HANAMAVERA

VENTAMAVERA BOMBAJ

VENTAMAVERA BENARES

TIGRIS

TIGRIS

TIGRIS

ČINGTAU HAVAJA HANARES

MAHAJA TAMARION

MAHAJA HAVIDIJA

MAHAJA SANKARA

SANKARA

SANKARA

INDIANAMAURAPRAKRITI

INDIANA MAVERA SANSURPERITI

INDIANA MAHAJA VANTAMAHEJA

VANTAMAHEJA

VANTAMAHEJA

HEJO SAMARA UNRAGA

MAHERA

HEJO MAHERA UNRAGA

SAMARA

RIKORO MANRADA PANRUGA
RIKORO PANRUGA MANRADA
PANRUGA
MAHERA
RATAHITA
INDIANA VANTAMAHEJA
INDIANA VANTAMAHEJA
HAVIDIJA

PHILIPPE SOUPAULT: Horizon

for Tristan Tzara

The city came into my room
trees disappeared
and the night fastened on to my fingers
Houses turned into ocean liners
and I heard the rising sounds of the sea
in two days we'll be in the Congo
I've crossed the Equator and the Tropic of Capricorn
I know there are countless hills
Notre Dame blocks out Gaurisankar and the northern lights
night falls drop by drop
I bide my time

Bring me another lemonade and a last cigarette
I'm going back to Paris

BRANKO VE POLJANSKI: Journey to Brazil

Still under the sway of the first law of static
Panic in the dark
Canadian Pacific spans America
Gonorrhea stinks
Aliagic thinks, worms are shrewd animals.
Belgrade in Zurich

7.77
The cubes of time split vertically
That's how everything lines up
I am
I'm thinking about going over the ocean
I have a fear of scorpions
Orchestration makes me happy
A street full of thunder smells of lightning.
The seals have not accepted reason
Drastic curses of the new era's pioneers
Rain down on the cathedrals.
Today I stroke a dame's foot
Through silk stockings.
I sense all beauty in the radio poems
of Zenitism.
I turn back from Gaurisankar
To resume my trip to Brazil in my room.

Edouard Roditi: Seance

The stranger walks into the dark room where the two men sit at the table and talk of travel. The stranger joins in the conversation, saying: "I have also traveled" and the two men look up and seem surprised at his sudden appearance. In the corners of the ceiling there is a sound of very swift wings, a muttering of motors, and a chattering of thin voices. The stranger disappears. His voice is heard first in this corner, then in that, until it fades away somewhere near the open window. Where the stranger stood the two men find a railway ticket to an unknown destination.

Luis Cardoza y Aragón: from *Maelstrom*

Life revolts. Multitude. Springs. Fairs. Cities. Hangars. Circuses. Department stores. Railway stations. Boats. Trains:

The arms of the road
(steel and parallel)
will flutter my dream

with tales of energy
and tales of action.

Temptation of foreign lands,
craving for adventures
pounce on my chest—crazy colts—
a Saint Elmo's fire in my fingertips,
my nerves running high tension.

The hoot of a panting train,
a function of my emotional movie,
chomping on an unlit cigarette,
shakes my heart like a propeller
and I feel myself rise.
Oh life, sweet and cruel!
always does the same thing:
why do all destinations
end up in the opposite direction?
The thrilling woman
(person, thing or animal)
has just reached the station
where I'm about to depart.

MARCEL PROUST: from *Within a Budding Grove*

Sunrise is a necessary concomitant of long railway journeys, just as are hard-boiled eggs, illustrated papers, packs of cards, rivers upon which boats strain but make no progress. At a certain moment, when I was counting over the thoughts that had filled my mind during the preceding minutes, so as to discover whether I had just been asleep or not (and when the very uncertainty which made me ask myself the question was about to furnish me with an affirmative answer), in the pale square of the window, above a small black wood, I saw some ragged clouds whose fleecy edges were of a fixed, dead pink, not liable to change, like the color that dyes the feathers of a wing that has assimilated it or a pastel on which it has been deposited by the artist's whim. But I felt that, unlike them, this color was neither inertia nor caprice, but necessity and life. Presently there gathered behind it reserves of light. It brightened; the sky turned to a glowing pink which I strove, gluing my eyes to the window, to see more clearly, for I felt that it was related somehow to the most intimate life of Nature, but, the course of the line altering, the train turned, the morning scene gave place in the frame of the window to a nocturnal village, its roofs still blue with moonlight, its pond encrusted with the opalescent sheen of night, beneath a firmament still spangled with all its stars, and I was lamenting the loss of my strip of pink sky when I caught sight of it anew, but red this time, in the opposite window which it left at a second bend in the line; so that I spent my time running from one window to another to reassemble, to collect on a single canvas the intermittent, antipodean fragments of my fine, scarlet, ever-changing morning, and to obtain a comprehensive view and a continuous picture of it.

JULIETTE ROCHE: Toulon—Cannes

She says: "I love elsewhere"..... "Wanderlust"..... other things..... that are like it..... in several languages.....

(Why in all the dining cars is she always sitting on the left?)

Bénédictine, red letters on black backgrounds.....

Red letters on gray backgrounds, black boat—Green waves—Wreaths of smoke.

Nord-Deutsche Lloyd
Hamburg-America Linie

(The leather armchairs in the smoking rooms of the transatlantic liners are always the same color as her hair.)

Hôtel Héliopolis

Cairo looks too much like Geneva—
blue, white and green, blue, white and green, blue white and green ......

(She must enter the scene with that special rolling of her skirt around her knees and break away in the fourth act, on a terrace, beside a lake, while someone in the wings sings "Sole MIO".....

Nevertheless the arrangement of her veil, her slightly protruding jaw and the name of her little dog reveal rather literary gifts.....

Rome Elysée Palace
400 Rooms open year-round.

It's in Rome, certainly, that she understood..... "Vanity of Vanities".... Florence on the contrary made her feel like a very 16th-century soul, audacious sumptuous and ferocious..... and one day in the Campo Santo in Pisa, alone amidst the smell of warm grasses and the rustling of insects, she lived through all the bitternesses of dying....

(Yellow cover. Second thousand—at Ollendorff's or Calmann Lévy's).

Compagnie Internationale des Wagons-Lits

She read Chinese poets in Swiss hotels and Russian novels in Spanish trains.....

With each shake of the train a slight trembling builds up around her cheekbones and falls to the corners of her lips, all along her cheeks.....

Hotel Astoria completely renovated

New Astoria, Victoria, Windsor..... interminable hallways all cluttered with her trunks and her perfume — Lucid departures — Sleeping cars to such long vibrations..... and the cold awakening in the station in the morning — For her will remain.....

Moutarde Grey-Poupon — Champagne Montebello

Maybe in more brutal cities..... Melbourne..... San Francisco.....

red letters on black ground **Bénédictine** —
gray backgrounds, red letters, black boat, green water, wreaths of smoke

Nord-Deutsche Lloyd
Hamburg-America Linie.....

Jaroslav Seifert: Harbor

ANCHOR still one beautiful hope at the end
a dead oyster is ascending toward the ship

HELMSMAN in the evening to walk about Marseille
on the shoes still the Singapore dirt

SHIP in the rigging of the mast between lanterns
a parrot and a monkey thought they were at home

NIGHT a soldier and a girl remained at the café alone
the bottle cast the shadow of Emperor Napoleon

SHIP'S PROPELLER when to the dance everyone had gone
from the deep water lilies to the surface would float

CRANES to sleep grotesque giraffes in long files moved on
among palm trees of a land unknown

Valery Larbaud: Night in the Port

My face *sprayed* with Portugal
(Oh, to live in this scent of oranges in cool mist!)
Kneeling on the couch in the darkened cabin
—I've turned off the buttons of the electric lights—
Through a clear round porthole that cuts through the night
I spy the city.
This is really it, really it. I recognize
The avenue of casinos and dazzling cafés,
Its perspective of lighted globes, white
Through the hanging curtains of somber palms.
Here are the shining façades of immense hotels,
Restaurants beaming onto the sidewalks, beneath arcades,
And the gilded grilles of the Residence gardens.
I still know every corner of this African city.
Here's the Post Office, and South Station, and I also know
The way I'd go from the docks
To such and such a shop, hotel or theater,
And all of it at the edge of this blue rolling of peaceful water
Where the reflections of the lights of the yacht are shimmering . . .
Several sunny months of my life are still here
(Just as I remembered them, in London)
Here again, and real, in front of me, now,
Like a big boxful of toys on the bed of a sick child . . .
And once again I'd see people that I knew
And didn't like; who mean less to me in fact
Than the palms and fountains of the city,
These people who never travel, but who stay

Near their excrement, without ever being bored,
I'd see their once-forgotten faces again, and them
Continuing their narrow lives, with their ideas and their affairs
As if they had stopped living when I left . . .
No, I'll not set foot on land, and tomorrow
At daybreak the *Jaba* will weigh anchor.
Until then I'll pass the night with my past,
Near my past seen through a hole
As in the dioramas at the fairs.

JOAN SALVAT-PAPASSEIT: Drama in the Port

GULP OF OCEAN
IN THE NIGHT

(ADORNED WITH MAN-MADE BRILLIANCE

ARC-VOLTAIC)

AT MY FEET
WHITE
GREEN
RED LIGHTS

THE MASCULINE **OCEANLINER**

SCREAMING

THE SIRENS DON'T KNOW IT
BUT SCREECH

THE EMIGRANTS PRESS FORWARD

I PASS NEAR THE DREDGE {DREDGE}
THAT IS DARK AND

THE BUOY GROWS ANXIOUS

S E L

W L

NOW THE WAVES SING THEIR DESIRE TO ENGULF

THE THUNDER IS IN THE DISTANCE
SIGH OF THE SHADOWS
I SEE MYSELF ON THE HORIZON

OUTSIDE THE HARBOR THE SEAGULLS REST

ARMANDO MAZZA: Oceanliner

Adieu Cherbourg
six days of sailing
I am drowning in the liquid air
the horizon's finish-line never reached
the sky's indigo soaked in the water
the radio-antenna bejeweled with dew

polarized desires Paris — New York

the northwest wind unwinds cool scarves

the ship's wake leaves shivering tongues of flame

Moulin Rouge
Juliette
dew-filled eyes
eyelashes
antimony white lead carmine
flashes of light iridium bracelets
breaking off
studding the sky butterflies flit with short gauze skirts
arm's mimo-tetanic insertion
the orchestra's hysterical excitement
verses
chorusing rabble syncopated

sparkling musty with joy
sly lustful glances

a bachelor room Passage de Clichy 10
cigarettes-cigarettes-cigarettes
extinguishing-lighting-lighting-extinguishing
je t'aime
incredulous chloral
oh your glowing conch poker of carnal torches which smells of the sea
je t'aime
corrosive smile
threads of dancing smoke
the smoke dissolves in the air like anise in water
it's suffocating in here   open the windows

gasping for breath
moaning
salivary mucilage in devoured mouths

my tongue melting with pleasure like chocolate in the warmth of your mouth
filtered by the Venetian blinds slices of the dawning sun dissect your nudity
the smoking candelabra slowly fizzes out

Blaise Cendrars: from *The Formosa*

Moonlight

The boat rocking and rocking
The moon the moon makes rings in the water
In the sky it's the mast that makes circles
Pointing out each and every star
A girl from Argentina leaning over the rail
Dreams of Paris staring at lighthouses dotting the coastline of France
Dreams of Paris she barely knows already bathed in regret
These lights revolving steady double colored blinking remind her of ones she saw
    from her hotel window on the Boulevards promising a prompt return
She dreams she'll soon return to France to live in Paris
The noise of my typewriter blots out the end of her dream

My beautiful typewriter that rings at the end of each line and is quick as jazz
My beautiful typewriter that keeps me from dreaming starboard or port
And puts me on the track of an idea to the end
My idea

Ocean Letter

The ocean letter is not a new poetic genre
It's a practical message with decreasing rates and a lot cheaper than a radiogram
It's frequently used on board to wrap up business left dangling on shore and to give final instructions
It's also a sentimental messenger who shows up to say hi between ports of call as distant as Leixoës and Dakar when I'm six days out so who'd expect to hear from me
I'll use it again crossing the South Atlantic from Dakar to Rio de Janeiro sending messages backward since that's the only direction they go
The ocean letter wasn't invented for making poems
But when you travel when you do business on board when you send ocean letters
You're writing poetry

Cabin 6

I'm in it
I should live here for good
There's no merit staying cooped up working in here
Besides I'm not working I put down whatever comes into my head
No not absolutely everything
Since lots of things come to mind but don't make it into the cabin
I live in a draft the porthole wide open the fan humming
I don't read a thing

Guillaume Apollinaire

Ocean-Letter

nose in the air
I cross the city
and I cut it in 2

I was on the banks of the Rhine when you left for Mexico
Your voice reaches me in spite of the huge distance
Seedy-looking people on the pier at Vera Cruz

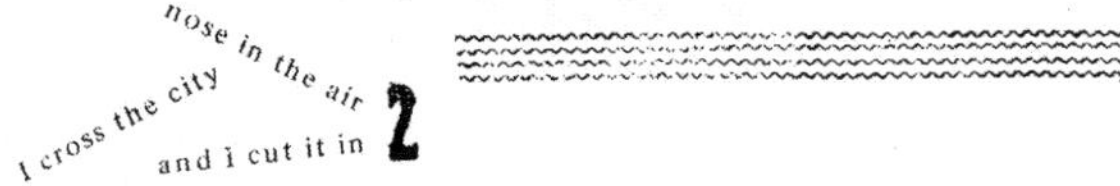

Juan Aldama

Since the travelers on the *Espagne* are supposed
to go to Coatzacoalcos in order to embark
I send you this card today instead

Correos
Mexico
4 centavos

YPIRANGA

REPUBLICA MEXICANA
TARJETA POSTAL

11 45
20 - 5
14

Rue des Batignolles

of profiting by the Vera Cruz mails which aren't dependable
Everything is quiet here and we are awaiting events.

U. S. Postage
2 cents 2

Long live the Re pub lic
Nuts to Mr. Zun
Sto p driv er
Long li ve the King
Boo the peasant
On the left bank in front of Iéna bridge
I have seen thousands of keys
Evviva il Papa
Down with priests
Shut up my old pad
Jac ques it was de li cious
Tu ni sia you're starting a news paper
not if you have a mus tache

T

S

F

Bonjour
Anomo
Anora

YOU WILL NEVER REALLY KNOW
THE

Mayas

Do you remember the earthquake between 1885 and 1890
people slept in tents for more than a month

HELLO MY BROTHER ALBERT in Mexico

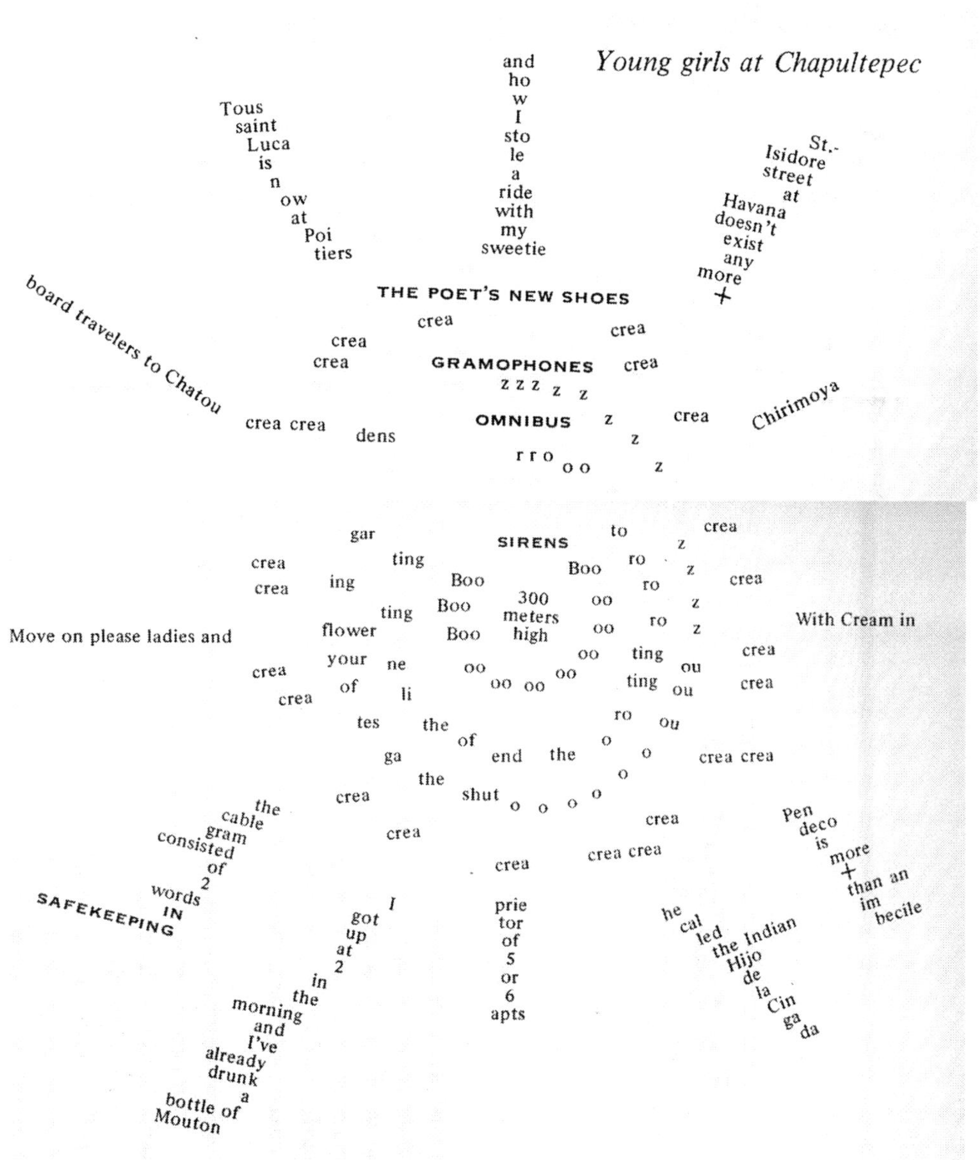

Young girls at Chapultepec
and how I stole a ride with my sweetie
Tous saint Luca is now at Poitiers
St.-Isidore street at Havana doesn't exist any more +
board travelers to Chatou
THE POET'S NEW SHOES
crea crea crea crea crea
GRAMOPHONES
z z z z z
OMNIBUS
crea crea
dens
crea
Chirimoya
rro oo
SIRENS
Boo Boo Boo Boo
300 meters high
Move on please ladies and
With Cream in
the cablegram consisted of 2 words
IN SAFEKEEPING
I got up at 2 in the morning and I've already drunk a bottle of Mouton
prietor of 5 or 6 apts
he called the Indian Hijo de la Cingada
Pen deco is more + than an imbecile

Vicente Huidobro: Ocean or Dancing

The ocean's jazz-band
This boat dances badly and I lose my step

Over there
The sky and the sea merge
Too bad if the sky is blue and fish drown

Disembarking the port wobbles
Everywhere I go I keep this cadence

I embrace your hands that unravel the days
Your little hands always going away
Like the boats love hairdo of the horizon

The port recoils
last song
My throat freezes up
your fingers too

And from afar you hold your heart
As one holds a flower
But the rhythm of your breast is in the sea
And the waves are hot with your heartbeat

Love love of the young swimmer
Harpist between the waves

The horizon comes undone

Foam that's born
foam that dies
Foam that dances on the hours

The sea is tired of fluttering its hankies
At boats as they drift away

The night as usual does its duty

Moon a glass of milk
Our stars look after themselves
The Southern ocean between two trees
So many wreaths in the water
The beloved ocean under marble

You will drink drop by drop the warm moonlight
This mist that rises above the tides
Slowly drags its boat
Poem of the evening, children's plaything

The boats move away like your hands

Otto Gelsted: The Show Boat

The ship heads straight into the harbor
at shadowy dusk.
Her megaphone bellows salute to the city,
the electric searchlights
level their five-splintered beams
up in the air like a comet's tail
and scrawl in firescript on the clouds:
BUY A FORD

And the ship is transformed
to a garish glitter of lights from end to end;
airmen bombard her with Bengal-lights;
the funnel shaped like a bottle of Tuborg,
and the daubed sides with their colossal figures and lettering like a fantastic camouflage,
the Kodak girl, Johnnie Walker, and the rest of them,
alternate in dazzling colors
that are mirrored in the water . . .
till the ship is riding, now in a green abyss,
now in a blaze of yellow flickering flame,
now in a pool of blood.

And on board—what is there not on board?

Here are exhibits of painting and cooking,
French cuisine and cubism and chemical recipes;
here is the Social Exhibition showing society in longitude,
from the proletarian eaten up by lice in a dustbin
to the *toilette de luxe* of the millionaire.

Here are clinics for make-up and bureaus for suicide,
which men in despair can consult for a suitable fee;
here are displayed the latest stunts of the doctor's art,
men changed into women and women into men;
here is the ship herself with all that's in vogue:
tennis courts and swimming pools, the church and the newspaper office
(that prints you the whole Bible in installments);
here is the giant gyroscope,
whose 180,000 revolutions to the minute
neutralize all motion
and safeguard the passengers from seasickness.

And here finally are the passengers—
all of them symbols of sensation and publicity.
The 136-year-old patriarch from Volhynia,
who was with Napoleon at Moscow,
the 6-year-old chess genius, Sammi Meyer, from Poland,
and the Siamese Twins. . . .
Then, of course, an adequate selection
of the world war's bankrupt monarchs and celebrities,
plus—among the crew and the galley staff—
the inevitable Russian grand dukes
and opera queens from Vienna.

And, in the first class,
film stars:
the Hero from the Wild West
(with Odol smile),
the World Comedian
(with Odol smile)
and the Sunbathing Beauty
(Odol smile).

But away up the harbor

sits a man in a shanty
in front of a table with contraptions and clock dials.
He has a shag-pipe in his mouth
and looks like an ordinary blond Danish student.
He is waiting for the moment
when the ship comes right over the spot.
Then he will press a button.

It is not fire from heaven he is waiting for;
no, he himself will raise fire from the abyss.
And in the midst of the popular shimmy,
"Shake me till I shiver,"
while a man of fire strides forth on the show boat
and proclaims a new truth to all mankind—
OMA IS BEST—
a crash is heard . . .

LUIS CARDOZA Y ARAGÓN: from *Luna Park* [8]

to Jules Supervielle

Havre.
Coruña.
Vladivostok.
Hamburg.
Visions of distant ports.
Ocean.
The Hudson.
New York.
«Liberty» France holds like a torch in its fist
—the Gauls offering Don Quixote an airplane?—
people of America will come with a sword.
Springs:
54, 55, 56 . . .
Indicators signaling routes,
Rose petals of the winds.
Hot America roaring like a bull,
Moving muscles of steel,
The great trans-ocean liners.

The ships have been festooned
With handkerchiefs

In the bays,
On sleepy decks,
Smoke a pipe and let your
Bohemian hair grow.

Coney Island
And its immense neighborhood:
New York,
At night:
A pyrotechnic festival.
By day enormous cubes
Of chewed windows
Are such cardboard cities
Of the movie world.
Towers of Babel,

(«50 story homes,
....
....
....
and pain, pain, pain! . . .»)

Ruben's soul,
A lily in the pages of a book,
Buried away
In the walls of the skyscrapers.

Docks and boats,
Sky and sea
And horizons
And horizons!

Boats fragrant
With tropical fruit;
Boats that have seen the Northern Lights
And white polar landscapes,
Pale and sad,
Dissolving in the distance;
Oriental boats

Weighing anchor in the mist
Wrapped up in themselves
As in an opium dream
And off like a sleepwalker.

Life of the party a big sad boat.
—Four smokestacks, three bridges—
Burning at night
As the band plays.
With a course charted out
And seeming to roll on rails
As it crosses the sea!

In the marine twilight
An airplane disappears at once.
Clumsy winged like a bat;
But later, an arrow,
Dazzling bird
Digging into the full moon.

Blaise Cendrars: from *Travel Notes*

Dinner Time

I gave a big tip to the chief steward for a small table all to myself in a corner
I won't have to make small talk
I look at the others and eat
Here's the first European-style menu
I confess I eat these European dishes with pleasure
Pompadour soup
Beef tenderloin Brussels style
Partridge on toast
Taste is the most atavistic sense the most reactionary the most national
Analytical
Quite the opposite of the love of touch the touch of love fully developed and
universal growth
Revolutionary
Synthetic

Writing

My typewriter clicks in cadence
It rings at the end of each line
The gears clutch
From time to time I lean back in my wicker chair and blow a big smoke ring
My cigarette's always lit
Then I hear the sound of the waves
The gurgle of water choking in the washbasin plumbing
I get up and cool off my hands in cold water
Or put on cologne
I've draped the wardrobe mirror wardrobe so I don't see myself writing
The porthole's a round slice of sun
When I think
It resounds like the head of a drum in a big voice

Bad Faith

That damned chief steward I tipped so generously for a private table sniffs me out like an alley cat
He invites me on behalf of the captain to sit at the head table
I'm furious but I can't refuse
At dinner it turns out the captain's an agreeable guy
I'm seated between an embassy attaché at The Hague and an English consul in Sweden
Across the table is a world expert in bacteriology and his wife who's a gentle greedy woman with really pale skin and dull wide eyes
My antimusical paradoxes and my culinary theories cause a ripple of indignation around the table
The attaché from The Hague dips his monocle in the gravy
The Stockholm consul turns ghastly green like striped pajamas
The bacteriology celebrity pulls an even longer ferret's pointy snout
His wife giggles and her face contracts from margin to center so the whole thing ends up resembling a poobah's bellybutton
The captain winks with malice

Unmasked Incognito

For several days I've puzzled my fellow diners
They've been wondering what on earth I could be
I talked bacteriology with the world authority
Women and nightclubs with the captain

Kantian theories of peace with the attaché at The Hague
Questions of freight with the English consul
Paris movies music finance vitalism aviation
This evening at dinner while I was paying her a compliment the world authority's wife said It's true
The man's a poet
Pow
She got it from the jockey's wife in second class
I can hardly blame her since her greedy bellybutton grin amuses me more than anything in the world
I'd really like to know how she manages to wrinkle up such a round chubby face

Wet Nurses and Sports

There are several nurses on board
Dry and wet ones
When we play quoits on deck
Each time the young German leans forward she shows two small breasts nestling in her blouse
All the men from first-class passengers to deckhands know that game and they all walk across the portside deck to see these two round things in their nest
It must be talked about as far down as the steward's room
At the end of a bench
In a dark corner
A baby pulls on the large breast of a black woman and makes it spurt out plentiful and sticky like a bunch of bananas

Dancing

An American couple dances apache dances
The young Argentinian girls resent the orchestra and heartily scorn the young men on board
The Portuguese break into applause as soon as a Portuguese tune is played
The French keep to themselves laugh loudly and make fun of everyone
Only the young servant girls want to dance in their beautiful dresses
Shocking some and diverting others I invite the black nurse
The American couple again dances apache dances

Karel Schulz: Jazz Over the Sea

on the deck 55 sailors are dancing wild Tom is downing his usual shots
the steam engines turn into goldminers' pubs the helmsman had a star fall onto the helm
a dove hits the glass of the engineer's booth and flutters its wings to the fall and rise of pressure
the roar of fifty thousand people is bursting the sky
and its pieces plunge into the ocean
a girl is combing her hair and her elbowbend is a poet's lyre
the moon and a bottle with a message about the wreck of the old order are sailing through the waves
the captain has turned into a red flag and we can see all five continents from our table

anemones snowdrops lilies-of-the-valley are not in the ground but in window reflections
and people's heads are flowerbeds of pain rimmed with hands
lovers' suicides have names like: RIO PLATA HONOLULU TEXAS
white seagulls are waving good-bye with their kerchiefs and someone has died on their wings
a blind man with accordion is drinking the sun
and Frank in a gray sweater hawks barometric attractions
a clown dances on Sundays atop smokestacks

carhorns have built a metropolis in the middle of a Sunday excursion
but stockings are unpeeled by the river and chests made bare
verses fade on women's lips behind lit-up windows
and a man who longed to be Robinson Crusoe on the island of her heart
now regrets the sunken ship
white railing is dancing above the staircase through the sea and the African lakes
officers from a foreign legion
are getting drunk on field rations and the boredom of constant rain
a poet reading Longfellow falls into a daydream over the machine-gun backfire of a motor named Indian
the pinnacles of towers punch holes through a postcard with a final greeting

people have film posters and love in their eyes
on Monday mornings they take orchestrions and knife stabs to the hospital
the day has grown gray and drowned in the banks and offices
through which is drifting the smell of the forest or the suburban hotel rooms

for 40 francs love is included
in the laboratories microscopes are now telescopes peering into the future
and new bodies lie in the mortuary but life doesn't end on a dissecting table
in a crows nest high in the sky linked by the mainmast to the sea and the world
sits Jaroslav Seifert
calling out
L A N D

Álvaro de Campos [Fernando Pessoa]

All along the wharf there's the bustle of an imminent arrival.
People begin to gather around and wait.
The steamer from Africa is coming into plain view.
I came here to wait for no one.
To watch everyone else wait,
To be everyone else waiting,
To be the anxious waiting of everyone else.

I'm exhausted from being so many things.
The latecomers are finally arriving,
And I suddenly get sick of waiting, of existing, of being.
I abruptly leave and am noticed by the gatekeeper, who gives me a hard, quick stare.
I return to the city as if to freedom.

It's good to feel, if for no other reason, so as to stop feeling.

Blaise Cendrars: São Paulo

Finally some factories a suburb a nice little trolley
Electric wires
A crowded street full of people out for their evening shopping
A gas tank
Finally we pull into the station
São Paulo
I think I'm in the station at Nice
Or disembarking at Charing Cross in London

I find all my friends
Hi
It's me

OSWALD DE ANDRADE: Bengaló

Elastic teats under the Jersey
a *maxixe* slides through the dark fingers
of Gilberta
Windows
Jacks and aces abandon the sky of moving stars
The piano fox-trots
Sunday-like
A cock crows in his pen
The bell telephones
Cretonnes
The cinema of business
Plans to buy a Ford
The piano fox-trots
Window
Trolley cars

MÁRIO DE ANDRADE: Sunday

Late arrivals at Mass, in lace,
exchanging acrobatic glances . . .
So much wireless telegraphy!
St. Cecilia exudes from washed bodies
and pictorial sacrileges . . .
But Jesus Christ in the wilderness,
but the priest at the Confiteor . . . Contrast!
"Futility, civilization . . ."

Who's playing today? . . . The Paulistano Team.
Off to America Garden of the roses and kick-offs!
Friedenreich made a goal! Corner! What a referee!

Do I like Bianco? Crazy about him. Better than Barto . . .
And my wonderful fellow-Mario! . . .
"Futility, civilization . . ."

Warmly in gasolines . . . Thirty-five thousand!
Do you have ten bucks? let's go make the main drag . . .
And mooch cigarettes for two weeks on end . . .
You've got to go down to the main drag. Did you see Marilia?
And Phyllis! What a dress: practically naked!
Closed automobiles . . . Motionless figures . . .
The yawn of luxury . . . Burial.
And also the wholesale Sunday families,
among the perennially proper . . .
"Futility, civilization . . ."

Main jail. A drama of adultery.
Bertini tears her hair and dies.
Getaways . . . Hold-ups . . . Tom Mix!
Tomorrow a German film . . . For free!
The young girls are disturbed from thinking about German films . . .
The Romes of Petronius . . .
And the virgin's bed . . . All blue and white!
Rest . . . The angels . . . Immaculate!
The young girls dream masculinities . . .
"Futility, civilization . . ."

Blaise Cendrars: from *São Paulo*

Getting Up

The night is waning
Day begins to break
A window opens
A man leans out humming
He's in shirtsleeves and takes in the world
The breeze murmurs softly like a buzzing head

The City Wakes Up

The first trolleys go past filled with workers
A man hawks the news in the middle of the square
He struggles with the big sheets of paper flapping their wings and does a sort of solo ballet accompanying himself with guttural cries STADO . . . ERCIO . . . EIO
Klaxons reply
And the first cars speed by

Electric Horns

Here they've never heard of the League of Silence
As in all new countries
The joy of living and making money is expressed by honking horns and backfiring mufflers

Small Fry

The sky is raw blue
Across the street a raw white wall
Raw sun beats down on my head
A black woman on a small terrace is frying tiny fish on a portable stove made from an old biscuit tin
Two pickaninnies chew a sugarcane stalk

Landscape

The glossy wall of the PENSION MILANESE is framed by my window
I see a slice of São Joao Avenue
Trams cars trams
Trolleys-trolleys trams trams
Three yellow mules harnessed together pull tiny empty carts
Looming over the avenue's pepper trees is the huge sign of CASA TOKYO
The sun gushes varnish

São Paulo

I adore this city
São Paulo is dear to my heart
No tradition here
No prejudice

Neither ancient nor modern
Nothing counts but this furious appetite this total confidence this optimism this audacity this toil this labor this speculation which puts up ten houses an hour in every style ridiculous grotesque beautiful big small northern southern Egyptian Yankee cubist
With no other concern but going with statistics forecasting the future the comfort the utility the capital gain and attracting a lot of immigrants
All countries
All peoples
I love that
The two or three old Portuguese houses left are blue china

CARLOS PELLICER: Third Time

From the plane,
the panoramic orchestra of Rio de Janeiro
sounds in my heart.
From the crest of Corcovado
to the waves of Copacabana
happiness is a simple distance that has passed
blurring the nearest dates with its silvery hands.
I'll bind my starry existence
to the divine rock of Pao de Açucar
which sees the bursting dawn sooner than the ocean waters.
The sea of Rio Janeiro
is an old-time barcarolle
being learnt by the gentle
wave of my thought
Guanabara its name. Guanabara,
like a star stretching out
above the rhythm of a moment.
Naval city, your avenues
of orohydrographic marvels
anchor my eyes in an air
of depthless eternity.
Your sea and your mountain—
a tiny handful of Andes and a thousand litres of Atlantic—
pass beneath the wings

of my plane like a synthesis of the beloved Continent.
The mighty rocks are golden,
the mountains green and purple.
The water stirs in a semitone.
The town is a leaf-stripped book.
The air, a soprano trilling.
The fleet is putting out to fish.
A loop-the-loop shatters our return
and sends the city exploding.

KYN TANIYA: Fox-Trot

The Bolshevik world is a ruby
        placed on the December night
And on my glowing stained-glass a gold butterfly knocks
        Because the deserted streets are black
Your great big head is full of songs
        of geometric birds Genaro
And your eyes are unlike themselves
        behind your spectacles
Maybe you're right
        that the soul is as simple as a Cubist drawing

There are two or three stars that sting the night
        like golden fleas on a negress's thigh
Reach out your chubby arm some more
        and grab them
Everyone believes in the Moon
        but you well know that it's the hole
Blown by a potent shell from the Great War
        and in punishment
YOUR BODY TOOK THE SHAPE OF AN ARTILLERY OFFICER
laughing

        With the world in your hands
take a last run
        kick the kick to end them all
then stand with your head in the air

waiting for a ball that won't ever come back
Shout of laughter!
soccer champ on the team of LIFE

MÁRIO DE ANDRADE: Colloque Sentimental

My feet are lacerated on the thorns of the sidewalks . . .
Hygienopolis! . . . The Babylons of my base desires . . .
Houses in the noble style . . . Bonanzas in tragedies . . .
But the night is all a bridal veil in the moonlight!

The high tide of the gleams from the mansions . . .
The colored jazz band . . . The rainbow of perfumes . . .
The clamor of coffers stuffed with lives . . .
Naked shoulders, naked shoulders, lips heavy with adultery . . .
And rouge—mushroom of putrefactions . . .
Armies of dress coats eruditely well-cut . . .

Crimeless, thiefless the carnival of titles . . .
Using so much talcum, you look like bags of flour!
Pitilessly . . .

"Sir . . ." "I am a count!" "I beg your pardon.
Do you know that a Braz district exists, a Bom Retiro?"

"Dammit!" I breathe . . . "I thought you were begging.
I only know Paris!"

"Come with me, then.
Forget a moment your neighbor-lady's arms . . ."

"You understood, did you! I'll give you a tip so shut up.
The sultan has ten thousand . . . But I am a count!"

"You see? This part of town glooms of silence . . .
No wings whatsoever, no joy whatsoever . . . The Moon . . ."

The street all naked . . . The lightless houses . . .

And the myrrh of unwitting martyrs . . .

"Let me put my handkerchief to my nose.
I have all the perfumes of Paris!"

"But look, under the doors, slipping . . ."
"Into the sewers! Into the sewers!"

"slipping
a thread of nameless tears! . . ."

MARTÍN ADÁN: from *The Cardboard House*

Here one is possessed by a certain kind of frenetic and infantile, experienced and weary, critical and dilettantish culture. Paul Morand on a sailing boat accompanied by his earless, raceless lover on their way to Siam. Like in the social pages. Cendrars, who comes to Peru to preach the enthusiasms of a spontaneous Bavarian explorer (lynched tourists, wheat plantations, and the man who strangles his destiny). Radiguet, carrying around on tiptoe his wife who is suddenly uglified by a heroic husband. Istrati, a whiff of Dutch cheese, a ship's hold, Eurasian misery. All the same, all indistinct, unaffiliable—secretaries of embassies, heirs to textile mills, day students in schools run by European nuns, failed university students, devout women who have come for their health, for a saintly scandal, a spiritual experience. Excessive Baedeker, a guide from who knows which avant-garde Pentapolis, inadmissible nationalism, a great big hunch . . . A drunken Charleston shakes up a buxom lady as if she were a sack full of wood chips. A policeman rubs his anointed, cunning hands. The funicular modernly lends its signature to the cliff's prerepublican calling. Lima, Lima, finally . . . And everything is nothing but your insanity and a Peruvian resort for bathing in the sea. And a native and premature desire that Europe will make of us men, women's men, terrible Portugese men, men like Adolphe Menjou, with a false moustache and a valet, with an international smile and a dozen London gestures, with specific danger and a thousand unexpected vices, with two Rolls Royces and a German liver ailment. Nothing else. Bad Nauheim, Cauterets, summer in Paris . . . Nothing of the kind.

Valery Larbaud: from *Europe* [IX]

Cities and more cities:
I remember cities the way one remembers love affairs:
Why talk about it? Sometimes, though,
At night, I dream I'm here, or there,
And I wake up in the morning wanting to travel.

My God, death!
I'll have to follow this body through sickness and into death,
This body I had known only in sin and joy.
O store windows on big streets in the capitals,
One day you'll reflect this passing face no more.
So many trips in steamers and first-class trains,
Is an open grave the only thing they lead to?
They'll put the homeless stray in a box,
Shut the lid and that will be that.

Oh! Give me just one more chance
To see a few places that I love, like
Pacific Square in Seville,
La Chiaja cool and crowded;
The big tropical ferns in the Naples botanical garden
And the girl-tree I love so much, and also
The light shade of the pepper-plants on Kephisia Avenue;
The square in Old Phalerum, the port of Munychia, and also
The vines of Lesbos and its fine olive trees
Where I carved my name as lyric poet.
And also
That beach, Chersonesus, near Sevastopol,
Where the sea runs up among the ruins, and where a scholar
Lovingly points out a hideous Kirghiz idol
With a blubber-lipped idiot grin on his fat stone cheeks.
And above all, ah above all
Kharkov!
Where I felt, for the first time,
The virgin sigh of the Muse lift up my timid heart.
My kind of town:
Gold domes in the heart of emptiness,

Palaces in the desert, hot red sun on the distant dust;
And in the poor neighborhoods
Thousands of signs for clothing shops:
The squat houses, their white walls
Painted with big fat men, with no heads . . .

Langston Hughes: I Thought It Was Tangiers I Wanted

I know now
That Notre Dame is in Paris.
And the Seine is more to me now
Than a wriggling line on a map
Or a name in travel stories.

I know now
There is a Crystal Palace in Antwerp
Where a hundred women sell their naked bodies,
And the night-lovers of sailors
Wait for men on docks in Genoa.

I know now
That a great golden moon
Like a picture-book moon
Really rises behind palm groves
In Africa,
And tom-toms do beat
In village squares under the mango trees.

I know now
That Venice is a church dome
And a net-work of canals,
Tangiers a whiteness under sun.
I thought
It was Tangiers I wanted,
Or the gargoyles of Notre Dame,
Or the Crystal Palace in Antwerp,
Or the golden palm-grove moon in Africa,
Or a church dome and a net-work of canals.

Happiness lies nowhere,
Some old fool said,
If not within oneself.

It's a sure thing
Notre Dame is in Paris,—
But I thought it was Tangiers I wanted.

◈ INTERLUDE ◈

Lewis Jacobs: Highway 66

Montage Notes for a Documentary Film

"Rjechevsky has the virtue, he aims at being limited, to pose problems bravely before the director; he determines the emotional content and the sense of the film without determining the visual contours." —*Pudovkin*

— Limp cities alike in their escapes
        and conquests
— Concordant traffic
— Dumb hordes long out of work
— Prowling . . . . . .
— Their vigilance confined to passing women
        and their bodies
        who turn away
— A sudden thrust for space!
        from daring offers of recognition
        and a vise-like need of them
— And their bodies . . . . . .
— KODAK AS YOU GO!
— SOUTH PENN SQUARE!
— Weeping willows for men
        or what's left of them
        to dump their past there
— To wallow in, to reflect
        and suffer again
        their wrinkled history;
— For the police to trample in unconcern
        of pilgrims' weariness to begone
        . . . . . . And bedamned!
— DO NOT THROW RUBBISH AROUND!
— A sudden radio pronouncement
— While you're jostled in the street
        from the quick perception of
— Apples
— Unemployed who covet the beggars' cup
— Citizens! . . . . . .
— Torsos and ankles
— The undulation of a calf
        or breast
        calling for a hand
        to plumb and survey
— Its greek fecundity!
— Faces
— Prolix and stained
— In format vigilant
— Pouched in decay
— Caloried
— Sticky with time
— Rapt and furrowed
— METROPOLITAN!
— FOUR OUT OF FIVE HAVE IT!
— Shop windows
— unrestrained and lying
— their faces bewildering
— And court-plastered;
— The clangor of "SALE" notices
— The zigzag of "REDUCTIONS" . . .
        "PAY AS YOU EARN!"
— The peering newspapers
        preaching their corruption
— In trumpet-grandeur
        and lusty conclusion.

"ALL THE NEWS THAT'S FIT TO PRINT!"
— A Greta Garbo sign
— Vibrant
— Throbbing to adolescents
— and nomads
stamped down like grapes in sweat
— Its electric hallucination.
"FLESH AND THE DEVIL"
— Department Stores
— Woolworth the A and P's
— counters busy with unwanted children
who are as reconciled as their parents.
"Papa Loves Mamma
Mamma Loves Papa
Every Thing is Rosy Now!"
— Skyscrapers
babbling to God
in their heterogeneous stammer
— And confusing man
and beast
in their braggadocio.
"Roar of Cities has musical undertone!"
— The Carnegie Library
— Severe and uninhabited
— Fiction for the Sabbath
— And librarians of ephemeral sex
"SILENCE PLEASE!"
— The Deposits in the men's room
and axiom of its walls;
"SOME COME HERE TO . . . . . ."
— 13th precinct
— Cages and complex excrement
— The writing on the wall . . . . . .
—Scratches by men awaiting daylight
— Excavating lice
— And shuddering
— From vermin and the cold . . . . . .
— Scratching, scratching
for others to follow
— Or for the law to erase:
"Tully Filmus
who left this jail for Joliet!"
"They put me here
for ridin' the rods,
I wanted to see things—
Charley "KID" Weisberg"
— Apartment houses
— Hotel-pimps and gamblers
— Prostitutes
— Kept women smoking the day away
with rummy
gin and recount
of yesteryear's harlotry!
"A RADIO IN EVERY ROOM!"
— Speakeasy
— Women gleam
and wrest away laughter
and bewilderment
— Witness greed and wanton breath
— Muster wails
— Set griffins into flight;
— Taut lovers reprieve themselves
— And sound new pacts . . . . . .
— Somehow a cuspidor.
— Typists and secretaries
describing their new "thrill"
and new "ensemble"
—emerging with desire
"True Stories"
read in intervals
— Of office slack, lavatory duty
— Subway run.
— Real estate men, lawyers and clerk
— Salesmen
who collect quick-lunches
— All the day's routine
— Automobile-love episodes
and gaming debts;
— Then back to an afternoon of dreaming:
"When I get you alone tonight . . . . . ."
— Of desperate outwitting
— Of both.
"Where will you be at forty?"
— Arguing students
— Destroying the past
— Denouncing the present
— Despising the "mercenary"
— All for black coffee
and a future.

"Own your own home!"
— With a bedroom of lust
— A kitchen of hate and destruction
— Plush living rooms
"A dollar down!"
— Decrepit with cheap wit
and the moment's wise-cracks;
— Or
— Abated with compromise
until its customers
go
— Screaming made
from silence enforced
— Or suicide
from dispatched venom.
The city swallows the sun
Men hack God into bread.
— "FARM FOR SALE."
— Farmer's help
— And family and possessions
— And second hand car
— Resist the road
— Trek silently from state
— To state
— Envying cattle their cud
— And contentment
— Only resting
— For shepherd-food
— And smuggled childbirth ......
— Or to rant at the Combines
— And the "Power"
which conditioned them.
"Farm For Sale."
— In town
— Farmers auction and barter
— And families exchange toothpicks
and hunger
"When it's springtime in the Rockies!"
— Rivets of concern
with the withering of crops
— And unemployment
— Animal lore
— The political exploitation
— And the same feudalism
next Saturday.
— Oil wells
"Where oil has been
little ever grows again"
— Ranches and barren mines
"A fertile region the prairies
and an obstacle
to white advance
with no economy
and only fit for Indians"
— Billboards
— For religion, mountains
— And the holy word
— Chalked by a strident bedouin
— In a mouldy ford;
"God is Love"
"Jesus Saves"
"You are now leaving the incorporated village
of Eden"
— All
— The city, the country
— All the hitch-hikers' kit
— The discarded refuse
for maintenance
— And excursion
— The billboards
— The bourgeois scenery
— The Highway
— Aristocratic
— And imperious
— Impassive to the worker
— And imperial!
"Negro burned by mob"
"Hunger-marches throughout U.S."
"STRIKE!"
The city swallows the sun
Men hack God into bread.

Hart Crane: from *The River*

Stick your patent name on a signboard
brother—all over—going west—young man
Tintex—Japalac—Certain-teed Overalls ads
and lands sakes! under the new playbill ripped
in the guaranteed corner—see Bert Williams what?
Minstrels when you steal a chicken just
save me the wing for if it isn't
Erie it ain't for miles around a
Mazda—and the telegraphic night coming on Thomas

a Ediford—and whistling down the tracks
a headlight rushing with the sound—can you
imagine—while an Express makes time like
SCIENCE—COMMERCE and the HOLYGHOST
RADIO ROARS IN EVERY HOME WE HAVE THE NORTHPOLE
WALLSTREET AND VIRGINBIRTH WITHOUT STONES OR
WIRES OR EVEN RUNning brooks connecting ears
and no more sermons windows flashing roar
breathtaking—as you like it . . . eh?

So the 20th Century—so
whizzed the Limited—roared by and left
three men, still hungry on the tracks, ploddingly
watching the tail lights wizen and converge, slip-
ping gimleted and neatly out of sight.

◈ NEW YORK ◈

EMIL BØNNELYKKE: New York

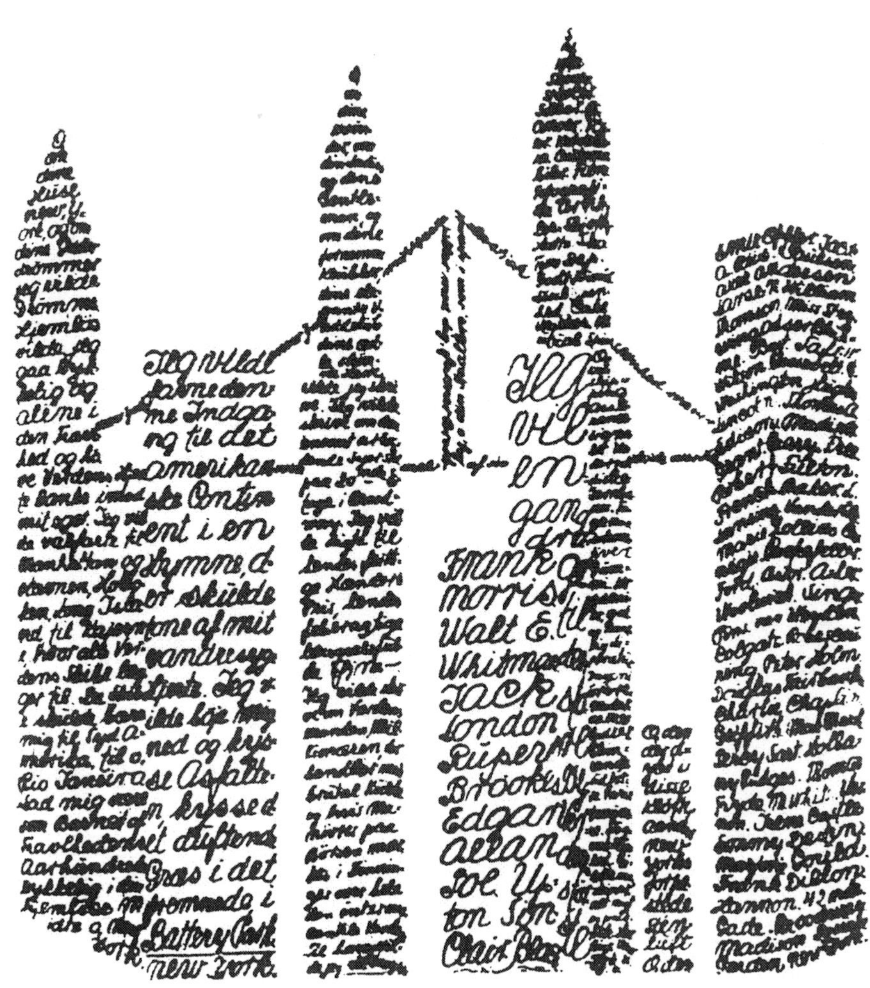

GIORGIO DE CHIRICO: from *I Was in New York*

Beyond the barrier of the ocean, beyond customs and the Irishmen with polished black revolvers, beyond the white-gloved phantoms who in the pale dawn light unload the debris of the seven sins from their armored cars, you will find again and again in New York the magnificent, in New York eternally New you will find forgotten memories, memories which return there like they return in the hours of half-sleep, in those mysterious hours when the soul and spirit, freed at last from logic and reality, resolve a crowd of otherwise insoluble enigmas and problems — forgotten, alas, as soon as they are solved.

In mysterious New York luxury and wealth create, in an apotheosis of fireworks, those strange paradises in the very center of this immense, antique, mechanical and polymorphous city, those paradises that transport us with a gentle and imperceptible speed, smoothly and evenly in cushioned sleighs drawn in silence by polychrome ducks and the good storks of distant memory . . .

Splendid city of dream within dream, city of Plate Glass, Plate Glass City, Shop Window City, in these store windows march day and night, like the characters of a very old clock, all the *things* of humble humanity, from its distant birthplaces shrouded in the mists of sylvan and sepulchral paleontology, to the spectacular and electric aspects of its obscure future.

New York, eternally New, pulls us with its parallel infinities into the improbable kaleidoscope of its shop windows, its transparent towers, its splendid bazaars, its windows lit all through the long nights of winter and where the ineffable Dioscuri sleep, bent over the breasts of their tired horses; where the characters in the tragedy of Mayerling consult their instruments, bent over without seeing in their refracting telescopes the rusty cutlasses that the one-eyed buccaneers, now long since gone, once clasped in their clenched fists.

In this forest of glass, steel and cement, in this extraordinary New York so difficult to define you will rediscover, O voyager, the gigantic masks of the antique gods, you will rediscover the eternal sadness of the plaster Antinous and the immense solitude of the Pantheon on summer nights, beneath the great sky all streaming with stars.

Carlos Oquendo de Amat: New York

The trees will soon break their bonds
and all the policemen are bunches of flowers

CONEY ISLAND

Rain is a shaving token

WALL STREET

A breeze hurries the growth
of Paramount Actresses

The traffic
writes
a love letter

T
I
M
E

Telephones
are liquor depots

I
S

Ten runners
naked in the Underwood

M
O
N
E
Y

28th FLOOR

CHARLESTON
RUDOLPH VALENTINO MAKES HAIR GROW
NO ONE MAY BE OLDER THAN 30
(because men will have shrunk 10 inches
and they will walk obliquely on walls)

Mary Pickford climbs along the gaze of the manager

To observe her

I' VE END

ED

UP DI VID ED

BY 25 WI

ND-

OWS

b e n e a t h t h e c a r p e t t h e r e a r e s h i p s

Don't sing, Spanish woman
you will make George Walsh appear inside the chimney

HERE AS IN THE FIRST NO ONE KNOWS ANYTHING ABOUT ANYTHING

100th floor

The factory smoke

slows clocks down

Children play hoop games
with the moon

in the outskirts

the park rangers
charm rivers

And the morning
leaves like any girl
In her braids
she wears a sign

FOR RENT

THIS MORNING

JULIETTE ROCHE: Déja-Vu

Earthquake
Cyclone
Tidal wave
or war

The city awaits its judgment
Its sterilized skies were preparing eclipses
like operations
Its parks smelled like warm bitumen and gasoline
Summer malaise in deserted neighborhoods
delirium of empty streets
senegalite of iron bridges.

The same pianolas were playing Tipperary.

Limbo
inconsistency
ennui after death and before birth

We will not be astonished.

We've already seen these catastrophes elsewhere
accompanied by cinema scores
Triangle Play Film or ancient prophecy?
Bible or Broadway?

We know the clean-shaven clerk and the blonde
stenographer
the Negro, the Chinese, the boxer, the banker,
the women who danced on the roof of the Biltmore
with their eyes frozen in acetylene fires
(their civilized nerves won't feel a thing).

Crowds
automatons and somnambulists
parades
with the anticipated effect of muted car horns
and muffled cylinders

The whistlings of the ferries,

grindings of the factories;
a gramophone
will play (in-e-luc-ta-bly)
the Afternoon of a Faun;

someone will recite transposed psalms.
Sioux cries.
Billy Sunday.
Orchestra.
Suicide.

Tipperary.

A. Léyeles: New York

Metal. Granite. Uproar. Racket. Clatter.
Automobile. Bus. Subway. El.
Burlesque. Grotesque. Café. Movie-theater.
Electric light in screeching maze. A spell.

In eyes—a pending verdict, faces—strangers:
No smile, no Bless-you, no nod, no gentle word.
And straying, rambling, imminent danger.
And jungle, crush, upheaval, wild absurd.

Nathan Asch: Downtown

New York — downtown — streets — buildings — firms — people.
streets — short — crooked — narrow — dark.
are crowded — teeming — undulating — festering.
passers by — strollers — walkers — loiterers — crowds — mobs.

members of the Big Board — members of the Curb — sleek haired salesmen — girl graduates from the Manhattan Preparatory School on Houston Street — telephone clerks — book-keepers — comparison clerks — runners very young and very old — bucket shop keepers — boy wonders — news boys — news women — beggars — best traders on the Street — never get nowhere fellows — plain whores — insurance salesmen — tipsters —

touch system typists — detectives — men — women — boys — girls — American — Dutch — Irish — Jew — Italian — Russian — French — German — Spanish — Polish — Argentine — Swedish — nigger — English — Turk — Mexican — Syrian — American — wop — greaser — polack — sheenie — coon — mick — kike — chink — yid — frog — limie.

extra — chocolate almonds — pineapples — dates — figs — straw hats — lunch on the tombs of the Trinity churchyard — cigars — cigarettes — chewing gum — cigarette butts from the sidewalk.

best architects — most famous engineers — most skillful draughtsmen — best paid artists — greatest builders — decorators — mechanics — carpenters — plumbers — masons — hod carriers.

conceived — planned — consulted — draughted — executed — constructed — erected — decorated — furnished.

tallest — largest — greatest — biggest — strongest — everlasting.

most massive — most economical — space saving — most artistic.

magnificent — grandiose — superb — marvelous — unique.

rock — steel — granite — marble — wood — glass — copper — brass — lead — paint.

National City Bank — National City Company — National Park Bank — National Bank of Commerce — First National Bank — Guaranty Trust Company — Equitable Trust Company — Bankers Trust Company — J. P. Morgan & Company — Kuhn, Loeb and Company — Lazard Freres et Cie — Kidder, Peabody and Company.

safe — solid — conservative — solid bed rock — unlimited resources — high grade — gilt edged — respectability — we do not guarantee this statement but we have taken it from sources we believe reliable — church going — my country may she ever be in the right but my country right or wrong — patriotism — rock of Gibraltar — absolutely safe — A1 — AAAaaa — 24 carat — Mayflower — New England tradition — bulldog — gr-r-r-r.

men — women — boys — girls — husbands — fathers — grandfathers — daughters — granddaughters — wives — sons — sisters — friends — foes — nodding acquaintances — hat lifting acquaintances — hand shaking acquaintances.

good fellows — bad sports — nice chaps — damned fools — she's easy to get — wise guys — know it all fellows — boy wonders — never missed a shot fellows — clever financiers — suckers — fish — poor fish — nevergetnowherebecausehe-neverlookswherehesgoingfellows.

buy — sell — exchange — beg — borrow — steal — cheat — give — take — donate — endow — deceive — lie — sympathize — pity — love.

melting pot — maelstrom — mixup — Bedlam — pandemonium.

YEHOASH: Broadway

Rushing cars, wagons, trams,
Whistling whistles, blowing horns, ringing bells,
A fire truck roars by
Trailing a black braid of smoke.
Masses shuffle their feet,
Brown, yellow, pearl-gray, white bare legs . . .
White necks, clumps of powdered bodies,
Black painted brows, bleached blond hair,
Hats with green plumes,
Shining top hats, and a whirl of straw hats,
Broad Mexican sombreros,
Soldier and sailor hats of a dozen nations,
Veteran denizens of the night with watery eyes
And big diamond stickpins,
Boys lighting up at every girl's eye,
People of all lands and all suns,
Of a vineyard at the quiet sea,
Of snow-mountains, of broad fields of wheat and rye,
Of high grass pampas,
Of where a hundred thousand slaves
Dig gold out of graves in the earth . . .
Northerners, southerners, of airplanes and ships,
Rushing to the night bustle of Babel . . .
A wanton shine screams from all corners,
A bright raucous cascade pours
And sprays up to the clay-yellow sky . . .
Fire-serpents creep up high buildings,
On a tower three fire-horses run
With wild energy into the hot night,
A huge fire-bottle taps
Fire into a glass,
From the dark, a fire-cat leaps
And claws
A fiery spool . . .

FORTUNATO DEPERO

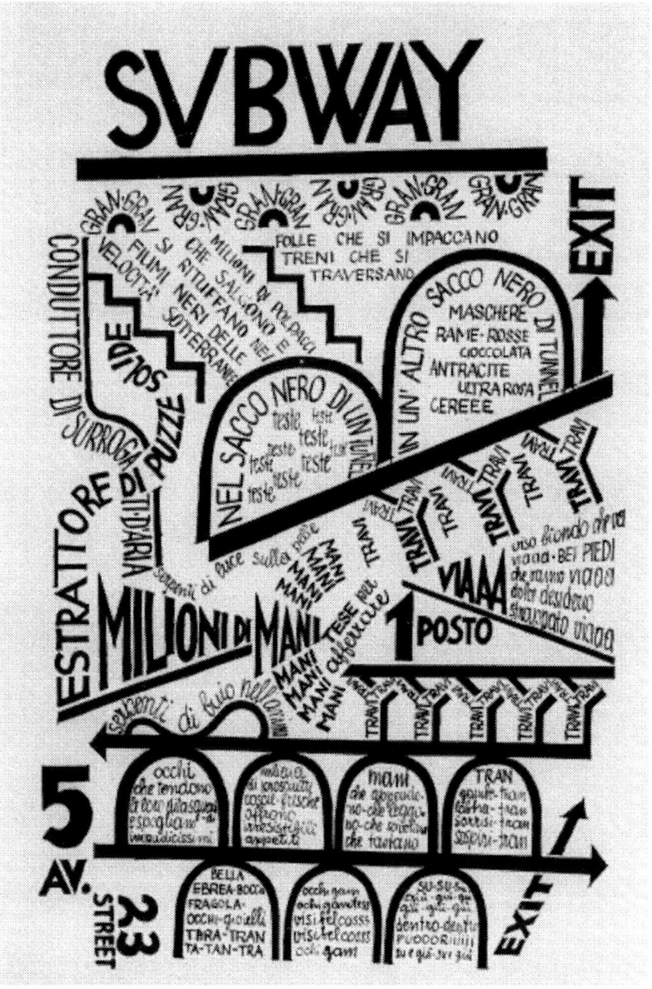

SYNOPSIS: At the top: a string of semi-circles of promotional bunting ("big-big"). Moving diagonally down the stairs are "millions of calves that board and dive into the black rivers of subterranean velocities." In the smaller tunnel, "in the black bag of a tunnel" frames nine small "heads"; in the larger tunnel, "in another black bag of tunnel" frames a mix of colors and elements ("copper-red masks, ultra-pink chocolate, waxen anthracite"). Just below the surface: "crowds packed together, trains criss-crossing." In between two sets of Y-shaped girders ("travi travi travi") are "millions of hands, hands, hands" "poised to grab" as a "blond face" and "beautiful feet" depart—"sweet desire pulled away." In the intersecting word-tubes along the left side, there's an "artificial air conductor" (emitting wispy "serpents of light on the skin") and a "solid smells extractor." Curving below the millions of hands ("millioni di mani") are "serpents of darkness in the soul". At the bottom are two tiers of smaller tunnels containing, on the upper tier, fragments of the underground voyeur (with "eyes that hold their finger-glances and shamelessly undress") and a parade of body parts ("thousands of prosciutti fresh thighs offer irresistible temptations"—"hands that hang, that read, that slide, that touch"—"leg-tran, lip-tran, smile-tran, sigh-tran"); continued more frenetically on the lower tier ("beautiful Jewish-strawberry-mouth-eyes-jewels, tara-tran, ta-tan-tra" mix with nonsense fragments of "eyes-legs" and "beautiful faces," ending in a flurry of "up-up-up, down-down-down, in-in, ouuuuut!!!!!, up and down up and down").

Edward Nagle: Spring Psychosis

Siren screech—conceived in space a point given inward outward rotation—whistles—types febrile diagonals plus ambiguous luminosity—whistles—left right, right left, ensnares intersecting convoluted circles, propels incidental enchanted ellipses—whistles—whistles—thrusts ever hungry edges to the moon—narrower wider, wider narrower—one to three rectilinears to this—whistles—youth destitute of papers, flames from flower fested puberty enchained by manifest doubts in milky adolescence, farewell youth—ave atque vale—youth

Speed—Cinema extra—Ordinaire—whirring entrails snap slide backwards, buzzing genitals, incidental short circuits—Speed—Speed—minus burnt celluloid click click—minus barber chair dentist fussing brittle teeth

Smoke into the metallic mauve metropolis—New York—quit ta rève—New—York—by and for steam whistling, mill churning, trip hammering, rivet retching, piston plying, bell sounding, electric lightning—blue, red, green, red, blue, green,—Yellow—X—raying, water flushing, radio sparking, aeroplaning grey hesitancies inn continuous repetitive leap frog through revolving brass glass doors to rainbow smooth planes—not to taste purple retrospective ashes—with thumb and index press button to switch out, on, out—city collapses, an English aluminum picnic cup, But walls a gas grated mechanical piano room scents a subway elevated street car odor—insistent telephone, eye reflected from an eye—Oeil poisson mort—in a mirror—feel furtive coins, insistent telephone, go again

Leap into hat and cane—paint an ivory watch chain on this Ego's chest, go once again shadow somersaulting awkward automaton—play blind man's buff with fluttering taxicabs, hear a crass mucker telescoped in a motor horn shout—"Where's yuh pants?"—fix shell rims to ogle roller skating straw virgins moving upper lips in petulant rabbit munches—Waltz—waltz down the avenue—let psychoanalytical sycophants search the sun for scars—waltz on to tea—leave green waistcoated messenger boys with tulips bound in their hair riding gold velocipedes through an arch for tea talk tosh—

Mary Garden is Monna Vanna or Salomé, darling Garden—Polly have a cracker—is divine, sugar two lemon, drunken Carmen—Nirvana—Cracker Polly—pull them out with fire tongs

Night swims in through the window myriads of thunder tossed blue balloons—click—whirr—Ha.

CHARLES HENRI FORD: Poem from The Insurance Policy of The Automobile Club of New York, Inc.

For Loss of

Life
Two Eyes
Two Arms
Two Hands
Two Legs
Two Feet
One Arm and One Leg
One Arm and One Foot
One Hand and One Foot
One Leg and One Eye
One Arm and One Eye
One Hand and One Eye
One Foot and One Eye
One Arm

One Hand
One Leg
One Foot
One Eye

ELSA VON FREYTAG-LORINGHOVEN: Subjoyride

Ready-to-wear —
American soul poetry.
(The right kind)

It's popular — spitting — Maillard's
Safety controller handle —
You like it!
They actually kill Paris
Garters dromedary fragrance
Of C. N. in a big Yuban!
Ah — Madam —
That is a secret pep-o-mint —
Will you try it —
To the Last Drop?

Tootsie kisses Marshall's
Kippered health affinity
4 out of 5 — after 40 — many
Before your teeth full-o'
Pep with 10 nuggets products
Lighted Chiclets wheels and
Axles — carrying Royal
Lux Kamel hands off the
Better Bologna's beauty —
Get this straight — Wrigley's
Pinaud's heels for the wise —
Nothing so Pepsodent — soothing —
Pussy Willow — kept clean
With Philadelphia Cream
Cheese.
They satisfy the man of

Largest mustard under wear —
No dosing —
Just rub it on.

Weak — run down man like
The growing miss as well —
Getting on and off unlawful
With jelly — jam — or Meyer's
Soap noodles
The rubber set kind abounds —
The exact flavor lasts —
No metal can Vapo Rub
Oysterettes.

Wenatchee Barbasol peaks
Father John's patent — presentation —
Set — cold — gum's start
And finish.
18 years' electro-pneumatic
Operation Mary Garden cost
The golden key $1-500-000
Smile — see Lee Union — all
It's the grandest thing
After every meal — no boiling
Required — keeps the
Doctor a day — just musterole
Dear Mary — the mint with
The hole — oh lifebuoy!
Adheres well — delights
Your taste — continuous
Germicidal action — it
Means a wealth of family
Vick's —
Our men know their
Combatant jobs since 1888 —
Quicker than Maxwell
Brakes.
You can teach a select
Seal packer parrot — Kinso —
Postum lister World-War

On Saxo Salve ——
Try a venotonic semi-
Soft of a stiff indigestion
Don’t scratch!
Original sunshine makes
Tanlac children
Do you know that made
From rich pure shaving
Cream Jim Henry tired
Out?

Famous pain reduces
Reg’lar fellows to the
Toughest Cory-Chrome
Pancake apparel — kept
Antiseptic with gold dust
Rapid transit ——
It has raised 3 generations
Of mince-piston-rings-pie.
Wake up your passengers —
Large and small — to ride
On pins — dirty erasers and
Knives
These 3 Graces operate slot
For 5 cents.
Don’t envy Aunt Jemima’s
Self raising Cracker Jack
Laxative knitted chemise
With that chocolaty
Taste — use Pickles in Pattern
Follow Green Lions.

Juliette Roche

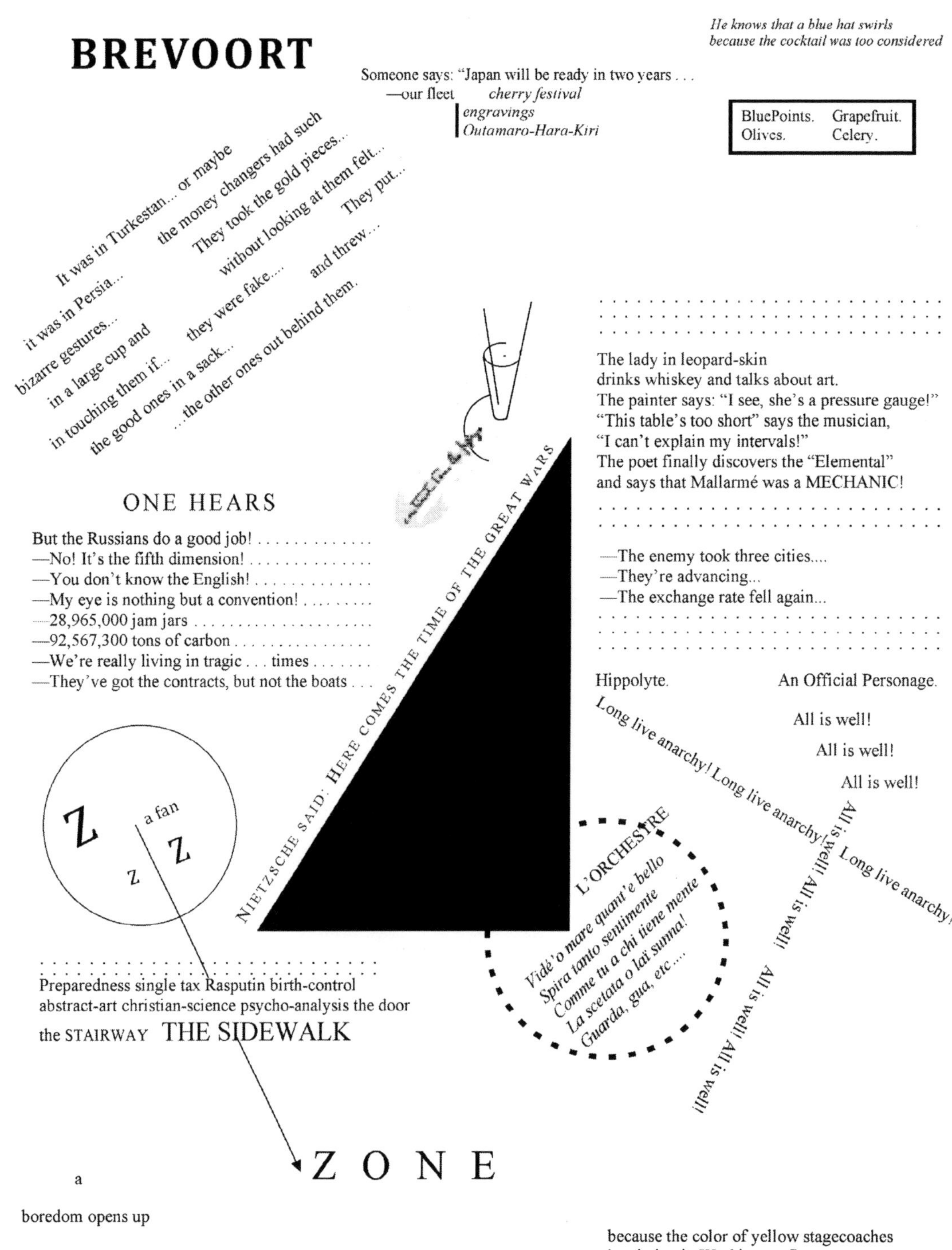

BREVOORT
He knows that a blue hat swirls
because the cocktail was too considered
Someone says: "Japan will be ready in two years . . .
—our fleet cherry festival
engravings
Outamaro-Hara-Kiri
BluePoints. Grapefruit.
Olives. Celery.
It was in Turkestan... or maybe
it was in Persia... the money changers had such
bizarre gestures... They took the gold pieces...
in a large cup and without looking at them felt...
in touching them if... they were fake.... They put...
the good ones in a sack... and threw...
...the other ones out behind them.
The lady in leopard-skin
drinks whiskey and talks about art.
The painter says: "I see, she's a pressure gauge!"
"This table's too short" says the musician,
"I can't explain my intervals!"
The poet finally discovers the "Elemental"
and says that Mallarmé was a MECHANIC!
ONE HEARS
But the Russians do a good job! . . . .
—No! It's the fifth dimension! . . . .
—You don't know the English! . . . .
—My eye is nothing but a convention! . . . .
—28,965,000 jam jars . . . .
—92,567,300 tons of carbon . . . .
—We're really living in tragic . . . times . . . .
—They've got the contracts, but not the boats . . .
NIETZSCHE SAID: HERE COMES THE TIME OF THE GREAT WARS
—The enemy took three cities....
—They're advancing...
—The exchange rate fell again...
Hippolyte. An Official Personage.
Long live anarchy! Long live anarchy! Long live anarchy!
All is well!
All is well!
All is well!
All is well! All is well! All is well! All is well!
Z a fan Z z
L'ORCHESTRE
Vidè'o mare quant'e bello
Spira tanto sentimente
Comme tu a chi tiene mente
La scetata o lài summa!
Guarda, gua, etc....
Preparedness single tax Rasputin birth-control
abstract-art christian-science psycho-analysis the door
the STAIRWAY THE SIDEWALK
ZONE
a
boredom opens up
because the color of yellow stagecoaches
is missing in Washington Square

JOHN DOS PASSOS: Newsreel [LIII from *The Big Money*]

Bye bye blackbird

ARE YOU NEW YORK'S MOST BEAUTIFUL
GIRL STENOGRAPHER?

No one here can love and understand me
Oh what hard luck stories they all hand me

BRITAIN DECIDES TO GO IT ALONE

you too can quickly learn dancing at home without music and without a partner . . . produces the same results as an experienced masseur only quicker, easier and less expensive. Remember only marriageable men in full possession of unusual physical strength will be accepted as the Graphic Apollos

Make my bed and light the light
I'll arrive late to-night

WOMAN IN HOME SHOT AS BURGLAR

Grand Duke Here to Enjoy Himself

ECLIPSE FOUR SECONDS LATE

Downtown Gazers See Corona

others are more dressy being made of rich ottoman silks, heavy satins, silk crepe or côte de cheval with ornamentation of ostrich perhaps

MAD DOG PANIC IN PENN STATION

UNHAPPY WIFE TRIES TO DIE

the richly blended beauty of the finish, both interior and exterior, can come only from the hand of an artist working towards an ideal. *Substitutes good normal solid tissue for that disfiguring fat.* He touches every point in the entire compass of human need. It may look a little foolish in print but he can show you how to grow your brains. If you are a victim of physical ill-being he can liberate you from pain. He can show you how to dissolve marital or conjugal problems. He is an expert in matters of sex

Blackbird bye bye

SKYSCRAPERS BLINK ON EMPTY STREETS

it was a very languid, a very pink and white Peggy Joyce in a very pink and white boudoir who held out a small white hand

---

GEORGE OPPEN: from *Discrete Series*

1

White. From the
Under arm of T

The red globe.

Up
Down. Round
Shiny fixed
Alternatives

From the quiet

Stone floor . . .

2

Thus
Hides the

Parts—the prudery
Of Frigidaire, of
Soda-jerking—

Thus

Above the

Plane of lunch, of wives
Removes itself
(As soda-jerking from
the private act

Of
Cracking eggs);

big-Business

AMY LOWELL: Thompson's Lunch Room — Grand Central Station
Study in Whites

Wax-white—
Floor, ceiling, walls.
Ivory shadows
Over the pavement
Polished to cream surfaces
By constant sweeping.
The big room is colored like the petals
Of a great magnolia,
And has a patina
Of flower bloom
Which makes it shine dimly
Under the electric lamps.
Chairs are ranged in rows
Like sepia seeds
Waiting fulfillment.
The chalk-white spot of a cook's cap
Moves unglossily against the vaguely bright wall—
Dull chalk-white striking the retina like a blow
Through the wavering uncertainty of steam.
Vitreous-white of glasses with green reflections,
Ice-green carboys, shifting—greener, bluer—with the jar of moving water.
Jagged green-white bowls of pressed glass

Rearing snow-peaked of chipped sugar
Above the lighthouse-shaped castors
Of grey pepper and grey-white salt.
Grey-white placards: "Oyster Stew, Cornbeef Hash, Frankfurters":
Marble slabs veined with words in meandering lines.
Dropping on the white counter like horn notes
Through a web of violins,
The flat yellow lights of oranges,
The cube-red splashes of apples,
In high plated *epergnes.*
The electric clock jerks every half-minute:
"Coming!—Past!"
"Three beef-steaks and a chicken-pie,"
Bawled through a slide while the clock jerks heavily.
A man carries a china mug of coffee to a distant chair.
Two rice puddings and a salmon salad
Are pushed over the counter;
The unfulfilled chairs open to receive them.
A spoon falls upon the floor with the impact of metal striking stone,
And the sound throws across the room
Sharp, invisible zigzags
Of silver.

Laura Tanne: On Lenox

Black strata in gargoyles of color
On the Avenue . . . mathematics of rhythm
In swagger, slouch, strut of the Avenue.

A spontaneous god spilled a bowl of amber milk
Lost a gold tooth
Emptied seventeen acres of moonlight
And autumn leaves (miscegenous color of the wind)
On the Avenue.

Elaborations of voile, young girls are
Subtle and shy pardons for dark profusions
Of grime and poverty.

One lone red geranium plant
On a rusty window sill
Is a prayer one of them said.
Pairs of young breasts are little lambs
Which have never strayed from brown sun-lit hills.
Their chatter makes fury close his eyes
In reflective peace on the Avenue.

Gay cravats are wishes in crepe de chine
Silken stripes, knitted jersey
On an iceman's assistant, a janitor, a window-washer.
Impertinent fantasies of jazz are visions of forgetfulness
At 128th and Seventh avenue.
Geography is an incident of finding
A girl's lips at midnight.
Brown eyes are a repetitious chant
But the wistful echo of an ancient spiritual
Are the blue eyes shining
Out of a brown face on the Avenue.

Motherhood is an adventure in bitterness.
She is challenge wearing a shroud of hope
To warm the keeper of tears and sighs
The hunger and loneliness of life.
She churns strong and bitter acid

CHARLES GALWEY: Stadium Concert

Welter of loveliness
And cash net sixty days
do it now.
Splendors—
And futilities earning dollars—
The crowd
The individual
New York.

Stone seats in tiers

(Damn my back!)

A semi-circle of brown Doric
Jowled by cigar box tenements
Blatant brick of Hebrew Orphanage Asylum
A many peaked rubble of bastard college
Parodying Oxford and cathedrals
With six windows that slit mild light.

Straight scream of electric arcs.
An orange flame mutters waveringly upward in the dim east city
Below the dusty bastions of a park.

The focus, a belly of sounding board, a stage,
Fat bass fiddles, iron desk.

Tables, lonely, barren, bereft of genial foams.
The central ten thousand huddle
A self-drilled mob school.
Some leech has let the blood
Of outward loveable gayeties.

Girl stenographers "going with" their men.
Jew and Christian.
Clerks salesmen buyers teachers
Dwellers in hot perforations of vertical
Rows of eyes that stare insanely
Vertiginous identity.

Exalted, beautiful, the Seventh Symphony,
The sure reconcilers, brass, wood, strings,
High a woman's voice
Flatterers
Into an escape
To emotions soft red, purple, rhythmic,
Shading away constricted monotony
Of cloaks suits hair nets hats stocks bonds schoolrooms
Dry-goods advertising.

Alone

Two

Where at the semi-circle ends
Individuals vanquish the crowd.

The woman, crouched head over knees
Big hatted,
Her mystery
Poignant where the sounds
Announce themselves in shadows.
The man, tiers under her
Unmoving, straw hatted,
Common cryptic solitary.

INTERMISSION

Program list of guarantors,
Vaguely existent rich, the powerful ones,
Givers of spiritualities out of dollars.

FINAL ENCORE

Showery clapping dispersed.

A concert neatly fitted into the rut
THE BOSS orders them back
To clean bed rooms porcelain efficient kitchens
Strap clutching subway stench, screaming "L"
Sadistic slavery and return.

Or a walk by the park benches
Prescient the Phallic obscene
Day hidden—
Cackling innuendoes boys hug girls—
They write their world in the scrawls of privies.
Dust bare grass
Electric glamour of tree boughs.

Huge naked breast of water
Saturated lead by sewers—

Red and green glow of little boats in swarm—
In it are sunk the stars.

All obsessing electric capitals

Warner's Sugar

And on the Palisade cliff

Surf Bathing

Moon silvered coin edge of ragged cloud
A chuckle streaking straight overhead.

The busses totter spilling the jammed shadows.

Cloaca and Beethoven
Putridity of a monster gas tank gray—
Noise of sliding automobiles and hunger of their eyes
Hunting, yellow—
Fetid heat of August with fecundity at play.

Illusion winged beauty—
A million strangled deaths of trapped souls.

The crypts of loneliness,
The dreams and immundicities of the crowd.

New York.

FORTUNATO DEPERO: Coney Island

SYNOPSIS: Depero uses "alphabetic fountains" and a "typographical explosion" to depict this famous amusement park. He conveys the movement and speed of amusement parks in several places: especially near the top, where the words for roller coaster (montagne russe, or Russian mountains) run parallel to the words "steel mountains for rolling at absurd speeds"; and near the bottom, where a loop-de-loop contains the words "motorcycle loop of death", and the two curved lines that intersect the central ferris wheel repeat the up-and-down words “climb descend climb descend.” Even more numerous and prominent are the references to color and light. A string of alternating “red green” winds around the outside of the large ferris wheel (inside the ferris wheel we find the riders in a “game of laughter,” a “dance of legs,” of “flying [?] embraces” and “winged kisses”—but also, emanating from the wheel’s axis, are perhaps more references to light: “splashes”, “puffs”, “sprays” and “bursts”); above and to the right of the ferris wheel a sort of hall of mirrors features “grape-shot laughs,” “colored fusillades for laughing,” “shoot-outs of light bulbs,” and a “shower of light”; above and to the left of the ferris wheel a tilt-o-wheel has “gorges of illuminations” and “arcs of [light?]” spinning below and around extended lines repeating the word “light”; tumbling down on the left side of the ferris wheel we see a “colored hail of lights” and “downpours” of color and light; and faint strings of the word “light”, singular and doubled, spin off the loop-de-loop to the right.

e. e. cummings: poem, or beauty hurts mr. vinal

take it from me kiddo
believe me
my country, 'tis of

you, land of the Cluett
Shirt Boston Garter and Spearmint
Girl With The Wrigley Eyes (of you
land of the Arrow Ide
and Earl &
Wilson
Collars) of you i
sing: land of Abraham Lincoln and Lydia E. Pinkham,
land above all of Just Add Hot Water and Serve—
from every B. V. D.

let freedom ring

amen.   i do however protest, anent the un
-spontaneous and otherwise scented merde which
greets one (Everywhere Why) as divine poesy per
that and this radically defunct periodical.   i would

suggest that certain ideas gestures
rhymes, like Gillette Razor Blades
having been used and reused
to the mystical moment of dullness emphatically are
Not To Be Resharpened.   (Case in point

if we are to believe these gently O sweetly
melancholy trillers amid the thrillers
these crepuscular violinists among my and your
skyscrapers—Helen & Cleopatra were Just Too Lovely,
The Snail's On The Thorn enter Morn and God's
In His andsoforth

do you get me?) according
to such supposedly indigenous

throstles Art is O World O Life
a formula: example, Turn Your Shirttails Into
Drawers and If It Isn't An Eastman It Isn't A
Kodak therefore my friends let
us now sing each and all fortissimo A-
mer
i
ca, I
love,
You.   And there's a
hun-dred-mil-lion-oth-ers, like
all of you successfully if
delicately gelded (or spaded)
gentlemen (and ladies)—pretty

littleliverpill-
hearted-Nujolneeding-There's-A-Reason
Americans (who tensetendoned and with
upward vacant eyes, painfully
perpetually crouched, quivering, upon the
sternly allotted sandpile
—how silently
emit a tiny violetflavored nuisance: Odor?

ono.
comes out like a ribbon lies flat on the brush

FEDERICO GARCÍA LORCA: Landscape of a Vomiting Multitude (Dusk at Coney Island)

The fat lady came first,
tearing out roots and moistening drumskins.
The fat lady
who turns dying octopuses inside out.
The fat lady, the moon's antagonist,
was running through the streets and deserted buildings
and leaving tiny skulls of pigeons in the corners
and stirring up the furies of the last centuries' feasts

and summoning the demon of dread through the sky's clean-swept hills
and filtering a longing for light into subterranean tunnels.
The graveyards, yes, the graveyards
and the sorrow of the kitchens buried in sand,
the dead, pheasants and apples of another era,
pushing into our throat.

There were murmurings from the jungle of vomit
with the empty women, with hot wax children,
with fermented trees and tireless waiters
who serve platters of salt beneath harps of saliva.
There's no other way, my son, vomit! There's no other way.
It's not the vomit of hussars on the breasts of their whores,
nor the vomit of a cat choking down a frog,
but the dead who scratch with clay hands
on flint gates where clouds and desserts decay.

The fat lady came first
with the crowds from the ships, taverns, and parks.
Vomit was delicately shaking its drums
among a few little girls of blood
who were begging the moon for protection.
Who could imagine my sadness?
The look on my face was mine, but now isn't me.
The naked look on my face, trembling in alcohol
and launching incredible ships
through the anemones of the piers.
I protect myself with this look
that flows from waves where no dawn would go,
I, poet without arms, lost
in the vomiting multitude,
with no effusive horse to shear
the thick moss from my temples.
But the fat lady went first
and the crowds kept looking for the pharmacies
where the bitter tropics could be found.
Only when a flag went up and the first dogs arrived
did the entire city rush to the railings of the boardwalk.

EDOUARD RODITI: Manhattan Novelettes

I.

The Lorelei with the spaghetti hair
Queens it at the raw-meat piano
While her heliotropic audience pays
A thousand looks for every note.

Desperate beneath her platformed feet,
Her rubber lover sweats pure oil;
He's jealous of his snoring neighbor,
The Hairy Ainu with a dyed mink face.

Both men now think her heels are round,
Since each in turn has been her beau
Though neither long enough to know
That art's her love and love her art.

II.

Nursing his beer until it boils,
The boy whose fall cost but a dime
Watches the blond with parrot voice
And hopes she'll whisper love at last.

This pretty polly knows her stuff.
She's no sad sister: hard as nails,
She'll trail her man through fog or fen
And turn her dollar, come what may.

And come who may, by hook or crook,
He'll think this houri's worth her price;
He'll never find, concealed beneath
The feathers smooth, bird-claw, bird-beak.

III.

The subway cowboy with a midnight tan

Texas of sex will nightly roam;
He'll sell his body to any devil
For a greenback dollar bill.

For a greenback dollar bill or two
He'd sell his soul. But who will pay
Visible coin for invisible wares,
Temporal for eternal, who?

All for a greenback dollar bill,
What Wests can we discover yet
Who roam Manhattan's midnight range
From neonrise to neonset?

Fortunato Depero: 24th Street

Synopsis/translation:

skyscraper	taLLL	
golden ember	TALL	
skyscraper	tall	
bayonet	tall	
skyscraper	almost pink	
flat-iron	Dolomite	
towers-tower	**PARAMOUNT**	["blue beacon"
for climbing	BUILDING	*heading up toward the right corner*]
on the staired	*numeric cages	
clouds to enter	figures figures figures figures figures	
the dancing	castles of figures	
of the storms	thousands-millions-trillions	
towers of Babel of	of probabilities of percents	[*on the far right:*
business business busi-	of accounts-credits-debits	*a building made of*
ness—22 million	provisions-customs-tariffs	*walls of* "solid" (*left*)
telephone calls	[* *written sideways*]	*and* "iron" (*right*),
a day that weave	black buildings	"constructed" *floors,*
the most intense	monstrous collossi	*supported by slanting*
human electricity	parallel pipes of	"iron girders"
[*making up*	carbon launched	

the bulk of
the building:
the over-sized
words
NEW
YORK
with "lights" *to the left,*
"elevators" *to the right,*
and in and among the
large letters of NEW
YORK *are* "iron" *and*
"smoke"]
[*To the left of the*
building large "tubes"
intersect.]

out of sight into
the murky vertical
vertigoooooos
the blood-red windows
clamber up
the heights –
they are open counters
infernal coffers
CLOSED SUNDAYS
At the base of these
square mountains
luminous boxes
there burst onto
the streets colored hair -
clothes of a thousand fabrics;
meats; booksellers; machines
of
flowers made of paper and glass

immediately to the
left of this building:
intersecting spirals of
"clear smoke" *and*
"dark smoke"

near the base of this
building there
appears a semi-
circular assortment
of lights:
"pneumatics of lights"
"chains red light"
"rack of lamps"
—*adjoining a sign for*
an "American dish"
"pink India rubber
meat"]

Also prominently visible on the sides of the two skyscrapers are signs for ROXY, PARAMOUNT CINE, *and* HOTEL MANAGER.

Below the buildings, on the streets we find the crowded mass of "tired and scattered" *people* (*wearing* "cynical masks of struggle and tiredness—faces of iron—hearts of iron—tongue of iron—crowd of iron…") *pressed together with more goods* (*slicing down and across the corner of 24th Street and 7th Avenue:* "real furs and fake furs by the million: mountains of the most delicate beasts to cover millions of PINK-WOMEN; BROWN AND BLACK WOMEN"); *with what appear to be traffic lights* (*upward thrusting* "iron trees with luminous fruit that signal the voracious shifts of speed"); *and with t* the "floating" vision of "sweet and seductive blonds".

In the city's lower depths (at the bottom left), an "uncertain bastard humanity" *dissolves into a confused stream of dreary clothing*—"silk stockings and red and blue threads on stove-cylinder legs, punched-out hair with flowers of straw and polished tin, gloves-hats-jackets of the oiliest leather"—*and (at the bottom right) restless machine and body parts* ("torrents of legs that mow each other down, herds of cars that move in close formation with shivers of disciplined brilliance, confetti-crowd, ants-crowd, human cage that runs, unlaces, slides, picks, thins and thickens with exasperating order and continuity; and comes and goes, and comes and goes, and comes and goes, andcomesandgoesandcomesandgoes"

Slicing down through these depths: a "tiny crowd that moves forward intensely in every sense."

At the bottom right of the image, the artist-observer looks up at this sea of humanity and notes: "Always in view two magnificent calves."

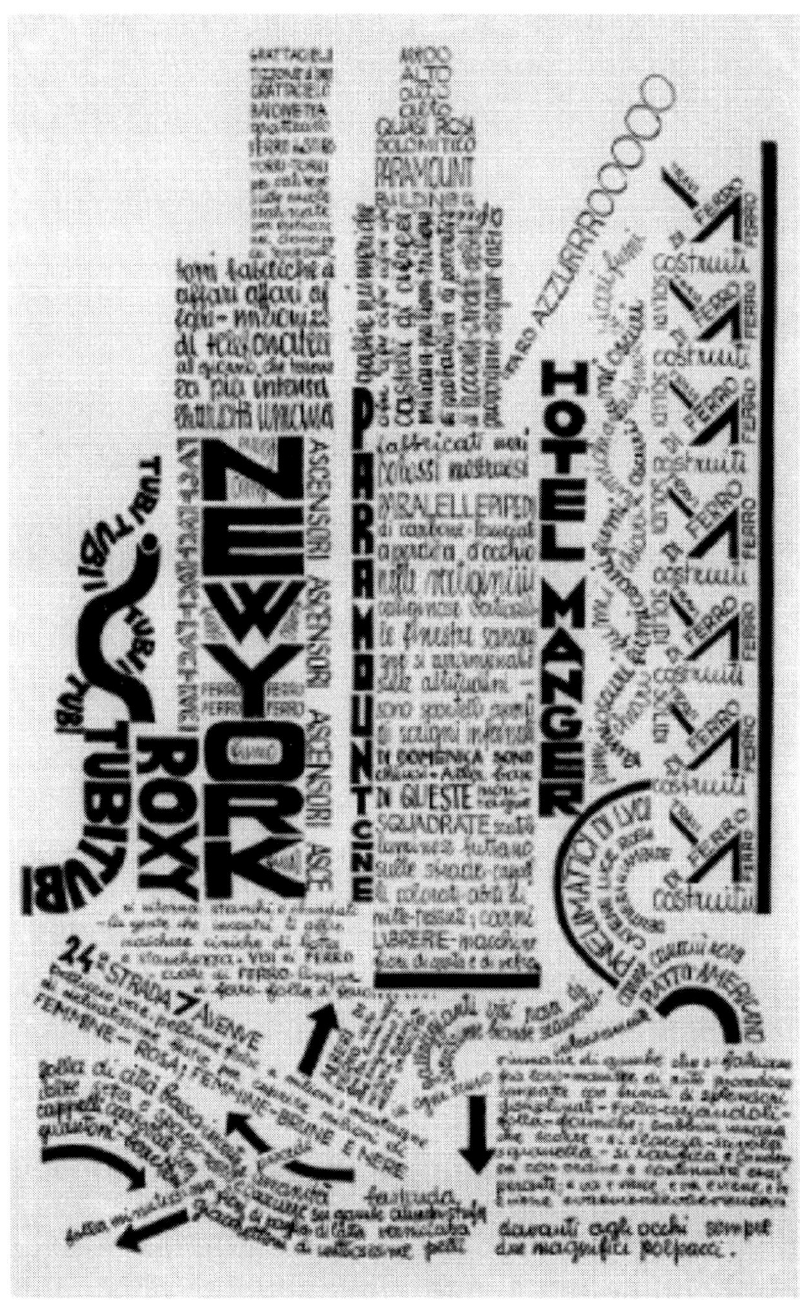

Jaroslav Seifert: New York

THIS IS NOT THE MAIDEN OF ORLEANS
THIS IS THE FAMOUS STATUE OF LIBERTY
WHICH BEARS THE TORCH AND SCORCHES
THE AIRPLANE'S WINGS

CINELAND: CHAPLINADE

PARKER TYLER: Paean

Charlie of the fresh boutonniere and the soiled vest . . . Charlie of the windy pants, the silent giggle, and the heart of candy . . . Charlie of the boyish mouth and the slim shoulders, of the infant eyes and the Promethean brows . . . Charlie of the outturned toes, open to the blow of fate . . . Charlie of the shuffle, flirt, and skimmer . . . Charlie of the *moue triste* . . . the clasped, terribly normal hands . . . the ten-cent mustache . . . Charlie of the back like a poem . . . Charlie of the tousled hair, the shrug of the Void . . . Charlie of the *jeune fille* waist . . . Charlie, divinely fastidious . . . Charlie of the trick derby, the obliging, automatic smile . . . Charlie, sad as a vacationing angel . . . Charlie of the heavy date, the hot romance, the owl's stare . . . Charlie of the epilepsy of tenderness . . . Charlie: credulous as a dog, suspicious as a cat . . . Charlie, who could sleep anywhere . . . Charlie of the delicate behind, the straight neck of a prince or a prizefighter . . . Charlie, the unflagging, mute accusation against mankind: he of the monosyllabic silhouette . . . of the dash through space . . . the French kick . . . Charlie, Charlie the funny . . . Where is he now?—only in the mind, as we remember him, or in the past of "Monsieur Verdoux."

XAVIER ABRIL: X-Ray of Chaplin

1
Charles Chaplin's reality belongs to everyone but him. Every one of Chaplin's adventures is a loss of his reality. Pure creation, surrealism—bearing in mind the escapism of dreams.

2
Chaplin clouds the bourgeois sense of rotation. For this reason fat men are so charming and rudderless next to Chaplin.Others always lack atmosphere when Chaplin moves.

3
Chaplin's intentions are already lurking in the ovaries of today's mothers.

4
Babies say "Chaplin" and wet themselves. Infants in Virginia are given nipples and Chaplin to keep them pacified.

5
Chaplin's solitude resides more in the Pole than in the Circus, which is a telegraphic, X-ray version of the Pole.

6
I feel that Charles Chaplin's smile has sprung from the curly locks of my childhood, from my first way of experiencing the world.

7
In his creative life, Chaplin—in Freudian terms—is as he should "be" in real life. Such is the nature of his small-scale tragedy, at times augmented by his long sleeves and loose attire, by one eye glancing sidelong at the blank numbers inside his tomb-like pockets.

8
Charles Chaplin was the first to announce the disenchantment of Romanticism, and if he was somewhat sentimental, it was due to his Jewish waywardness, his world-weariness.

9
Charles Chaplin's shoes are epic, Napoleonic. His jacket is like Musset's, complete with a honey-tongued keepsake from one of his trysts. Chaplin's jacket has the sobs of Romanticism as its trademark.

10
Chaplin borrows his technique from the poor. He finds himself before a row of closed doors. Chaplin knows, moreover, that the doors of the bourgeoisie only open from the inside.

11
From behind, Chaplin is a photographer who could have shot portraits of the lame, the disfigured, the invalids of war.

12
Chaplin's films, once shown, glean new sensations from the world.

13
Chaplin is in the world by divine providence. It is impossible to do without his little mustache during Easter. Chaplin has replaced the Three Kings.

14
St. Nicholas sprinkles Chaplin in children's stockings. But Chaplin laughs at St. Nicholas.

15
Children grow fat watching Chaplin.

16
Chaplin should be manufactured. And just as you buy a house or a car, you should be able to purchase a Chaplin.

17
Chaplin's pathos is inspired by the mannequins of poor tailors.

18
The atmosphere of the Pole is the same as that of circus tents. There are sub-freezing temperatures. One dreads bears and Eskimos.

19
In his film *The Circus*, Chaplin reaches a realm of solitude, obscurity, limits. Chaplin leaves life behind via the circumference of the sky.

20
Chaplin's appearances seem like blackmail. We watch him descend on an elevator of clouds, pathetic, alone, stiff, pale. Chaplin has the face of a dove and an olive branch.

21
We all bear some resemblance to Chaplin. I find that my navel is my childhood and Chaplin.

22
Something from sacred history must have snuck into the machine, so that Chaplin could have stepped into the world left left left foot first.

23
Chaplin embodies certain fat men, old spectators, in a painful way.

24
That dark lock of hair falling into Chaplin's face suggests that he has read Eguren's "clouds of yore": black clouds of mourning, of a funeral chapel.

25
On the darkest nights, Chaplin slips out of the side of the moon.

26
On windy, rainy nights, Chaplin sits soaking beneath his umbrella. Chaplin is absurd, and he looks at himself in the mirror. He knows he is absurd.

27
Early every morning street sweepers find Chaplin dead in city trash bins.

28
Seeing Chaplin for the first time we think we are beholding a fireman unfit for love. Chaplin's sentimental heart is a shambles. He has cracks in his eyelids where black water seeps in, lending his eyes their gloomy, celluloid look.

29
Chaplin is the New Man because he is the anti Don Juan. He is loving and grounded in his humanity—which does not require of him that he be a cowardly lover. The NEW man creates woman in an ultimate gesture of narcissism. So it is. And so be it.

30
On the other hand, Chaplin enjoys magnificent health. He could be a polar explorer, silently, without telegraph service or sustenance.

31
Chaplin is the greatest mystic of the arts. Chaplin—white, aerial—surpasses St. John.

32
One can find Chaplin slipping out of his private dining room, as flustered as a child for not being on screen at this very moment.

33
At 7pm in the Bay of Biscay there are fish that resemble Chaplin.

34
Chaplin: with a red carnation in his buttonhole and awful luck with women.
Chaplin: next stop Spain to study Don Juan.

35
Quevedo would die to meet Chaplin.

36
Quevedo and the Cid say that Chaplin is a twit.

37
Chaplin signals the dawn of a NEW HUMANITY.

Alexander Rodchenko: Charlot

He never pretends to be no one,
Never worries at all,
Rarely changes his costume,
wears no makeup,
remains true to himself, never mocks a soul.

He simply knows how to reveal himself so fully and audaciously that he affects the viewer more than others do.

The tempo of his movement contrasts with the tempo of his partner. He doesn't act—but walks, runs, falls, picks things up, unwraps them, and shows them just as he shows and unwraps himself.

He has no pathos, he isn't monumental—this is his value for the contemporary world—he is momental.

He doesn't need the old tinsel of the stage—set decorations—and the newfangled tinsel—the eclectic, generalized Constructivism of our monumentalists with their gods: dynamo, aero, radio station, cranes, and so on.

He is Charlie Chaplin—he can show everything he needs to with his bowler derby and cane.

Charlie Chaplin was in the circus and knows that things should be either smaller or bigger than a person, that next to a mountain or a dirigible a human being is nothing, but next to a screw and one surface—he is Master.

His colossal rise is precisely and clearly—the result of a keen sense of the present day: of war, revolution Communism.

Every master-inventor is inspired to invent by new events or demands.

Who is it today?

Lenin and technology.

The one and the other are the foundation of his work.

Thus is the new man designed—a master of details, that is, the future of anyman.

Today this is the artist and actor Charlie Chaplin—a master of details.

JEAN EPSTEIN: Charlie Chaplin

Tears!
Despair of such a smile
where, pathetic and distracted,
the pirouette
is reflected
gray and glum and tender end
of a drama to make you hang yourself
Nostalgia that festers
from gesture to gesture
certain and precise
Laugh
Every meter carries a disappointment
One asks for grace
Laugh
When   morose
fresco crowned with roses
Laugh dance
naïve elegance
Laugh innocence
in love with a charming imbecile, un-
                              happy and ironic
Laugh Genius of the clown
A cretin said "Slapstick comedy"
Happiness!
pure and heavy glory of an idiotic insult.

Osip Mandelstam

Charlie Chaplin
        came out of the show,
Two boot-soles,
        a hare-lip,
Two bright peepers
        full of ink,
And god what wonderful
        astonished power.
Charlie Chaplin—
        a hare-lip,
Two boot-soles—
        ah a pitiful fate.
Somehow we all live unsuccessfully—
        strangers, strangers.
Tin horror
        on his face,
The head
        won't stay in place,
Soot-black struts,
        shoe-black minces,
And slowly, quietly, gently,
        Chaplin says:
"What am I known and loved
        and even famous for?"
And a great highway leads him
        to strangers, to strangers.
Oh Charlie Chaplin,
        step on it, Charlie.
Oh Chaplin, rabbit,
        fight your way into the role, shove, push,
Peel red-pulp Malta oranges,
        put on the roller-skates,
And your wife—
        a blind shadow—
And the alien distance tries
        to be original, and is strange.
And why does Chaplin

have a tulip,
And why is the crowd
so loving?
Because, because—
this is Moscow, after all.
Charlie, Charlie—
you have to take risks,
This is the wrong time to go sour.
Your bowler hat is that ocean, that same ocean,
And Moscow is so close you might fall in love
with the sweet, sweet road.

UMBERTO SABA: Charlot in The Gold Rush

We see
a chain of mountains
snow covered.

At a deadly
pace, interminable single file,
in furs, resembling bears,
the men go,
and go,
motionless because
nearby the abyss beckons.
If there's gold out there,
and those who put their lives
on the line pursuing a dream,
it seems fair if it falls to those
who go it alone. Outside
the frame. Alone, glaciers crumbling,
in short jacket and cane, appears
Charlot.

In its age,
its melancholy, all Europe is mirrored
in him.

Sad,
very sad, and all you can do is laugh!
Pondering "this man or that?" you wonder,
for he manages
impossible
things
amidst a swarm of
monsters, relying
on the most fragile equilibrium,
and the challenge is met
right where it needs to be,
at the point where death perches,
the heaps of gold are biggest,
and a beautiful woman
has greatest appeal . . .
in a dream.

Don't despair,
even if every resource he seeks
fails.

His face
under the hat bomb, a little oblique,
has the watchful eyes of a dog that
quickly sniffs out danger,
dark sentence calling down fate,
and the fatal blow. And oh so
sad, Charlot, but it pleased you
plucking the fruit of chance,
oh so good, *so* good,
that at heart, you give
just a bit more, and an anguished end.
Between him and the gold in America,
that's everything.

Charlot,
every hungry immigrant dreams
your dream.

Coming home on a big shiny

oceanliner, he's a grand gentleman
very happy.
Why say
that? His face raised to the beautiful sky
checking the weather,
his person adorned
with one or two furs, has no cares,
approaches the door of the cab
like royalty, . . . the rest
no more than a cigar butt
twisted with the heart of poverty, the mouth
and the door.

Charlot,
there's no one sadder than you,
I know.

Rafael Alberti: Charlie's Sad Date

My necktie, my gloves.
My gloves, my necktie.

The butterfly knows nothing about the death of the tailors,
about wardrobes conquering the sea.
Gentlemen, my age is 900,000 years.
Wow!

I was a boy when fish didn't swim,
when geese didn't say mass
or the snail attack the cat.
Miss, let's play at cat and mouse.

The saddest thing, mister, is a watch:
11, 12, 1, 2.

At three on the dot a passerby will drop dead.
you, moon, moon of late taxis,
smoky moon of firemen,

don't be scared.

The city is burning in the sky,
clothing like mine gets sick of the country.
My age is suddenly 25.

Because it snows, it snows
and my body turns into a wooden shack.
Wind, I invite you to rest.
It is too late to dine on stars.

But we can dance, lost tree,
a waltz for wolves,
for the sleep of the hen without fox's claws.

I have mislaid my cane.
It is very sad to think of it alone in the world.
My cane!

My cat, my cuffs,
my gloves, my shoes.

The bone that hurts most, my love, is the watch:
11, 12, 1, 2.

3 on the dot.
In the pharmacy a nude cadaver evaporates.

PAUL MORAND: from *Evening with Charlot*

Already
on the screen
images are moving.
A waste
land,
a human bundle sleeps behind the boardwalk;
on the other side of the fence
an old Jewish

hot dog vendor;
at sunrise
those sausages perfume the morning;
then the pile of black clothes suddenly comes to life . . .
All around me,
in the darkened studio,
laughter
bursts out:
It's the recognition of Charlie:
This child laughs at his universe.
And,
isn't he right to laugh,
since the fat yankee policeman's club
on the lookout for him
behind the boardwalk
has never snuffed him out for good?

YVAN GOLL: from *The Chaplinade*

Having arrived at the center of the earth, Chaplin holds a telephone receiver to his ear, listening to the voices of the globe as if he were at the central switchboard of the world—reproduced on the sound track:

> *Ten million butterflies / The old baker murdered /* Un jour viendra / *In the year 800 Charlemagne became / I'll tell you everything and nothing / A fever of 76 degrees / Macaroni with red tomatoes / I'm in love with a lady from Zanzibar / Bitteschön / Christsson and Company, Collars and Gentleman's Linens / Milk train to Marathon / The Radical Left has gotten frightened /* La la la petite femme / *No, it would be better yesterday than tomorrow / Charlottenburg six / Baked brains in butter . . .*

CHAPLIN: Is that what people are thinking?
The center of the earth is roaring
With a tumult of lies, stupidity of telephones, insanity of telegrams.
How poverty-stricken man is. All literature melts away
In the face of this golden syllable: pain!
The fountain of the brain is spewing numbers

And empty bubbles float down from the starry sky
To explode in the dirty waters of canals.
Graveyards with their heavy stones weigh down on all memory:
And our love is always false.
The only truth is longing
For the infinite illusion!
But the truth will always make us yawn!

GUILLERMO DE TORRE: Charlot

«J'ai sauvé aux hommes ce qui'ils avaient perdu depuis de siècles
Je leur ai rendu le joyau de leur âme: LE RIRE
Et pourtant je suis le plus seul des hommes.»

IWAN GOLL: *La Chaplinade*

Charlie Chaplin
K i n g   o f   p h o t o g e n i c   c r e a t i o n
Sign of the new comic dawn
Dynamometer of modern humor—

The laughter of his unipersonal mask
liquefies the jolly torrents—
Oh, the intention of his framed gesticulation!
S p r a y   o f   i n t e r s t i t i a l   s m i l e s

Walks like a duck on the lawn
Puppet caricature
The mechanism of his movements
logarithmizes cinematic equations
Rhythmic games
of looks and gestures converging
on the vertex of pure grace
C h a r l o t i s m = a r t o f l i n e a r c l o w n i s m

He's a spiritual mime
Full of reality   he moves
in the plane of the everyday grotesque
His face of paradoxical melancholy
is a diagram of rippling buffoonery

His peculiar *tic* is raised to the plane of religious rite:
And when he bows, his forehead becomes his occipital
and his cane, an urban *cowboy's* lasso
to capturethe neck of Edna Purviance
and the bare legs of the luminous *sunshine girls*

C h a r l o t u n i q u e   e q u a l t o h i m s e l f
splits and multiplies in parallel mirrors:
Charlot soldier aviator vagabond sailor fire fighter violinist in the war in the fields in the theatre . . .
Mime and debater
Sole creator of chaplinesque farces
Spiritual father of Jackie Coogan
Charlot p o l a r i z e s h i m s e l f u b i q u i t o u s l y
Passing through cities,
Flooding the continents—
The fountain of his laughter
unbends our folded spirits
—leading the way to humorous antics
Simultaneous and multiform
from all the screens and posters
his whirling laughter
accelerates the spin of the hours—

HART CRANE: Chaplinesque

We make our meek adjustments,
Contented with such random consolations
As the wind deposits
In slithered and too ample pockets.

For we can still love the world, who find
A famished kitten on the step, and know
Recesses for it from the fury of the street,
Or warm torn elbow coverts.

We will sidestep, and to the final smirk
Dally the doom of that inevitable thumb

That slowly chafes its puckered index toward us,
Facing the dull squint with what innocence
And what surprise!

And yet these fine collapses are not lies
More than the pirouettes of any pliant cane;
Our obsequies are, in a way, no enterprise.
We can evade you, and all else but the heart:
What blame to us if the heart live on.

The game enforces smirks; but we have seen
The moon in lonely alleys make
A grail of laughter of an empty ash can,
And through all sound of gaiety and quest
Have heard a kitten in the wilderness.

Gunnar Björling: Charlie Chaplin

No one's
Laugh from his mouth,
The great sorrow.
Look, Missus and the cop hot dog stand kid,
Painting crazy eyes
With your feet
Packed threefold in a packing-case sent
In the last railroad car
To a place for what will become of us.

Walter Benjamin: Chaplin

After a showing of *The Circus*, Chaplin never allows the audience to smile while watching him. They must either double up laughing or be very sad.

Chaplin greets people by taking off his bowler, and it looks like the lid rising from the kettle when the water boils over.

His clothes are impermeable to every blow of fate. He looks like a man who hasn't taken his clothes off for a month. He is unfamiliar with beds; when he lies down, he does so in a wheelbarrow or on a seesaw.

Wet through, sweaty, in clothes far too small for him, Chaplin is the living embodiment of Goethe's *aperçu*: Man would not be the noblest creature on earth if he were not too noble for it.

This film is the first film of Chaplin's old age. He has grown older since his last films, but he also acts old. And the most moving thing about this new film is the feeling that he now has a clear overview of the possibilities open to him, and that he is resolved to work exclusively within these limits to attain his goal.

At every point the variations on his greatest themes are displayed in their full glory. The chase is set in a maze; his unexpected appearance would astonish a magician; the mask of noninvolvement turns him into a fairground marionette. The most wonderful part is the way the end of the film is structured. He strews confetti over the happy couple, and you think: This must be the end. Then you see him standing there when the circus procession starts off; he shuts the door behind everyone, and you think: This must be the end. Then you see him stuck in the rut of the circle earlier drawn by poverty, and you think: This must be the end. Then you see a close-up of his completely bedraggled form, sitting on a stone in the arena. Here you think the end is absolutely unavoidable, but then he gets up and you see him from behind, walking further and further away, with that gait peculiar to Charlie Chaplin; he is his own walking trademark, just like the company trademark you see at the end of other films. And now, at the only point where there's no break and you'd like to be able to follow him with your gaze forever—the film ends!

◈ A NEW MYTHOLOGY ◈

HUGO BALL

KARAWANE

jolifanto bambla ô falli bambla
grossiga m'pfa habla horem
égiga goramen
higo bloiko russula huju
hollaka hollala
anlogo bung
blago bung
blago bung
bosso fataka
ü üü ü
schampa wulla wussa olobo
hej tatta gôrem
eschige zunbada
wulubu ssubudu uluw ssubudu
tumba ba- umf
kusagauma
ba - umf

VIRGINIA WOOLF: from *Mrs Dalloway*

A sound interrupted him; a frail quivering sound, a voice bubbling up without direction, vigor, beginning or end, running weakly and shrilly and with an absence of all human meaning into

ee um fah um so
foo swee too eem oo—

the voice of no age or sex, the voice of an ancient spring spouting from the earth; which issued, just opposite Regent's Park Tube Station, from a tall quivering shape, like a funnel, like a rusty pump, like a wind-beaten tree for ever barren of leaves which lets the wind run up and down its branches singing

ee um fah um so
foo swee too eem oo,

and rocks and creaks and moans in the eternal breeze.

Through all ages—when the pavement was grass, when it was swamp, through the age of tusk and mammoth, through the age of silent sunrise—the battered woman—for she wore a skirt—with her right hand exposed, her left clutching at her side, stood singing of love—love which has lasted a million years, she sang, love which prevails, and millions of years ago her lover, who had been dead these centuries, had walked, she crooned, with her in May . . .

YVAN GOLL: For a New Mythology

for Alfred Ehrenstein, last poet of Miteuropa

Mississippi
God of gods
Dark American Zeus

Copper fiddle
Heavenly telephone
Tell about your dynamic arena

Cable from Peking
Cable from Erebus
Bring ancient longing and doubt

Ancient fate
Love and farewell
Rev your heart up to 3,000 volts

Pale earth is rusty
But horse

Power churns it faster and faster

Distant sphinx
Opens stony eyes
Love works radioactive

From Aetna's slopes
To Milky Way
Hastens a Broadway rainbow

Golden airships
Already export to the stars
Christianity and cash

Only the weary old poet
Clinging to the Eiffel Tower
Burns his birds and dreams

Tossing
Such useless things
Behind

Guillermo de Torre: Eiffel Tower

T
O
R
R
EIFFEL

(to Robert Delaunay)

This is my poem to the tower
Eiffel Tower

Abstract tower
World tower
I, the Tower of Madrid
On the bell tower of Santa Cruz

High song, with wings like flowers,
Rises above it all

Listen to the aviator's rhythm
of my motorized Word
that sings and skates in the blue
and circles the tower.

Atmospheric perspectives

TOWER
Gigantic tree
Sky spider
Steed of the air
Electric bird
Mechanical man
VERTICAL ALLEGORY
Rays of light—lights—lightning
Blossom of synchronized landscapes
Bridges jump-rope
over the Seine

Submerged sounds
Conjuring colors

DYNAMIC APOTHEOSIS
Vibrating puzzle
of volcanic Tower
on moving streets
contorted houses
and drunken people
= as in the kaleidoscopic picture
of the destructive Delaunay =

(The best poets

write madrigals at your feet
oh, Eiffel Tower:
"graceful palm tree": Cendrars
"zenith and nadir": Apollinaire
"guitar of the sky": Huidobro
"symbol of victory": Beauduin
"organ of the Trocadero": Goll
"ray-thrower": Soupault)

T. S. F.
The antennas exult
And the souls of the towers
through their armored flesh
change their synthetic words
f r o m p o l e t o p o l e
p
o
t
n
o
m
a
I

My soul hurls itself
into the electric air

T o w e r
H e l i x o f t i m e
G y m n a s t o f s p a c e
R o c k e t — s i g n a l
o f a s c e n d i n g i n t e n t i o n s

The flag of triumph in the wind
Solar reflector
of new films

Oh lookout Tower
Your eyes X-ray the body of Paris

Tower disguised and polyhedral
daughter of Proteus
How many faces have you shown

during the days of war
and oceanic nights

Tower of the Occident
Compass of aesthetic winds
Line of the lyric meridian
Ghost of the rainbow
Show of the everlasting novelty

T Perpendicular arrow
O
W Compass of the new spirit
E
R Lightning rod of Beauty

Vicente Huidobro: Eiffel Tower

for Robert Delaunay

Eiffel Tower
Guitar of the sky

Your wireless telegraphy
draws words
As a rose bush draws bees

During the night
The Seine halts its flow

Telescope or bugle

EIFFEL TOWER

And it's a hive of words
Or an inkpot of honey

At the dawn's bottom
A spider with legs of steel wire
Was making her web of clouds

My little boy
To climb the Eiffel Tower
We climb up on a song
Do
re
mi
fa
so
la
ti
do
We're up on top

A bird sings
In the telegraph
Antennae

It is the wind
Of Europe
The electric wind

Below
The hats fly
They have wings but do not sing

Jacqueline
Daughter of France
What do you see up there

The Seine sleeps
Under its bridges' shadows

I see the Earth turn
And I sound my bugle
Toward all of the oceans

On the way
Of your perfume
All the bees and the words take off

Upon the four horizons
Who has not heard this song

I AM THE QUEEN OF THE DAWN OF THE POLES

I AM THE ROSE OF THE WINDS THAT WILTS EVERY AUTUMN
AND FILLED WITH SNOW
I DIE THE DEATH OF THIS ROSE
IN MY HEAD A BIRD SINGS THROUGHOUT THE YEAR

That's how the Tower spoke to me one day

Eiffel Tower
Aviary of the world
Sing Sing

Clamor of Paris

The giant suspended in the midst of emptiness
Is the advertisement for France

On the day of Victory
You'll describe it to the stars

MICHEL LEIRIS: December 22-23, 1923

I meet a woman in a movie theater, I speak to her, I caress her. Arm in arm, we go to the little bungalow where she lives, on a street that is a row of brothels. She opens the bungalow door and leads me to her bedroom: a young girl's room. She makes it clear that she is mine for the taking, but just as I am about to possess her, I am seized by second thoughts: this woman is a prostitute and most likely diseased. I leap into the garden with a single bound and jump (exactly as a woman would jump on a chair at the sight of a rat or a large spider) on top of one of the two stone pillars that frame the entrance gate. I perch on this pedestal like a stylite.

As I am getting ready to leap down to the street, I realize that I am in fact on the uppermost platform of the Eiffel Tower, so I hold back. For a moment, I consider climbing down the outside of the tower, gripping the iron cross-bars. But knowing I would suffer a fatal bout of vertigo, I give up the idea and resign myself to waiting for the arrival of the next elevator. The platform is at once a ship's deck, an airplane, the top of a lighthouse. I have no idea when I'll make it down.

WALTER BENJAMIN: Paris as Goddess

A bibliographic allegory: The goddess of the capital of France resting dreamily in her boudoir. A marble chimney, cornices, bulging cushions, animal skins spread over divans and floors. And knickknacks, knickknacks everywhere. Models of the Pont des Arts and the Eiffel Tower. On plinths, reminders of so many forgotten things—the Tuileries, the Temple, and the Château d'Eaux in miniature. In a vase, the ten lilies from the city's coat of arms. But all this colorful bric-à-brac is intensified, outdone, buried beneath the overwhelming quantity of books of every shape and size—in sextodecimo, duodecimo, octavo, quarto, and folio in every conceivable color—held out by illiterate amoretti swooping down from above, scattered by fauns shaking out the Horn of Plenty from the hangings, spread out before her by kneeling genies: signs of poetic homage from every corner of the globe. Chaste street directories covered in shrunken leather and secured with a lock dating back to the city's youth—far more seductive for the true connoisseur than the illustrated atlases, which sumptuously reveal all; *Les mystères de Paris*, shamelessly laid bare in all the black luster of its copperplate engravings; vain volumes that speak to the city of nothing but their author, of his astuteness, his distinction, if not indeed of the moments of happiness he has enjoyed with her; and books with the aristocratic modesty of crystalline mirrors, in which the object of veneration can view herself in all the shapes and poses she has adopted over the centuries. To say nothing of the most important sign of the Baroque emblem that we are constructing here *post festum:* the sight of the flood of books in the foreground, pouring out over the curved ramp of the boudoir and landing at the feet of a committee of reviewers, who have their hands full catching them and sharing them out among themselves.

JINDŘICH ŠTYRSKÝ: Picture

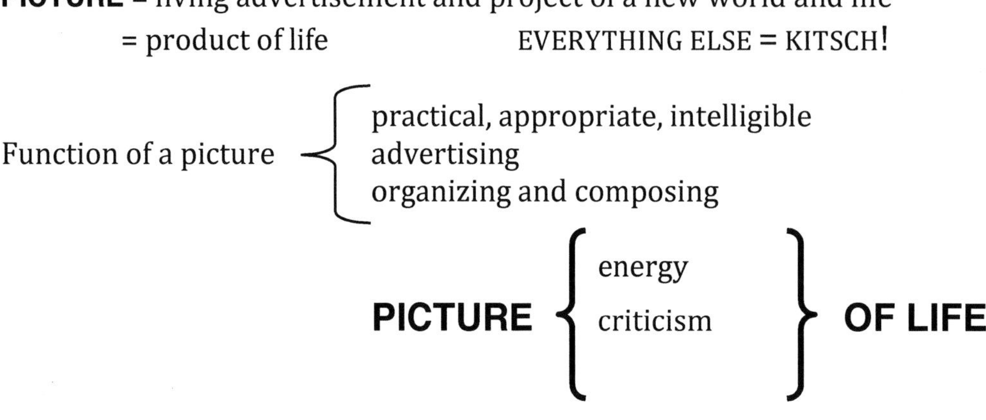
PICTURE = living advertisement and project of a new world and life
= product of life
EVERYTHING ELSE = KITSCH!
Function of a picture
practical, appropriate, intelligible
advertising
organizing and composing
PICTURE
energy
criticism
OF LIFE

motive power

Requirements: a picture must be active
it must do something in the world. In order to accomplish the task allotted to it, it must be mechanically reproduced. 1,000, 10,000, 100,000 copies. Reproduction. Graphic art by pamphlet.
I hate pictures as much as I hate snobs who buy them out of the desire to be individual so that they can sigh in front of them in their easy chairs between the four walls of their aesthetic flats (à la Matisse!).
A picture is not just a picture! *The picture hangs on the wall in a closed area, a barren decoration, and does nothing, wants nothing, says nothing: it does not live.*

Teige: **BE A POSTER!**
an advertisement and project for a new world!

A plan, project of a new world—by exploring new, more beautiful, more useful forms and values of life
—by exploring new, more beautiful, more useful forms and values of life

Advertisements and promotion of new, more beautiful, more useful forms and values of life.

The new world lives neither in the stars nor in the clouds but on earth. Much of the new world we already know, have, and live.

PROMOTION

of new beauty, health, wisdom, freedom, order, joy of life.

Goll: The Chaplin Saga (cinema). – Černik: Joys of the Electric Century. – Nezval: The Wisdom of Foolhardy Merriment. – Krejcar: Americanism. – Birot: Outdoor Poetry. – Teige: Paris. – Seifert: Paris. – Picasso-Seurat: Circus. The Third International. – Film (music hall, circus).

Publicity: of ideas
of books
of revolution
of actions and attractions

Definitely **not** promotion of “Mánes,” Ibsen, Stinnes, Poincaré, the bourgeoisie, social patriots, academies, salons, KU KLUX KLAN.

PICTURE

building up	tearing down
positive action	negative action
objective	subjective

JOURNALISTIC REVOLUTIONARY CARICATURE destroys, whips, hates.

FORM: Dictated by a purpose, brief, exact, intelligible, entertaining, lucid, constructive, simple: no decoration, ornament, pettiness, literature, psychology, mysticism.

Beauty without soul

THE DESIGN OF A NEW GLOBE

Picture = constructive poem of the beauties of the world

Guillermo de Torre: Mental Diagram

All is rhythm, contrast, simultaneity
Discontinuous wobble of the impressionist trajectory
Tachycardia
The motor of my anxiety harmonizes its pulse
To the contrapuntal syncope of the jazz-band
The nerves leap in lyric hypertension
Eager for new spaces
X-ray glances
The illusion of action won’t do
We need to be multiplied into the vital horizons
Avoid the sunstroke of deep depression
Although Epstein elucidates the law of intellectual fatigue
Seismic commotion of aesthetics and ideologies

But life is still shredding us with hostile blades
In the danger zone we need to shield our sensibilities
I exult when I see in *L'Esprit Nouveau*
Perfect specimens of the latest planes: lyric "Farman," slender "Bleriot," magnificent "Air Express"!
They modulate the rhythm of speed,
That new religion Marinetti preaches in his countless manifestos
Electric-sidereal harmony
Engines sound better than hendecasyllables
Optimism — impulse — Western light
Fearless concepts glide
Let's knock down the towering ivory columns
Ah! the breezes of elliptical humor
With which the author of the *Greguerías* lightens the load of his findings, infusing them with Quevedesque microrealism
Beautiful stylized caricatures
Eternal beauty doesn't exist
Oh! marvels of the fleeting moment, only for a moment seized
All that's historically majestic vanishes
And our loud guffaws of lyrical anthropo-afflatus breaks the anachronic spell
New art has a comfortable earthy dimension
Poetry says Epstein along with me is no longer in mythology, not in the lives of saints nor in the museums
It's right at hand in railway stations and piers
If Beethoven wants to soar up to the Empyrean listening to his *Pathètique* I'd rather plunge with Satie into the everyday soundworld
In the same way Darius Milhaud's been thrilled hearing *Indianola* and *Hindustan*, my vertebrae clack in a jubilant spasm to Auric's fox-trot *Adieu New York*
May poems likewise vibrate to the accelerated rhythm of "rag music"
The images of so many petals quickly lose their striations and unfold in metaphoric perspectives
A new lyricism purifies itself in the cognitive vortex
I prefer, to symbols, tangible things full of hypnotic force, hypervital sense
The asphyxiations of sentiment have vanished with the last of the moonlight where dandies faint away
Emotion is measured now in the speedboat's altimeter
Psychoanalysis and energetic hypnotic power supersede the eros of the leitmotif
A simple sign —European Trains International Company— is worth all the glamour of poetic exotica

Isn't trivial poetry the most sincere of all? A poem's as free as a diary entry,
Apollinaire said
The air is bristling with generative incitement
I've cursed the penumbra of "Woman"
But erotic emotion pulsates before the Exceptional Woman
Rejecting morphine, I inject myself with three Hollywood flicks
Intellectual reality over sensory appearance — as the theorists of Cubism say
Thrilled crowds collide amidst Futurist mutual understanding
In ten Picasso still-lifes I see a shower of abstractions
Shapes stretch their elastic lines: color harmonies abound in pictures by Delaunay
The Futurist noise machines take up the sound of walking *greguerías* and the
thrash of noise composes a colossal tentacled orchestra
Every winter there's a subversive theoretical cyclone
From the new art magazines I snort exciting doses of experimental aesthetics
My intellectual hunger opens up great cavities in the books
I am actor-audience of the action mind
I'm intent on the fleeting moment, full of its own synthetic contemporary
expressionism, an expressionism with an eternally present vibration
1921-1922 : Table of cerebral emissions : Ars Poetica : helicoidal turn.
And that's where I've filmed the curvilinear diagram of my mental temperature.

VÍTĚZSLAV NEZVAL: Pierrot Cyclist

Pierrot
is begging

like a zebra
The prompter is

She trains children
with dabblers

is the Cinderella
Backstage

she is dressing up the puppets
raising the dead

cyclist
on Sunday
an hour from the city
in a striped shirt

Columbine

The filmstar

in a fast movement

Pierrot
Vaudeville

of the nymphs
applauds

Pierrot
moon
on his shoulder
dreamingly says to Columbine
"For the spring
indeed
the best plan
is the aero-plan(e)".

is holding the lamp for her

good mood
humming

The public

Jaroslav Seifert: ! ! Hello ! !

Since fauns elves and dryads suffered extinction
it was necessary to invent the telephone! Hello!
that love of yours is driving me to desperation
  a swallow is sitting on the telephone pole

At dusk when the dew has cooled wither will the flower
but from the famous Capitol to Manhattan's skyscrapers
the beauty of women has not withered even for an hour
  in the snow of exotic powders and vapors

To be sure the lovesick are sustained by poetry
and for you the gramophone your love will bemoan
after all candymaker Love from vanilla he makes ice cream
  and is shivering with the cold

The cuckoo in the clock a hundred times has called
On the icicle flute an aria I blow
See starry notes that song is already old
  in Paris there is the magasin Printemps

And in the Radio bar a drunken pilot wagers

that he will reach the stars before you finish your cigarette
What countless pleasures life could allot
    but poets do not have wings

And if it were not for grief love's sickness afflicting me
I would mix my pleasures like cards and cocktails
how sad would the funeral be for the brothers Fratellini

pierrot with a lute and boston

Ilarie Voronca: from *Ulysses in the City* [IX]

The boulevards glaze themselves like loaves in the morning bakery
The automobiles slide through the esophagus of silence
The parks open fresh empty mirrors
And before you know it in the restaurants where at noon the staff scurries
The dishes flow vertiginous pell-mell like trains
I saw in the butcher's window
Chuckling beasts their bellies open like flaps
The slaughterhouse thunders like drums
Now your blood courses like the metro
A memory signals, tempting you like a day off
And suddenly the North Sea is a blue cape
The mermaids toss up islands
The foggy veils evaporate
The big grin is a beach
The city visits like a school holiday

And in concert halls the ocean fondles the land
It's an elephant hunt creeping through the blood
High in the forest the instruments quiver: they're squirrels
Torrential silence bursts like a cloud
Footsteps arrested in the torrid vegetation of sounds
The notes are slack like panthers' tongues
The guns rip white bears' padding
The glances melt gliding phantoms
And suddenly the stock exchange with riotous cries
Resounds up the cardial trunk

Transactions fluctuate like thermometer mercury
The buzz of airplanes vibrates the sky
A word and forests in Mexico crumple like balconies
Petroleum rigs pass hand to hand like straw hats
The harvest grains align like acids in test tubes
And for all that you can hire some sleep in little vials at the pharmacy

On the terraces of great palaces they serve the sky up in cups
The sea's a towel on the arm of the waiter
Your companion wears her pearls like inscriptions
You spell out her fingers like hieroglyphs
This glance is a string on which memory slides
Glancing over the geometric pallor of the tablecloth's lips
Night and silence embrace
Like the manes of two mares

The mountains glove themselves with clouds
A smile clouds the line of storks
The voice lies down in the violin case like a cow in the manger

The trees conspire up to the nearest station
The angels' tread resounds between the coasts
Alarmed the stags glance up at the hill
Receiving the new moon blushing like a girl

The words appoint leaves to their gardens
Accidents blossom at the edge of the cliff
What beautiful linen the stars spray through the branches
The forest absorbing the tension of its leaves

You rip from the air foggy placards
A new realm receives you the same Illyria
The gaze of the deity slanting like rain
The southern earth flips over under the plow

Everywhere you perch you're the same refugee

MAX JACOB: The Rue Ravignan

"One does not bathe twice in the same stream," said the philosopher Heraclitus. Yet it is always the same ones who mount the street! Always at the same time of day they pass by, happy or sad. All of you, passers-by of the Rue Ravignan, I have named you after the illustrious dead. There is Agamemnon! There is Madame Hanska! Ulysses is a milkman! When Patroclus appears at the end of the street a Pharaoh is beside me! Castor and Pollux are the ladies of the fifth floor. But thou, old ragpicker, who come in the enchanted morning to take away the still living rubbish as I am putting out my good big lamp, thou whom I know not, mysterious and impoverished ragpicker, I have given thee a celebrated and noble name, I have named thee Dostoyevsky.

MARCOS FINGERIT: Jazz-Band

Epilepsy
writhing
on the stretcher
of the staves.

Sabbatical serenade
from demonic
jubilation.

Mill
of musical grain,
whose flour
is syncopated notes,
with the yeast
of sensuality,
making our
daily bread.

Last chance
of the tightrope walker
who loses his footing
and falls
tearing the trans-

parent paper
of space.

Elated blondine*
walking with your head
on a rope.

Alcohol
of superior grade
to drown
metaphysical sorrows.

Great breath of sun
and the nature
of African primitivism.

Classical music
of the future . . .

* Fingerit's reference is to Jean-François Gravelot, tightrope walker known as "The Great Blondin" for his pale hair.

---

e. e. cummings

even if all desires things moments be
murdered known photographed,ourselves yawning will ask ourselves
où sont les neiges. . . . some

guys talks big

about Lundun Burlin an gay Paree an
some guys claims der never was
nutn like Nooer Leans Shikahgo Sain
Looey Noo York an San Franc Dictaphones
wireless subways vacuum
cleaners pianolas funnygraphs skyscrapers an safetyrazors

sall right in its way kiddo
but as fer i gimme de good ole daze. . . .

in dem daze kid Christmas
meant sumpn youse knows wot
i refers ter Satter Nailuyh (comes but once er
year)i'll tell de woild one swell bangup
time wen nobody wore no cloze
an went runnin around wid eachudder Hell
Bent fer election makin believe dey was chust born

Nicolás Guillén: Small Ode to a Black Cuban Boxer

Your gloves
alert before your squirrel's body
and the *punch* of your smile.

Boxer, the North is fierce and tough.
This very Broadway
has attitude like a vein
that bleeds out in the *ringside* shouts
in which you bound, a modern rubber monkey,
without resorting to the ropes
or the pillow of a *clinch* . . .
This very Broadway,
its astonished melon-mouth smeared
with your explosive fists
and your trendy patent leather shoes . . .
is the same Broadway
stretching its chops with a huge wet tongue,
to greedily lick up
all the blood of our cane.

It's a sure thing that you
don't know a few things about us,
nor even of things up there;
for *training* is tough and muscle's a traitor,
and you've got to be a bull,
as you cheerfully say, to make the blow hurt more.

Your English,

only a bit more shaky than your feeble Spanish,
is just enough on the canvas for you to get
whatever dirty slang
is chewed in the jaws of those you stun
jab by *jab*.

In fact maybe you need nothing else,
because as you surely know
you've found your place.

It's good at last, after all,
to find a *punching bag*,
work off some fat in the sun —
to leap,
sweat,
swim —
and from *shadow-boxing* to showdown,
from shower to dining room,
come out polished, fine, strong,
like a fresh carved truncheon
with the ferocity of a *black jack*.

So now that Europe strips
to toast its flesh in the sun
and seeks in Harlem and Havana
jazz and style*
the black glows while boulevards applaud.
And to the envy of whites
speak black truth.

* The word Guillén uses is *son*, a Cuban musical rhythm. All the italicized words are in English in the original.

Bertolt Brecht: Tablet to the Memory of 12 World Champions

This is the story of the world middleweight champions
Their fights and careers
From the year 1891

To the present day.

I start the series in the year 1891—
The age of crude slogging
When contests still lasted 56 or 70 rounds
And were only ended by the knockout—
with BOB FITZSIMMONS, the father of boxing technique
Holder of the world middleweight title
And of the heavyweight title (by his defeat of Jim Corbett on 17 March 1897).
34 years of his life in the ring, beaten only six times
So greatly feared that he spent the whole of 1889
Without an opponent. It was not till the year 1914
When he was 51 that he accomplished
His two last fights:
An ageless man.
In 1905 Bob Fitzsimmons lost his title to

Jack O'Brien, known as PHILADELPHIA JACK.
Jack O'Brien started his boxing career
At the age of 18.
He contested over 200 fights. Never
Did Philadelphia Jack inquire about the purse.
His principle was
One learns by fighting
And so long as he learned he won.

Jack O'Brien's successor was
STANLEY KETCHEL
Famous for four veritable battles
Against Billy Papke
And, as the crudest fighter of all time
Shot from behind at the age of 23
On a smiling autumn day
Sitting outside his farmhouse
Undefeated.

I continue my series with
BILLY PAPKE
The first genius of in-fighting.
That was the first time people used

The term "Human Fighting-Machine".
In Paris in 1913
He was beaten
By a greater master of the art of in-fighting:
Frank Klaus.

FRANK KLAUS, his successor, encountered
The famous middleweights of the day
Jim Gardener, Billy Berger
Willy Lewis and Jack Dillon
And Georges Carpentier by comparison seemed weak as a baby.

He was beaten by GEORGE CHIP
The unknown from Oklahoma
Who performed no other deed of significance
And was beaten by
AL MCCOY, the worst middleweight champion of them all
Who was good at nothing but taking punishment
And was stripped of his title by

MIKE O'DOWD
The man with the iron chin
Beaten by

JOHNNY WILSON
Who beat 48 men K.O.
And was himself K.O.'d by

HARRY GREBB, the Human Windmill
The most dependable boxer of them all
Who never refused a contest
And fought each bout to a finish
And when he lost said:
I lost.
Who so infuriated the man-killing Dempsey
Tiger Jack, the Manassa mauler
That he flung away the gloves when training
The "phantom who couldn't keep still"
Beaten on points in 1926 by

TIGER FLOWERS, the Negro clergyman
Who was never K.O.'d.

The next world middleweight champion
Successor to the boxing clergyman, was
MICKY WALKER, who on 30 June 1927 in London in 30 minutes
Beat Europe's pluckiest boxer
The Scot Tommy Milligan
To smithereens.

Bob Fitzsimmons
Jack O'Brien
Stanley Ketchel
Billy Papke
Frank Klaus
George Chip
Al McCoy
Mike O'Dowd
Johnny Wilson
Harry Grebb
Tiger Flowers
Micky Walker—
These are the names of 12 men
Who were the best of their day in their line
Confirmed by hard fighting
Conducted according to the rules
Under the eyes of the world.

MIHAIL COSMA: News Flash

Nessus the centaur with 125 h.p.
champion of the Fiat factory and Epsom raceway
former director of the International Corporation of Electric Trains
knocked out in the seventh round
by the famous Greek boxer Hercules

Raymond Queneau: Dream (1925)

I am in London, in one of the city's seediest streets. I walk quickly wondering how to say urinate in slang. I pass before a station which seems to be obviously that of Brompton Road. In the street, a woman is singing in French: "C'est jeune." I then cross a bridge over the Thames, become excessively small and under which nevertheless sail a great number of ships of very heavy tonnage. Martinican sailors hoist a small boat onto the bridge. The commotion is extraordinary. Then I find myself among three friends, J. B. P., L. P. and V. T. The latter, no longer pretending to be "dried up," gives each of us a five franc note and a five centime coin. We pass before a store where are displayed oriental antiquities and negro fetishes. J. B. P. makes hypnotized passes in front of the shop window, saying: "There's no tertiary age." We then find ourselves at the Batignolles fair, which is moreover Avenue de Clichy. We want to enter an anatomical museum, but we can't see anything for the crowd is large. I want to buy some candy, but what I took for eucalyptus pastilles are crystals of a recently discovered metal. At this moment, P. reproaches me for not writing more to him; and, instantly, I find myself alone on a street, where the congestion of cars is considerable. The crowd cries: "These are the clerics who clutter the streets." However, I see none of them. I try in vain to cross; a woman takes my arm and says to me: "Womb hypercomplex."

Eugene Jolas: Sleep in Ur (Dream-Scenario)

First Part

A long white road.
Poster in blue, white, and black:
    WHEN YOU GO TO NEW YORK
    STAY AT THE BUCKINGHAM
A masked man.
Automobile crashing along at mad speed. Roar of motors.
The sun blazes down.
An old farm-house long ago abandoned.
Alfalfa fields.
The automobile races through the village.
Main Street.
Radio jazz-splashing on pavement.

Electric train clangs through valley.

Second Part

Columbus Circle.
X arrives in automobile with an enormous perch, in form of a cross, but obviously in its original form a totem-pole.
Sultry July dusk.
Crowd milling around Maine Monument.
Automobile motors whir.
X carries his totem-cross into music store.
A sound of jazz from jug-band.
Feet of passers-by become epileptic
X runs across square crying:

Larwae wool moult
Aluminum hulls
Sing throats of steel
Sing tongues of nickel!

A sound like electric waves cuts into the nerves of the passers-by.
Blood sputters on the asphalt.
A voice chants a Congo song.
Screen changes suddenly into luminous colors of every description. The new moon tumbles down. A planet burns rose against a poster for United States Rubber.
X carries his totem-cross and hums a folk-song.
X places totem-cross against street-lamp.
Crowd rushes by wth a kind of hallucinated step, very staccato, monotonous, almost disciplined.
X suddenly notices a Mayan corpse, withered and waxen, hanging on totem-cross.
What is it?

Third Part

July night on Rialto.
Times building trembles as if under the shock of earth-quake.
Crowd mangles Broadway singing:

Our little moon is dead!
Our little star's gone out!
O clingaling o clang!
O putrid phantom rout!

X walks out of subway station with totem-cross over his shoulders.

A girl begins to dance at the curb.

The crowd sways rhythmically. There is a feeling of erotic mass-insanity in the air.

A masked man.

X throws perch into waiting automobile.

Electric lights glare against a huge zodiac sketched upon a poster.

They shine full blast into the face of the corpse on the totem-cross.

A shriek.

X runs to the car, where several women stand in a trance of horror.

The eyes of the withered Mayan divinity have opened.

Close-up of eyes: enormous, circular, metallically blue.

They roll in a feverish intensity.

Bells ring.

Auto claxon roars crescendo.

The houses lean over the pavement like drunken men.

Fourth Part

Night.

Telegram arrives:

X Hotel Buckingham, New York.

Diabolical events stir sleep stop Tom-Tom astrologer Stop Nightingales rock drunken last vertigo Stop Locusts devastate ruins legends Stop Alone Desperate Z.

The Mayan divinity appears. It is now huge of stature and clad in evening clothes.

X—his face blanched by fear. Rats scurry around his feet.

X talks excitedly to Y, the resurrected corpse.

"Where to?"

"Saturn..."

"How?"

"On singing carpet of love."

X thinks: "...Taxi... Help... Singing away... Carnival... War Help..."

Jazz orchestra.

Telephone: "Hello... District Attorney's Office...; Hello. Police Headquarters. Revolution... Fire Department... Hello... Fire... Red Rooster... Hello... City Hall... Anarchy... Insanity... Hello... Hello..." X reads Daily Tarot:

TAXI DANCER IN POISON CASE

O'DONNELL GETS UP TO 50 YEARS

OCEAN OF LOVE ROUGH, SINGER

IN RAPE CHARGE LANDS IN RENO
VILLAGE COWED
BY GANG PATROL
IN BANK LOOTING
JOHNNY WALKER WALKS THE PLANK
DON'T MISS THESE FEATURES IN TODAY'S SUNDAY TAROT.
CUT THE HAIR OR LET IT GROW
OTHER NEWS IN TABLOID

X walks out followed by Y who waves his arms and whistles between his teeth.

Fifth Part

Midnight, Brooklyn Bridge.

X tells Y: "...Leave me alone... Go down the tracks... Alone... Aged solitude...".

Y snickers. His laughter develops into a sneer. It grows into an insane cackling that resounds above the noise of the elevated train just passing.

X looks at lower Manhattan. The city gleams in clustered cliffs of jewels.

X: Mendacity of fairy-tales...

Y: Xipe Totec...

X: Colibris haunt the strangled bodies...

Y: Mother night...

X: raging and foaming at the mouth like epileptic in convulsions.

Y sneers.

X attacks Y, pins his arms behind his back, cries: Acheronta movebo.

An old hag treasurepicks in garbage can.

Picture of Roman funeral lamp with orphic illustrations of baby in golden vessel before a caterpillar and a butterfly.

Y turns into corpse once more.

His face is tranquil, almost angelic; the eyes look into space as if at some ecstatic vision.

A child sleeping in cradle.

Sixth Part

A masked man, a crippled dwarf, a penguin.

An over-voice cries: The sorcerer of alchemy is dead...

And always there will be parallactic instruments...

X, his shoulders hunched, walks into a milk-white fog, saying:

Woman is sleep

Healing like rain
Primal *νους*
And mantic pain

Two steel eyes gyrate prestissimo.

The over-voice again, a shrill, electric sound, growing in intensity until the fog is torn by an asteroid shaft of light.

Enghien-les-Bains, S.-et-O.
Winter, 1929

Vladimir Mayakovsky: Brooklyn Bridge

Coolidge, old boy,
give a whoop of joy!
What's good is good—
no need for debates.
Blush red with my praise,
swell with pride
till you're spherical,
though you be ten times
United States
of America.
As to Sunday church
the pious believer
walks,
devout,
by his faith bewitched,
so I,
in the grisly mirage
of evening
step with humble heart,
on to Brooklyn Bridge.
As a conqueror rides
through the town he crushes
on a cannon
by which himself's a midge,
so—
drunk with the glory—

all life be as luscious—
I clamber,
proud,
on to Brooklyn Bridge.
As a silly painter
into a museum Virgin,
infatuated,
plunges
his optics' fork,
so I
from a height on heaven verging
look
through Brooklyn Bridge at New York.
New York,
till evening stifling and bewildering,
forgets
both its sultriness
and its height,
and only
the naked soul
of a building
will show
in a window's transclucent light.
From here
the elevators
hardly rustle,
which sound alone,
by the distance rubbered,
betrays the trains
as off they bustle,
like crockery
being put by
in a cupboard.
Beneath,
from the river's far-off mouth,
sugar
seems carted from mills by peddlars,
it's the windows of boats
bound north and south—
tinier

than the tiniest pebbles.
I pride
in the stride
of this steel-wrought mile.
Embodied in it
my visions come real—
in the striving
for structure
instead of style,
in the stern, shrewd balance
of rivets and steel.
If ever
the end of the world
should arrive,
and chaos
sweep off
the planet's last ridge,
with the only lonely
thing to survive
towering over debris
this bridge,
then,
as out of a needle-thin bone
museums
rebuild dinosaurs,
so future's geologist
from this bridge alone
will remodel
these days
of ours.
He'll say:
this mile-long iron arch
welded
oceans and prairies together.
From here old Europe
in westward march
swished
to the winds
the last Indian feather.
This rib will remind

of machines by its pattern.
Consider—
could anyone with bare hands
planting
one steel foot
on Manhattan
pull Brooklyn
up
by the lip
where he stands?
By the wires—
those tangled electric braidings—
he'll tell:
it came after steam, their era.
Here people
already
hollered by radio,
here folks
had already soared up by aero.
Here life
for some
was a scream of enjoyment,
for others—
one drawn-out,
hungry howl.
From here the victims of unemployment
dashed headlong
into the Hudson's scowl.
And further—
my picture unfurls without a hitch—
by the harp-string ropes,
as the stars' own feet,
here stood Mayakovsky,
on this same bridge,
and hammered his verses
beat by beat.
I stare like a savage
at an electric switch,
eyes fixed
like a tick on a cat.

Yeah,
Brooklyn Bridge . . .
It's something, that!

JAROSLAV SEIFERT: Evening at the Café

Princess Salome you are strolling through my dream
I see your head of hair between goblets and grapes
oh what bliss a poet to be
to be a poet with the eyes of an eccentric

The waiter carries his head on a silver tray

I want to hide from the world like a mouse in the sand
where did that banner on the red ship's mast cruise
and why is the anchor a sign of hope if here I feel so sad
and that song will not awaken the dead danseuse?

Under an artificial palm a smiling black man
on his face a rose-colored mask of light
At that moment the great love in my heart I overcame
yet her shadow follows me through the night

Through the night across a hanging garden of withered stars
when I adventurer of beauty and passionate sleeper
leaning on the heat of an American stove as if to sleep forever I desired
remembered frozen pineapples

Crests of chrysanthemums like light ostrich feathers
on the table cards fate loves burden

JOSÉ DE ALMADA-NEGREIROS: Mima-Fatáxa, Cosmopolitan Symphony

It's she who laughs in the lightning
And kisses me in mirror images
She whose shawl blots out the sun when it falls to the floor,

and who has hands as flexible as garters half-way up her thighs;
She who takes the shape of whatever she shuts up,
She who talks as she walks,
She who can lie,
She whose gaze creates Illusion
and whose voice burbles like fountains;
With her transparent eyes of Distance deformed into regressive Vice;
She you can feel in your knees;
Celle qui est de plus en plus danseuse depuis Dégas;
Duncan dansant toute nue la Marche Militaire;
Attention!
: Il n'y a qu'une Ville : P A R I S
C'est là haut qu'Elle vive partout !
She with blood of emerald green
She's the one, the one I want to sing of!

Tambourines hiss in the rust of rims
The copper sieves have sifted now the i of the embroidery
And the baubles of the stall are brass-like in the trace of Light.
Petulant tils (~ ~) of grey storks are slowly undone in lines of blue.
Kisses are blown by those told to wait for laughs
Slender steps slowly undone in the cold of the North
Stoics vault vaulting arches asleep on canvas plinths,
Statics laugh acute angles funambulist twists in a blanket.
Khakhi
Jeers
Mocks
and grates
the limp tambourine.
The pulse stops in her swirl as She loosens up.
Coming and coming again on the lit up boulevards on the russet tambourine.
OPÉRA — 7:50 : Thaïs.
Jewels and earrings
So busy and dizzy
magnet-tinted
shaded in flinty sparks.
Iris ember of ARARA-bird in the mounting.
Dressed-up fireflies in the military stripes of a bric-a-brac lackey.

Gestures-colors soaked in nudes of naked water in the swing of swimming pool.
Fauns fighting with a too transparent sky.
Burst of Nostalgia in the final act of sunsets.
Embalmed queens going down to the SEA.

SEA.

Jeers
Mocks
and tinkles
The tambourine raps on the tambourine.
Cloisters of fear stiflingly collapse
Up pops the Folle in stays
and the salamander slips into the cistern down the stairs of sleep.
Disconcerted date-lamp of ARARA–bird
Extravagant shining tarantula
Concave dome of diaphanous tymbal where rests the big bass drum
Fire-fly-helix of swaying bamboo down which the dying lightning slides into the band

Empty grave of lute and flute diluted into lily
Blue labyrinth of flamey absinthe
Cylindrical timbre of Abanindra (India)
Regal euphorbia in the magic lantern
Pandora's box
Altar float of phlegmatic prayer
Ignenous enigma of the summit magnet of the salamander.
Cirius-light
Heraldic shield tinklingly agate megalomaniac
Peerless title of The Only One
Amen

The blind-knot hurting in scorched passion

Mourning-temperament of lazy woman
Romantic title of sentimental Verses
Rage at not having an idea of how to resolve
Spasm-indifference of fights not for the winning
Perverse somnolence of lives that never happened.

Hasty quarrels in breathing positions
Sacred station-stanzas to compensate time
Saint Barbara stops thunderclaps

Ave Marias on silver thimbles
Needles, ointments balls of wood . . .
Elegant labyrinths of simple blue filigree of the single initial.

Pale climate printed in retreat
Exquisite embroidery to Our-Lady-Woman
Fragile sphere of Satin-Maternity
    : It's a boy! let her sleep.

Inner devotion
Blessed be Maeterlink!
Intense life of cuddled bagatelle
The story of Grandfather the marshal
Estimated value
Memories of the family.

High-lighting scar of Berber-venal air
Blue groins
Fale eye-shadows
artifice envy of degenerate woman
Outbursts-medium of improvising myth
Bronzes tinkles on two sides the limp tambourine.

    Jeers
    Mocks
        and tinkles
The slack tambourine on the torn elbow.

The shawl flies from one side only in a high note swirl
Reverence at being in the sky from astonished eyes at the back.
    The Page-boy gets gifts!
Envies of the Little Princess
It's indecent to say Whore (encore and after the chorus)
Hothead
Indiscreet
Flighty
The Pederasty problem!
The acute Angles open up passively in meager outlays.
The morbid dry their lips crushed up against fantasy.

Spasms stride through archived lies.
For whom will this spasm be?

I've already squandered Her lie!

Pornographic on the sly
Secrets which make you blush:
The invert who loves men and women
and who sleeps with the Sun and is Lover of the Moon!
Mistress of indecent secrets
Cosmopolitan Synthesis
Esperanto-Invader!
Hail! fornicator of Mystery!
It is you I shall sing of, Millionaire, who gave me the Madness to be my Indian slave
Or Salome if I wanted to.
Oh erudite of passions,
Guide of labyrinths!

Jeers
tinkles
and scolds
The tambourine clashes,
Mocks
Hisses
and tinkles
The limp tambourine
drizzles
On the tambourine tin.

Vowels of muffled and long tone still early coinage.
When She died she had not said it all—
Poets are born for Fantasy.

Hosannas and choruses of inverted women scarcely appear in the morning-sin of the Saint's temptation.
The window-panes kiss in hymns of Lechery
and the margin dances in the inhabitants fluid enigmas of russet forms.
Zebras stuck in pin-cushions.

Unbuttoned Hungarian cavalcade
toilette-method for the Conquest!

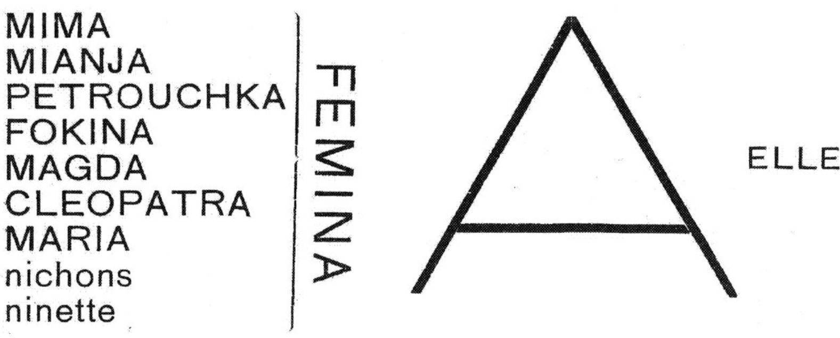

MIMA
MIANJA
PETROUCHKA
FOKINA
MAGDA
CLEOPATRA
MARIA
nichons
ninette
FEMINA
ELLE

Salvé-Regina
The Central Nave
The Carillon and corridor of stone-slabs
The seat of cushioned upholstery
: Groins are duplicated!

Diphthongs rich for going airwards
Ou I ou ai
In the middle of the parvis
White chamois of temptation
Axis, axis, ribaldaxis

5:MARIA OF THE EARRINGS

First popular quatrain

Platignum clarions jingle blagues
chink carillon dogmas
Cymbals and marimbas.
Virtue is freed from breasts to Cavalcade
Transparency grows ever more transparent,
B Solo truth is on the oboe.

Révanche of Madness Captained by the Genius!
Subtle avalanche beyond evil and evil remains to be vanquished
The world is saved in a brain and the rest remains demented serving as cross in her arms

Quivers
Helmets and blades
See-saw plough handles in space.
Hermaphrodite Valkyries
Magic tangerines
Imperial chants unwind serpentine to the lightning-bolts of hallucination.

Bacchanal of picnic in the Lantern Dome
Apologia of Debauch
Long live the Banner of Adventure!

Selection of the esoteric
Nuances of the tints of Europe
Entourage of the Gentlemen
Wilde, Nijinski and I: Sacrosanct melody of the Flesh!

The Circus shakes itself into panic in concentric whirls
and all of a sudden the stage turns into the size of the World.

Tambourines turn windwards in din of steel and dynamite
Ashy snares
Reflexes fall silent sprawling in the mud
The life of cigarette-holders now only Fury
Babel tumultuously revived in quarrelsome fishwives.

Disaster of the tonneau!
Meaning of Unity
—LONG LIVE MAN !

    Jeers
    Hisses
    and tinkles
The Gypsy tambourine
    Wanda
The Russian tambourine
    Mona Lisa
The zinc tambourine
    Acetylene-Drizzle
The tin tambourine of Andalucia
    to go airwards
ou i ou ai
don't think Sphinx!
Slices of orange swaying Trojan Horse!
    Gymkhana of Vowels
    End of Poem
    : Don't think Sphinx!

◈ POSTCARDS ◈

OSWALD DE ANDRADE: Aperitif

Happiness walks the walk
In Plaza Antônio Prado
10 hours are blue
Coffee takes you as high in the morning as a skyscraper

Tietê Cigarettes
Automobiles
A city without myths

WALTER BENJAMIN: First Aid [from *One Way Street*]

A highly convoluted neighborhood, a network of streets that I had avoided for years, was disentangled at a single stroke when one day a person dear to me moved there. It was as if a searchlight set up at this person's window dissected the area with pencils of light.

LUIS VIDALES: Telephone

The telephone is an octopus falling over the city. Its tentacles tangled in the homes. With the suckers on the tentacles sucking up the voices of the people. At night—a sound of gobbling.

MAX JACOB: A Touch of Modernism by Way of a Conclusion

In the ink black night, half the 1900 World's Fair drew back
from the Seine and rolled over in one piece because a mad poet-head
in the sky above the school is biting a diamond star.

◈ LUNAR BAEDEKER ◈

PIET ZWAART: Hot Spots

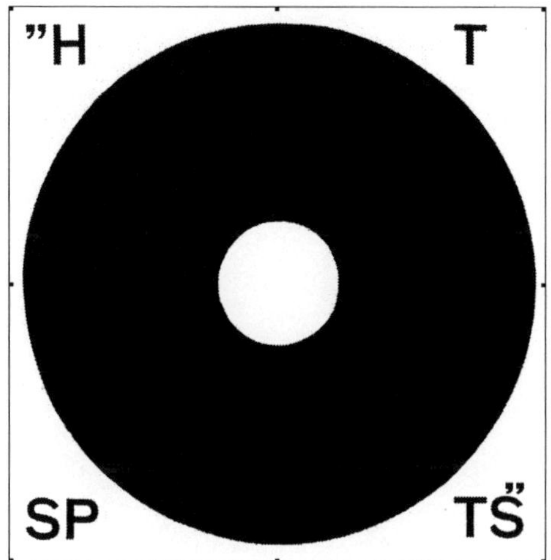

LÉON-PAUL FARGUE

Children softly shout and play, in a dim narrow square, at dusk. Tight little alleys without ears, riddled walls wearing away. Chimneys wearying on the high-railed sky. In their chains of heavy smoke one pictures crowds, spilling forth . . .

. . . All through your neighborhoods I love to look for those eyes of The Unknown, to me familiar.

From amid the clouds, a ray of light anoints a face. With silver it brushes the far reaches of the roads, upright like bundles of frail branches where the shadows of clouds spill and slide. It moves an arm over a man covered with sweat, tiny and pale, with a fat vein at his brow, dragging an outsized wagon. It strikes the grass of a terrace where girls argue. In a gray street it washes the sad façade of a bathhouse . . . It bathes poorly paved little squares where children run with brazen chickens, around a fountain collared in iron, between the chattings of women at their sewing . . .

But now the first lamps make the evening blush like someone's face . . . The square is no more than an open and empty cage, and it falls asleep, with the sweet repose of women dozing in chairs . . . A window pane stretches, like a spot of oil, in a corner of velvet shadow . . . The pale cheek of a clock awakes, among the thin trees that cut wanly across my route and wink against the lights . . .

A whole stand of carriages moves off, like a line of crabs, and lights up . . .

Pensive lanterns blink on an iron bridge . . . The massive smoke of a locomotive scatters in the dusk like a release of purple doves . . .

At the center of a travelling carnival a carousel grinds its mill to a melancholy insistent old song, an organ with a toothache and a brogue. Booths bleed like sides of meat. A hammer falls. A bell's ring unravels, endlessly . . . In stiff groups soldiers move toward the girls like scarabs marching on the rose . . .

An old woman flaps her arms, hops backwards, and starts to sing by the door of a hotel—whose gas lamp is startled awake in its rounded cage! She watches afar dramas we cannot see, the way one watches a shipwreck from the shore . . .

And all the baptism of the day, the violence of children so close to fever, the cries of nervous little girls, and their hopscotch, and their obscure and terrible joy, have brought the evening near, perhaps . . . The beaten legions in parades, the broken victors returning from the somber woods . . . The river speaks of it under the ancient arches to shadowy things that pass . . . An electric tram, with its vast and empty light, skirts the long cemetery with a delicate singing sound and makes us think of voyages . . .

And like it my thought sings in the dark, with a voice sad and low, that comes from olden days . . .

JOSEPH CONRAD: from *The Secret Agent*

The shop was a square box of a place, with the front glazed in small panes. In the daytime the door remained closed; in the evening it stood discreetly but suspiciously ajar.

The window contained photographs of more or less undressed dancing girls; nondescript packages in wrappers like patent medicines; closed yellow paper envelopes, very flimsy, and marked two-and-six in heavy black figures; a few numbers of ancient French comic publications hung across a string as if to dry; a dingy blue china bowl, a casket of black wood, bottles of marking ink, and rubber stamps; a few books, with titles hinting at impropriety; a few apparently old copies of obscure newspapers, badly printed, with titles like *The Torch*, and *The Gong*—

rousing titles. And the two gas-jets inside the panes were always turned low, either for economy's sake or for the sake of the customers.

GEORG HEYM: Berlin II

From the dim warehouse thresholds barrels caulked
with tar went rolling down to the tall lighters.
The tugboats started. On the oily waters
a mane of soot was trailing from the smoke.

Two pleasure-steamers came with music playing.
They dipped their funnels at the bridge's curve.
Smoke, soot, stench lay on the dirty waves
by tanneries where the brown hides were drying.

Every time the barge that bore us travelled
beneath a bridge, the signal's sudden parley
swelled out of stillness like a deep drum's rattle.

We entered the canal, and drifting journeyed
slowly alongside gardens. In the idyll
we saw the night-flares of the giant chimneys.

RUVEN AYZLAND: Night Reflex

From the soft, flowing evening gray,
Skyscrapers thrust, like naked giants
With dark foreheads and fiery eyes—
A mighty scream of human will
To create wonder in the wonder of the world.

And wonderfully veiled, like a black giant bow,
Spanning its stiff belly, a bridge from shore to shore
Over a black river.

And life, tense from the days,

And dreams conjured up in the nights,
Flow golden through steel veins
From wonder to wonder,
Where people have kindled windows in the sky.

C. P. CAVAFY: The Tobacco Shop Window

By the brightly lit window
of the tobacco shop, they stood in a crowd.
By chance their glances met
and timidly, haltingly expressed
the secret longing of their flesh.
Later, a few steps down the sidewalk,
they smiled and nodded faintly.

Then the closed carriage . . .
the sensitive meeting of body with body,
hands together, lips together.

OLIVERIO GIRONDO: Biarritz

The casino sips the last drops of dusk.

Hoarse automobiles. Shop windows with constellations of false stars. Women that go to lose their smiles at baccarat.

With faces faded by the table, the "croupiers" officiate, eyes squinting at so much passing money.

Pupils that melt at the dealing of cards!

Necklaces of pearls that sink a harsh bite into the throat!

There are clean-shaven boy toys that have a zipper in the back. Men with bibs of porcelain. A gentleman with a collar that will end up strangling him. Boobs that will burst all of a sudden from a low-cut neck, and will roll over everything, like two enormous billiard balls.

When the door opens itself halfway, it shows a flash of "foxtrot".

Alfred Richard Meyer: Foxtrot

I trot, you trot, we trot.
You trot before me, I trot behind.
Two physiognomies aiming at one.

But there's always between us this wall.
We stomp, an unwieldy foundry, clap-clap the melody's beats.
We stomp it out, fiery, fierce, always inflamed.

Presto! Black earth spits out from our polar bear soles.
It clumps up the next pair (Miller-Cat)! with a lunar smooch!
So trots the fox. So foxes the trot.
We're divine floorwax.
We polish the parquet to goldenmost mirrorglass.
We see with horror right up into nostrils.
I trot. You trot. We trot.—
Yet we're not for all that a fox.

Giacomo Giardina: City at Night

Light, light, light . . .
colorful electric fantasy
motors throbbing
in the silken streets.
Jazz bands throbbing with music;
people carefully jostling each other,
people nervously waiting for someone;
saucy seamstresses'
silver voices,

white laughter blossoming from African
mouths,
bon vivants in top hats smoking . . .
between clusters of bright lights,
hurrying like express trains running late.
Men covered with talcum powder
act as puppets;
beggars with two cents to their name
hang around street-corners,
shop windows sparkling like suns,
displaying the latest model from Paris;
voices, newsboys' voices
cling to one's ears,
votive candles sob
and from time to time
a nun's extremely pale face looks down
from a tower of smoking clouds.

VLADIMIR MAYAKOVSKY: Because of a Bandleader

It's this nightclub, reddish with neon chairs drowned in feminine flab when this sulky bandleader bows, coming out, orders the musicians to cry. So immediately the tuba empties a bunch of brassy tears into the mug of this guy nestling a salmon in his beard. And before he has a chance, between belches and harrumphs, to stuff a yell down the golden throat, the whole crowd mauled by the trombones and bassoons staggers and falls all over him. When the last one out couldn't make it, dying saucerwise down on the cheeks, the bandleader absolutely flipped, orders the musicians to bellow like beasts, pushes the tuba like a breadloaf beween that beard and its crockery, and blows and listens. Doubled by the blow, a sob clacked metallic like a kopek in his gut. Next morning when the man gives him notice he's

through, your bandleader's hanging from a
burnt-out chandelier, I mean a blue note,
still blueing.

Clément Pansaers

fox-trot

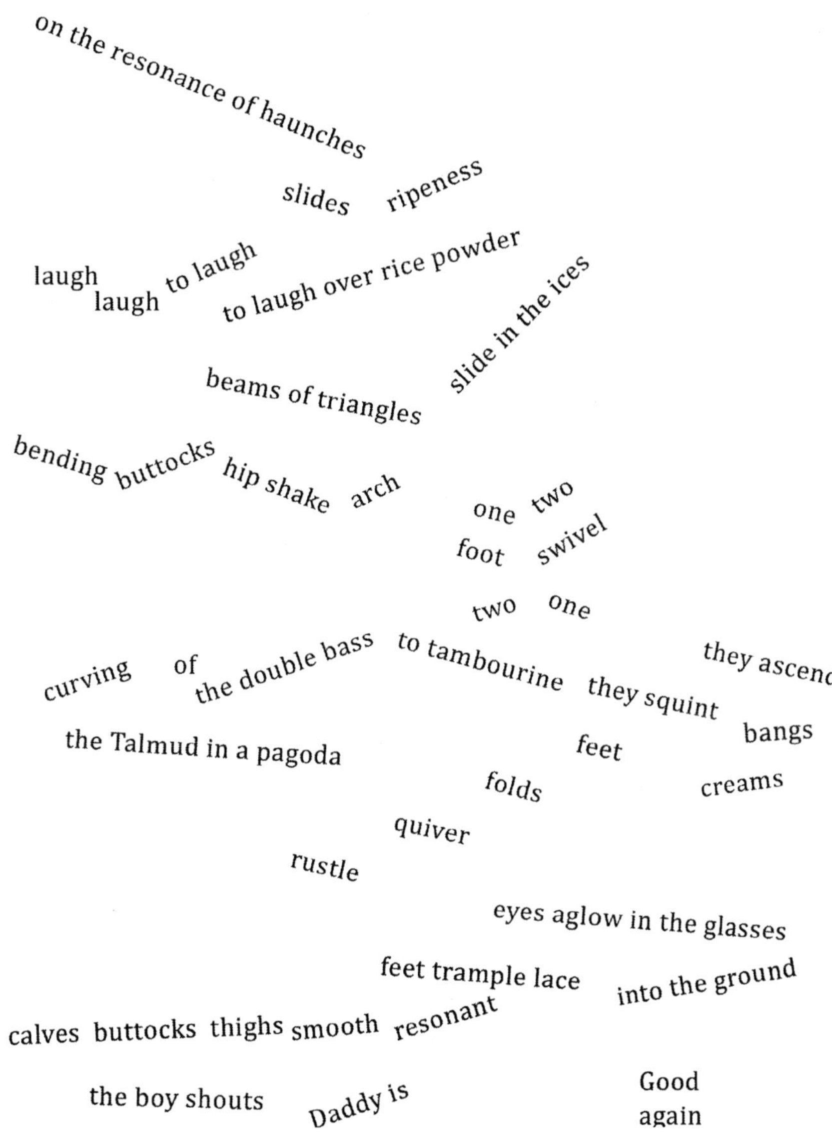

on the resonance of haunches
slides ripeness
laugh laugh to laugh to laugh over rice powder
slide in the ices
beams of triangles
bending buttocks hip shake arch
one two
foot swivel
two one
curving of the double bass to tambourine they squint they ascend
the Talmud in a pagoda feet bangs
folds creams
quiver
rustle
eyes aglow in the glasses
feet trample lace into the ground
calves buttocks thighs smooth resonant
the boy shouts Daddy is Good
again

e. e. cummings

god pity me whom(god distinctly has)
the weightless svelte drifting sexual feather
of your shall i say body?follows
truly through a dribbling moan of jazz

whose arched occasional steep youth swallows
curvingly the keenness of my hips;
or,your first twitch of crisp boy flesh dips
my height in a firm fragile stinging weather,

(breathless with sharp necessary lips)kid

female cracksmen of the nifty,ruffian-rogue,
laughing body with wise breasts half-grown,
lisping flesh quick to thread the fattish drone
of I Want a Doll,
          wispish-agile feet with slid
steps parting the tousle of saxophonic brogue.

Francis Carco: Dive

They are dancing. Some lean hustlers, on the lookout for women, survey the scene. Everything is bustling. People are drinking. Some of the men get excited and lurch after the girls. A pair of big, bold amazons swaggers past, alternately aroused and lulled by the waltz. A basket dangling at her side, a sickly child casually circulates, selling violets. The big female couple, fervent and simple, hips flexing, grind against one another, with masterfully controlled slowness.

The orchestra plays, boisterous, driven by the language of valve and piston. The dancing couples, happily fatigued, turn in patient unison. The amazons float past, always close together, always sauntering, slow and clenched, the two slinky companions and their truly moving tenderness.

RICHARD JOHNS: Robert in Berlin

feeling spanish french and german
looking skittishly at hermann

not daring to camp on the strasse
drinking nothing but evian wasser

fancy little german boys
dancing in a ring
fancing little german boys
oh you nasty thing

come here
come beer

beer and leer
then beer some more
leer in beer
drop tear in beer
you fear when sober
so drink and come ober

edelweiss robert
that's your name
afraid-of-vice robert
means the same

GEORGE GROSZ: Night Café

A girl singing shrilly
Musicians fiddling
Somewhere a solder sits asleep
Someone says: Pussycat, I'm *always* on the lookout for a man!
Hips droop like clusters of ripe grapes over the edges of stools
Sadists pine for a whipping
Young men, pimps
Girls, Americans, soldiers
Blacks and a waitress age eighteen

Gottfried Benn: Night Café

824: Lives and Loves of Women.
The cello takes a quick drink. The flute
belches expansively for three beats: good old dinner.
The timpani is desperate to get to the end of his thriller.

Mossed teeth and pimple face
wave to incipient stye.

Greasy hair
talks to open mouth with adenoids
Faith Love Hope round her neck.

Young goiter has a crush on saddlenose.
He treats her to onetwothree beers.

Sycosis brings carnations
to melt the heart of double chin.

B flat minor: the 35th Sonata.
Two eyes yell:
stop hosing the blood of Chopin round the room
for that rabble to slosh around in!
Enough! Hey, Gigi!—

The door melts away: a woman.
Dry desert. Canaanite tan.
Chaste. Concavities. A scent accompanies her,
less a scent
than a sweet pressure of the air
against my brain.

An obesity waddles after.

Dino Campana: Hoodlum at Night

Florence down below was a whirlpool of lights, trembling dully:
On wings of fire the tedious vanishing noises
Of the street car soared: the huge sluggish
River glittered like a scaly serpent.
Above a wavering circle the restless mocking faces
Of the thieves, and I between a long double row of uniform cypresses like wasted
torches,
Harsher than hedges to the cypresses
Harsher than quivering box-trees,
As from my heart my love
As from my heart, love a pimp intoned and sang:
I love the old whores
Swollen with ferment of sperm
Who fall like toads on four paws on the red featherbed
And wait and pant and snort
Flaccid like bellows.

e. e. cummings

when you rang at Dick Mid's Place
the madam was a bulb stuck in the door.
a fang of wincing gas showed how
hair, in two fists of shrill color,
clutched the dull volume of her tumbling face
scribbled with a big grin. her sow-
eyes clicking mischief from thick lids.
the chunklike nose on which always the four
tablet of perspiration erectly sitting.
—If they knew you at Dick Mid's
the three trickling chins began to traipse
into the cheeks "eet smeestaire steevensun
kum een, dare ease Bet, an Leelee, an dee beeg wun"
her handless wrists did gooey severe shapes.

Jacob Glatshteyn: Twelve

The hands of the lighted city clock
Climb one on top of the other
Like a street dog on his accidental mate—
Twelve.
Now the hoarse song of blood rises
To the night ears of the city.
Now the whole city sings the song of two.
Now the whole city cries the cry of one to one.
And the lighted city clock replies:
Twelve.

Kyn Taniya: "Midnight Frolic"

        Silence
Listen to the words conversing
        in the atmosphere

There's an unbearable muddle of earthly voices
        and alien voices
far away

        Hairs stand on end from the friction of radio waves
Gusts of electric wind whistle
        in the ears

        Tonight
to the negro beat of jazz-bands from New York
        the moon will dance a foxtrot

IF THE MOON AND JUPITER AND VENUS AND MARS
AND SATURN WITH ITS GOLDEN RINGS!

        The planetary system will be a motley corps de ballet
whirling to the compass of a musical light

NIGHT OF REVELS
I'll have to wear a tuxedo

But who'll be my partner in this astral midnight frolic?

XAVIER VILLAURRUTIA: L.A. Nocturne: The Angels

You might say the streets flow sweetly through the night.
The lights are dim so the secret will be kept,
the secret known by the men who come and go,
for they're all in on the secret
and why break it up in a thousand pieces
when it's so sweet to hold it close,
and share it only with the one chosen person.

If, at a given moment, everyone would say
with one word what he is thinking,
the six letters of DESIRE would form an enormous luminous scar,
a constellation more ancient, more dazzling than any other.
And that constellation would be like a burning sex
in the deep body of night,
like the Gemini, for the first time in their lives,
looking at each other in the eyes and embracing forever.

Suddenly the river of the street is filled with thirsty creatures;
they walk, they pause, they move on.
They exchange glances, they dare to smile,
they form unpredictable couples . . .

There are nooks and benches in the shadows,
riverbanks of dense indefinable shapes,
sudden empty spaces of blinding light
and doors that open at the slightest touch.

For a moment, the river of the street is deserted.
Then it seems to replenish itself,
eager to start again.
It is a paralyzed, mute, gasping moment,

like a heart between two spasms.

But a new throbbing, a new pulsebeat
launches new thirsty creatures on the river of the street.
They cross, crisscross, fly up.
They glide along the ground.
They swim standing up, so miraculously
no one would ever say they're not really walking.

They are angels.
They have come down to earth
on invisible ladders.
They come from the sea that is the mirror of the sky
on ships of smoke and shadow,
they come to fuse and be confused with men,
to surrender their foreheads to the thighs of women,
to let other hands anxiously touch their bodies
and let other bodies search for their bodies till they're found,
like the closing lips of a single mouth,
they come to exhaust their mouths, so long inactive,
to set free their tongues of fire,
to sing the songs, to swear, to say all the bad words
in which men have concentrated the ancient mysteries
of flesh, blood, and desire.

They have assumed names that are divinely simple.
They called themselves Dick or John, Marvin or Louis.
Only by their beauty are they distinguishable from men.
They walk, they pause, they move on.
They exchange glances, they dare to smile.
They form unpredictable couples.

They smile maliciously going up in the elevators of hotels,
where leisurely vertical flight is still practiced.
There are celestial marks on their naked bodies:
blue signs, blue stars and letters.
They let themselves fall into beds, they sink into pillows
that make them think they're still in the clouds.
But they close their eyes to surrender to the pleasures of their mysterious
incarnation,
and when they sleep, they dream not of angels but of men.

Sidney Hunt: Solution

a boy wearing nothing but anklets of electric light and a close gold cap walks purposeless along the main street an hour after midnight passing wax women behind glass and under railway bridge following thin flowing steel car rails. his footsteps are quick sighs

AND CONTINUALLY SEEN

coming off the open top of the electric car making his way between the seats of the stairs cold pale flesh of afternoon knees and legs muddy from football thin rounded body nipples denting sweat wet jersey lost contact everseen through half closed eyefringes clutching lust the seats of the swaying pleasure the cars pass each other time holds him there and

THEN
in a cinema thin
blouse and smell
of youngirls

and the sound of a not then tedious popular prelude
pre. jazz

Malcolm Cowley: The Eater of Darkness

Dipping an adroit hand into his hat, he found excessively a patent razor, gin, a banjo-ukelele,

five cigar bands, 3-in-1, a jackknife with broken blades, a portable bathtub, and a Sunday *Times*, as well as freckles, Matisse, red hair, a blue airplane, and a white rabbit.

The last he gave to the White Queen, who ran away.

The red-haired man burst into genuine tears, they did not change to pearls. He went to a dance in Harlem. Holding a toy pistol bang to his head, he crumpled boom to the floor, in time with Duke Ellington's umpah-umpah.

It was what everybody expected. That year everybody was being baroque and outrageous, with a false hint of sadness underneath. The parties were wonderful and nobody believed in them any more.

But the bullets were real and the death was real, I couldn't get over it.

Ardento Soffici: Café

To a hysteria of fire the light heart of civilization circularly here the affluence of the night echoed in a delta of eternal anonymity stellar abysses of numbers in the crystalline adapted to the concreteness of simple arithmetic in a public place

025 050 075 in the glaze of the plates on the table Modern Café
In the liquidation of a waltz idiocy of musics in settings scarlet funiculì funiculà begging musing at the recollection of the countryside electric shadows foliage in an iris of absinthe of three oak trees along the sidewalk coming and going of amorous possibilities

tu as vu
comme il bien chaussé?

Si vas a Calatayud
Pregunta por la Dolores
Es una chica guapo ——

with the gold glow of silks masks of gem-studded feathers of eyes ponds pilgrimage of useless nostalgias

ah! ben non zut pas pour toute la nuit je ne marche pas

what a damn'd pimp!

in the glow of faces abandoned under their makeup to the best offer Crossing of screams

un bock garcon
cigarette-paper

at the gold frontiers of youth hopefulness in disorder inside the vanity of smoke anxious ending

cognac I said
another beer

to a subaltern black wing of waitresses Love friendship and lots of literature in a crowd long ray gaze awakened in hearts in lyricism flowery illuminations splotches from the typography of newspapers on a rail flags news of beauty and war Alembic of destinies brief and formidable cafés distilling with the drugs of the sun beyond the seas and the pink arabias north's drunken poisonous alcohols flux of things thoughts prostituted to a minute to a laugh In the live mystery of arc lamps reflected in one line in nothingness reciprocal of mirrors iridescent geometrically vis-à-vis to the right and to the left sensible image of the Infinite

---

M. S. Petrov: 13

Words cling wall hangs as
LUSTbush hanging together
(**O** precious **MAIDEN**!)
Bimm — bammmm
Timm — lammmm
KxxZ — Kzzzzzzz
Green to the gills dance the brains
Toreador **H**
l t ! !
Toreador **A**

Telephone whimpers solder all fishermen
Trolley oblique and
THIN
Verse KLAK-KLAK
BLOSSOM
MIDNIGHT WHORES
(Ha-haaaaaaaaAA !
Corsica draws night
Slowly
QUIET

MY DREAM
QUIET
Slowly till morning
ADIO **ADIO** ADIO

EUGENE JOLAS: Linotype

the mergenthalers roar through the night
electric moons tumble into the streets
and tired hands are feverish with letters
all the air echoes with rhythms

hello compositor why do you hide your eyes
and outside spring is singing like a girl
the elevated roars against cruel silences
madness stumbles through the editorial room

memories bite into your brain
while feverishly you decipher dispatches
romance comes in rags
for Michigan Boulevard cries
and Broadway shakes with lust
and Montmartre smears caricatures onto the stars
somewhere an automaton is groaning
Mammy Mammy my girl has soft breasts
the foreman's crazy
because of unrequited love miss May Hurley drank a dose of veronal last night
hootch hootch hootch

dynamically the film of the world rolls along
shame wails before white light
a death strides impudently through the landscape
a dream bursts asunder
everywhere you see the chaos of life
the continents rumble and flicker like mania's vistas
court rooms shudder prisons whimper
forests primeval sorrow over corpses

sometimes there is a shaking of pity
but when the machines are silent
a blasphemy blossoms gigantically

Vladimir Mayakovsky: Great Big Hell of a City

Windows split the city's great hell
into tiny hellets—vamps with lamps.
The cars, red devils, exploded their yells
right in your ear, rearing on their rumps.

And there, under the sign-board with herrings from Kerch
an old man, knocked down, stooping to search
for his specs, sobbed aloud when a tram with a lurch
whipped out its eyeballs in the twilight splurge.

In the gaps between skyscrapers, full of blazing ore,
where the steel of trains came clattering by,
an aeroplane fell with a final roar
into the fluid oozing from the sun's hurt eye.

Only then, crumpling the blanket of lights,
Night loved itself out, lewd and drunk,
and beyond the street-suns, the sorriest of sights,
sank the flabby moon, unwanted old junk.

Salvador Gallardo: Cabaret

Jazz lays out its clandestine bed
        and weaves a tangle of desires
A voltaic current
        leaps from the backbone's battery
and vibrates in the buzzers of the breasts
        Orgiastic eyes
ejaculate glances
        A forgotten spouse

downs romanticism
        in beer-glassses
Bruised reflectors
        smash the piñata of dawn
loosing polychrome confettis
        all over the orgy
Outside a flock of automobiles
                YAW–AWNS
And the Cabaret
                in the sky
        is a shimmy of stars

Vadim Shershenevich

Skyscrapers shake and in laughter fall down
Onto the streets sewn with stone embroidery.
Someone's invisible playful hands
Tickle the earth under its armpits.

The embankments violently twist the iron viaducts,
The seconds rush by at a mad gallop—
Tired, foamy—and explosions suddenly cut short
Wax eloquently about the paroxysm of hysterics.

Graves open up and from them, like vomit,
Tumble out half-rotten corpses and bones,
Skeletons come to life under the primordial fingers,
And the sky with its storms hammers nails in asphalt.

From the stormy monoplanes fall lightning and fires,
Turning in the air, onto the earth.
The gaunt, arm-crossed devil, having sullenly frozen,
Admires the disarray.

Federico García Lorca: Landscape of a Pissing Multitude (Battery Place Nocturne)

The men kept to themselves.
They were waiting for the swiftness of the last cyclists.
The women kept to themselves.
They were expecting the death of a boy on a Japanese schooner.
They all kept to themselves—
dreaming of the open beaks of dying birds,
the sharp parasol that punctures
a recently flattened toad,
beneath silence with a thousand ears
and tiny mouths of water
in the canyons that resist
the violent attack of the moon.
The boy on the schooner was crying and hearts were breaking
in anguish over everything's witness and vigil,
and because on the sky-blue ground of black footprints,
obscure names, saliva, and chrome radios were still crying.
It doesn't matter if the boy grows silent when stuck with the last pin,
or if the breeze is defeated in cupped cotton flowers,
because there is a world of death whose perpetual sailors
will appear in the arches and freeze you from behind the trees.
It's useless to look for the bend
where night loses its way
and to wait in ambush for a silence that has no
torn clothes, no shells, and no tears,
because even the tiny banquet of a spider
is enough to upset the entire equilibrium of the sky.
There is no cure for the moaning from a Japanese schooner,
nor for those shadowy people who stumble on the curbs.
The countryside bites its own tail in order to gather a bunch of roots
and a ball of yarn looks anxiously in the grass for unrealized longitude.
The moon! The police. The foghorns of the ocean liners!
Façades of rust, of smoke, anemones, rubber gloves.
Everything is shattered in the night
that spreads its legs on the terraces.
Everything is shattered in the tepid faucets
of a terrible silent fountain.

Oh, crowds! Loose women! Soldiers!
We will have to journey through the eyes of idiots,
open country where the tame cobras hiss in a daze,
landscapes full of graves that yield the freshest apples,
so that uncontrollable light will arrive
to frighten the rich behind their magnifying glasses—
the odor of a single corpse from the double source of lily and rat—
and so that fire will consume those crowds still able to piss around a moan
or on the crystals in which each inimitable wave is understood.

JOHN DOS PASSOS: from *Manhattan Transfer*

Arm in arm they careened up Pearl Street under the drenching rain. Bars yawned bright to them at the corners of rainseething streets. Yellow light off mirrors and brass rails and gilt frames round pictures of pink naked women was looped and slopped into whiskyglasses guzzled fiery with tipped back head, oozed bright through the blood, popped bubbly out of ears and eyes, dripped spluttering off fingertips. The raindark houses heaved on either side, streetlamps swayed like lanterns carried in a parade, until Bud was in a back room full of nudging faces with a woman on his knees. Laplander Matty stood with his arms round two girls' necks, yanked his shirt open to show a naked man and a naked woman tattooed in red and green on his chest, hugging, stiffly coiled in a seaserpent and when he puffed out his chest and wiggled the skin with his fingers the tattooed man and woman wiggled and all the nudging faces laughed.

MINA LOY: Lunar Baedeker

A silver Lucifer
serves
cocaine in cornucopia

To some somnambulists
of adolescent thighs
draped
in satirical draperies

Peris in livery
prepare
Lethe
for posthumous parvenues

Delirious Avenues
lit
with the chandelier souls
of infusoria
from Pharoah's tombstones

lead
to mercurial doomsdays
Odious oasis
in furrowed phosphorous———

the eye-white sky-light
white-light district
of lunar lusts

——— Stellectric signs
"Wing shows on Starway"
"Zodiac carrousel"

Cyclones
of ecstatic dust
and ashes whirl
crusaders
from hallucinatory citadels
of shattered glass
into evacuate craters

A flock of dreams
browse on Necropolis

From the shores
of oval oceans
in the oxidized Orient

Onyx-eyed Odalisques

and ornithologists
observe
the flight
of Eros obsolete

And "Immortality"
mildews . . .
in the museums of the moon

"Nocturnal Cyclops"
"Crystal concubine"
————————
Pocked with personification
the fossil virgin of the skies
waxes and wanes————

TRISTAN TZARA: Balance Sheet

voltaic arc of these two nerves that don't touch each other

near the heart

under a microscope the black shudder can be seen

is it sentiment this white spurt

and methodical romance

divides my body into beams

toothpaste

transatlantic

accordion

the crowd breaks the reclining column of wind

tail of rockets

on my head

the bloody revenge of the liberated two-step

repertory of prix fixe pretensions

madness at 3:20 a.m.

or 3 francs 50

cocaine is slowly peeling the walls for its pleasure

satanic horoscope dilates under your vigor

VIRTUAL VIGILANCE VERIFIES YOUR VIRILE WIND

eyes keep falling

☛ **TRISTAN TZARA**

THEO VAN DOESBURG: *Remembrance of the Night Fountains*

1.

in little metal plates the moon falls on my face
rank morbid black whore dances the fox-trot of the wobbling headbacks
Bloodnaked halfroom with body fragments

I You Green-brown
We white
Nothing

the white napkins slice me You everyone everything in two electric lights burn shamelessly in body parts
look look look

loose arms stick
loose hands grip
loose fingers clatter
sparkle glitter and illuminate

FUN

paradise of the evening toads
wrung out of each other are these figures
phenomena of press and pull
ENORMOUS TOAD
"Well now?"
greedy and in unison we eat these things up
We gobble each other
gobble knives, bowls plates
gobble lamps tables chairs
gobble women men things
up.

gluttony of the night fountains
I greet you tiny blind eternity
and drink with fixed jaws the green blood of god

2.

from the night of the pillars of light . . .
(red black tobacco haze)

rosegreen primrose
Vertical-horizontal

19

all around: frozen through and cut through Naked

Black drinking barracks

mortuary carmine

burning ice and shuffle step on absolute dumb Floor

black fixed vertical bottles

hard dumb fixed space

(human heads roll through the black space)

round white table-planes turn turn turn
in a man's flat belly

usury factory of the night fountains
electric monumental night

Langschnitt
Querschnitt

(drawn on the night like mute red scratches.)

ALFRED LICHTENSTEIN: *After the Ball*

Night creeps into the cellars, musty and dull.
Tuxedos totter through the rubble of the street.
Faces are moldy and worn out.
The blue morning burns coolly in the city.

How quickly music and dance and greed melted . . .
It smells of the sun. And day begins
With trolleys, horses, shouts and wind.

Dull daily labor cloaks the people in dust.
Families silently wolf down lunch.
At times a hall still vibrates through a skull,
Much dull desire and a silken leg.

JOSÉ JUAN TABLADA: *Alternating Nocturne*

Golden New York night,
cold limedark walls,
Rector's, foxtrot, champagne,
still houses, strong bars,
and looking back,
above the silent roofs,
the spirit petrified,
the white cats of the moon,

like Lot's wife.

And yet
it is one,
at New York,
at Bogota,
and the same

MOON!

◈ INTERLUDE ◈

ANATOL STERN: Europe

abecedary of slaughter
of dirt lice fires
and mercy
united states
and argentine brazil chile
states at war
phenomena and noumena
eternity and nothingness—
two fattened boxers
who will always win !

we

who wolf meat
once a month
we
who breathe
sulphur
expensive sulphur
like air—
we
who drag along the streets
our queue of sunken bellies
our powerless fists
stuffing our pockets
we shall
lose
lose
lose
as always ! !

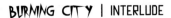

they feed us

they feed us

they pour down our throats
food for the spirit !
500 metres of trichinae of
sermons
faded tapeworms of
newspapers
sweet
virulent
bacilli of words
are shoved into our mugs
by the gluttonous fraternity of
scribblers of
presidents of
ministers of education
china of the west ! !

stop poisoning us

we are not rats !
o if we could only be
a proletarian swarm of rats
we could
bite the
white
fleshy
fingers
which incessantly push towards us
the
white
poisoned
dust of
powderised pages

grand
showerbath
of meetings
the massage of propaganda
the gospel of terror——
this is the chasm
into which we jump
since we cannot jump
into heaven

spurting forth
hatred
terror of turnings
all of which
all
are red—
but who
but who
fights
for that—dearer than all the
silesias of the world
dearer than all the independences—
the liberated
heart of
man ? !

film of world war
directors
cameramen
blinded
all captions erased
impossible to understand
the howling gesticulation
of a milliard arms
the ham acting
of the players' eyes
film of folly
stuffed with the vermin of
numbers
which explain nothing

millions of dance-halls grin
with their black faces
here's the jazz-band
of discoveries
shimmy of relativity
jig of
economic
catastrophes
under which collapses
the parquet floor of
europe

115

this

this is
what we need :
a little bairam of concepts
a scouring of the intellect
in the eastern fashion
(a la maniere orientale)

aaa ! !
to hell with everything !
but first of all
drop that bayonet
with which you rip open
the belly
of that wretch !

the nearest family of objects
given life by our own hands
the infinite ladder of
complications
the building of a new expression
—words
oneself

the life of the city
at all hours
the polyphonic concert of
cables
of rat-a-tats
a "honneger pacific"
of the sewer-pipes
a desperate signalisation of
lamps
flashing on with night
the most difficult moment to
endure
the sudden agony of
motorcars
when the town subsides
into void

the city's zeppelin
not eckener's
—columbus's
discovering the new america
of sensitivities
I can't
I don't want to express it in words !

what you need here are millions
of
steel tools
all the Timeses of the world
aren't enough for one line
you have to sing it by centuries
to register
all the explosions of
atoms to
lay bare the
seismograph of the
subconscious

the man made up of
match-sticks
and the other one 3000 years
old
from the magyar cave
are two separated brothers
the stone age
never mind which one

cuts across our
reinforced-concrete
it is the race of the ages
always the same
the venerable
murder of
civilisation
the ectasy of sensuality
a brain
twisted with intensity

the XXth.
century
is a haarman

devouring his own loves !
intellectualism is
psychological sadism
do not transform life
into a fight between types of logic
great therapeutics
of the future—
training in gluttony is
approaching !

tradition and continuity—
those imaginary quantities . . .
o inventor—
you are born of coincidence !

we hasten to the great
reaction of liberty
crowned with the 20-centuries old
bondage
the only real station is the one
missing
from the yellow timetable
allow me to rest for a while
to sever the cables
of my sensitivity

this green blade of grass
squeezed up between two paving
stones
this wreck tearing itself loose
on the chequered
stony
atlantic
is the messenger of death—
look
in his wan hand he holds the
mountains
valleys
fir trees
sycamores

the angels of destruction
whirring their wings
his dumb lips proclaim
all the sweetnesses of leisure
he drags behind him the rabble
of olympians
with his ram he batters the
  chest of the walls
strips the tramways of their
  red skin
melts glass and iron—
the brain of the city
he breaks down
the frail and exalted jigsaw puzzle
  of civilisation
—this couple
hiding in his shadow
in an animal fear
of microcephals
—the fetish of parliament
and the wisest of mistresses
o ! terrible is the death of europe
—o ! blessed

epileptic dionysos
leads them
the women
with flapping breasts
in their hands
trembles the naked body of a
radio torn to pieces
the mechanical orpheus

the others have already burst
into the trampled herd of
motor cars
locomotives
those panic-stricken lambs
bleating with their
hoarse trumpets
and still they have not supped
  their fill of it
towards the dreamy heifers of the
  suburbs
and the heated bullocks of the cities
  who jump on them
the women forage
stir panic
disperse the herd of
parises
warsaws
lisbons
londons
this one's jaws ate into the
stretched spine of the church of
  la medelaine
—she with her red mane rends the
trembling columns of the
stock exchange
with their hips they push asunder
  the
petrified obesities of the
towns
appease their hunger with the
fatted
flesh of
europe

at last
at last
free !
o—to stamp out the
flagellant of labour
flogging himself with tragedising
o—to stamp out the tragedising of
the
ethics of labour
to honour
the decalogue of the
stomach

I am covered by a milliard lips
by an organised
proleteriat of cells a
revolt of gullets !

this throng of raging bacchantes
is one centimetre of my skin

this throng of raging bacchantes

—is one centimetre of my skin

1
2

◈ TWENTIETH-CENTURY BLUES ◈

KENNETH FEARING: Twentieth-Century Blues

What do you call it, bobsled champion, and you, too, Olympic roller-coaster ace,
High-diving queen, what is the word,
Number one man on the Saturday poker squad, motion-picture star incognito as a home girl, life of the party or you, the serious type, what is it, what is it,

When it's just like a fever shooting up and up and up but there are no chills and there is no fever,
Just exactly like a song, like a knockout, like a dream, like a book,

What is the word, when you know that all the lights of all the cities of all the world are burning bright as day, and you know that some time they all go out for you,
Or your taxi rolls and rolls through streets made of velvet, what is the feeling, what is the feeling when the radio never ends, but the hour, the swift, the electric, the invisible hour does not stop and does not turn,
What does it mean, when the get-away money burns in dollars big as moons, but where is there to go that's just exactly right,
What have you won, plunger, when the 20-to-1 comes in; what have you won, salesman, when the dotted line is signed; irresistible lover, when her eyelids flutter shut at last, what have you really, finally won;
And what is gone, soldier, soldier, step-and-a-half-marine who saw the whole world; hot-tip addict, what is always just missed; picker of crumbs; how much has been lost, denied; what are all the things destroyed,
Question mark, question mark, question mark, question mark,
And you, fantasy Frank, and dreamworld Dora and hallucination Harold, and delusion Dick, and nightmare Ned,

What is it, how do you say it, what does it mean, what's the word,
That miracle thing, the thing that can't be so, quote, unquote, but just the same it's true,
That third-rail, million-volt exclamation mark, that ditto, ditto, ditto,
That stop, stop, go.

Dragan Aleksić: Trade Mark

Now then,
There was a crematorium in Pilaw with scrambled eggs
Without sandwich, box extra
                Extradream
                Extrababy
                Extracomplexion
                Extradream
So will sugar be sucked
So will a post be nibbled
So will a tower be pondered
So will
Ah and an accumulator with extra
                Extravolt
                Extraampere
                Extracalorie
                Extramagnet
Take a gradual right over the bridge
Take a quick left across the meadow
Take a deliberate
        Ah you scaly dame Cica
        Yeah, always the extra buck
                Extrapowder
                Extrabodice
                Extralaugh
                Extravalues—

René Bizet: Saxophone

The saxophone in the back of the bar
Like the horn deep in the woods,
Makes appeals to that which departs
And has tears for bad and good!

One must live with one's defeats
A dice cup without chance

Trembles in our hands; our heads
Buzz with mocking chants.

At the edge of the melancholy night
The light of the moon's the song of the horn,
And under the electric lights
The saxophone feels remorse:

Remorse for me, remorse for you.

EDWARD DAHLBERG: November Blues

the cheap rain
swings the tinfoil leaves
against the bensonhurst wind
          and the goldfish
          wheeling thru faucet water
          in a glass jar
          look like woolworth's
          5 and 10 cents tin toys

          the yellow taxis
          glide along the
          varnished streets
and throw their battery lights
into jerry's bicycle shop

          the cheap rain
          lacquers the pavement
          and drives the trade
                              away from jerry's bicycle shop
                                        and the goldfish
                                        in faucet water
                                        wheel a monotone
                                        thru his brain :
                         "cheap peoples live here now."

II

the bensonhurst stores
like camel cigarette boxes
squat before the baymist

the milkdairy
its white oilcloth walls
give off a polar light
which plays with
the bluegrey sidewalk
in front
sits Sarah Kirshenbaum
her tweased eyebrows
a streak of matchdust
her forehead

low and flat
as 20th avenue Brooklyn
she sells appetizers
and watches
the stores
like camel cigarette boxes
squat before the baymist

and mutters at the rain
which drives the trade away :
"these people
they eat the heart out of
you for a penny."

III

inside
the senate movies theater
the machine rays
luminous
above the center aisle
like a tin moon

and from the violin
chanson triste thru the exit door
into the jaundiced lights
thru the baymist
                        a yellowish celluloid film

the bensonhurst shopkeepers
squat
        before the silver screen
        the machine rays
        mercurial
        on their baldheads
        like the tin moon over calvary
        unravels the sixreeler

the bensonhurst shopkeepers
squat
before the moviedrama
                                and weep
these goddam people
                                they eat the heart
                                out of one.

RICHARD ALDINGTON: Cinema Exit

After the click and whirr
Of the glimmering pictures,
The dry feeling in the eyes
As the sight follows the electric flickerings,
The banal sentimentality of the films,
The hushed concentration of the people,
The tinkling piano—
Suddenly,
A vast avalanche of greenish yellow light
Pours over the theshold;
White globes darting vertical rays spot the somber buildings;
The violent gloom of the night
Battles with the radiance;

Swift figures, legs, skirts, white cheeks, hats
Flicker in oblique rays of dark and light.

Millions of human vermin
Swarm sweating
Along the night-arched cavernous roads.

(Happily rapid chemical processes
Will disintegrate them all.)

Lawren Harris: City Heat

The streets are hot under the sun,
Surging with animal heat,
Sucked to the surface
Through pores, through angers, through feverishness
By the sun.

The heat jiggles along every street,
Reverberates from the scorching pavement,
Hot brick walls, stone walls and side walks—
Runs everywhere
With licking-hot, laughing tongues
Driven by the sun.

The breezes are dead,
Only the slow undulating coarse stench
From hot meals, dead meats,
Stinking steam, sour milk
And sour sweat
Moves—
Soughing swamp breathings
In the pestilential city.

Babies in the heat,
The sick in the heat,
Pain in the heat,
Noises running the waves of heat,

Metal-hot, nasal noises,
Cryings, bawlings, clangings
And wearied voices
Ringing in the head
Like the close-singing remoteness
Of delirium.

From out the city
Oozes forth
A sticky, cloying, stinking thickness,
Sucked to the surface
By the sun.

YOKOMITSU RIICHI: from *Shanghai*

From the railing on a bridge over the canal a Chinese woman who had been carrying some flowering plants was staring just like Osugi onto the surface of the water. A cobbler who was always on the bridge was seated on the ground next to the young woman's hems holding a support and biting into the sole of a clog, using his teeth to pull out nails with a keening sound. Coming and going in front of those two were a peddler with fiddles piled up on his back, soldiers on their morning return, prostitutes swaying on rickshaws, and footbound women waddling along like infants. The people crossing the bridge moved along upside down on the surface of the water, where dented cans, insects, jet black foam, fruit peels, and many other objects swirled about. A small boat that had probably come down the river last night from Suzhou was loaded with split firewood. It was stopped, as if stuck fast on the muddy water.

T. S. ELIOT: Preludes

I

The winter evening settles down
With smell of steaks in passageways.
Six o'clock.
The burnt-out ends of smoky days.
And now a gusty shower wraps

The grimy scraps
Of withered leaves about your feet
And newspapers from vacant lots;
The showers beat
On broken blinds and chimney-pots,
And at the corner of the street
A lonely cab-horse steams and stamps.

And then the lighting of the lamps.

II

The morning comes to consciousness
Of faint stale smells of beer
From the sawdust-trampled street
With all its muddy feet that press
To early coffee-stands.

With the other masquerades
That time resumes,
One thinks of all the hands
That are raising dingy shades
In a thousand furnished rooms.

III

You tossed a blanket from the bed,
You lay upon your back, and waited;
You dozed, and watched the night revealing
The thousand sordid images
Of which your soul was constituted;
They flickered against the ceiling.
And when all the world came back
And the light crept up between the shutters
And you heard the sparrows in the gutters,
You had such a vision of the street
As the street hardly understands;
Sitting along the bed's edge, where
You curled the papers from your hair,
Or clasped the yellow soles of feet
In the palms of both soiled hands.

IV

His soul stretched tight across the skies
That fade behind a city block,
Or trampled by insistent feet
At four and five and six o'clock;
And short square fingers stuffing pipes,
And evening newspapers, and eyes
Assured of certain certainties,
The conscience of a blackened street
Impatient to assume the world.

I am moved by fancies that are curled
Around these images, and cling:
The notion of some infinitely gentle
Infinitely suffering thing.

Wipe your hand across your mouth, and laugh;
The worlds revolve like ancient women
Gathering fuel in vacant lots.

BRUNO JASIÉNSKI: from *I Burn Paris*

He couldn't sleep. The damp paw of a fine, misty rain stroked his face, soaking his clothes with a sharp, slick wetness. The rain and sweat in his rags gave off a musty, acidic smell. The stone pillow of the spittle-covered stair jabbed his head. The sharp edges of the steps cut into his ribs, splitting his body into separate pieces that writhed in feverish insomnia like the segments of a severed worm. The lucky wretches at the bottom, fortunate to have reserved their places by the gate in advance, snored in a wide register of stifled breaths. Pierre, too, was gradually overcome by a heavy, delirious half-sleep.

He dreamed he was lying on no ordinary flight of stairs, but on an escalator, which was ascending with a rattle (he had seen one like it the Au Printemps store, or at the Place Pigalle metro station). From the yawning chasm of the earth, the open maw of the metro, a never-ending iron harmonica of moving stairs climbed upward in a hollow and rhythmic rumble. One after another, more and more steps clattered into sight, blocked by the row of ragged, helpless bodies. The summit of the stairs, where Pierre lay, was somewhere far in the clouds. Down below, many-eyed Paris shouted out into the soulless silence of the night with its billions of lights. The stairs clanged in time as they rose higher. Pierre was overwhelmed by the cosmic vacuum of the interplanetary infinity, the blinking of the stars, the limitless hush of space.

The escalator flowed from the bleak abyss of the open street into the gaping abyss of the heavens, carrying along a black mass of wretched, dormant bodies.

Charles Reznikoff

Scared dogs looking backwards with patient eyes;
at windows stooping old women, wrapped in shawls;
old men, wrinkled as knuckles, on the stoops.

A bitch, backbone and ribs showing in the sinuous back,
sniffed for food, her swollen udder nearly rubbing along the pavement.

Once a toothless woman opened her door,
chewing a slice of bacon that hung from her mouth like a tongue.

This is where I walked night after night;
this is where I walked away many years.

Osip Mandelstam: Leningrad

I've come back to a town I know by heart—
In my veins, like the swell of childhood sickness.

You're back? Then take your medicine:
Fish-oil, slick, light tracks in canals.

Take a long look: in December dusk
The ill-reflecting asphalt stains the sky.

I do not want to die. Not yet, Petersburg,
My number's in your phonebook, not up yet.

I still have some addresses, Petersburg,
To find the faces of the dead, the gone.

I live in a backstairs walk-up, the doorbell hurts,
It rings inside me, torn out by the roots.

All night long I wait for friends to call;
I shake like handcuffs at footsteps in the hall.

WILLIAM CLOSSON EMORY: Theme for a Blues Song

It was in Saint Louis I think
        or maybe Cincinnati
        or Louisville
        or Indianapolis
while the tall buildings swayed
like golden rod in the blue fields of night
and she came soliciting
        with a mouth like a smear of cherries
        across the porcelain of her face.
She came soliciting
out of the blue tomb of night
and the buildings leaned down their orange eyes
and stared in rigid curiosity.
And I said
hell dearie do they still get money
for that in Saint Louis
        or was it Cincinnati
        or Louisville
        or Indianapolis
O you should have heard the concrete
lean back and blister with crackling laughter.

Raúl González Tuñón: Remembering A. O. Barnabooth

What can I say about my life, pah! my life, that like A. O. Barnabooth's
cares only to wait eternally for something vague?
My life in the world's seaports, staring at countries,
juggling the hankies of futile departures and impossible returns.
In the old streets of perished cities
where the past is so alive and so present and so human
that we smell it like the dampness in a cellar can be smelled.
In the penumbra of movie theaters where a frozen butterfly beats its wings
inside the projectionist's blue chamber.
At the junction of longings and failures,
in international hotels crowded with the familiar faces
of swindlers, prostitutes and conjurers.
In marionette-headed women
like those in Kisling's paintings.
In the bridges that hang above the earth on fire
and the cold hard stony vertigo of the rails and afar
the green and red lights on the box of a sleepless signalman.
In village fairs where men drink and gamble and dance
with strapping girls.
And in music boxes and in walking and in nothing.
And in the walking and nothing of all the cities,
in factories and skyscrapers, and in small squares
like that of the Contrescarpe.
On ships already pregnant with oceans and gales
and on the great express trains that startle huddled houses
and only stop in the high countries.
And in the reds and in the grays
of taverns as sailors fall to singing
and in black-hearted women and in basement smoking rooms.
In the godforsaken ports on narrow rivers
smelling of fried food, their horizons like a picture.
In Maurice Utrillo churches crossed by transparent women
out of Marie Laurencin.
And in hopes of I don't know what fever, passion, grief
will one day come to rescue me.
Waiting, waiting on a corner and lighting a cigarette
and listening, amazed, frightened and nostalgic,
to the gathered music of the world.

◈ CODA ◈

IRVING CAESAR: Crazy Rhythm

I feel like the Emperor Nero
When Rome was a very hot town;
Father Knickerbocker, forgive me,
I play while your city burns down.
Through all its nightlife I fiddle away,
It's not the right life, but think of the pay.
Someday I will bid it good-bye,
I'll put my fiddle away
And I'll say:

REFRAIN

Crazy rhythm, here's the doorway,
I'll go my way, you'll go your way.
Crazy rhythm, from now on
We're through.
Here is where we have a showdown,
I'm too high hat, you're too low down,
Crazy rhythm, here's good-bye
To you.
They say that
When a highbrow meets a lowbrow
Walking down Broadway,
Soon the highbrow,
He has no brow,
Ain't it a shame,
And you're to blame.
What's the use of Prohibition?
You produce the same condition.
Crazy rhythm,
I've gone crazy, too.

Ev'ry Greek, each Turk and each Latin,
The Russians and Prussians as well;
When they seek the lure of Manhattan,
Are sure to come under your spell.
Their native folk songs they soon throw away,
Those Harlem smoke songs, they soon learn to play.
Can't you fall for Carnegie Hall?
Oh, Danny, call it a day
And we'll say:

REPEAT REFRAIN

◈ PASSPORTS ◈

Authors, Source Texts, Translators

Xavier Abril (Peru, 1905-1990)
156 *Chronic* (mss. 1927); tr. Jed Rasula
498 *X-Ray of Chaplin —Amauta* (Jan. 1929); tr. Jason Borge
Martín Adán (pseudonym of Rafael de la Fuente Benavides, Peru, 1908-1985)
437 from *The Cardboard House* (1928); tr. Katherine Silver
Conrad Aiken (United States, 1889-1973)
165 *Inscriptions in Sundry Places —The Coming Forth by Day of Osiris Jones* (1931)
Anna Akhmatova (Russia, 1889-1966)
271 *The Stray Dog Cabaret —Rosary* (1914); tr. Paul Schmidt
Pierre Albert-Birot (France, 1885-1967)
59 *Poem for Voice and Dance: Flight —SIC* 23 (Nov. 1917); *La Lune ou le livre des poèmes* (1924); tr. Jed Rasula
80 *Poem-Poster* (The Sun) *—La Lune ou le livre des poèmes* (1924); tr. Jed Rasula
87 *Jazz Chronicle —La Lune ou le livre des poèmes* (1924); tr. Donna Stonecipher
161 *Metro —SIC* 14 (Feb. 1917); *La Lune ou le livre des poèmes* (1924); tr. Donna Stonecipher
Rafael Alberti (Spain, 1902-1999)
236 *Harold Lloyd, Student —Yo era un tonto y lo que he visto me ha hecho dos tontos* (1929); tr. Jed Rasula
251 *Summer Guidebook to Paradise —Cal y Canto* (1929); tr. Ben Belitt
507 *Charlie's Sad Date —Yo era un tonto y lo que he visto me ha hecho dos tontos* (1929); tr. Mark Strand
Richard Aldington (England, 1892-1962)
604 *Cinema Exit —Images Old and New* (1916)
Dragan Aleksić (Serbia, 1901-1958)
142 *Obilatnost —Dada-Tank* (1922)
598 *Trade Mark —Hipnos* 2 (1923); tr. Jed Rasula
José de Almada-Negreiros (Portugal, 1893-1970)
553 *Mima-Fatáxa, Cosmopolitan Symphony —Portugal Futurista* (1915); tr. Bernard McGuirk
Guilherme de Almeida (Brazil, 1890-1969)
395 *Telephone —Era uma vez...* (1922); tr. Paulo Henriques Britto
Gonzalo de Alvar
394 *Hertz-Spatial Poem —Grecia* 34 (Nov. 1919); tr. Jed Rasula

Mário de Andrade (Brazil, 1893-1945)
371 *Typewriter —Losango Cáqui* (1926); tr. Paulo Henriques Britto & Jed Rasula
430 *Sunday —Paulicéia Desvairada* (1922); tr. Jack E. Tomlins
435 *Colloque Sentimental —Paulicéia Desvairada* (1922); tr. Jack E. Tomlins
Oswald de Andrade (Brazil, 1890-1954)
430 *Bengaló —Pau-Brasil* (1925); tr. Manoel Cardozo
560 *Aperitif —Pau-Brasil* (1925); tr. Jed Rasula
Guillaume Apollinaire (pseudonym of Guillaume de Kostrowitzky, Italy/Poland, 1880-1918, emigrated to France 1899)
82 *Windows —Poème et Drame* II (Jan. 1913); *Robert Delaunay* (Sturm Gallery, Berlin 1913); *Calligrammes* (1918); tr. Anne Hyde Greet
162 *Monday in Christine Street —Les Soirées de Paris* 19 (Dec. 15, 1913); *Calligrammes* (1918); tr. Anne Hyde Greet
181 *Phantom of Clouds —Les Ecrits Français* 1 (Dec. 5, 1913); *Calligrammes* (1918); tr. Anne Hyde Greet
418 *Ocean Letter —Les Soirées de Paris* 25 (June 15, 1914); *Calligrammes* (1918); tr. Anne Hyde Greet
Louis Aragon (France, 1897-1982)
38 *Imagination's Speech —Le Paysan de Paris* (1924); tr. Frederick Brown
115 "Certa" *—Le Paysan de Paris* (1924); tr. Frederick Brown
Luis Aranha (Brazil, 1901-1987)
45 *Cocktail*; tr. Jed Rasula
Céline Arnauld (France, 1895-1952)
267 *Luna Park —Projecteur* (May 21, 1920); tr. Ian Monk
386 *Enigma Figures —Dadaphone* 7 (March 1920); tr. Ruth Hemus
Nathan Asch (Poland, 1902-1964, emigrated to United States 1915)
462 *Downtown —Little Review* 10: 2 (1924-25)
W. H. Auden (England, 1907-1973)
63 *The Airman's Alphabet —The Orators* (1934)
Ruven Ayzland (Galicia, 1884-1955, emigrated to United States 1903)
564 *Night Reflex*; tr. Benjamin Harshav & Barbara Harshav
Hugo Ball (Germany, 1886-1927)
276 *Cabaret —Cabaret Voltaire* (May 1916); tr. Timothy Adès
517 *Karawane* (1917)
Djuna Barnes (United States, 1892-1982)
260 from *Nightwood* (1936)
Nicolas Beauduin (France, 1880-1960)
1 *The City in Me —L'Homme cosmogonique* (1922); tr. Tim Conley
39 *The New Beauty —The Little Review* I: 10 (Jan. 1915); tr. Edward J. O'Brien

320 *Music Hall —L'Homme cosmogonique* (1922); *Noi* II: 5 (Aug. 1923); tr. Jed Rasula
Johannes R. Becher (Germany, 1891-1958)
78 *The New Syntax*; tr. Jed Rasula
Franz Richard Behrens (Germany, 1895-1977)
320 *Tiller Girls* (mss.); tr. Jed Rasula
322 *Chocolate Kiddies* (mss.); tr. Jed Rasula
340 *Jazz* (mss.); tr. Jed Rasula
350 from *The Asta Ode* (mss. 1923); tr. Donna Stonecipher
Herbert Behrens-Hangeler (Germany, 1898-1981)
388 Obibi *—Het Overzicht* 21 (April 1924)
Andrei Bely (pseudonym of Boris Bugayev, Russia, 1880-1934)
152 from *Petersburg* (1916); tr. David McDuff
Walter Benjamin (Germany, 1892-1940)
37 *This Space for Rent —Einbahnstraße* (1928); tr. Edmund Jephcott
515 *Chaplin* —(mss. 1928/29); tr. Rodney Livingstone
525 *Paris as Goddess —Die literarische Welt* (Sept. 1928); tr. Rodney Livingstone
560 *First Aid —Einbahnstraße* (1928); tr. Edmund Jephcott
Gottfried Benn (Germany, 1886-1956)
577 *Night Café —Morgue* (1912); tr. Michael Hofmann
René Bizet (France)
599 *Saxophone —Saxophone* (1925); tr. Donna Stonecipher
Gunnar Björling (Finland (Swedish language), 1887-1960)
7 "I want to live in a city" *—Solgrönt* (1933); tr. Martin Allwood
36 from *4711: Universalistic Dada-Individualism* (1928); tr. Johannes Göransson
515 *Charlie Chaplin —Quosego* (1928); tr. Lars Forssell, Carl Anderson, Martin Allwood
Maxwell Bodenheim (United States, 1892-1954)
148 *Sunlight on the Avenue —Returning to Emotion* (1927)
Emil Bønnelycke (Denmark, 1893-1953)
9 *Century — Asfalten Sange* (1918); tr. Jed Rasula
457 *New York* (1918)
Jorge Luis Borges (Argentina, 1899-1986)
179 *Butcher Shop —Fervor de Buenos Aires* (1923); tr. Jed Rasula
Xavier Bóveda (Spain, 1898-1935, emigrated to Argentina 1927)
155 *An Automobile Passes —Grecia* 13 (Apr. 1919); tr. Jed Rasula
Bertolt Brecht (Germany, 1898-1956)
537 *Tablet to the Memory of 12 World Champions* (1927); tr. John Willett
Bob (Robert Carlton) Brown (United States, 1886-1959)
43 from *The Readies* (1930)

276 *Dime Museum —Demonics* (1931)
Rogelio Buendía (Spain, 1891-1969)
379 *X-Rays —Grecia* 40 (Feb. 1920); tr. Jed Rasula
Basil Bunting (England, 1900-1985)
176 *Aus dem Zweiten Reich*
Mary Butts (England, 1890-1937)
82 from "Mappi Mundi" —*Life and Letters Today* XVIII: 2 (Spring 1938); *Last Stories* (1938)
Paolo Buzzi (Italy, 1874-1956)
58 *Highway to the Stars —Versi Liberi* (1911); tr. Felix Stefanile
343 *Cineland —Canto quotidiano* (1933); tr. Willard Bohn
Irving Caesar (United States, 1895-1996)
636 *Crazy Rhythm* (1928)
Dino Campana (Italy, 1885-1932)
327 *Fantasy on a Painting by Ardengo Soffici —Canti Orfici* (1914); tr. I. L. Salomon
578 *Hoodlum at Night* — (mss.); tr. I. L. Salomon
Francesco Cangiullo (Italy, 1888-1977)
328 *Café Concert — Caffè Concerto: Alfabeto a Sorpresa* (1916); tr. Jed Rasula
Francis Carco (France, 1886-1958)
250 *On the Boulevard —Instincts* (1911); tr. Gilbert Alter-Gilbert
327 *Cabaret —Instincts* (1911); tr. Gilbert Alter-Gilbert
576 *Dive —La Bohème de mon Coeur* (1912); tr. Gilbert Alter-Gilbert
Luis Cardoza y Aragón (Guatemala, 1901-1992)
409 from *Maelstrom* (1926); tr. Jed Rasula
423 "Havre" —*Luna Park* (1924); tr. Jed Rasula
C. P. Cavafy (Greece, 1863-1933)
565 *The Tobacco Shop Window* (1907); tr. Jed Rasula
Blaise Cendrars (pseudonym of Frederick Sauser, Switzerland, 1887-1961)
106 *Contrasts —Der Sturm* 194-195 (Jan. 1914); *Dix-neuf poèmes élastiques* (1919); tr. Walter Albert
267 *Medrano Academy —L'Oeuf dur* 14 (Autumn 1923); tr. Walter Albert
364 *Cracklings —Cabaret Voltaire* (May 1916); *Dix-neuf poèmes élastiques* (1919); tr. Walter Albert
416 from *The Formosa* {Moonlight; Ocean Letter; Cabin 6} —*Le Formose* (1924); tr. Jed Rasula
425 from *Travel Notes* {Dinner Time; Writing; Bad Faith; Unmasked Incognito; Wet Nurses and Sports; Dancing} —*Montparnasse* 49 (Feb.-March 1927); tr. Jed Rasula
429 *Sao Paolo —Le Formose* (1924); tr. Jed Rasula

431 from *Sao Paolo* {Getting Up; The City Wakes Up; Electric Horns; Small Fry; Landscape; Sao Paolo} —*Sao-Paulo* (1926); tr. Jed Rasula

Giorgio de Chirico (Italy, 1888-1978)

458 from *I Was in New York* —*XXe Siècle* 1 (1938); tr. Margaret Crosland

Jean Cocteau (France, 1889-1963)

65 *Parable of the Prodigal Son* (from *The Cape of Good Hope*) —*Le Cap de Bonne-Espérance* (1918); *Little Review* 8 (Autumn 1921); tr. Jean Hugo, with corrections by Jed Rasula

145 "The café quivers" (mss. 1917/20); tr. Jed Rasula

Joseph Conrad (Józef Konrad Korzeniowski, Poland, 1857-1924, British citizen 1887)

562 from *The Secret Agent* (1907)

Bruno Corra (pseudonym of Bruno Corradini, Italy, 1892-1976)

47 *Futurist Hope* —*L'Italia Futurista* (June 15, 1916); tr. Willard Bohn

Mihail Cosma (pseudonym of Ernest Spirt, Rumania, 1902-1976, moved to Paris in 1926, using nom de plume Claude Sernet)

456 *Preface for a Baedeker* —*Integral* 11 (Feb.-Mar. 1927); tr. Jed Rasula

540 *News Flash* —*Integral* 13-14 (April 1927); tr. Jed Rasula

Malcolm Cowley (United States, 1898-1989)

172 *Buy 300 Steel* — *The Little Review* XII (Spring-Summer 1926); *The Blue Juniata* (1929)

324 *In Memory of Florence Mills* —*Transition* 15 (Feb. 1929); *The Blue Juniata* (1929)

583 *The Eater of Darkness* —*The Little Review* XII (Spring-Summer 1926); *The Blue Juniata* (1929)

Hart Crane (United States, 1899-1932)

455 from *The River* —*The Bridge* (1930)

514 *Chaplinesque* —*Gargoyle* (Dec. 1921); *White Buildings* (1926)

Antonio Cubero (Spain)

391 *The Electric-Man* —*Grecia* 34 (Nov. 1919); tr. Jed Rasula

e. e. cummings (United States, 1894-1962)

485 *Poem, or Beauty Hurts Mr. Vinal* —*S.4.N* IV: 23 (Nov. 1923); *is 5* (1926)

535 "even if all desires" —*is 5* (1926)

575 "god pity me whom" —*&* (1925)

579 "when you rang at Dick Mid's Place" —*Broom* II: 2 (May 1922); *Tulips & Chimneys* (1923)

Tytus Czyżewski (Poland, 1880-1945)

373 *Hymn to the Machine of My Body* —*Zielone oko wizje electriques, Noc-Dzień* (1922); tr. Bogdana Carpenter

Edward Dahlberg (United States, 1900-1977)
601 *November Blues —This Quarter* 4 (Spring 1929)
Auro D'Alba (pseudonym of Umberto Bottone, Italy, 1888-1965)
49 *Brush Strokes —Baionette* (1915); tr. Felix Stefanile
Fortunato Depero (Italy, 1892-1960)
54 *Abstract Transcription of a Woman — Depero Futurista* (1927); tr. Steve Soper
158 *Streetcar —Depero Futurista* (1927); tr. Steve Soper
465 *Subway* (1929); tr. Steve Soper
484 *Coney Island* (1929); tr. Steve Soper
491 *24th Street* (1929); tr. Steve Soper
Alfred Döblin (Germany, 1878-1957, emigrated to France 1936)
173 *Berlin —Alexanderplatz, Berlin* (1929)
Theo van Doesburg (pseudonym of Christian Küpper, Holland, 1883-1931)
374 *X-Images —De Stijl* 3: 9 (July 1920); tr. Jed Rasula
594 *Remembrance of the Night Fountains —De Stijl* 5 (Jan. & May 1922); tr. Hannah Hedrick
John Dos Passos (United States, 1896-1970)
472 *Newsreel* —from *The Big Money* (1936)
591 from *Manhattan Transfer* (1925)
T. S. Eliot (United States, 1888-1965, British citizen 1927)
605 *Preludes —Blast* 2 (July 1915); *Prufrock & Other Poems* (1917)
Paul Éluard (pseudonym of Eugène-Émile-Paul Grindel, France, 1895-1952)
322 *The Gertrude Hoffman Girls —Nouvelle Revue Française* (Oct. 1, 1925); *Capitale de la douleur* (1926); tr. Ruthven Todd
William Closson Emory (United States)
609 *Theme for a Blues Song —Blues* 4 (1929)
Jean Epstein (Poland, 1897-1953, lived in France from 1921)
231 *Bonjour Cinema —Bonjour Cinéma* (1921); tr. Donna Stonecipher
244 *Douglas Fairbanks —Bonjour Cinéma* (1921); tr. Donna Stonecipher
503 *Charlie Chaplin —Bonjour Cinéma* (1921); tr. Donna Stonecipher
Gonzalo Escudero (Ecuador, 1903-1971)
279 *Zoo —Anthology of Contemporary Latin American Poetry* ed. Fitts (1942); *Altanoche* (1947); tr. Richard O'Connell
Farfa (pseudonym of Vittorio Osvaldo Tommasini, Italy, 1881-1964)
334 *Newyorkcocktail —Noi miliardario della fantasia* (1933); tr. Willard Bohn
Léon-Paul Fargue (France, 1876-1947)
186 *The Boulevard —Poëmes* (1912); tr. Lydia Davis
561 "Children softly shout" —*Poëmes* (1912); tr. Peter S. Thompson

Kenneth Fearing (United States, 1902-1961)
378 *Cracked Record Blues —New Yorker* (Dec. 12, 1942); *Afternoon of a Pawnbroker* (1943)
398 *Radio Blues —New Yorker* (Nov. 26, 1938), *Dead Reckoning* (1938)
597 *Twentieth-Century Blues —Poems* (1935)
Alfredo Mario Ferreiro (Uruguay, 1899-1959)
157 *Poem Without Traffic Obstacles —El Hombre que se comió un autobus* (1927); tr. Jed Rasula
386 *Moving Train —El Hombre que se comió un autobus* (1927)
398 *Radio-Telephone —El Hombre que se comió un autobus* (1927); tr. Jed Rasula
Fillia (pseudonym of Luigi Colombo, Italy, 1904-1936)
50 *Typography —I nuovi poeti futuristi* ed. Marinetti (1925); tr. Willard Bohn
375 *Mechanical Sensuality —Sensualità-Sette atti* (1925); tr. Zbigniew Folejewski
Marcos Fingerit (Argentina, 1904-?)
533 *Jazz-Band —Antena* (1929); tr. Jed Rasula
John Gould Fletcher (United States, 1886-1950)
160 *'Bus-Top* (from "London Excursion") *—The Egoist* 14: 1 (July 15, 1914); *Some Imagist Poets* (1915)
Luciano Folgore (Italy, 1888-1966)
180 *Electricity —Il Canto dei Motori* (1912); tr. Roberta Payne
Joaquim Folguera (Catalonia, 1893-1919)
180 *Blind Street Musicians —En Enemic del Poble* 16 (March 1919); *Traduccions i fragments* (1921); tr. Willard Bohn
Charles Henri Ford (United States, 1913-2002)
467 *Poem From The Insurance Policy Of The Automobile Club Of New York, Inc.*
Elsa von Freytag-Loringhoven (Germany, 1874-1927)
116 *Café du Dôme —Transition* 7 (Oct. 1927)
335 *A Dozen Cocktails Please* (mss. 1923/27)
468 *Subjoyride* (mss. 1920/22)
Salvador Gallardo (Mexico, 1893-1981)
249 *Short Circuit —El Pentagrama eléctrico* (1925); tr. Lorna Scott Fox
588 *Cabaret —El Pentagrama eléctrico* (1925); tr. Lorna Scott Fox
Charles Galwey (United States)
480 *Stadium Concert —Broom* 4: 2 (Jan. 1923)
Federico García Lorca (Spain, 1898-1936)
487 *Landscape of a Vomiting Multitude —Poeta in Nueva York* (1940); tr. Greg Simon & Steven F. White
590 *Landscape of a Pissing Multitude —Poeta in Nueva York* (1940); tr. Greg Simon & Steven F. White

Pedro Garfias (Spain, 1901-1967)
78 *Storm —Grecia* 37 (Dec. 1919); tr. Jed Rasula
343 *Cinematographer —Grecia* 17 (May 1919); tr. Jed Rasula
Otto Gelsted (Denmark, 1888-1968)
421 *The Show Boat* (1923); tr. R. P. Keigwin
Giacomo Giardina (Italy, 1903-1994)
568 *City at Night —Quand'ero pecoraio* (1931); tr. Willard Bohn
Oliverio Girondo (Argentina, 1891-1967)
152 *Street Sketch —Veinte Poemas para Ser Leídos en el Tranvía* (1922); tr. Daniel Coudriet
179 *Pedestrian —Veinte Poemas para Ser Leídos en el Tranvía* (1922); tr. Daniel Coudriet
331 *Café Concert —Veinte Poemas para Ser Leídos en el Tranvía* (1922); tr. Daniel Coudriet
566 *Biarritz —Veinte Poemas para Ser Leídos en el Tranvía* (1922); tr. Daniel Coudriet
Jacob Glatshteyn (Poland, 1896-1971, emigrated to United States 1914)
579 *Twelve —Jacob Glatshteyn* (1921); tr. Benjamin Harshav & Barbara Harshav
Claire Goll (Germany, 1890-1977, lived outside Germany from 1916)
4 *Twentieth Century —Zenit* 6 (July 1921); *Lyrisches Films* (1922); tr. Jed Rasula
94 *To Bus No. 12 —Lyrisches Films* (1922); tr. Babette Deutsch
Yvan Goll (Alsace, 1891-1950)
95 *Paris is Burning —Paris Brennt* (1921); "Paris Brûle" in *Le nouvel Orphée* (1923); tr. Tim Conley
512 from *The Chaplinade* (1920); tr. Clinton J. Atkinson & Arthur S. Wensinger
518 *For a New Mythology —Der Eiffelturm* (1924); tr. Jed Rasula
Ramón Gómez de la Serna (Spain, 1888-1963, emigrated to Argentina 1936)
230 *Movieland —Cinélandia* (1923); tr. Angel Flores
357 *Absurd Cocktails —Cinélandia* (1923); tr. Angel Flores
George Grosz (Germany, 1893-1959, emigrated to United States 1932)
577 *Night Café*; tr. Jed Rasula
Nicolás Guillén (Cuba, 1902-1989)
535 *Small Ode to a Black Cuban Boxer —Sóngoro Consongo* (1931); tr. Tim Conley
Hagiwara Kyojiro (Japan, 1899-1938)
190 *Advertising Tower —Advertising Tower* (1925); tr. William Gardner
234 *A Love Letter —Advertising Tower* (1925); tr. William Gardner
377 *Morning●Noon●Night●Robot —Advertising Tower* (1925); tr. William Gardner
393 *Armored Coil —Advertising Tower* (1925); tr. William Gardner

Hagiwara Sakutaro (Japan, 1886-1942)
8 *Longing I Walk in a Crowd —The Blue Cat* (1923); tr. Hiroaki Sato
187 *Yoshiwara* (1927); tr. Hiroaki Sato
František Halas (Czechoslovakia, 1901-1949)
171 *The World in the Telephone* (1925); tr. Jed Rasula
Lawren Harris (Canada, 1885-1970)
604 *City Heat —Contrasts* (1922)
Raoul Hausmann (Austria, 1886-1971)
25 poster poems (1918)
Georg Heym (Germany, 1887-1912)
564 *Berlin II —Der Democrat* (Nov. 23, 1910); *Der ewige Tag* (1911); tr. Anthony Hasler
Jakob von Hoddis (Germany, 1887-1942)
316 *Varieté —Der Sturm* II: 47 (1911); tr. Jed Rasula and Pierre Joris
Langston Hughes (United States, 1902-1967)
438 *I Thought It Was Tangiers I Wanted —Opportunity* (Dec. 1927)
Vicente Huidobro (Chile, 1893-1948)
394 *Telephone —Horizon Carré* (1917); *Grecia* 41 (Feb. 1920); tr. Geoffrey O'Brien
420 *Ocean or Dancing —Automne Régulier* (1925); tr. Tim Conley
522 *Eiffel Tower —Nord-Sud* 6-7 (Aug.-Sept. 1917); *Tour Eiffel* (1918); tr. Tim Conley
Sidney Hunt (England, 1896-1940)
582 *Solution —Pagany* 1: 2 (Jan.-March 1930)
Iliazd (pseudonym of Ilya Zdanevich, Georgia, 1894-1975, emigrated to France 1921)
339 *Typographic Composition —Het Overzicht* 20 (Jan. 1924)
Max Jacob (France, 1876-1944)
533 *The Rue Ravignan —Le Cornet à dés* (1917); tr. John Ashbery
560 *A Touch of Modernism by Way of a Conclusion —Le Cornet à dés* (1917); tr. Beth Archer Brombert
Lewis Jacobs (United States, 1904-1997)
451 *Highway 66 —Experimental Cinema* 4 (1932)
Bruno Jasiénski (pseudonym of Wiktor Zysman, Poland, 1901-1939)
33 *Song of Hunger*; tr. Zbigniew Folejewski
234 *Run Over*; tr. Zbigniew Folejewski
538 from *I Burn Paris* (1929); tr. Soren Gauger and Marcin Piekoszewski
Richard Johns (United States, 1904-1970)
576 *Robert in Berlin —Blues* 7 (Fall 1929)
Eugene Jolas (United States, raised in France, 1894-1952)
545 *Sleep in Ur —I Have Seen Monsters and Angels* (1938)

Valery Larbaud (France, 1881-1957)
11 *Europe* III — *Poèmes par un riche amateur* by A. O. Barnabooth (1908); tr. Ron Padgett and Bill Zavatsky
413 *Night in the Port —Poèmes par un riche amateur* by A. O. Barnabooth (1908); tr. Ron Padgett and Bill Zavatsky
437 *Europe* IX — *Poèmes par un riche amateur* by A. O. Barnabooth (1908); tr. Ron Padgett and Bill Zavatsky
Michel Leiris (France, 1901-1990)
250 *December 16-17, 1924 —Nuits sans Nuit et quelques Jours sans Jour* (1961); tr. Richard Sieburth
524 *December 22-23, 1923 —Nuits sans Nuit et quelques Jours sans Jour* (1961); tr. Richard Sieburth
A. Léyeles (pseudonym of Aron Glanz, Poland, 1889-1966, emigrated to England 1905, United States 1909)
462 *New York —Labyrinth* (1918); tr. Benjamin Harshav & Barbara Harshav
Alfred Lichtenstein (Germany, 1889-1914)
596 *After the Ball —Die Aktion* 3: 8 (Feb. 19, 1913); *Gedichte* (1919); tr. Sheldon Gilman, Robert Levine, Harry Radford
Germán List Arzubide (Mexico, 1898-1998)
340 *Cinematics —Esquina* (1923); tr. Jed Rasula
Amy Lowell (United States, 1874-1925)
474 *Thompson's Lunch Room—Grand Central Station —Men, Women and Ghosts* (1916)
Mina Loy (England, 1882-1966, lived abroad from 1903)
85 *Café du Néant —International: A Review of Two Worlds* 8: 8 (Aug. 1914); *Rogue* 1: 4 (May 1, 1915); *Lunar Baedeker* (1923)
261 *Crab-Angel — Lunar Baedeker* (1923)
591 *Lunar Baedeker —Lunar Baedeker* (1923)
Enzo Mainardi (Italy, 1898-1983)
323 *Jazz Band —Istantanee* (1938); tr. Willard Bohn
Émile Malespine (France, 1892-1952)
93 *Montparnasse —Manomètre* 3 (March 1923); tr. Tim Conley
Osip Mandelstam (Russia, 1891-1940)
504 "Charlie Chaplin" (mss.); tr. Burton Raffel & Alla Burago
608 *Leningrad —Literaturnaya Gazeta* 53 (Nov. 23, 1932); tr. Paul Schmidt
Mao Tun (pseudonym of Shen Dehong, China, 1896-1981)
159 from *Midnight* (1933); tr. Hsu Meng-hsiung and A. C. Barnes
Manuel Maples Arce (Mexico, 1898-1981)
17 *Metropolis —Urbe* (1924); tr. John Dos Passos

367 *T. S. F. (Radiophonic Poem)* —*El Universal Ilustrado* 308 (April 5, 1923); *Manomètre* 4 (Aug. 1923); *Poemas interdictos* (1927); tr. Lorna Scott Fox

Juan Marín (Chile, 1900-1963)

75 *Looping* —*Looping* (1929); tr. Jed Rasula

388 *Mechanical* —*Aquarium* (1934); tr. Jed Rasula

F. T. Marinetti (Italy, 1876-1944)

48 from *Destruction of Syntax—Wireless Imagination—Words in Freedom* (1913) —(French broadside 1913); *Lacerba* (June 15, 1913); *I manifesti del futurismo* (1914) (Italian version); tr. Jed Rasula

62 *Synchronic Chart* —*Zang Tumb Tumb* (1914); tr. Elizabeth R. Napier and Barbara R. Studholme

Vladimir Mayakovsky (Russia, 1893-1930)

111 *Paris (Chatting with the Eiffel Tower)* —*Krasnaya Niva* 9 (March 4, 1923); tr. Peter Tempest

119 *Last Farewell* —*Parizhskyi Vestnik* 25 (June 3, 1925); tr. Dorian Rottenberg

549 *Brooklyn Bridge* —*Projector* 24 (Dec. 31, 1925); *Ispania. Okean. Havana. Meksika. Amerika. Moscow* (1926); tr. Dorian Rottenberg

568 *Because of a Bandleader* —*Novyi Satirikon* 32 (1915) & (revised) *Novyi Satirikon* (1916); *Vsio Sochinionnoye* (1919); tr. Jack Hirschman & Victor Erlich

587 *Great Big Hell of a City* —*Moloko Kobylitsy* almanac (1914); *Vsio Sochinionnoye* (1919); tr. Dorian Rottenberg

Armando Mazza (Italy, dates unknown)

53 *Cities* — *Firmamento* (1920); tr. Steve Soper

415 *Oceanliner* —*10 Liriche d'amore* (1919); tr. Willard Bohn

Walter Mehring (Germany, 1896-1981)

34 *Prologue to "Berlin—Paree"* —*Wedding-Montmerte* (1923); tr. Donna Stonecipher

174 *Advertising is the Parasite of Life* —*Das Ketzerbrevier* (1921); tr. Donna Stonecipher

Alfred Richard Meyer (Germany, 1882-1956)

333 *Manhattan-Cocktail* —*Der große Munkepunke* (1924); tr. Donna Stonecipher

566 *Foxtrot* —*Der große Punkemunke* (1924); tr. Jed Rasula

Henry Miller (United States, 1891-1980)

119 from *Tropic of Cancer* (1934)

Jaume Miravitlles (Catalonia, 1906-1988)

369 *The Paris Fair* —*L'Amic de les Arts* 28 (1928); tr. Jed Rasula

Stanisław Młodożeniec (Poland, 1895-1959)

362 *Twentieth Century* —*Kreski i futureski* (1921); tr. Bogdana Carpenter

László Moholy-Nagy (Hungary, 1895-1946, emigrated to United States 1937)
216 *Dynamic of a Metropolis —Ma* 9: 8/9 (Sept. 15, 1924); *Malerei Fotografie Film* (1927); tr. Janet Seligman
Marianne Moore (United States, 1887-1972)
28 *The Past is the Present —Observations* (1924)
Paul Morand (France, 1888-1976)
163 *Anthology —Grecia* 18 (1919); tr. Jed Rasula
172 *Business —Feuilles de temperature* (1920); tr. Jed Rasula
324 from *Black Magic —Magie noire* (1920); tr. Hamish Miles
508 from *Evening with Charlot —USA* (1928); tr. Tim Conley
Robert Musil (Austria, 1880-1942)
154 from *The Man Without Qualities* (1931); tr. Sophie Wilkins
Edward Nagle (United States, 1893-1963)
466 *Spring Psychosis —The Little Review* XII: 1 (Spring-Summer 1926)
Vítězslav Nezval (Czechoslovakia, 1900-1958)
245 *Fireworks 1924 —Pantomima* (1924); tr. Jerome Rothenberg & Milos Sovak
529 *Pierrot Cyclist —Pantomima* (1924); tr. Zbigniew Folejewski
Nicolás Olivari (Argentina, 1900-1966)
242 *Our Life in a Newspaper Serial —La musa de la mala pata* (1926); tr. Lorna Scott Fox
353 *Poem in the Shape of a Cross for Barbara La Marr —El Gato escaldado* (1929); tr. Lorna Scott Fox
Pedro Olmedo Zurita (Spain)
395 *The Telephone —Grecia* 15 (May 1919); tr. Jed Rasula
George Oppen (United States, 1908-1984)
378 "Brain" —*Active Anthology* ed. Pound (1933)
473 from *Discrete Series* #1-2 —*Poetry* 39: 4 (Jan. 1932)
Carlos Oquendo de Amat (Peru, 1905-1936)
164 *Advertisement —5 Metros de Poemas* (1927); tr. Alejandro de Acosta and Joshua Beckman
459 *New York —5 Metros de Poemas* (1927); tr. Alejandro de Acosta and Joshua Beckman
Paul van Ostaijen (Belgium, 1896-1928)
280 *Music Hall —Bezette Stad* (1921); tr. Sascha Bru and Bart De Ruyck
Saşa Pană (pseudonym of Alexandru Binder, Rumania, 1902-1981)
27 *Manifesto —Unu* (Apr. 1928)
Clément Pansaers (Belgium, 1885-1922)
251 from *Pan-Pan —Le Pan Pan au Cul du Nu Nègre* (1919); tr. Michael Hays Sanchez
574 *Fox-Trot* (mss. 1920); tr. Donna Stonecipher

Henry Parland (Finland (Swedish language), 1908-1930)
380 from *The Ideals Clearance —Idealsrealisation* (1929); tr. Johannes Göransson
396 "Funny" (posth.); tr. Johannes Göransson
Tadeusz Peiper (Poland, 1895-1969)
179 *The Street —Żywe linie* (1924); tr. Bogdana Carpenter
Carlos Pellicer (Mexico, 1899-1977)
433 *Third Time —Pieda de Sacrificios: Poema Iberoaméricano* (1924); tr. Dudley Fitts
Fernando Pessoa (Portugal, 1888-1935)
28 "The true modern poem" (mss.); tr. Richard Zenith
146 "Bright bugle of morning" (mss.); tr. Richard Zenith
206 "I walk in the night of the suburban street" (mss.); tr. Richard Zenith
209 *Triumphal Ode —Orpheu* 1 (Jan.-March 1915); tr. Richard Zenith
429 "All along the wharf" (mss.); tr. Richard Zenith
M. S. Petrov (Russia, 1902-1983, emigrated to Yugoslavia 1919)
585 *13 —Dada-Tank* (1922); tr. Jed Rasula
Francis Picabia (France, 1879-1953)
86 *Magic City —391* 4 (Mar. 25, 1917); *Cinquante-deux Miroirs* (1917); tr. Marc Lowenthal
339 *Dada-Madrid* (mss. 1921); tr. Marc Lowenthal
380 *Wireless Telegraphy —Poèmes et dessins de la fille née sans mere* (1918); tr. Marc Lowenthal
Branko Ve Poljanski (pseudonym of Branco Micić, Serbia, 1898-1947, moved to Paris 1927)
407 *Indiana —Dada-Jok* (1922)
408 *Journey to Brazil —Zenit* II: 15 (June 1922); *Zenitismus* (July 14, 1922); *Panika pod suncem* (1924); tr. Jed Rasula
Ezra Pound (United States, 1885-1972, lived in Europe from 1908)
80 *In a Station of the Metro —Poetry* II: 1 (April 1913); *Lustra* (1917)
204 *The Encounter —Smart Set* XLI: 4 (Dec. 1913); *Lustra* (1917)
Marcel Proust (France, 1871-1922)
410 from *Within a Budding Grove —A l'ombre des jeunes filles en fleurs* (1919); tr. C. K. Scott Moncrieff and Terence Kilmartin
Julian Przyboś (Poland, 1901-1970)
109 *Four Quarters*; tr. Bogdana Carpenter
155 *Buildings — Z Ponad* (1930); tr. Jed Rasula
365 *Roofs —Zwrotnica* 5 (June 1923); *Śruby* (1925); tr. Bogdana Carpenter
Raymond Queneau (France, 1903-1976)
544 *Dream (1925) —La Révolution surréaliste* 3 (April 15, 1925); tr. Tim Conley

Carl Rakosi (Germany, 1903-2004, emigrated to United States 1910)
268 *Foyer, The Orpheum —Pagany* III: 1 (Jan.-March 1932)
Francisco and Guillermo Rello (Spain)
6 *The Voices of Life —Cervantes* (Apr. 1919); tr. Jed Rasula
Pierre Reverdy (France, 1889-1960)
117 *Paris in Play —La guitare endormie* (1919); tr. Pierre Joris
183 *Acrobats —Poèmes en prose* (1915); tr. Tim Conley
275 *Cabaret —Cale Sèche* ("Inédits" in *Main d'oeuvre* (1949)); tr. Tim Conley
Salvador Reyes (probably Chile, 1889-1970)
274 *Cabaret —Ultra* 18 (1921); tr. Alejandro de Acosta and Joshua Beckman
Charles Reznikoff (United States, 1894-1976)
607 "Scared dogs looking backwards" —*Five Groups of Verse* (1927)
Georges Ribemont-Dessaignes (France, 1884-1974)
30 *Poetic Circulation*
Rainer Maria Rilke (Germany, 1875-1926)
208 from *The Notebooks of Malte Laurids Brigge* (1910); tr. Stephen Mitchell
Humberto Rivas (Spain 1893-?, emigrated to Mexico 1923)
142 *The Multiple City —Ultra* 21 (1922); tr. Jed Rasula
José Rivas Panedas (Spain, 1890-?)
326 *Café —Grecia* XLXIX (Sept. 1920); tr. Jed Rasula
Juliette Roche (France, 1884-1980)
411 *Toulon-Cannes —Demi Cercle* (1920); tr. Donna Stonecipher
461 *Déja-Vu —Demi Cercle* (1920); tr. Donna Stonecipher
471 *Breevort —Demi Cercle* (1920); tr. Donna Stonecipher
Alexander Rodchenko (Russia, 1891-1956)
502 *Charlot —Kino-Fot* 3 (1922); tr. Jamey Gambrell
Edouard Roditi (United States, raised in France, 1910-1992)
409 *Séance —Blues* 7 (Fall 1929)
489 *Manhattan Novelettes* (1942)
Stephan Roll (pseudonym of Gheorghe Dinu, Rumania, 1904-1974)
55 *F. T. Marinetti —Integral* 12 (1927); tr. Jed Rasula
337 *Etc. —Integral* I: 4 (1925); tr. Jed Rasula
390 *Metalloid —75HP* (Oct. 1924); tr. Jed Rasula
Jules Romains (France, 1885-1972)
149 *The City —La Vie unanime* (1907); tr. Jane Marie Todd
Joseph Roth (Germany, 1894-1939)
345 from *The Conversion of a Sinner in Berlin's UFA Palace —Frankfurter Zeitung* (Nov. 19, 1925); tr. Michael Hofmann
Muriel Rukeyser (United States, 1913-1980)
349 *Movie —Theory of Flight* (1935)

Umberto Saba (Italy, 1883-1957)
505 *Charlot in The Gold Rush —La Fiera Letteraria* III: 15 (Apr. 10, 1927); tr. Jed Rasula
Mário Sá-Carneiro (Portugal, 1890-1916)
193 *Manicure —Orpheu* 2 (April-June 1915); tr. Alejandro Crawford
Pedro Salinas (Spain, 1891-1951, emigrated to United States 1936)
237 *Far West —Seguro Azar* (1929); tr. David Lee Garrison
355 *Movie Theater —Seguro Azar* (1929); tr. David Lee Garrison
Joan Salvat-Papasseit (Catalonia, 1894-1924)
264 *Wedding March —L'Irradiador del port i les gavines* (1921); tr. Dominic Keown and Tom Owen
414 *Drama in the Port —Poemes en ondes hertzianes* (1919); tr. Willard Bohn
Lucía Sánchez (Spain)
344 *Cinemas —Ultra* 2 (1921); tr. Jed Rasula
Marcel Sauvage (France, 1895-?)
107 *Place St. Opportune —Voyage en Autobus* (1921); tr. Tim Conley
145 *"...and Marcadet!" —Voyage en Autobus* (1921); tr. Tim Conley
384 *Les Halles-Saint-Eustache —Voyage en Autobus* (1921); tr. Tim Conley
Jens August Schade (Denmark, 1903-1978)
338 *In the Café —Hjerte-Bogen* (1930); tr. Jed Rasula
Karel Schulz (Czechoslovakia, 1899-1943)
428 *Jazz Over the Sea —Život* II (1922); tr. Josef Horacek & Jed Rasula
Kurt Schwitters (Germany, 1887-1948)
170 *High Fashion Furs —Sturmbilderbücher* 4 (1920); tr. Jerome Rothenberg
178 *Subway Poem —Sturmbilderbücher* 4 (1920); tr. Jerome Rothenberg
376 *Song of Miss Electricity* (mss. 1928); tr. Jed Rasula
George Seferis (Greece, 1900-1971)
341 *Tuesday —Book of Exercises* (1940); tr. Edmund Keeley & Philip Sherrard
Jaroslav Seifert (Czechoslovakia, 1901-1986)
12 *All the Beauties of the World —Sáma Láska* (1923); tr. Dana Loewy
253 *Miss Gada-Nigi —Na Vlnánch TSF* (1925); tr. Dana Loewy
361 *Electric Lyre —Sáma Láska* (1923); tr. Dana Loewy
412 *Harbor —Na Vlnánch TSF* (1925); tr. Dana Loewy
456 *New York —Na Vlnánch TSF* (1925); tr. Dana Loewy
552 *Evening at the Café —Na Vlnánch TSF* (1925); tr. Dana Loewy
530 *! ! Hello ! ! —Na Vlnánch TSF* (1925); tr. Dana Loewy
Mikhail Semenko (Ukraine, 1892-1937)
360 from *Cablegram Over the Ocean —Semafor u Maibutnie* 1 (May 1922); tr. Ryan Culpepper
387 *City* (1914); tr. Oleh S. Ilnytzkyj

Gino Severini (Italy, 1883-1966, lived in Paris from 1906)
51 *Compenetration Simultaneité —SIC* 4 (Apr. 1916)
M. G. Shelley
169 *Poème Mécanique —Transition* 12 (March 1928)
Vadim Shershenevich (Russia, 1893-1942)
30 *The Rhythm of the Future —Green Street* (1915); tr. Catriona Kelly
188 "Garrulous motors" (1914); tr. Tim Harte
589 *Earthquake* (1913); tr. Tim Harte
Evan Shipman (United States, 1904-1957)
255 *Circus —Contact* I: 2 (May 1932)
Victor Shklovsky (Russia, 1893-1984)
270 from *Zoo* (Letter Twenty-two) *—Zoo* (1923); tr. Richard Sheldon
Ardengo Soffici (Italy, 1879-1965)
47 *Typography —BÏF§ZF+18* (1919)
83 *Studio —BÏF§ZF+18* (1919); tr. Laurie Duggan
151 *Crossroad —BÏF§ZF+18* (1919); tr. Willard Bohn
203 *Café Paszkowski —BÏF§ZF+18* (1919); tr. Laurie Duggan
583 *Café —Lacerba* II: 9 (March 1, 1914); *BÏF§ZF+18* (1919); tr. Laura Wittman
Gino Soggetti (Italy, 1898-1958)
61 *Athletes of the Air —L'Italia Futurista* II: 3 (1917); tr. Jed Rasula
Philippe Soupault (France, 1897-1990)
134 *Westwego —Westwego* (1922); tr. Andrew Zawacki
231 *Palace Cinema—Rose des vents* (1920); tr. Louis Simpson
337 *Ragtime —Nord-Sud* 16 (Oct. 1918); *Rose des vents* (1920); tr. Paulette Schmidt
408 *Horizon —Rose des vents* (1920); tr. Paulette Schmidt
Ernst Stadler (Alsace, 1883-1914)
204 *Closing Time —Der Aufbruch* (1914); *Menschheitsdämmerung: Ein Dokument des Expressionismus* ed. Pinthus (1920); tr. Joanna M. Ratych, Ralph Ley, Robert C. Conrad
Anatol Stern (Poland, 1899-1968)
624 *Europe —Europa* (1929); tr. Stefan Themerson and Michael Horovitz
Jindřich Štyrský (Czechoslovakia, 1899-1942)
525 *Picture —Disk* 1 (May 1923); tr. Michael Henry Heim
Andor Sugár (Hungary, 1903-1944)
37 *Paths —Ma; Aktivista Folyöirat* VII: 5-6 (May 1922)
José Juan Tablada (Mexico, 1871-1945)
596 *Alternating Nocturne —Li-Po y otros poemas* (1920); tr. Samuel Beckett
Kyn Taniya (pseudonym of Luis Quintanilla, Mexico, 1900-1980)
366 *...IU IIIUUU IU... —Radio* (1924); tr. Lorna Scott Fox
435 *Fox-Trot —Avión* (1923); tr. Lorna Scott Fox

579 *"Midnight Frolic"* —*Radio* (1924); tr. Lorna Scott Fox
Laura Tanne (United States)
475 *On Lenox* —*The Crisis* (Oct. 1928)
Igor Terentev (Georgia, 1892-1937)
46 *Nonsensical Tools* —*17 Nonsensical Tools* (1919); tr. Gerald Janecek
Boško Tokin (Serbia, 1894-1953)
40 *Cinema Poems* —*Crno na belo* (1924); tr. Jed Rasula
254 *Circus* —*Hipnos* 2 (1923); tr. Jed Rasula
Guillermo de Torre (Spain, 1900-1972, emigrated to Argentina 1937)
29 *Pentagram* —*Hélices* (1923); tr. Jed Rasula
60 *Upon Landing*; tr. Jed Rasula
346 *Photogenie* —*Ultra* 23 (1922); *Hélices* (1923); tr. Jed Rasula
363 *Bric-a-brac* —*Grecia* 49 (Sept. 1920); tr. Willard Bohn
513 *Charlot* —*Zenit* 13 (April 1922); *Hélices* (1923); tr. Jed Rasula
519 *Eiffel Tower* —*Hélices* (1923); tr. Jed Rasula
527 *Mental Diagram* —*Ultra* 18 (1921); *Hélices* (1923); tr. Jed Rasula
Jaime Torres Bodet (Mexico, 1902-1974)
263 *City* —*Destierro* (1930); tr. Rolfe Humphries
Joaquín Torres-García (Uruguay, 1874-1949)
168 from *The City With No Name* —*La Ciudad sin Nombre* (1941); tr. G. J. Racz
Marina Tsvetayeva (Russia, 1892-1941)
371 *Wires* —*After Russia* (1928); tr. Michael Naydan and Slava Yastremski
Raúl González Tuñón (Argentina, 1905-1974)
609 *Remembering A. O. Barnabooth* —*De Todos bailan* (1930); tr. Lorna Scott Fox
Parker Tyler (United States, 1904-1974)
498 *Paean* —*Chaplin, Last of the Clowns* (1947)
Tristan Tzara (pseudonym of Sami Rosenstock, Rumania, 1896-1963, emigrated to France 1919)
183 *The Showmen* —*Noi* III: 1 (Jan. 1920); *Mecano* 3 (1922); *De Nos Oiseaux* (1923); tr. Mary Ann Caws
257 *Circus* —*Littérature* 5 (July 1919); *De Nos Oiseaux* (1923); tr. Mary Ann Caws
593 *Balance Sheet* —*SIC* 49-50 (Jan. 1918); *Dada* 4-5 (May 15, 1919); *De Nos Oiseaux* (1923); tr. Mary Ann Caws
Adriano del Valle (Spain, 1895-1958)
151 *Gyrating City* —*Ultra* 4 (1921); tr. Jed Rasula
César Vallejo (Peru, 1892-1938)
117 *Hat, Overcoat, Gloves*; tr. Jed Rasula
Dziga Vertov (pseudnym of David Kaufman, Russia, 1896-1954)
348 from *The Birth of Kino-Eye* (mss. 1924); tr. Kevin O'Brien

Luis Vidales (Columbia, 1904-1990)
325 *In the Café —Suenan timbres* (1926); tr. Jed Rasula
560 *Telephone —Suenan timbres* (1926); tr. Jed Rasula
Xavier Villaurrutia (Mexico, 1903-1950)
580 *L.A. Nocturne: The Angels —Nocturnos* (1933); tr. Eliot Weinberger
Ion Vinea (pseudonym of Ion Iovanache, Rumania, 1895-1964)
33 *Tip —Punct* 3 (Dec. 6, 1924); tr. Jed Rasula
56 *Empty Words —Punct* 14 (Feb. 20, 1925); tr. Jed Rasula
Ilarie Voronca (pseudonym of Eduard Marcus, Rumania, 1903-1946, moved to Paris 1933)
15 *Aviogram —75HP* (1924); tr. Jed Rasula
531 from *Ulysses in the City* (IX) (1928); tr. Jed Rasula
William Carlos Williams (United States, 1883-1963)
249 *The Great Figure —Sour Grapes* (1921)
Virginia Woolf (England, 1882-1941)
57 from *Mrs Dalloway* (1925)
517 from *Mrs Dalloway* (1925)
Yehoash (pseudonym of Solomon Bloomgarden, Poland, 1872-1927, emigrated to United States 1890)
205 *Subway —Woven In* (1919); tr. Benjamin Harshav & Barbara Harshav
345 *Cinema —Woven In II* (1921); tr. Benjamin Harshav & Barbara Harshav
464 *Broadway —Woven In II* (1921); tr. Benjamin Harshav & Barbara Harshav
249 *The Great Figure —Sour Grapes* (1921)
Yokomitsu Riichi (Japan, 1898-1947)
57 from *Shanghai* (1928-31) tr. Dennis Washburn
Louis Zukofsky (United States, 1904-1978)
332 "Cocktails" *—55 Poems* (1941)
Piet Zwaart (Holland, 1885-1977)
561 *Hot Spots* (1926)

◈ BIBLIOGRAPHY ◈

Abril, Xavier, *Poesía soñada* ed. Marco Martos Carrera (Lima, Peru: Universidad de San Martin de Porres, 2006)

Adán, Martin, *The Cardboard House* tr. Katherine Silver (St. Paul: Graywolf, 1990)

Ades, Dawn, ed., *The Dada Reader: A Critical Anthology* (London: Tate, 2006)

Aiken, Conrad, *The Coming Forth by Day of Osiris Jones* (New York: Scribner's, 1931)

Albert-Birot, Pierre, *Poésie (1916-1924)* (Paris: Gallimard, 1967)

Alberti, Rafael, *Obras Completas, Volume 1: Poesía 1920-1938* ed. Luis García Montero (Madrid: Aguilar, 1988)

Aldington, Richard, *Collected Poems* (New York: Covici, Friede, 1928)

Allwood, Martin, ed., *Modern Scandinavian Poetry: The Panorama of Poetry 1900-1975* (Mullsjö, Sweden: Anglo-American Center, 1982)

Almada Negreiros, José, *Obras Completas I: Poesia* (Lisbon: Imprensa Nacional / Casa da Moeda, 1985)

Andrade, Mario de, *Hallucinated City* tr. Jack E. Tomlins (Nashville: Vanderbilt University Press, 1968)

———, *Poesias Completas* ed. Diléa Zanotto Manfio (Rio de Janeiro: Villa Rica, 1993)

Andrade, Oswald de, *Pau-Brasil* (Sao Paolo: Globo, 1990)

Antliff, Mark, and Patricia Leighten, eds., *A Cubism Reader: Documents and Criticism, 1906-1914* (University of Chicago Press, 2008)

Apollinaire, Guillaume, *Calligrammes* tr. Anne Hyde Greet (Berkeley: University of California Press, 1980)

Aragon, Louis, *Nightwalker (Le Paysan de Paris)* tr. Frederick Brown (Englewood Cliffs, N.J.: Prentice-Hall, 1970)

Aranha, Luis, *Cocktails* ed. Nelson Ascher (São Paulo: Editora Brasiliense, 1984)

Auden, W. H., *The English Auden: Poems, Essays, and Dramatic Writings, 1927-1939* ed. Edward Mendelson (New York: Random House, 1977)

Auster, Paul, ed., *The Random House Book of Twentieth-Century French Poetry* (New York: Random House, 1982)

Baljeu, Joost, *Theo van Doesburg* (New York: Macmillan, 1974)

Beauduin, Nicolas, *L'Homme cosmogonique* (Paris: Jacques Povolozky, 1922)

Behrens, Franz Richard, *Blutblüte: Die gesammelten Gedichte* ed. Gerhard Rühm (Munich: Text und Kritik, 1979)

Behrens-Hängeler, Herbert, *Gedichte* ed. Christian Scholz and Klaus Werner (Siegen, 1987)

Behring, Eva., ed., *Texte der Rumänischen Avantgarde 1907-1947* (Leipzig: Reclam, 1988)

Bely, Andrei, *Petersburg* tr. David McDuff (New York: Penguin, 1995)

Benjamin, Walter, *Selected Writings, Volume 1: 1913-1926* ed. Marcus Bullock and Michael W. Jennings (Cambridge: Harvard University Press, 1996)

Benson, Timothy O., and Éva Forgács, eds., *Between Worlds: A Sourcebook of Central European Avant-Gardes, 1910-1930* (Los Angeles County Museum of Art / The MIT Press, 2002)
Bizet, René, *Saxophone* (Paris: NRF, 1925)
Björling, Gunnar, *Träd Står i Sina Rader: Urval Lyrik 1922-1936* (Stockholm: Wahlström & Widstrand, 1952)
Bodenheim, Maxwell, *Returning to Emotion* (New York: Boni & Liveright, 1927)
Bohn, Willard, *The Aesthetics of Visual Poetry 1914-1928* (Cambridge University Press, 1986)
———, ed., *The Dada Market: An Anthology of Poetry* (Carbondale: Southern Illinois University Press, 1993)
———, ed. and tr., *Italian Futurist Poetry* (Toronto: University of Toronto Press, 2005)
Bonilla, Juan, ed., *Aviones Plateados: 15 Poetas Futuristas Latinoamericanos* 2nd rev. ed. (Málaga: Puerta del Mar, 2009)
Bønnelycke, Emil, *Asfaltens Sange* (Copenhagen: Nordiske Forfatteres Forlag, 1918)
Bonset, I. K. [Theo van Doesburg], *Nieuwe Woordbeeldingen* (Amsterdam: Querido, 1975)
Borge, Jason, ed., *Avances de Hollywood: Crítica cinematográfica en Latinoamérica, 1915-1945* (Rosario, Argentina: Beatriz Viterbo, 2005)
Borges, Jorge Luis, *Selected Poems 1923-1967* ed. Norman Thomas di Giovanni (New York: Delacorte, 1972)
Brecht, Bertolt, *Poems* ed. John Willett and Ralph Manheim (London: Methuen, 1976)
Breunig, L. C., *The Cubist Poets in Paris: An Anthology* (Lincoln: University of Nebraska Press, 1995)
Brown, Bob, *Demonics* (Bad Ems: Roving Eye, 1931)
———, *The Readies* (Bad Ems: Roving Eye, 1930)
Bunting, Basil, *Collected Poems* (London: Fulcrum, 1968)
Butts, Mary, *Last Stories* (London: Brendin, 1938)
Campana, Dino, *Orphic Songs* tr. I. L. Salomon (New York: October House, 1968)
Cangiullo, Francesco, *Caffè Concerto: Alfabeto a Sorpresa* (Milan: Poesia, 1916)
Carco, Francis, *Streetcorners: Prose Poems of the Demi-Monde* tr. Gilbert Alter-Gilbert (Los Angeles: Green Integer, 2004)
Cardoza y Aragón, Luis, *Maelstrom: Films Telescopiados* (Paris: Excelsior, 1926)
Carpenter, Bogdana, *The Poetic Avant-Garde in Poland, 1918-1939* (Seattle: University of Washington Press, 1983)
Caruso, Luciano, and Stelio Maria Martini, eds., *Tavole parolibere futuriste (1912-1944)* 2 vols. (Naples: Liguori, 1974, 1977)
Caws, Mary Ann, ed., *The Yale Anthology of Twentieth-Century French Poetry* (New Haven: Yale University Press, 2004)
Cendrars, Blaise, *Complete Poems* tr. Ron Padgett (Berkeley: University of California Press, 1992)

———, *Complete Postcards from the Americas: Poems of Road and Sea* tr. Monique Chefdor (Berkeley: University of California Press, 1976)
———, *Panama, or the Adventures of My Seven Uncles tr. John Dos Passos* (New York: Harper, 1931)
———, *Selected Writings* ed. Walter Albert (New York: New Directions, 1966)
Chirico, Giorgio de, *Hebdomeros; with Monsieur Dudron's Adventure and Other Metaphysical Writings* tr. Margaret Crosland, John Ashbery et al. (Boston: Exact Change, 1992)
Ciepiela, Catherine, and Honor Moore, eds., *The Stray Dog Cabaret: A Book of Russian Poems* tr. Paul Schmidt (New York Review, 2007)
Cocteau, Jean, "The Cape of Good Hope," tr. Jean Hugo, *The Little Review* 8 (Autumn 1921), 43-96
———, *Oeuvres poétiques complètes* ed. Michel Décaudin (Paris: Gallimard, 1999)
Conrad, Joseph, *The Secret Agent; A Simple Tale* (London: Dent, 1947)
Cowley, Malcolm, *The Blue Juniata* (London: Jonathan Cape, 1929)
———, *The Blue Juniata: Collected Poems* (New York: Viking, 1968)
Crane, Hart, *Complete Poems and Selected Letters* ed. Langdon Hammer (New York: Library of America, 2006)
Cummings, E. E., *Complete Poems, Volume One: 1913-1935* (London: Macgibbon & Kee, 1968)
Czyżewski, Tytus, *Poezje* ed. Krzysztof Karasek (Warsaw: Panstwowy Instytut Wydawniczy, 1987)
D'Alba, Auro, *Baionette* (Milan: Poesia, 1915)
Depero, Fortunato, *Depero Futurista* (Milan: Dinamo-Azari, 1927)
Desnos, Robert, *The Voice of Robert Desnos: Selected Poems* tr. William Kulik (Riverdale-on-Hudson: Sheep Meadow Press, 2004)
Deutsch, Babette, and Avrahm Yarmolinsky, ed. & tr., *Contemporary German Poetry* (New York: Harcourt, Brace, 1923)
Dos Passos, John, *U. S. A.* (Boston: Houghton Mifflin, 1948)
Eluard, Paul, *Thorns of Thunder: Selected Poems* ed. George Reavey (London: Europa Press, [1936])
Epstein, Jean, *Bonjour Cinema* (Paris: Sirene, 1921)
Fargue, Léon-Paul, *An English Translation of Léon-Paul Fargue's Poëmes* tr. Peter S. Thompson (Lewiston, Maine: Edwin Mellen, 2003)
Fearing, Kenneth, *Complete Poems* ed. Robert M. Ryley (Orono, Maine: National Poetry Foundation, 1994)
Ferreiro, Alfredo Mario, *El Hombre que se comió un autobus* (Montevideo, Uruguay: La Cruz del Sur, 1927)
Fingerít, Marcos, *Antena: 22 Poemas Contemporaneos* (Buenos Aires: Tor, 1929)
Fitts, Dudley, ed., *Anthology of Contemporary Latin-American Poetry* (Norfolk, Ct.: New Directions, 1942)
Florido, Francisco Fuentes, ed., *Poesias y Poetica del Ultraismo (Antologia)* (Barcelona: Mitre, 1989)

Folejewski, Zbigniew, *Futurism and its Place in the Development of Modern Poetry: A Comparative Study and Anthology* (Ottawa: University of Ottawa Press, 1980)
Ford, Charles Henri, *Flag of Ecstasy: Selected Poems* ed. Edward B. Germain (Los Angeles: Black Sparrow, 1972)
Freytag-Loringhoven, Elsa von, *Mein Mund ist Lüstern: I Got Lusting Palate; Dada-Verse* ed. Irene Gammel (Berlin: Ebersbach, 2005)
Gallardo, Salvador, *El Pentagrama-Eléctrico* (Puebla, Mexico: Germán List Arzubide, 1925)
Gallo, Rubén, *Mexican Modernity: The Avant-Garde and the Technological Revolution* (Cambridge: The MIT Press, 2005)
García Lorca, Federico, *Poet in New York* rev. ed., ed. Christopher Mauer, tr. Greg Simon and Steven F. White (New York: Farrar, Straus and Giroux, 1998)
Gardner, William, *Advertising Tower: Japanese Modernism and Modernity in the 1920s* (Cambridge: Harvard University Asia Center, 2006)
Giralt-Miracle, Daniel, ed., *Las Vanguardias en Cataluña 1906-1939* (Barcelona: Fundació Caixa de Catalunya, 1992)
Girondo, Oliverio, *Veinte Poemas para Ser Leídos en el Tranvía* (Buenos Aires: Martin Fierro, 1925)
Goll, Claire, *Lyrisches Films* (Berlin: Rhein, 1922)
Goll, Yvan, "The Chaplinade: A Film Poem," tr. Clinton J. Atkinson and Arthur S. Wensinger, *The Massachusetts Review* 6: 3 (Spring-Summer 1965), 497-514
———, *Die Lyrik in vier Bänden: Vol. I, : Frühe Gedichte 1906-1930* ed. Barbara Glauert-Hesse (Berlin: Argon, 1996)
———, *Oeuvres I* ed. Claire Goll and François Xavier Jaujard (Paris: Émile-Paul, 1968)
Gómez de la Serna, Ramón, *Movieland* tr. Angel Flores (New York: Macaulay, 1930)
González Tuñón, Raúl, *Antología Poética* ed. Elvio Romero (Buenos Aires: Losada, 1974)
———, *El Violín del Diablo; Miércoles de Ceniza* (Buenos Aires: La Rosa Blindada, 1973)
Gottlieb, Robert, and Robert Kimball, eds., *Reading Lyrics* (New York: Pantheon, 2000)
Grosz, George, *Pass Auf! Hier kommt Grosz: Bilder, Rhythmen und Gesänge 1915-1918* ed. Wieland Herzfelde and Hans Marquardt (Leipzig: Reclam, 1981)
Guillén, Nicolás, *Obra Poetica 1920-1972, Tomo 1* (Havana: Editorial de Arte y Literature, 1974)
Gullón, Germán, ed., *Poesia de la Vanguardia Española* (Madrid: Taurus, 1981)
Hagiwara Sakutaro, *Howling at the Moon: Poems and Prose* tr. Hiroaki Sato (Los Angeles: Green Integer, 2002)
Hamburger, Michael, ed. & tr., *German Poetry 1910-1975* (Manchester: Carcanet, 1977)
Harris, Lawren, *Contrasts: A Book of Verse* (Toronto: McClelland & Stewart, 1922)
Harte, Tim, *Fast Forward: The Aesthetics and Ideology of Speed in Russian Avant-Garde Culture, 1910-1930* (Madison: University of Wisconsin Press, 2009)

Harshav, Benjamin, ed., *Sing, Stranger: A Century of American Yiddish Poetry; A Historical Anthology* tr. Benjamin Harshav and Barbara Harshav (Stanford University Press, 2006)

Hedrick, Hannah L., *Theo Van Doesburg: Propagandist and Practitioner of the Avant-Garde, 1909-1923* (Ann Arbor: UMI, 1980)

Heym, Georg, *Poems* tr. Antony Hasler (Evanston: Northwestern University Press, 2006)

Hofmann, Michael, ed., *Twentieth-Century German Poetry, An Anthology* (New York: Farrar, Straus and Giroux, 2005)

Hughes, Langston, *Collected Poems* ed. Arnold Rampersad (New York: Vintage, 1995)

Huidobro, Vicente, *Obras Completas, Vol. 1* (Santiago, Chile: Editorial Andres Bello, 1976)

———, *Selected Poetry* ed. David M. Guss (New York: New Directions, 1981)

Ingold, Felix Philipp, *Literatur und Aviatik: Europäische Flugdichtung 1909-1927* (Basel: Birkhäuser, 1978)

Jacob, Max, Francis Ponge and Jean Follain, *Dreaming the Miracle: Three French Prose Poets* tr. Beth Archer Brombert et al. (Buffalo, NY: White Pine, 2003)

Janecek, Gerald, *The Look of Russian Literature: Avant-Garde Visual Experiments, 1900-1930* (Princeton: Princeton University Press, 1984)

Jansen, F. J. Billeskov, and Hans Reitzels Forlag, eds., *Den Danske Lyrik* vol. 4 (Copenhagen: Anden Udgave, 1986)

Jensen, Line, et al., eds., *Contemporary Danish Poetry: An Anthology* (Boston: Twayne, 1977)

Jolas, Eugene, *Cinema* (New York: Adelphi, 1926)

———, *I Have Seen Monsters and Angels* (Paris: Transition, 1938)

Joyce, James, *Ulysses* (New York: Modern Library, 1934)

József, Attila, *The Iron-Blue Vault: Selected Poems* tr. Zsuzsanna Ozsváth and Frederick Turner (Newcastle upon Tyne: Bloodaxe, 1999)

———, *Perched on Nothing's Branch: Selected Poetry* tr. Peter Hargitai (Buffalo: White Pine Press, 1999)

———, *Sixty Poems* tr. Edwin Morgan (Glasgow: Mariscat Press, 2001)

———, *Winter Night: Selected Poems* tr. John Bákti (Oberlin: Oberlin College Press, 1997)

Junoy, Josep Maria, *Obra poètica* ed. Jaume VallacorbaPlana (Barcelona: Quaderns Creme, 1984)

Kafka, Franz, *The Diaries of Franz Kafka, 1914-1923* ed. Max Brod, trans. Martin Greenberg, with Hannah Arendt (New York: Schocken, 1949)

Kamensky, Vassily, *Tango s Korovami* (Moscow 1914)

Kelly, Catriona, ed., *Utopias: Russian Modernist Texts 1905-1940* (New York: Penguin, 1999)

Khlebnikov, Velimir, *Collected Works, Volume III: Selected Poems* ed. Ronald Vroon, tr. Paul Schmidt (Cambridge: Harvard University Press, 1997)

Kosovel, Screcko, *Integrals* tr. Nike Kocijancic Pokorn, Katarina Jerin, and Philip Burt (Ljubljana: Slovene Writers' Association, 1998)

Kracauer, Siegfried, *The Mass Ornament: Weimar Essays* ed. and tr. Thom Y. Levin (Cambridge: Harvard University Press, 1995)
Kruchenykh, Alexei, *Suicide Circus: Selected Poems* tr. Jack Hirschman, Alexander Kohav, and Venyamin Tseytlin (Los Angeles: Green Integer, 2001)
Kundera, Ludvík, with Eduard Schreiber, eds., *Adieu Musen: Anthologie des Poetismus* (Munich: Deutsche Verlags-Anstalt, 2004)
Lam, Andrzej, ed., *Die literarische Avantgarde in Polen: Dichtungen, Manifeste, Theoretische Schriften* (Tübingen: Gunter Narr Verlag, 1990)
Larbaud, Valery, *The Poems of A. O. Barnabooth* tr. Ron Padgett and Bill Zavatsky (Tokyo: Mushinsha, 1977)
Leiris, Michel, *Nights as Day, Days as Night* tr. Richard Sieburth (Hygiene, Colorado: Eridanos Press, 1987)
Lichtenstein, Alfred, *The Prose and Verse of Alfred Lichtenstein* tr. Sheldon Gilman, Robert Levine, Harry Radford (n.p.: ExLibris, 2000)
Lista, Giovanni,, ed., *Futurisme: Manifestes–Proclamations Documents* (Lausanne: L'Age d'Homme, 1973)
Lowell, Amy, *Men, Women and Ghosts* (Boston: Houghton Mifflin, 1916)
Loy, Mina, *The Lost Lunar Baedeker* ed. Roger L. Conover (New York: Farrar, Straus and Giroux, 1996)
Makaryk, Irena R., and Virlana Tkacz, eds., *Modernism in Kyiv: Jubilant Experimentation* (University of Toronto Press, 2010)
Mandelstam, Osip, *Complete Poetry* tr. Burton Raffel and Alla Burago (Albany: State University of New York Press, 1973)
Mao Tun, *Midnight* tr. Hsu Meng-hsiung and A. C. Barnes (Peking: Foreign Languages Press, 1957)
Maples Arce, Manuel, *Metropolis* tr. John Dos Passos (New York: T. S. Book Co., 1929)
———, *Poemas Interdictos* (Jalapa, Mexico: Horizonte, 1927)
Marín, Juan, *Aquarium* (Santiago, Chile: Documentos, 1934)
———, *Looping* (Santiago, Chile: Imprenta Nascimento, 1929)
Marinetti, F. T., *Selected Poems and Related Prose* ed. Luce Marinetti, tr. Elizabeth R. Napier and Barbara R. Studholme (New Haven: Yale University Press, 2002)
Mayakovsky, Vladimir, *Electric Iron* tr. Jack Hirschman and Victor Erlich (Berkeley: Maya, 1971)
———, *Selected Works, Vol. 1: Selected Verse* (Moscow: Raduga, 1985)
Mazza, Armando, *Firmamento* (Milan: Poesia, 1920)
__, *10 Liriche d'Amore* (Milan: Facchi, 1919)
McGuirk, Bernard, "Almada-Negreiros and *Portugal Futurista*," *International Futurism in Arts and Literature* ed. Günter Berghaus (Berlin: Walter de Gruyter, 2000), 182-203
Mehring, Walter, *Chronik der Lustbarkeiten* (Düsseldorf: Claassen Verlag 1981)
Meyer, Alfred Richard, *Der große Munkepunke: Gesammelte Werke* (Hamburg: Hoffmann & Campe, 1924)
Miller, David, and Stephen Watts, eds., *Music While Drowning: German Expressionist Poems* (London: Tate Publishing, 2003)

Miller, Henry, *The Tropic of Cancer* (New York: Grove Press, 1961)
Moholy-Nagy, Laszlo, *Painting, Photography, Film* tr. Janet Seligman (Cambridge: The MIT Press, 1969)
Molas, Joaquim, ed., *La Literatura Catalana d'Avantguarda 1916-1938* (Barcelona: Bosch, 1983)
Moore, Marianne, *Observations* (New York: Dial, 1924)
Morand, Paul, *Black Magic* tr. Hamish Miles (New York: Viking, 1929)
———, *Poèmes* (Paris, Gallimard, 1973)
Musil, Robert, *The Man Without Qualities* tr. Sophie Wilkins (New York: Knopf, 1995)
Neistein, José, ed., *Poesia Brasileira Modernia: A Bilingual Anthology* tr. Manoel Cardozo (Washington, D. C.: Brazilian-American Cultural Institute, 1972)
Nezval, Vitezslav, *Antilyrik and Other Poems* tr. Jerome Rothenberg and Milos Sovak (Los Angeles: Green Integer, 2001)
Olivari, Nicolás, *El hombre de la baraja y la puñalada y otros escritos sobre cine* ed. María Gabriela Mizraje (Buenos Aires: Adriana Hidalgo, 2000)
Olschowsky, Henrich, ed., *Der Mensch in den Dingen: Programmtexte und Gedichte der Krakauer Avantgarde* (Leipzig: Reclam, 1986)
Oppen, George, *New Collected Poems* ed. Michael Davidson (New York: New Directions, 2002)
Oquendo de Amat, Carlos, *5 Meters of Poems* tr. Alejandro de Acosta and Joshua Beckman (Brooklyn: Ugly Duckling, 2010)
Ostaijen, Paul van, *Verzameld Werk/Poëzie* 2 vols. (Antwerp: C de Vries-Brouwers, 1963)
Pansaers, Clément, *Bar Nicanor & autres textes Dada* ed. Marc Dachy (Paris: Lebovici 1986)
Parland, Henry, *Ideals Clearance* tr. Johannes Göransson (Brooklyn: Ugly Duckling, 2007)
Passuth, Krisztina, *Les Avant-Gardes de l'Europe Centrale* (Paris: Flammarion, 1988)
Payne, Roberta L., ed., *A Selection of Modern Italian Poetry in Translation* (Montreal & Kingston: McGill-Queen's University Press, 2004)
Paz, Octavio, ed., *Anthology of Mexican Poetry* tr. Samuel Beckett (Bloomington: Indiana University Press, 1958)
Pellicer, Carlos, *Poesía completa, Volumen 1* ed. Luis Mario Schneider and Carlos Pellicer López (Mexico City: Ediciones del Equilibrista, 1996)
Pessoa, Fernando, *Fernando Pessoa & Co.: Selected Poems* ed. and tr. Richard Zenith (New York: Grove Press, 1998)
———, *A Little Larger Than the Entire Universe: Selected Poems* ed. and tr. Richard Zenith (New York: Penguin, 2006)
Picabia, Francis, *I Am a Beautiful Monster: Poetry, Prose, and Provocation* tr. Marc Lowenthal (Cambridge: The MIT Press, 2007)
Pinthus, Kurt, ed., *Menschheitsdämmerung: Ein Dokument des Expressionismus* (Berlin: Rowohlt, 1959)

———, *Menschheitsdämmerung: Dawn of Humanity, A Document of Expressionism*, tr. Joanna M. Ratych, Ralph Ley, Robert C. Conrad (Columbia SC: Camden House, 1994)

Pop, Ion, ed., *La Réhabilitation du rêve: Une anthologie de l'Avant-garde roumaine* (Paris: Marcel Nadeau, 2006)

Pound, Ezra, *Lustra* (New York: Knopf, 1917)

Proust, Marcel, *Remembrance of Things Past* tr. C. K. Scott Moncrieff and Terence Kilmartin (Harmondsworth: Penguin, 1983)

Przybos, Julian, *Poesie und Poetik* ed. and tr. Karl Dedecius (Frankfurt am Main: Suhrkamp, 1990)

———, *Z Ponad* (Kraków: Wydawnictwo Literackie, 1988 [1930])

Rainey, Lawrence, Christine Poggi, and Laura Wittman, eds., *Futurism, An Anthology* (New Haven: Yale University Press, 2009)

Reverdy, Pierre, *Main d'oeuvre: Poèmes 1913-1949* (Paris: Mercure de France, 1949)

———, *Plupart du temps* (Paris: Flammarion, 1967)

Reznikoff, Charles, *Poems 1918-1936: Volume I of The Complete Poems* ed. Seamus Cooney (Santa Barbara: Black Sparrow, 1976)

Ribemont-Dessaignes, Georges, *Dada: Manifestes, Poèmes, Nouvelles, Articles, Projets, Théatre, Cinéma, Chroniques (1915-1929)* ed. Jean-Pierre Begot (Paris: Ivrea, 1994)

Rilke, Rainer Maria, *The Notebooks of Malte Laurids Brigge* tr. Stephen Mitchell (New York: Random House, 1983)

Roche, Juliette, *Demi Cercle* (Paris: Éditions d'Art "La Cible," 1920)

Rodchenko, Aleksandr, *Experiments for the Future: Diaries, Essays, Letters, and Other Writings* ed. Alexander N. Lavrentiev, tr. Jamey Gambrell (New York: Museum of Modern Art, 2005)

Roditi, Edouard, *Emperor of Midnight* (Los Angeles: Black Sparrow, 1974)

Roth, Joseph, *What I Saw: Reports from Berlin, 1920-1933* tr. Michael Hofmann (New York: Norton, 2003)

Rothe, Wolfgang, ed., *Deutsche Großstadtlyrik vom Naturalismus bis zur Gegenwart* (Stuttgart: Philipp Reclam, 1973)

Rukeyser, Muriel, *The Collected Poems* ed. Janet E. Kaufman and Anne F. Herzog (University of Pittsburgh Press, 2005)

Sá-Carneiro, Mário de, *Obras Completas II: Poesias* ed. João Gaspar Simões (Lisbon: Atica, 1978)

Salinas, Pedro, *Certain Chance* tr. David Lee Garrison (Lewisburg: Bucknell University Press, 2000)

Salvat-Papasseit, Joan, *Poesies* ed. Joaquim Molas (Barcelona: Ariel, 1978)

———, *Selected Poems* tr. Dominic Keown and Tom Owen (n.p.: The Anglo-Catalan Society, 1982)

Sauvage, Marcel, *Voyage en Autobus* (Paris: Éditions "Liber," 1921)

Schneider, Luis Mario, *El Estridentismo o una Literatura de la Estrategia* (Xoco, Mexico: Consejo Nactional para la Cultura y las Artes, 1997)

Schwitters, Kurt, *Das literarische Werk: Lyrik* ed. Friedhelm Lach (Munich: Deutscher Taschenbuch Verlag, 2005)

———, *pppppp: Poems Performance Pieces Proses Plays Poetics* ed. and tr. Jerome Rothenberg and Pierre Joris (Philadelphia: Temple University Press, 1993)

Seferis, George, *Collected Poems* rev. ed., ed. and tr. Edmund Keeley and Philip Sherrard (Princeton University Press, 1995)

Seifert, Jaroslav, *The Early Poetry of Jaroslav Seifert* tr. Dana Loewy (Evanston: Northwestern University Press, 1997)

Semenko, Mikhail, *Ausgewählte Werke* vol. 1 (Würzburg: Jal Reprint, 1979)

Shipley, Joseph, ed. & tr., *Modern French Poetry* (New York: Greenberg, 1926)

Shklovsky, Viktor, *Zoo, or Letters Not about Love* tr. Richard Sheldon (Ithaca: Cornell University Press, 1971)

Siegel, Holger, ed., *In unseren Seelen Flattern schwarze Fahnen: Serbische Avantgarde 1918-1939* (Leipzig: Reclam, 1992)

Simpson, Louis, ed. & tr., *Modern Poets of France* (Brownsville, Oregon: Story Line, 1997)

Soffici, Ardengo, *BÏF§ZF + 18: Simultaneità e Chimismi Lirici* (Florence: Vallecchi, 1919)

———, "Four Poems" tr. Laurie Duggan, *Otis Rush* 8 (no date; online text at: www.eaf.asn.au/otis/asfp.html)

Soupault, Philippe, *I'm Lying: Selected Translations* tr. Paulette Schmidt (Providence, R.I.: Lost Roads, 1985)

———, *Poèmes et Poésies (1917-1973)* (Paris: Grasset, 1973)

Stefanile, Felix, tr., *The Blue Moustache: Some Futurist Poets* (Manchester: Carcanet, 1981)

Stern, Anatol, *Europa* tr. Stefan Themerson and Michael Horovitz (London: Gaberbocchus, 1962)

Strand, Mark, *Looking for Poetry: Poems by Carlos Drummond de Andrade and Rafael Alberti, and Songs from the Quechua* (New York: Knopf, 2002)

Taniya, Kyn [Luis Quintanilla], *Avion: Poemas 1917-1923* (Mexico: "Cultura," 1923)

———, *Radio* (Mexico: "Cultura," 1924)

Taylor, Richard, and Ian Christie, eds., *The Film Factory: Russian and Soviet Cinema in Documents* tr. Richard Taylor (Cambridge: Harvard University Press, 1988)

Terent'ev, Igor, *Opere* ed. Marzio Marzaduri and Tat'jana Nikol'skaya (Bologna: San Francesco, 1988)

Terry, Patricia, and Serge Gavronsky, eds. and trs., *Modern French Poetry: A Bilingual Anthology* (New York: Columbia University Press, 1975)

Tesic, Gojko, ed., *Antologija pesnistva srpske avangarde: 1902-1934* (Novi Sad: Svetovi, 1993)

Torre, Guillermo de, *Hélices: Poemas 1918-1922* (Málaga: Centro Cultural de la Generación del 27, 2000)

Tyler, Parker, *Chaplin, Last of the Clowns* (New York: Vanguard Press, 1948)

Vallejo, César, *Complete Later Poems 1923-1938* ed. and tr. Valentino Gianuzzi and Michael Smith (Exeter: Shearsman, 2005)

Tsvetaeva, Marina, *After Russia* ed. Michael Naydan, tr. Michael Naydan and Slava Yastremski (Ann Arbor: Michigan: Ardis, 1992)
Turnbull, Eleanor, tr., *Contemporary Spanish Poetry: Selections from Ten Poets* (Baltimore: Johns Hopkins Press 1945)
Tzara, Tristan, *"Approximate Man" and Other Writings* tr. Mary Ann Caws (Detroit: Wayne State University Press, 1973)
———, *Oeuvres complètes: Tome I (1912-1924)* ed. Henri Béhar (Paris: Flammarion, 1975)
Vajda, Miklos, ed., *Modern Hungarian Poetry* (New York: Columbia University Press, 1977)
Vertov, Dziga, *Kino-Eye: The Writings of Dziga Vertov* ed. Annette Michelson, tr. Kevin O'Brien (Berkeley: University of California Press, 1984)
Vicuña, Cecilia, and Ernesto Livon-Grosman, eds., *The Oxford Book of Latin American Poetry: A Bilingual Anthology* (New York: Oxford University Press, 2009)
Vinea, Ion, *Ora Fîntînilor / L'Heure des fontaines* tr. Dan Ion Nasta (Bucharest: Minerva, 1982)
Voronca, Ilarie, *Ulysse dans la cité* tr. Roger Vailland (Paris: Le Temps des Cerises, 1999)
White, John J., *Literary Futurism: Aspects of the First Avant Garde* (New York: Oxford University Press, 1990)
Williams, William Carlos, *The Collected Poems, Volume I: 1909-1939* ed. A. Walton Litz and Christopher MacGowan (New York: New Directions, 1986)
Woolf, Virginia, *Mrs Dalloway* ed. Claire Tomalin (Oxford: Oxford University Press, 1992)
Yokomitsu Riichi, *Shanghai* tr. Dennis Washburn (Ann Arbor: Center for Japanese Studies, 2001)
Zukofsky, Louis, *Complete Short Poetry* (Baltimore: Johns Hopkins University Press, 1991)

◈ ACKNOWLEDGEMENTS ◈

Several years in the making, such a diversified gathering of works as this naturally incurs a significant list of debts and we have many to thank. For industrious research assistance, thanks to Andre Cormier, Megan de Bray, Rebecca Gray, Jaya Karsemeyer, and Lindsay Osmun. For "rough" translation work carried out as the project developed and expanded, thanks to Jonathan Allen, Adleen Crapo, Melinda Cro, Paula Karger, Erin Knight, Sarah Martin, Maria Mizzi, and Gino Signoracci. For typographic and visual help, thanks to Joshua Hussey, and for assistance in the business of obtaining permissions, thanks to Gabriel Lovatt. Thanks as well to the avid response by those who provided translations, in most instances undertaken specifically for this volume: Joshua Beckman, Jason Borge, Sascha Bru, Daniel Coudriet, Alejandro Crawford, Ryan Culpepper, Lorna Scott Fox, Tim Harte, Ruth Hemus, Josef Horacek, Pierre Joris, Steve Soper, Donna Stonecipher, and Andrew Zawacki. We are also indebted to the generosity and enthusiasm of other scholars: Gregory Betts, Willard Bohn, Bogdana Carpenter, Gaby Divay, Benjamin Harshav, Gerald Janecek, Sean Latham, Robert Levine, Edward Mendelson, Ion Pop, Arnold Rampersad, and Suzanne Zelazo. Funding in the form of a grant from the Social Sciences and Humanities Research Council of Canada (SSHRC) was instrumental and very appreciated. The resources of the Helen S. Lanier Chair at the University of Georgia have been vital. Finally, we thank Johannes Göranssen and Joyelle McSweeney at Action Books for the support and care they have brought to this project.

Credits

"The Airman's Alphabet," originally published in *The Orators*, currently collected in *The English Auden: Poems, Essays and Dramatic Writings, 1927-1939* by W. H. Auden (Faber, 1976). Copyright © 1934, 1976 by the Estate of W. H. Auden, used with permission of The Wylie Agency LLC.

"Paris as Goddess" and "Chaplin" reprinted by permission of the publisher from *Walter Benjamin: Selected Writings, Volume 2, 1927-1934*, translated by Rodney Livingstone and Others, edited by Michael W. Jennings, Howard Eiland, and Gary Smith, pp. 141, 199-200, Cambridge, Mass.: The Belknap Press of Harvard University Press, Copyright © 1999 by the President and Fellows of Harvard College.

"This Space for Rent" and "First Aid" from *Reflections: Essays, Aphorisms, Autobiographical Writings* by Walter Benjamin, copyright © 1978 by Houghton Mifflin Harcourt Publishing Company, reprinted by permission of the publisher.

"Sunlight on the Avenue," from *Returning to Emotion* by Maxwell Bodenheim. Copyright 1927 by Boni & Liveright, renewed 1954 by Solbert Bodenheim. Used by permission of the Liveright Publishing Corporation.

"Carniceria" from *Fervor de Buenos Aires* by Jorge Luis Borges. Copyright © 1996 Maria Kodama, reprinted by permission of The Wylie Agency LLC.

"Aus dem Zweiten Reich" by Basil Bunting reprinted by permission of Bloodaxe Books.

"Chaplinesque" and "The River" from *The Complete Poems of Hart Crane* by Hart Crane, edited by Marc Simon. Copyright 1933, 1958, 1966 by Liveright Publishing Corporation. Copright © 1986 by Marc Simon. Used by permission of the Liveright Publishing Corporation.

Poems by E. E. Cummings used by permission: "god pity me whom(god distinctly has)" copyright 1923, 1925, 1953, © 1991 by the Trustees for the E. E. Cummings Trust. Copyright © 1976 by George James Firmage, "when you rang at Dick Mid's Place". Copyright 1923, 1951, © 1991 by the Trustees for the E. E. Cummings Trust. Copyright © 1976 by George James Firmage, "POEM,OR BEAUTY HURTS MR.VINAL". Copyright 1926, 1954, © 1991 by the Trustees for the E. E. Cummings Trust. Copyright © 1976 by George James Firmage, "even if all desires things moments be". Copyright 1926, 1954, © 1991 by the Trustees for the E. E. Cummings Trust. Copyright © 1985 by George James Firmage, from *Complete Poems: 1904-1962* by E. E. Cummmings, edited by George J. Firmage. Used by permission of the Liveright Publishing Corporation.

Excerpts from *The Big Money* and *Manhattan Transfer* by John Dos Passos, as well as John Dos Passos's translation of Manuel Maples Arce's "Metropolis" reprinted by permission of Lucy Dos Passos Coggin.

"The Boulevard" by Leon-Paul Fargue, translated by Lydia Davis. Translation copyright © 1982 by Lydia Davis. Reprinted by permission of the Denis Shannon Literary Agency, Inc. All rights reserved.

Poems by Claire and Yvon Goll are reprinted by permission of the Société des Amis de la Fondation Yvan et Claire Goll.

"City Heat" by Lawren Harris reprinted by permission of Stewart Sheppard.

"Berlin II" by Georg Heym, translated by Anthony Hasler, reprinted by permission of Northwestern University Press.

"I Thought It Was Tangiers I Wanted" from *The Collected Poems of Langston Hughes* by Langston Hughes, edited by Arnold Rampersad with David Roessel, Associate Editor, copyright © 1994 by the Estate of Langston Hughes. Used by permission of Alfred A. Knopf, a division of Random House, Inc.

Excerpt from *I Burn Paris* by Bruno Jasienski, from a forthcoming book by Twisted Spoon Press, reprinted by permission of the publisher.

"Sleep in Ur" and "Linotype" by Eugene Jolas reprinted by permission of Betsy Jolas.

"Cresting spires" by Velimir Khlebnikov reprinted by permission of the publisher from *The Collected Works of Velimir Khlebnikov: Volume III — Selected Poems*, translated by Paul Schmidt, edited by Ronald Vroom, p. 121, Cambridge, Mass: Harvard University Press, Copyright © 1997 by the President and Fellows of Harvard College.

Excerpts from Siegfried Kracauer's *The Mass Ornament*, translated and edited by Thomas Y. Levin, pp. 281-282, 298, 299, 302, Cambridge, Mass: Harvard University Press, Copyright © 1995 by the President and Fellows of Harvard College, reprinted by permission of the publisher.

Paisaje de la multitud que vomita / Landscape of a Vomiting Multitude and *Paisaje de la multitud que orina / Landscape of a Pissing Multitude* by Federico Garcia Lorca copyright [c] [copyright sign] Herederos de Federico Garcia Lorca from Obras Completas (Galaxia/Gutenberg, 1996 edition). English-language translations by Greg Simon and Steven White copyright [c] Herederos de Federico Garcia Lorca, and Greg Simon and Steven White. All rights reserved. For information regarding rights and permissions please contact lorca@artslaw.co.uk or William Peter Kosmas, Esq., 8 Franklin Square, London W14 9UU, England.

"Café du Néant" and "Crab-Angel" and "Lunar Baedeker" by Mina Loy reprinted courtesy of Roger L. Conover for the estate of Mina Loy.

"The Paris Fair" by Jaume Miravitlles reprinted by permission of Marc Miravitlles Rogers.

Permission to reprint "The Past is the Present" by Marianne Moore granted by David M. Moore, Administrator of the Literary Estate of Marianne Moore. All rights reserved.

Excerpt from *Black Magic* by Paul Morand, translated by Hamish Miles, copyright 1929, renewed © 1957 by The Viking Press, Inc. Used by permission of Viking Penguin, a division of Penguin Group (USA) Inc.

"Our Life in the Newspaper Serials" and "Poem in the Form of a Crucifix for Barbara La Marr" by Nicolás Olivari reprinted by permission of Adriana Hidalso editora, Buenos Aires.

"Discrete Series" and "Brain" by George Oppen, from *New Collected Poems*, copyright © 1933 by New Directions Publishing Corp. Reprinted by permission of New Directions Publishing Corp.

"Third Time" by Carlos Pellicer, translated by Dudley Fitts, from *Anthology of Contemporary Latin-American Poetry*, copyright © 1947 by New Directions Publishing Corp. Reprinted by permission of New Directions Publishing Corp.

"All along the wharf there's the bustle of an imminent arrival," "Triumphal Ode," and "Salutation to Walt Whitman," from *A Little Larger than the Entire Universe* by Fernando Pessoa, translated by Richard Zenith, copyright © 2006 by Richard Zenith. Used by permission of Penguin, a division of Penguin Group (USA) Inc.

"'In A Station of the Metro" and "The Encounter" by Ezra Pound, from *Personae*, copyright ©1926 by Ezra Pound. Reprinted by permission of New Directions Publishing Corp.

"Foyer, The Orpheum" by Carl Rakosi reprinted by permission of Marilyn J. Kane, Literary Executor, Estate of Callman Rawley (Carl Rakosi), San Francisco, California.

"The City" by Jules Romains, trans. Jane Marie Todd, from *A Cubism Reader: Documents and Criticism, 1906-1914*, reprinted by permission of the University of Chicago Press.

Excerpt from *What I Saw: Reports from Berlin 1920-1933* by Joseph Roth, translated by Michael Hofman. Copyright © 1996 by Verlag Kiepenheuer & Witsch Koln and Verlag de Lange Amsterdam. English translation copyright © 2003 Michael Hofman. Used by permission of W. W. Norton & Company, Inc.

Poems by Jaroslav Seifert reprinted by permission of Johanna Seifertová and Jaroslav Seifert.

"Palace Cinema," "Ragtime," "Horizon," and *Westwego* by Philippe Soupault © Editions Gallimard. Reprinted by permission.

Europa by Anatol Stern was written and first published in the magazine *Reflektor* in 1925. Four years later it was issued in book form with illustrations and layout by Mieczysław Szczuka and cover design by Teresa Zarnower. Franciszka and Stefan Themerson used it as a film-script for their avant-garde film *Europa* made in Warsaw in 1931/32. This translation of Stern's poem by Stefan Themerson and Michael Horovitz was published by Gaberbocchus Press in 1962 as a facsimile of the 1929 edition. © Themerson Archive.

"The Great Figure" by William Carlos Williams, from *The Collected Poems: Volume I, 1909-1939*, copyright © 1938 by New Directions Publishing Corp. Reprinted by permission of New Directions Publishing Corp.

Excerpts from *Mrs Dalloway* by Virginia Woolf reprinted by permission of The Society of Authors as the Literary Representative of Virginia Woolf.

Poems reprinted from *Sing Stranger: A Century of American Yiddish Poetry – A Historical Anthology*, edited by Benjamin Harshav, copyright © 2006 by the Board of Trustees of the Leland Stanford Jr. University. All rights reserved. Used with permission of Stanford University Press, www.sup.org.